Contact with Reality

Contact with Reality

Michael Polanyi's Realism and Why It Matters

ESTHER LIGHTCAP MEEK

CASCADE Books • Eugene, Oregon

CONTACT WITH REALITY
Michael Polanyi's Realism and Why It Matters

Copyright © 2017 Esther Lightcap Meek. All rights reserved. Except for brief quotations in critical publications or reviews, no part of this book may be reproduced in any manner without prior written permission from the publisher. Write: Permissions, Wipf and Stock Publishers, 199 W. 8th Ave., Suite 3, Eugene, OR 97401.

Cascade Books
An Imprint of Wipf and Stock Publishers
199 W. 8th Ave., Suite 3
Eugene, OR 97401

www.wipfandstock.com

PAPERBACK ISBN: 978-1-4982-3983-7
HARDCOVER ISBN: 978-1-4982-3985-1
EBOOK ISBN: 978-1-4982-3984-4

Cataloguing-in-Publication data:

Names: Meek, Esther L., 1953–

Title: Contact with reality : Michael Polanyi's realism and why it matters / Esther Lightcap Meek.

Description: Eugene, OR: Cascade Books, 2017 | Includes bibliographical references and index.

Identifiers: ISBN 978-1-4982-3983-7 (paperback) | ISBN 978-1-4982-3985-1 (hardcover) | ISBN 978-1-4982-3984-4 (ebook)

Subjects: LCSH: Polanyi, Michael, 1891–1976 | Knowledge, Theory of

Classification: B945.P584 M44 2017 (paperback) | B945.P584 (ebook)

Manufactured in the U.S.A.   05/02/17

For my mother, Edith Harvey Lightcap
—gratefully.

For the Polanyi Society
—convivially.

We can account for this capacity of ours to know more than we can tell if we believe in an external reality with which we can establish contact. This I do. I declare myself committed to the belief in an external reality gradually accessible to knowing, and I regard all true understanding as an intimation of such a reality which, being real, may yet reveal itself to our deepened understanding in an indefinite range of unexpected manifestations.

—Michael Polanyi

Contents

Acknowledgements | ix

Introduction | 1

Part 1: Early Consideration of Contact with Reality

Preface to Part 1 | 11

1. Personal Knowledge | 16
2. The Structure of Knowledge | 29
3. Scientific Discovery | 38
4. Polanyi's Realism | 55
5. The Reality Statement | 64
6. Contact with Reality | 75
7. Criteria of Reality | 86
8. Polanyi and Contemporary Realist Issues (I): Progress | 108
9. Polanyi and Contemporary Realist Issues (II): Truth, in Particular Correspondence | 148
10. Polanyi and Contemporary Realism | 180
11. Grounding Polanyi's Realism: Merleau-Ponty | 205

Part 2: Re-Calling Contact with Reality

Preface to Part 2 | 239

12. Polanyi and *Retrieving Realism* | 244
13. The Current Conversation: The Difference Polanyi Would Make | 260
14. Recovering Reality | 278

Bibliography | 299
Name Index | 307

Acknowledgements

In bringing this work to publication, I am grateful to the following institutions: Temple University, Geneva College, and the Polanyi Society. The following persons deserve my gratitude: Edith Lightcap, my mother, for leading me into philosophy, for any inherited capacity for articulation, and for (literally) typing the dissertation; James Meek, for early encouragement; my children, for amicable coexistence with my philosophical preoccupation over the years; my colleagues and friends in the Polanyi Society; my editor, Robin Parry, for his commitment to this project since 2004; (the galactic) Andrew Calvetti, editorial assistant on this project; Zac Hummel, indexer; and my Geneva Philosophy Program colleague and friend Robert Frazier, for sustaining the vision of this work with me.

Introduction

Michael Polanyi was a premier scientist-turned-economist-turned-philosopher whose career spanned the first decades of the twentieth century. A Hungarian of Jewish descent, his life story is deeply marked by the tumultuous ravages of Europe in those years. Born in 1889 in Budapest to a wealthy industrialist and mother whose living room salons were filled with intelligentsia of Hungary's gilded age, Polanyi's career moved him to and through Berlin to Britain, where he died in 1976.

He was a prominent physical chemist, to whose lab scientists came from around the world to apprentice and collaborate, whose work involved him in interchanges with Albert Einstein (to name only the most generally known of a cadre of great scientists), whose discoveries contribute to many fields, including the technology of X-rays, and whose efforts spawned Nobel Prize winning scientists—including his own son, John Polanyi. Turning to philosophy in the 1940s, Polanyi gave the prestigious Gifford Lectures in Natural Religion in the early 1950s. These became his *magnum opus*, *Personal Knowledge*, in 1958. He traveled to the U.S. repeatedly to give lectures and seminars at prestigious universities. With the help of American philosopher Marjorie Grene, he oversaw study groups which included premier philosophers such as Charles Taylor, Hubert Dreyfus, and Alasdair MacIntyre. His work played a major, misrepresented, role in the thought of influential historian of science Thomas S. Kuhn. Polanyi was among the first in modernity to identify key dimensions of inquiry and knowing that now have come to be more widely appreciated—for example, tradition, apprenticeship, and connoisseurship, and the vision of a society of explorers.[1]

---

1. Scott and Moleski, *Polanyi: Scientist and Philosopher* is the definitive biography of Polanyi. See also Breytspraak and Mullins, "Polanyi and the Study Groups."

Public intellectual Wilfrid McClay deems Polanyi the greatest underrated public intellectual of the twentieth century.[2] Despite his greatness, Polanyi's insights and even influence are little remembered or identified. Those who do keep his work alive wonder at this and lament it. How can this be? Various factors are commonly cited. Polanyi, a polymath, over his career contributed work in multiple areas, offering a wider interdisciplinary vision that it would be misrepresentative to reduce to—and perpetuate in—a single area of study. Further, in philosophy and philosophy of science, he contributed a wider epistemic vision that was fundamentally innovative. The vision was so deeply challenging that his work was unheard and dismissed in a time dominated by the presumptions and detail of analytic philosophy. Additionally, Polanyi did not write like an analytic philosopher—nor would he have cared to. His work is characterized, someone has said, by strings of quick, creatively brilliant insights.[3] On a positive side, precisely because his writing is so lustrous, efforts in secondary literature—such as this one—pale in comparison. That makes it a challenge to disseminate it. And my own personal theory regarding Polanyi's partial eclipse: Polanyi's epistemology is so personally liberating that the recipient is freed to be him- or herself—and tends to forget the liberator in the conviction that the work is his or her own.

This book concerns one of those creatively brilliant insights: Polanyi's idea of contact with reality. At the heart of what Polanyi was about, especially in his stepping away from science to do philosophy, was his concern to offer a fundamentally different epistemology that, rather than undercutting science (not to mention all of Western culture)—as he felt the prevailing paradigm was doing—would save it and enhance it. It was as a premier scientific discoverer that he offered an account of knowing that accords with discovery. This is in contrast to a prevailing epistemology that remained preoccupied, instead, with explanation or justification. Now, over fifty years since the publication of *Personal Knowledge*, his proposals remain innovative and healing. They ring true to what we actually do when we come to know—when we know, that is, not only in frontline scientific research and discovery, but throughout all the byways of ordinary life. Polanyi's distinctive epistemology is featured throughout his philosophical writings. Also lacing those discussions is a frequently repeated insight regarding the making of a discovery. How do we know that we have made contact with reality? We know because our discovery is accompanied, and therein attested to, by a sense of unspecifiable future prospects of what we have found. In

---

2. Personal conversation, 2006.

3. Amartya Sen's assessment in his foreword to the 2009 edition of Polanyi's *Tacit Dimension*. Sen, "Foreword," in Polanyi, *Tacit Dimension*, xv.

this the inquirer experiences the characteristic signature of reality as she or he contacts it: the real is that which manifests itself indeterminately and inexhaustibly in the future. It is this repeated, tantalizing, "reality statement" that I examine in this book, along with the distinctive realist stance that Polanyi therein maintains.

The first part of this book is my until-now unpublished 1985 Ph.D. dissertation. I found Polanyi's work around 1978 during my graduate studies. I had been a kind of skeptic even as a child: unreasonable though it seemed, I felt that I had no proof that reality existed outside my mind—that it was there, independently of my knowing it.[4] This was the seemingly unsolvable concern that drove me into philosophy as a teenager. Truth to tell, Polanyi's distinctive, repeated utterance of this remarkable notion about contact with reality, when I first heard it some years later, struck me as the one glimmer of hope, the one hint of water in a desert, of something I desperately needed. "Contact with reality" was the very thing that I longed for. Thus, eventually, in the dissertation I was trying to develop a viable response to my urgent childhood question, which remained, to me, the most critical question there could be.[5]

The approach of the dissertation to this problem of realism was as follows: to explore and analyze all of Polanyi's frequent expressions of the reality statement, to endeavor to connect his work with prevailing contemporary discussion of realist issues, such as progress in science, the realism vs. anti-realism debate, and truth (required by my dissertation supervisor, philosopher Joseph Margolis at Temple University), and then to craft a fuller defense of what Polanyi was offering by drawing on the resources of the convergent work of contemporary Continental phenomenologist Maurice Merleau-Ponty. In this last component I was following the personal guidance of Dr. Marjorie Grene, at that time a visiting professor to my philosophy department.[6]

At the time of its completion, I felt that the dissertation was only partially successful in proving realism. For one thing, it was timidly offered in the acerbic atmosphere of a highly analytic philosophy department. The

---

4. Born into a faithfully practicing Christian family, I also asked, how do I know that God exists? But it was obvious to me that the questions were related—in fact, crucial each to the other.

5. Polanyi never seems to have posed the skeptical question, even though I took what he was saying as hope for mine. His posture, as evidenced in any expressions of the reality statement, was unquestioned and presumptively confident. I will explore this presently.

6. See her own work on this: Grene, "Tacit Knowing and the Prereflective Cogito," in Langford and Poteat, eds., *Intellect and Hope*; see also her *Philosophical Testament*, ch. 4.

dissertation lacked both confidence and conclusions. But neither did the dissertation make a believer of me, the young Cartesian skeptic—a believer in the real. I felt that Polanyi didn't provide exhaustive—or even any—justification of his realism. Then, although Merleau-Ponty's work expanded and joyously corroborate key aspects of Polanyi's vision, one could walk away from it feeling both that it lacked a key Polanyian insight and that it ultimately fell short of the hoped-for proof of realism.

In spite of that, through the decades from then until now, through long-lived reflection on Polanyi's realism, it turns out that I have grown to embrace it. This lived reflection has leavened my epistemology, and it is continuing now further to leaven my sense of reality. Out of it has grown my own epistemic proposals, which I call covenant epistemology.[7] I have moved from child skeptic to seasoned intoxicated realist. Because of this, I believe that publishing the dissertation only *now*, with the addition of fresh chapters and an overall reframing, allows me to convey a felt sense of the very transformation in outlook that Polanyi's contact with reality has brought about—and can bring about for readers.

From this vantage point, I can finally see that the dissertation, driven as it was by the prevailing agenda of analytic philosophy and the artificial structures of a dissertation project, not to mention my own inherited modernist epistemic default, took what is perhaps fundamentally an informal Polanyian insight and endeavored to formalize and systematize it, and seek its exhaustive justification. In this, the dissertation—by definition an analysis—partly defaces the very insight that has brought me life and hope of reality. That is precisely why the dissertation, now reframed, can that much more effectively address the need of the day.

The "problem of realism" is driven by presumptions so deep that we cannot entirely see how they are playing out in our best efforts to respond to it. Presenting my early systematization affords the reader a felt sense of the ultimate unsuitability of analysis to the endeavor to lay hold of this brilliant informal insight of Polanyi's. Key to the mismatch of Polanyian insight and early Meekian treatment of it is the matter of indwelling—itself a brilliant

---

7. See Preface to pt. 2 for a brief summary of covenant epistemology. Meek, *Longing to Know*; *Loving to Know*; *Little Manual*. One way I came to express it in *Longing to Know* was to say that reality doesn't answer your questions so much as explode them—or to start questioning you (ch. 16). I must note that having children and living life ought to make a realist out of you. As Grene quipped of her revised take on Kant as a result of her life as a farmer: "My first ten years farming I found I had lost any ear for the sacred text. We had a great gray Percheron mare named Kitty; I couldn't look at her and ask, was she an appearance or a thing in herself.... Come to think of it, I don't know why one's offspring don't have the same effect: babies are not just phenomenal either (or not in the Kantian sense!)" (*Philosophical Testament*, 35.)

insight of Polanyian epistemology. Simply put: if you are to contact reality, you must be subsidiarily indwelling its clues. If you are staring at them focally—as in a formalized presentation—you are therein prevented from the insight that is making contact with reality. Just as, to see the moons of Jupiter, you can't look at the telescope but must rather give yourself to it to look through it, the committed posture of indwelling alone sidesteps the problem. The "problem of realism" proves to be not so much answered as obviated.

So why resurrect this dissertation? For one thing, as Polanyi stipulated, analysis is destructive only if you permanently ensconce it focally. Temporary reversion to focus on what should be indwelt subsidiarily is both necessary and helpful. It is only permanent reversion to the focal which blinds—and which futilely typifies modernist epistemology, to be frank. Contexting my focal analysis of Polanyian realism with the wider vision it is meant subsidiarily to support appropriately accredits the analysis, while enabling us in the future to indwell it with greater expertise and artistry. As we will see in the early chapters, this is just how knowing works, according to Polanyi.

The dissertation is studiously full of the many dimensions and prospects of Polanyi's remarkable notion of contact with reality, as well as of my sustained endeavor to set these alongside major claims of the prevailing philosophical discussion of realism. Even apart from the recent updating and reframing, the dissertation's focus beams life and hope. This idea of contact with reality needs to be heard and taken deeply to heart.

Additionally, I have deliberately preserved the dissertation with only minor revisions, out of respect for my colleagues in the Polanyi Society. It was this dissertation which, even though unpublished, in 2000 led them to draw me into their convivial communion. I continue to value their criticism as much as I value their affirmation. I commend their Polanyian conviviality to others: Polanyi Society conferences are the most delightful professional meetings to attend.

But the most critical reason that I resurrect the dissertation is that I am not alone in tending to be a skeptic regarding contacting reality. Modernity has deeply marked us all in the West, cutting us off from the natural trust and communion with reality that lies at the heart of humanness. People need not have raised the question in the form it took for me in eighth-grade: how do I know that reality exists outside my mind? Distrust of reality figures in decisions regarding life, time, nature, and culture. Modernity itself is centrally characterized by the Baconian vision of human mastery over nature. This outlook tacitly implies a distrust of reality, pitting us against it in our unceasing effort to triumph over it for entirely utilitarian purposes of self-aggrandizement. Postmodernity so utterly distrusts it and dismisses it that it is common to feel that we can make reality however we want it—and that we must. In this we also deface our own humanness. I offer this book—the dissertation freshly reframed—not only as the critical backdrop to all my other work, but as a healing, hope-filled challenge to modern culture quite generally.

This work submits the thesis that Polanyi's innovative notion of contact with reality and related claims render Polanyi an epistemic realist, a position especially surprising and intriguing given his celebrated but misunderstood commitment to the personal dimension of knowledge. Given that his philosophy challenges fundamental parameters of the philosophical debate, then and now, regarding realism and anti-realism in philosophy of science and in epistemology, it is both unsurprising that his position is not widely entertained or engaged, and it is difficult to attempt to do so. For all that, it is a telling and valuable exercise to identify Polanyi's potential contributions to that conversation.

Further, this book endeavors to develop, in the apparent absence of his own concern to provide one, a thorough justification for Polanyi's realist claims. To this end, I examine Maurice Merleau-Ponty's phenomenology of perception to elucidate the area of prethetic or subsidiary contact of our lived bodies with the world. In the final analysis, however, I conclude, as I have suggested above, that Polanyi's own realism is both the best realism to hold and contains the best justification for it.

The book ends with a foray along a different path perhaps more accordant with Polanyi's vision: I raise the question of whether the characteristic "indeterminate future manifestations" that signify our having made contact with reality are such because reality itself is characterized by indeterminate future manifestations. An affirmative answer to this presents the culminating claim that reality itself justifies realism. Taken together, these theses offer hope of restoration to truly human knowing and being, in healing challenge to the recalcitrant, deadening themes of modern Western thought and culture.

The work consists of two parts. Part I is the 1985 dissertation, minimally revised to supply the conclusions and coherence it lacked, but also modestly framed with opening and closing comments to link it to my current understanding. In addition to an extended systematization of Polanyi's notion of contact with reality, it includes a lengthy effort to relate Polanyi's theses to the then-current discussions in philosophy of science surrounding realism. This engagement of an earlier era of the ongoing realist vs. anti-realist debate nevertheless remains valuable, for it attends to the thought of philosophers still deemed to be giants in the area, and it proceeds along the lines of fundamental presumptions that continue to hold sway as the debate continues.

Part 2 is fresh and current work, representing the vantage point from which the entire project may be apprehended. It contains three chapters which together serve to update the contemporary realist debate, to assess afresh Polanyi's continuing potential contribution to it, and to offer what I now feel to be a better resolution to "the problem of realism." This resolution is one that opens out into future prospects for me personally and, I hope, for others. *Reality* solves the problem of realism. In this, it is true to the very notion of contact with reality itself: the real is that which promises to manifest itself indeterminately in the future. And just as it took some centuries, according to Polanyi, to uncover some of the hints that Copernicus sensed in his vision of the planetary system as heliocentric, it is appropriate that it be the work of decades to display earlier proposals at the time only felt to be insightful.

In my recent early reading of the work of contemporary Swiss Catholic theologian Hans Urs von Balthasar, I find that he has uncannily and aptly portrayed the philosophical trajectory of my life—and possibly yours.

> No philosophical question can be simply resolved, definitively settled, and then left behind. The same basic questions keep coming back, at a new level, as we wind higher around the spiral, or as we drill more deeply into the mysterious abyss of being. One of these questions is the question: Does truth in fact exist? . . . Our very inquiry into the essence of truth throws us back upon our starting point, which lies in the naked, unassured question of whether truth or being exists at all.
>
> And yet there is an elemental wonderment over the sheer fact of existence, essence and truth that, for the genuine thinker, does not decrease but only steadily increases in the course of his research. But this astonishment, this ever more reverent, ever more amazed marveling at the stupendousness of the object of his knowledge, indeed, of his knowledge itself, looks less and less like the schoolboy's abstract and fruitless doubt of the existence of being and truth. His intellectual life may have begun with such doubt, when, as a freshman, he made his first tentative efforts at thinking with the help of an epistemology textbook, but this starting point now seems touchingly naïve measured against the sheer weight of so many years lived in company with the truth . . . .
>
> That is why, when the novice hesitates before the problem of truth, not knowing where to begin, he should take the advice of those philosophers who urge him to start by diving into the

current, to find out what water is and how to make headway in it through direct, physical contact with the flowing stream. They will tell him, and rightly so, that . . . the man who does not dare to jump into the truth will never attain the certainty that truth in fact exists.[8]

In other words, over time, life—and hopefully this book as part of it—should make philosophers and realists of us all.

Aliquippa, Pennsylvania
Summer, 2016

---

8. Balthasar, *Theo-Logic*, I, 24–25. Balthasar's work abounds with phrases consonant with the Polanyian vision of contact with reality with its inexhaustible indeterminate future manifestations. Ch. 14 of this work features an analysis of D. C. Schindler's Balthasar-inspired proposals.

PART 1

Early Consideration of Contact with Reality

Preface to Part 1[1]

The purpose of this inquiry is to examine and evaluate a little-known and probably not seriously enough considered aspect of Michael Polanyi's thought: his realism. Polanyi is known best for his contribution to philosophy of science and epistemology, specifically, for his advocacy of the role of personal commitment and appraisal in knowledge, and his development of the subsidiary-focal structure of knowledge. Polanyi's realism—that is, in part, his conviction that reality exists independently of any knowledge of it, and confidence that human knowers are generally successful in establishing contact with reality in their acts of learning and discovery—is less well known, even though it lies close to the heart of his theory of knowledge.

At least one legitimate reason for its comparative obscurity is the fact that Polanyi nowhere gives his realism systematic treatment. His realism is evident and often explicit throughout his works, but these passages are for the most part short, and the subject is often introduced and disposed of without the kind of logical development and the explanation of concepts that the reader would like. Polanyi's realism is also obscured by the great popularity (or notoriety) of his fiduciary program, such that it is probably difficult to believe that a philosopher so concerned with presenting the ultimately fiduciary character of the foundation of knowledge could also be concerned about any sort of contact with extramental reality—let alone

---

1. This Preface stood as the Introduction to Meek, "Contact With Reality: An Examination of Realism in the Work of Michael Polanyi" (PhD diss, Temple University, 1983). The dissertation's chapters were grouped in parts: Part I: Polanyian Epistemology; Part II: Contact With Reality; Part III: Polanyi and Realism in Contemporary Philosophy of Science; Part IV: Grounding Polanyi's Realism. I have erased these part divisions for purposes of the current publication, using part headings to denote my 1983 and 2016 work.

that if he had such a concern, his proposals could possibly be considered successful.

In this work, I propose to make the case for Polanyi being called a realist. I will offer a systematization of his idea of contact with reality and a demonstration of his realism. Then, I will endeavor to bring his ideas into the arena of contemporary discussion of the matter. It must then be determined whether Polanyi has in fact substantiated his claim: whether the knower does in fact lay hold of the real in his epistemic activity. These are the questions that I hope to address in the coming chapters. The very first chapters are for the most part introductory, offering a sketch of Polanyi's fiduciary program and his structure of knowledge that will provide the important context for the realism discussion. Special attention will be given to Polanyi's analysis of the process of discovery, for it is closely tied to his realism.

It shall be seen that reality for Polanyi is epistemically independent, and that even so, it is substantially accessible to the knower. We shall see that Polanyi defines reality as that which inexhaustively manifests itself. For him successful contact with reality is attested to by virtue of its accompanying intimations of an indeterminate range of future manifestations, as well as by virtue of the experience of a sudden and far-reaching integration. These theses not only reveal the character of Polanyi's realism but also bear implications for questions of truth and correspondence.

In comparing Polanyi's thought with that of other contemporary philosophers of science with respect to the issues of realism, we will gain a better sense of the nature of Polanyi's realism as I piece together his position on such issues as progress and rationality in science, the nature of truth, and various current realist theses. It will be seen that, although Polanyi would espouse key doctrines of contemporary realism, the peculiar character of his realism is such that he would give a qualified and fresh interpretation to each.

The concluding chapter of this part explores the Polanyian notion of indwelling in its attempt to ground and justify as well as amplify Polanyi's realism. This is done by way of a short excursus into the work of Maurice Merleau-Ponty. Merleau-Ponty's phenomenologically portrayed concepts of preobjective experience, and the lived body in particular, closely parallel Polanyi's ideas. As a result, it is hoped that Merleau-Ponty's fuller development of these notions will provide Polanyi's realism with fuller justification. It becomes apparent that realism is a viable option by virtue of the fact that the knower, as a physical being, is already rooted in and part of the world prior to any distinction between subject and object. What is more, he constantly reaches beyond himself to something else—this by reason of his very nature.[2] Human knowledge, then, is rooted in the tacit and hence rooted in the world, but is integrative in character and hence always reaches beyond the knower to incorporate the known.

The reader unfamiliar with Polanyi may find it helpful at this juncture to be given some sense of Polanyi's relative position with respect to contemporary philosophy of science, even though a more expansive analysis appears in chapters 8–10. Harold I. Brown, in his 1977 *Perception, Theory and Commitment: The New Philosophy of Science*, considers Polanyi's *Personal Knowledge* to be one of the founding works of a new approach to science: a movement that has been united in its attack upon the methods and conclusions of logical empiricism.[3] Subsequent exponents of this new image of science, according to Brown, include Stephen Toulmin, Thomas S. Kuhn, and Paul Feyerabend. In the new approach, study of the history of science replaces formal logic as the primary tool for analysis of science. The concern is less with the logical structure of completed theories and more with the rational basis of scientific discovery and theory change. The central claim is that a presupposed theoretical framework is more fundamental to scientific knowledge than is a group of data (which can no longer be considered theory-independent). The framework itself guides the determination of the nature and significance of data as well as the choice and solution of problems. The framework is modified only from within, especially in the event of a major discovery. Brown deems Karl Popper a transitional, in fact, an equivocal, figure. On one interpretation Popper conforms to the principles of logical empiricism despite his proposing falsificationism, and on another interpretation (Imre Lakatos among others) he attempts to embrace some of the motivating concerns of the new movement.

Let us add to Brown's assessment the following: Polanyi's critique of empiricism compares favorably with that of Feyerabend's, differing from it primarily because of Feyerabend's disregard of any questions of rationality—something Polanyi fervently maintains in a revised form. In contrast to Kuhn, Polanyi does not concern himself with a *structure* of scientific revolutions or with a distinction between normal and abnormal science. The fact that Polanyi is concerned with the *process* of a scientific discovery allows Kuhn's developments to be brought into line with his. Although Kuhn develops the Polanyian notion of the scientific community and acknowledges in particular the foundational role of tacit knowing, Kuhn's proposals

2. In preparing this for publication, I have opted to retain masculine pronouns in the body of the 1983 text, as in all quotations in which it occurs. In the body of the 2016 text in Part II, I will use exclusively feminine ones, attempting a balance meant to honor all persons while maintaining the integrity of different eras.

3. Brown, *Perception, Theory and Commitment*.

contain no epistemological structure like Polanyi's. Finally, there are hints of what may turn out to be a fundamental difference of characterization of reality and truth—a topic to be discussed more fully in chapter 9. Some similarity exists between Popper and Polanyi, especially on the more recent interpretation of Popper. Lakatos, who is deeply critical of Polanyi's proposals, has himself nevertheless emphasized the role of human judgment in intellectual performances, in his development of Popper's position; nor does he consider his own position to be any the less rational for it.

In concluding this introduction, I make two disclaimers. First, Polanyi's concern with the real extends beyond the issue of the possibility of contact with it. It somewhat naturally involves him in the consideration of what sorts of things are real, and his conclusions concern a whole spectrum of things from atoms and physical objects to minds, works of art, concepts, and universals. Polanyi also attempts to develop a metaphysical doctrine of emergent levels of being, the connection of which to his theory of knowledge is, in my opinion, problematic. Neither of these topics will given a full-fledged exposition in this work.[4]

Secondly, the philosopher who reads Polanyi's work is liable to find that it fails to live up to the rigorous standards of reasoning, explanation, and critique that are generally held within philosophical circles; it does not manifest the philosophical formality that we might be used to. He introduces terms and topics without reference to the standard discussions; the evidence and rationale that he proffers for his peculiar concepts seem inadequate, not to mention unphilosophical. For all that, we would be foolish to write off his work without further consideration. It is helpful to realize that, in contrast to most philosophers, Polanyi's early and formative training was in science—not even philosophy of science, but science. His interests then expanded over the range of social studies, including political science and economics. Finally, he turned his hand to more philosophical questions as a result of his dissatisfaction with the reigning philosophical interpretation of the nature of scientific inquiry. In this philosophical venture, what he was attempting to do was to replace what he felt was an inadequate, misleading, in fact false, epistemology with one that rang true to the scientific enterprise as he knew it to be. Thus, at least to some extent, we would do well to put up with seemingly shoddy philosophical analysis for the sake of fresh and expert insight resulting from his scientific perspective. Indeed, his concepts, perhaps rough-hewn and flawed, are seminal, elegant, significant, and profound, not to mention useful.

---

4. However, I do return to consider reality in the final chapter of this book. But that chapter does not work closely with Polanyi's specific metaphysical claims.

Further, it is helpful to realize that Polanyi claims that his ideas represent a radical rejection of the status quo, especially in philosophy of science, but also in philosophy. In an upcoming chapter, we will consider the issue of incommensurability of theories. To whatever extent there exists a core of truth in this notion, incommensurability apparently pertains when we compare Polanyi's claims with the wider conversation in philosophy of science, and philosophy in general. To some extent, the thinker who would develop a radical approach in philosophy or science is barred from doing so within the principal methodological medium of the system(s) that he rejects. Polanyi is self-consciously aware of this state of affairs; in fact he preaches it enthusiastically. He tells us that as a result, the one who would understand a new way of thought must trust his teacher, not blindly, but truly, purposefully bringing himself under that teacher's authority. Such a move does not inhibit either criticism or rationality, to Polanyi's way of thinking; it is rather a move that is absolutely essential if there is to be any comprehension whatsoever. Thus, my basic stance throughout this work has been first of all sympathetic with respect to Polanyi. This is not meant as a prejudicing preacceptance, but so as to allow him extra time to speak in order to compensate for the initial dullness of our hearing with respect to Polanyian themes. Yet, comparison and criticism are not impossible, as the reader will see. In fact, since the time of Polanyi's writing, the general shift of thought in philosophy of science has been in the direction of his concepts, thus rendering his early message more commensurable with respect to contemporary thinking.

1

Personal Knowledge

In order to accurately portray Polanyi's realist claim, we must locate it in the larger context of his overarching proposal that knowledge is personal. This chapter will show what Polanyi means by "personal knowledge," and why he thinks we should understand knowledge this way. The demonstration of the personal character of all of knowledge is Polanyi's consuming concern in his *magnum opus* and thus is where he himself begins.[1] Tacit knowing and subsidiary-focal awareness are concepts that pervade *Personal Knowledge* more or less implicitly. Polanyi later recognized their importance and explicated them more fully as part of his structure of tacit knowing in several essays.[2] In *Personal Knowledge*, however, his concern is to state in

---

1 Polanyi, *Personal Knowledge*. For an extremely helpful account of the evolution of Polanyi's thought, see Grene, "Tacit Knowing: Grounds," 164–71. *Personal Knowledge* was not Polanyi's first publication. He wrote several articles, pamphlets, and books both in science and in social and philosophical areas. The complete listing of the latter two categories of his publications through 1968 has been compiled by Richard L. Gelwick: "Bibliography," in *Intellect and Hope*, 432–43. The most notable of these for the purposes of this exposition is *Science, Faith and Society*, in which can be found in seminal form concepts Polanyi develops and carries through his entire philosophical career. But *Personal Knowledge*, Polanyi's *magnum opus*, is the first and only work in which Polanyi develops systematically the foundational role of personal appraisal and commitment.

2. Polanyi, *Tacit Dimension*; as well as the following essays in *Knowing and Being*, ed. Grene: "Knowing and Being," 123–37 (orig. pub. in *Mind* 70 n.s. [1961] 458–70); "The Logic of Tacit Inference," 138–58 (orig. pub. in *Philosophy* 41 [1966] 1–18, though probably written in 1964); and "Tacit Knowing: Its Bearing on Some Problems of

general the case for recognizing the personal root of all knowledge, in condemnation of what he takes to be the prevailing, presumed to be impersonal, approach in epistemology. His development of the notion of the personal culminates most explicitly in his discussion of his notion of commitment and in his "fiduciary programme."[3] Along the way it encompasses a whole range of ideas, such as tacit knowing, subsidiary awareness, indwelling, and the bodily rootedness of all thought—all terms that this introductory section will introduce. The sketch in this chapter patterns itself roughly after that development.

This overarching context of the personal character of knowledge has often been viewed as a weakness and as grounds for dismissing Polanyi's proposals without any consideration. It is Polanyi's emphasis on the all-encompassing framework of commitment and belief that has provoked such stereotypical labels as "irrationalism" and "mysticism."[4] It has opened his system to the charge of subjectivism, as he himself realizes. But the very fact that Polanyi's thought embraces a personal stance, whatever he might take that to be, makes it, on the surface, that much more surprising that he should positively espouse realism and not anti-realism. It would seem that rendering knowledge as personal would hinder, not help, his realism. But in fact, Polanyi will argue that apart from personal epistemology as he describes it, not even knowledge is possible, let alone realism. Positively, he will view realism as integral to personal knowledge and vice versa. Personal knowledge thus lends a characteristic flavor to Polanyian realism. A brief examination of his case for the personal will serve to give us a better grasp of it and also of the challenges his realism must meet.

Polanyi's critique of impersonal knowledge has three interwoven emphases, which I shall somewhat arbitrarily distinguish and describe in order. The contrasting nature of personal knowledge will become clear in the process. We will then briefly consider what Polanyi calls the paradox of self-set standards as a preface to looking at the fiduciary program and the notion of responsible commitment, which he develops in response to the charge of subjectivism.

Philosophy," 159–80 (orig. pub. in *Reviews of Modern Physics* 34 [1962] 601–16).

3. Polanyi, *Personal Knowledge*, 264.

4. Lakatos, "Falsification," in Lakatos and Musgrave, eds., *Criticism and the Growth of Knowledge*, 115. Why it is that Polanyi's work should not be so labeled should become clear in this and the coming chapters.

The False Ideal of Objectivity

Chapter 1 of *Personal Knowledge* comprises Polanyi's main critique of "the false ideal of objectivity"; thus, the Polanyian assessment of objectivity is a good place to start. The matter of objectivity, as we shall see, interweaves a variety of other Polanyian themes, such as the personal element in knowing, the unacceptability of positivism, the role of human appraisal in the justification of knowledge, the inherent rationality of science, and the rationality of nature—all of which we will encounter again in our discussion.

Contemporary science (or philosophy of science),[5] Polanyi claims, believes itself to be objective in a sense that is impossible and absurd, and in a sense in which science, in fact, is not objective. The prevailing interpretation would have us believe that the ideal is a science free of human input. If science were a discipline devoid of human perspective or commitment to human values, Polanyi argues at the beginning of *Personal Knowledge*, it would mean that science must devote itself, not to the study of things interesting to mankind, but rather to those aspects of the universe that are proportionally the greatest. "This would result in a lifelong preoccupation with interstellar dust, relieved only at brief intervals by a survey of incandescent masses of hydrogen—not in a thousand million lifetimes would the turn come to give man even a second's notice."[6] Obviously, we do not think of the concerns proper to science in this way. Science, rather, is intimately concerned with human perspective and human values.

A primary sense in which science sees itself as striving to be impersonal, and hence "objective," is that the practice of science must be as free as possible of human input. Thus, science, it is claimed, is based directly and exclusively upon repeatable observation and experimentation; scientific theories, once derived, must not extend in scope beyond that which is testable and the scientist must be prepared to dismiss a theory the moment conflicting evidence comes to light. The scientist must therefore remain personally aloof from his work. Effectively, in contrast to what we come to recognize as a distinctly Polanyian claim, science must be free of reliance upon human appraisal or judgment to whatever extent is possible.

Polanyi's criticism of this understanding of objectivity has a *de facto* and a *de jure* emphasis. In fact, this simply isn't an accurate representation of science. Scientific theories are often formulated independently of and in

---

5. Polanyi is writing in the 1950s; since that time, thanks in part to his work, this overall stance has been greatly modified. Yet even today, the idea of relinquishing the following principles, which Polanyi describes as false objectivity, can encounter substantial resistance.

6. Polanyi, *Personal Knowledge*, 3.

advance of observation. They are embraced by the scientific community despite the absence of verification, and they are not dropped despite the revelation of apparently conflicting evidence. Moreover, scientists become passionately involved in and committed to such theories.

All of these claims Polanyi makes and demonstrates particularly in connection with Einstein's work. His case for the role of skilled human appraisal and judgment in all disciplines of science spans several chapters and works, and to present his argument and evidence would be to duplicate what he himself has done expertly in *Personal Knowledge*. In short, what he does is demonstrate, mostly by example upon example, that in fact the scientist or epistemic agent is involved in his claim by virtue of his skilled appraisal or assessment of the claim in light of standards that are not explicitly identifiable. Even critical verification requires such human involvement.

In principle, Polanyi also argues, science would not be possible if this false ideal of objectivity were achieved. Knowledge and science would be principally impossible—it would cease to exist—were it not for this fundamental human element. This is the heart of Polanyi's message. In contrast to the claims to impersonality by the false ideal of objectivity, Polanyi would have us recognize and accept the power of the human mind to discover and exhibit a rationality that governs nature, and to endorse our acknowledgment of beauty and profundity in order to account for our acceptance of scientific theories.[7]

These typically Polanyian phrases lead us to another point in his argument concerning objectivity. The false ideal of objectivity seeks to define "scientific theory" in such a way that it is reduced to a mere convenient contrivance, an economic description of facts, a mere working hypothesis from which are drawn various empirical inferences.[8] These are the tenets of traditional positivism, a stance which is presumed to allow the scientist greater intellectual detachment with respect to his theories. This anti-metaphysical bent thus presumably preserves objectivity in science. Such a trend has evolved, Polanyi believes, from the gradual separation of mathematical knowledge from empirical knowledge over the course of the history of science. This divorce led to the loss of the notion of the intrinsic excellence of scientific theory. Polanyi wishes to restore this idea. In contrast to conventional understanding, Polanyi claims that science, and any legitimate scientific theory, is inherently rational. A theory possesses intrinsically an independence, authority, and persuasive power which result from its being in contact with a natural world that is inherently rational. A theory's

---

7. Ibid., 15.
8. Ibid., 6–9.

"peculiar intellectual harmonies" reveal more profoundly and permanently than sense experience the presence of objective truth.[9] Thus, in contrast to the false ideal, a theory is truly objective in the sense that it possesses an inherent quality of rationality that independently commands respect and acts persuasively to evoke universal acceptance by rational creatures. This inherent rationality implies that the theory has made contact with reality, and hence truth, and implies an indeterminate range of future confirmations. It is in this "wholly indeterminate scope of true implications," Polanyi says, that the deepest sense of a theory's objectivity lies; this is the sense in which a theory speaks for itself.[10] These distinctive Polanyian phrases are foreign to the wider conversation in philosophy of science. They will receive full treatment in later chapters, for they are central to his distinctive realism. It should, however, be noted that objectivity in this Polanyian sense preserves the involvement of the epistemic agent and thus remains personal. As he says, inquirers thereby may hope to conceive of a rational idea which will authoritatively speak for itself.

The Impossibility of "Explicit" Knowledge

The second strand of Polanyi's critique of impersonal knowledge has to do with explicit knowledge. Polanyi's problem with explicit knowledge is bound up with his case for the existence and fundamental nature of tacit knowledge. This case pervades and dominates his work. Chapter 2 will describe the structure of tacit knowledge and some of its applications, but will not assess Polanyi's defense of it. My purpose at this point is simply to note Polanyi's criticism of explicit knowledge as it fits into his criticism of impersonal knowledge and his proposal of a different approach in epistemology. One of the more representative passages on this subject is Polanyi's essay, "The Logic of Tacit Inference"; I use it here as my major reference for this brief discussion.[11]

To hold that all knowledge is explicit means, according to Polanyian philosopher Marjorie Grene, that all knowledge consists of pieces of information immediately present to the mind and impersonally transferable from one mind to another.[12] Polanyi claims that explicit knowledge is the

---

9. Ibid., 16.
10. Ibid., 4–6.
11. Polanyi, "Logic of Tacit Inference," in Grene, ed., *Knowing and Being*, 138–58. See also Grene, *Knower and Known*, in which the entire first part is devoted to this subject.
12. Grene, *Knower and Known*, 31.

ideal of contemporary science: it is derived from mechanics and aims at a mathematical theory connecting tangible, focally observed objects in such a way that everything is above-board, open to public scrutiny, and wholly impersonal.[13] Keying off Grene's definition, we may organize Polanyi's critique around the two claims of explicit knowledge, namely, that all knowledge is pieces of information immediately present to the mind and that it is impersonally transferable from one mind to another. With respect to the first, we can already guess at Polanyi's difficulty on the basis of his understanding of true objectivity: the deepest sense in which a theory is objective has to do with its range of indeterminate future confirmations. This phrase describes one aspect of the indeterminacy or unspecifiability which Polanyi believes to be an essential ingredient of any knowledge: no "piece" of information is able to capture explicitly all that we know or mean by it. Polanyi offers the aphorism, "We know more than we can tell."[14] On the other hand, there is a second indeterminacy: to coin a matching aphorism, "we say more than we know."[15] That is to say, any "piece" of information itself implies a spectrum of implications of which we at a particular time are not explicitly aware. For these two reasons, we cannot style any piece of information as being "immediately present to the mind" nor restrict our definition of knowledge to this sort of information.

Another difficulty with such a claim is that, according to Polanyi, there exist realms upon realms of something which deserves to be called knowledge but which does not consist in pieces of information focally or explicitly stated. He has in mind all skills in which "information" is held tacitly, more as an understanding of how to do something rather than as an explicitly stated procedure. In fact, he argues, all knowing is to some extent skillful knowing—a point that cannot be pursued here. To the extent that our universe of knowledge includes skills and skillful knowledge, however, it consists of knowledge that is entirely tacit in character.

The claim that knowledge is impersonally transferable from one mind to another bears critically, for Polanyi and for Grene, on the matter of whether learning and discovery are justifiable procedures. Discovery involves the transference of information, not from one mind to another, but into the mind in the first place. If knowledge is wholly explicit, there can be no learning, no discovery, and thus no scientific knowledge. Discovery, as we shall see in chapter 3, involves the germination of new hunches and ideas and the pursuit of those hunches despite the absence of any sort of

---

13. Polanyi, "Logic of Tacit Inference," in Grene, ed., *Knowing and Being*, 151.
14. Polanyi, *Tacit Dimension*, 4.
15. Polanyi, *Personal Knowledge*, 95.

justification. Discovery has to involve the epistemic agent's coming to know something in some sort of non-explicit way before coming to know it focally or explicitly. The progress of science, Polanyi says, is determined at every stage by indefinable powers of thought.[16] There exist no explicit rules that govern the germination of good ideas, and no explicit rules even for verification and refutation. Yet the fact remains that discovery, learning, and progress in scientific knowledge do exist. To this Polanyi the scientific discoverer attests; thus, it is a point that his opponents must concede. Hence, knowledge cannot be wholly explicit.

Is it the case, then, that there is no explicit knowledge? Yes and no. Yes, in the sense defined originally; there is no knowledge that is immediately present to the mind and impersonally transferable from one mind to another. Such knowledge, Polanyi claims, would be useless, for it would be cut off from both knower and known. Some knowledge, in fact, is wholly tacit: not present to the mind in this explicit sense at all. But no: there is explicit knowledge in the sense that our knowledge is in some measure articulable precisely because of its tacit root. Explicit knowledge, in this sense, exists by virtue of being ever tacitly understood and applied. All knowledge, therefore, is either tacit or rooted in the tacit; without the tacit it would cease to exist.[17]

The False Ideal of Certainty

The third strand of the Polanyian critique has to do with the prospect of certainty in knowledge. Polanyi does not speak of certainty per se.[18] In chapter 9 of *Personal Knowledge*, he offers his critique of doubt—that is, of the claim that all opinions or beliefs must be subjected to doubt, or critical scrutiny, if truth is to be established. He demonstrates the invalidity of such a process: in contrast to what Descartes claimed for his era-shaping method, you cannot doubt everything simultaneously. This is a point made also by language

---

16. Polanyi, "Logic of Tacit Inference," in Grene, ed., *Knowing and Being*, 138.

17. I have come, in recent years since this dissertation was first written, to believe that it can be said that there is no meaningful explicit knowledge. The best articulated statements, as we express them or understand them, are therein indwelled subsidiarily by us just as we would a hammer we are using. This is just what renders them meaningful. By contrast, a truly explicit statement would be one, perhaps, written on a chalkboard in quotes: "The door is open." But even then it would be difficult to construe this gesture of ours as being utterly devoid of subsidiary dimensions.

18. It is Grene who uses the term in connection with the Polanyian critique. Grene, *Knower and Known*, Part I.

philosopher Ludwig Wittgenstein, and philosopher of science Karl Popper.[19] So all knowers do and must hold on to beliefs that, in principle, cannot be subjected to critical scrutiny but are nevertheless legitimately retained. Polanyi says that this impossible method of doubt "is a logical corollary of objectivism. It trusts that the uprooting of all voluntary components of belief will leave behind unassailed a residue of knowledge that is completely determined by the objective evidence. Critical thought trusted this method unconditionally for avoiding error and establishing truth."[20]

Although Polanyi does not use the word, it is fair to describe the unattainable goal as certainty, especially the certainty of a foundational class of beliefs. We can also see from this passage how such a goal participates in the ideal of impersonal knowledge, which Polanyi seeks to undermine. Although the legitimacy of this method has been undermined as modern philosophy has unfolded since Descartes, nevertheless, Polanyi believes the unattainable ideal is retained, blinding contemporary thinkers to the actual state of affairs in epistemology.

Certainty is out of the question for Polanyi because the ultimate justification for what we claim to be true consists of our deepest convictions. These convictions, of which we are for the most part unaware, serve to justify all claims; as such they cannot themselves be justified, except in circular fashion. This is not to say that this epistemological bedrock[21] is self-evident in the usual, explicit sense; it is not even infallible. That is why it undercuts the possibility of certainty. Furthermore, with regard to scientific knowledge, Polanyi is saying that the most appropriate paradigm is not verification, but rather discovery. In discovery, as Marjorie Grene says, uncertainties cannot be avoided. Also, if it is the case that knowledge can never be made wholly explicit, it is difficult to imagine that it could ever be rendered certain. Finally, experience is inexhaustible, with interconnected aspects and overlapping meaning. Where such a state of affairs prevails, the idea of certainty becomes problematic.

Personal Knowledge and the Fiduciary Program

Knowledge, therefore, is objective by virtue of responsible personal involvement, explicit by virtue of its tacit root, and examinable by virtue of our foundational commitments. As a result of this sketch of Polanyi's critique

---

19. Wittgenstein, *On Certainty*, 16e, 18e, 23e, 38e, 47e; Popper, *Conjectures and Refutations*, 238.
20. Polanyi, *Personal Knowledge*, 269.
21. Gill, "Saying and Showing," 279–90.

of impersonal knowledge, we can see that by personal knowledge he means the following: that the epistemic agent is necessarily and legitimately involved in knowledge by virtue of his acts of commitment, appraisal, and reliance upon inexplicit forms of knowledge. Polanyi further clarifies personal knowledge in connection with what he calls the paradox of self-set standards. In every domain of knowledge and experience, Polanyi claims, the most basic standards by which we evaluate the legitimacy of the object in question do not come to us from an external source. Instead, they grow out of the very experience to which we apply them. This places the ultimate responsibility for the choice of such standards squarely at the feet of the one who chooses and embraces the relevant experience in the first place. Thus, our most basic standards of evaluation are self-set and appear paradoxical: how can self-set standards be standards at all? "We are faced once more," Polanyi says, "with the existentialist dilemma of how values of our own choice can have authority over us who decreed them."[22] Thus, personal knowledge appears to devolve into subjectivism.

In answer to the paradox of self-set standards, Polanyi develops his fiduciary program.[23] The fiduciary program wholeheartedly embraces the prospect of our "ubiquitous participation in the shaping of truth,"[24] legitimating it simply by elaborating it more fully and in such a way as to remove the air of paradox. He calls for the accreditation of our own judgment as the paramount arbiter of all our intellectual performances. He calls us to recognize belief as the source of all knowledge—that is, the fact that no intellectual act, not even the reformation of our ultimate convictions, can take place except within the fiduciary framework of those convictions. This is to recognize the existence of "the whole set of acceptances that are logically prior to any particular assertions of our own, prior to the holding of any particular piece of knowledge."[25] There is no other way for justification ultimately to be consistent with itself.

The program is justified, negatively, by Polanyi's critique of doubt. Doubt, he has demonstrated, is itself a form of belief; *comprehensive* doubt is impossible. His positive tack is to develop this framework of commitment. Polanyi revises old concepts of belief, facts, and truth, distinguishes the personal from the subjective, and demonstrates the extent of commitment's foundational role through all aspects of life. Facts and truth are what they

---

22. Polanyi, "Creative Imagination," 90–93; *Personal Knowledge*, 104, 195, 203, 204, 256, 299, 309; "Commitment to Science," in *Duke Lectures*, 25–26.
23. Polanyi, *Personal Knowledge*, ch. 10.
24. Ibid., 204.
25. Ibid., 256, 264–68.

are only within the framework of commitment: "truth is something that can be thought of only by believing it."[26] For someone to say that *p* is true is for him to say, "I believe *p*," although the former emphasizes more heavily what Polanyi calls the external pole of commitment. How can such a view not be subjective? Because each claim to truth is made with universal intent, that is, with the expectation that it should be believed by everyone because of its successful contact with a reality independent of and shared by everyone. This universal intent compels the knower to responsibility in his judgment: to search until one has found the truth. "The paradox of self-set standards is eliminated, for in a competent mental act the agent does not do as he pleases, but compels himself forcibly to act as he believes he must."[27] In this way Polanyi distinguishes the personal from the subjective.[28]

Standing by itself, the fiduciary program may not appear convincing in its attempt to distinguish personal knowledge from subjectivism. As Marjorie Grene says, the argument has a way of dissolving "like Cinderella's coach, without even a pumpkin left behind."[29] She came to believe, however, that the fiduciary program was itself justified by the structure of tacit knowing. The subsidiary-focal integrative structure of knowledge—to be considered in chapter 2—is Polanyi's explanation of the nature of knowledge and the way knowing works. It is, on the whole, more explicitly developed and more fully justified in terms of our everyday experience than is the fiduciary program. Thus, it strengthens Polanyi's case if a connection between the two were demonstrated to exist. That the two are related is, in fact, evident in the early pages of *Personal Knowledge,* which was written even before his interest shifted from the fiduciary program to the structure of tacit knowing.[30]

26. Ibid., 303–5. Polanyi's understanding of truth will receive extensive consideration in ch. 10.

27. Ibid., 315.

28. Ibid., 300, 324. There exists an indisputable *public* aspect to Polanyian epistemology. Although he speaks of *personal* knowledge, *self*-set standards, and the problem of *subjectivism*, Polanyi believes that knowledge develops in the context of the community. He has written much concerning the character that such a community ought to have—take, for example, his lecture, "A Society of Explorers" in *Tacit Dimension*. His concern has been primarily to criticize the planned approach to research that characterizes totalitarian thought. This topic exceeds the bounds of this exposition. However, let us note that, in saying that knowledge is personal, Polanyi does not mean to make a distinction between the singular and the plural, excluding the latter. The problem of subjectivism is accompanied by the problem of conventionalism (which he opposes vehemently), and self-set standards are meant to include those embraced subsidiarily by the community in general. (Thus, by the way, Polanyi is dismissed by some people as a psychologist, by others as a sociologist!)

29. Grene, "Tacit Knowing: Grounds," 168.

30. For Polanyi's acknowledgement of this shift, see *Tacit Dimension*, x. In *Personal*

Here, he speaks of the "two kinds of awareness." His primary example of subsidiary awareness is our reliance upon tools as we use them. He then asserts that beliefs, interpretative frameworks, and the like, function the way tools do, in our knowledge. Our subsidiary awareness of tools, and also of these basic beliefs, comes about as they we assimilate them into ourselves, making them part of our existence. This occurs, with respect to most of our presuppositions, as we learn to speak of things in a certain language. The incorporation of objects or beliefs as tools by subsidiary reliance upon them is what Polanyi calls indwelling—a topic to be described in greater depth at a later point.

The Premises of Science

To this early evidence of the connection between the fiduciary framework and the structure of tacit knowing we may add, I believe, Polanyi's later discussion of the premises of science. I find this latter claim far more helpful than the fiduciary program when it comes to removing the air of paradox from the notion of self-set standards. Presenting it at this point necessitates the use of concepts that I will introduce formally in the next chapter about the structure of tacit knowing. But since this notion pervades his and our work, they will become clear as we go.

Polanyi's "premises of science" are our bedrock beliefs as they relate to scientific inquiry. They include general criteria of scientific value, standards of intellectual satisfaction that guide our information-gathering and conception-shaping, and our beliefs about the nature of things—beliefs bound closely with our language.[31] Such premises are revised in advance of the advent of new, especially major, discoveries. Is such a procedure a matter of arbitrary choice? This is, in effect, the question of the paradox of self-set standards. Polanyi responds in the negative, developing his answer more explicitly in his 1967 article, "The Creative Imagination."[32] These premises, like all of our beliefs, are for the most part subsidiarily held—they cannot be implemented unless they are subsidiarily held, as we shall see. Although they can be made explicit, we are often not even aware of them.

Knowledge, see 58–59.

31. Polanyi, *Personal Knowledge*, 160–71. Note that similar concepts are propounded by Thomas Kuhn, *Structure of Scientific Revolutions*, 4, 11, 15–17, 62, 103, 204; "Reflections on My Critics," in *Criticism and the Growth of Knowledge*, Lakatos and Musgrave, eds., 277; also, by Paul Feyerabend, *Against Method*, 66, 77, 98, 154–55, 225, 254, 266, 267, 269, 270, 284.

32. Polanyi, "Creative Imagination," 91–92.

Premises are indeed altered during discovery; but it is not a change of which we are focally aware, let alone have control of in an explicit way, until much later. What happens is that, in the course of our search for the answer, our premises are subsidiarily modified as part of our imaginative, anticipative integration of subsidiary clues. By the time the discovery is made, the new premises are already in place. Subsequent examination of the implications of the discovery may bring them to light, possibly to the consternation of the discoverers. But there is no sense of the arbitrary about such a change. Technically, perhaps, we have chosen them, but it seems more true to experience to say that they have imposed themselves on us. Contrast this, for example, with the kind of choice that, as we shall see, Imre Lakatos embraces: by contrast scientific choices as he characterizes them appear at best conventional—and Lakatos considers this to be rationality.[33] Or we may contrast Polanyi's account with a pragmatism in which the decision is based upon considerations of simplicity, fruitfulness, and so forth. The difference is that change in basic beliefs is for the others an explicit, or at least a focal, process; for Polanyi it is first of all subsidiary, as are the beliefs themselves. It is this unique move of Polanyi's—in which he explains that premises of science, as well as all other kinds of self-set standards and beliefs, are subsidiarily embraced and maintained—that removes from them the air of subjectivism or conventionalism. Personal knowledge, as a result, is more clearly distinguished from these.

In Conclusion

Thus, personal knowledge is a positive epistemic proposal that Polanyi is developing that he believes, in contrast to the prevailing false ideals of objectivity, explicit knowledge, and certainty, accurately represents how knowledge works, and also is positively conducive to its working better. Contemporary science should embrace the fact that knowledge necessitates and thrives on the basis of all of the following generally unacknowledged, but nevertheless operative, factors: the knower's responsible commitments to self-set standards, his appraisal of the value, strategy, and success of any inquiry, responsible submission with universal intent, the fiduciary framework of all truth claims, the fact that premises of science to which the scientist is committed are tacitly altered to a rationality that accommodates an impending discovery—else there is no discovery, and the subsidiary-focal structure of

---

33. Lakatos, "Falsification and the Methodology of Scientific Research Programmes," in *Criticism and the Growth of Knowledge*, Lakatos and Musgrave, eds., 106–12, 131.

all knowing (more of this in the next chapter). Personal knowledge does not exclude realism, but rather, in Polanyi's mind, implies it. Polanyian realism is rooted integrally in this epistemic vision, embracing its fundamental commitments. But far from proving a limitation or compromise, as the skewed ideals of contemporary science might anticipate, it unleashes realism to a qualitatively superior expression. In turn, Polanyian realism will offer personal knowledge the justification and objective anchoring it needs. Since this realism grows out of the concepts of objectivity and the rationality of scientific theories mentioned in this chapter, we shall return to them in later discussions.

2

The Structure of Knowledge

Personal knowledge furnishes Polanyian realism with its most general context and presupposition. Tacit knowing, Polanyi's foremost concern and contribution, concretely articulates the positive account of knowing that his realism presupposes, reflects, and in turn shapes. It infuses his realism with its distinctive character and figures significantly in its justification. This chapter offers only a short sketch, compiled from the whole breadth of his writings. While other more substantial secondary accounts exist, reading Polanyi's elegant work itself is by far the best way to further one's grasp of this central concern of his vision.

Origins of the Structure of Tacit Knowing

Polanyi's exposition of these concepts did not reach its fullest development until a few years after the writing of *Personal Knowledge*, which appeared in 1958. The concepts of focal and subsidiary awareness appear in a minor way in that book, but we have Marjorie Grene's testimony that Polanyi afterwards felt that this distinction was its most original concept.[1] Polanyi's convictions that the knower actively shapes his knowledge, and that the relevant result bears similarities to a gestalt, are also extant in *Personal Knowledge*.[2] These

---

1. Grene, "Tacit Knowing: Grounds," 168. See Polanyi, *Personal Knowledge*, 55, where the terms are first introduced.

2. See for example, Polanyi, *Personal Knowledge*, 132, 55–58.

ideas are developed further in *The Study of Man*, which appeared a year later.³ But the term "integration" appears in 1961 in "Knowing and Being," and in 1962, Polanyi elaborates the full structure of tacit knowing in the Terry Lectures, subsequently incorporated into the book *The Tacit Dimension*. In the 1966 introduction to this book, Polanyi notes that his reliance on the necessity of commitment has been reduced as he has developed the structure of tacit knowing.⁴ The structure itself accounts for the various unspecifiabilities that Polanyi sought to elucidate in *Personal Knowledge*. As has already been noted, Grene believes that the structure furnishes the requisite justification for the fiduciary program.

Reflecting over his extensive writing about the structure, we can infer major insights of Polanyi's which lead to his developing his proposal of tacit knowing. The first is the extent to which unspecifiability pervades what is presumed to be an entirely specified or specifiable discipline—the pursuit of knowledge, in particular, scientific knowledge. "Upon examining the grounds on which science is pursued," Polanyi says in reflection on the point from which he started in 1946, "I saw that its progress is determined at every stage by indefinable powers of thought."⁵ Apparently, Polanyi was constantly preoccupied with unspecifiability. In the course of developing his structure of tacit knowing, Polanyi elaborates five or perhaps six particular kinds of unspecifiability in knowing, as we shall see. Polanyi employs the aphorism, "We know more than we can tell."⁶ It has been helpful to me to realize that, for Polanyi, indeterminacy has what I call a "retrospective" and a "prospective" aspect, as I will develop in a later chapter. Not only does a particular articulated claim embrace and rely on particulars of which the knower is not aware, but the claim also anticipates particular implications of which we can, at present, have no explicit idea. By contrast, we may express this prospective indeterminacy as, "We say more than we know."

Other key insights are as follows. A second contributing insight is Polanyi's further recognition of "the strange way in which, in all knowledge, the inarticulate outruns and outweighs its articulate aspect"; the articulate is in fact rooted in the inarticulate.⁷ This has been evident in the development of the framework of belief as the foundation for knowledge. It receives formal exposition in the development of the from-to relationship of subsidiar-

---

3 Polanyi, *Study of Man*. These were his Lindsay Memorial Lectures at the University College of North Staffordshire.

4. Polanyi, *Tacit Dimension*, x.

5. Polanyi, "Logic of Tacit Inference," in Grene, ed., *Knowing and Being*, 138; compare Polanyi, *Science, Faith and Society*, ch. 1.

6. Polanyi, *Tacit Dimension*, 4.

7. Grene, "Tacit Knowing: Grounds," 168.

ies to focus. A third Polanyian insight, already noted, is the active role and the extent of participation of the knower in the shaping of knowledge. It is this personal element that has stood in need of accreditation. It is eventually captured in the notion of integration. Further, we have Polanyi's testimony that from the very beginning, he believed that the act of perception was paradigmatic for scientific discovery, and, in fact, for all forms of knowing. Thus, the structure of tacit knowing develops out of insights into perceptual activity and is successfully applied far beyond the boundaries of perception. Finally, Polanyi appropriates the findings of Gestalt psychology as a way to cast the structure of knowing.[8] This insight, I believe, is key to his innovative account; his adaptation of it offers him a positive integration of all his other insights into the structure of tacit knowing he proposes.

Subsidiary-focal Integration

Out of these insights grew Polanyi's structure of tacit knowing.[9] The heart of the doctrine is the claim that every act of knowing consists of the knower's active integration of a variety of particulars into a comprehensive whole. The nature of the integration is such that the knower relies on these particulars to attend to the whole. He attends from the particulars to the whole —hence Polanyi's denotation of it as a from-to structure. The knower's action involves two kinds of awareness: his focal awareness of the comprehensive whole to which he is attending and his subsidiary awareness of the particulars. The latter concept involves the notion that the knower is aware of these particulars only in terms of the whole into which they have been integrated. This is not to say that the knower cannot ever be focally aware of these particulars. It is to say that he cannot be focally aware of them if he is relying on them to attend to the first comprehensive whole. Knowledge of subsidiaries is not exactly a form of subconsciousness, for they are known within the structure of the whole. But what does become clear as Polanyi elaborates his theory is that the class of particulars on which the knower may rely includes even subliminal bodily clues, of which we cannot properly be said to be aware.[10] Again, what makes these particulars subsidiaries, as

8. Polanyi, *Personal Knowledge*, vii.

9. Perhaps the most methodical development of the structure of tacit knowing appears in the first lecture of *Tacit Dimension*. But it is also developed in the relevant articles in *Knowing and Being*. The concept and its implications are featured prominently in virtually all of Polanyi's later writings. This exposition is therefore culled from a great variety of sources.

10. Polanyi insisted on retaining the term, "awareness," even after he himself had applied it to cases in which awareness could hardly be said to be an appropriate

they may be called, is the sort of relationship that they have to the focus within the integrative feat.

For example: I am asleep in a campground. I am awakened by a strange and disturbing noise. My ears strain to make sense of what I am hearing; my eyes search the darkness intently in the direction of the sound, and I struggle to make out what it is I see. Suddenly, the moving shapes stand out from the shapeless background, and the noise becomes recognizable as so much scratching and chewing. The situation becomes understandable: raccoons have invaded my picnic basket. In this example, I have been confronted with an array of perceptual particulars, some of which I can specify—for example, some kind of sound and movement; some of which I have not specified, such as my latent knowledge of the layout of the camp and where in particular the picnic basket is in relation to my sleeping bag. As I struggle to make sense of the situation, I subsidiarily integrate these clues; I come to rely on them as I attend to a focus. The once independent particulars are suddenly fitted into a coherent pattern, and integration has been achieved.

Integration, as has been said, consists of the personal and active shaping of a comprehensive whole. It is, most basically, not an automatic performance. It involves, in critical cases, an often prolonged struggle to shape a coherent pattern, or gestalt, on the basis of particulars from which it could never have been deduced. It could never have been deduced from the particulars because not all the subsidiaries are or can be known explicitly. Further, even if the subsidiaries could, in another situation, be known explicitly, the integrated pattern remains logically out of reach by virtue of the integrative synthesis, attainable only by a personal act of insight. Once the feat of integration is accomplished, it is irreversible in the sense that the knower is never able willfully to return to his previous state of ignorance and perform the same feat again; from that point on that particular act of knowing is more a matter of routine or perhaps remembering.

---

description, and even after the matter had been called to his attention (Grene, "Tacit Knowing: Grounds," 170). But he himself defuses the problem—and undercuts the meaning of the word: "Let me say, therefore, once more that when I speak of my 'subsidiary awareness' of something, I do not describe an awareness of it in the usual sense; I merely refer to the *function* of an event in affecting my awareness of its meaning, as observed at the focus of my attention. When understood this way—which is the way I defined it from the start—subsidiary awareness will be found and accepted at all levels of consciousness" (Polanyi, "Logic and Psychology," 38–39).

The Structure of Knowledge

Integration—Four Aspects

Polanyi elaborates four distinct aspects of integration, consideration of which sheds more light on its nature. The *functional aspect* of integration consists of the fact that what makes a particular a subsidiary particular is its function as a pointer with respect to its focus. The *phenomenal aspect* of tacit knowing concerns the fact that particulars qua particulars and particulars qua subsidiaries often appear differently. The effect of the integration is often to transform their appearance—one can think of visual puzzles that operate on this principle (e.g., how many animals can you find hidden in this picture?). Closely related is the *semantic aspect:* the subsidiaries gain their meaning in terms of the focus; the comprehensive whole constitutes the joint meaning of the particulars. This is, of course, best illustrated by the words of a language, the meaning of whose spoken syllables or written characters is derived from the concepts toward which they point. Finally, the *ontological aspect* of integration may result from the phenomenal and semantic aspects. It concerns the fact that the successful accomplishment of a feat of integration is accompanied by the conviction that the resultant comprehensive entity is real. Of this last aspect in particular, more must be said at a later point.

The Subsidiary

Let me say a little more about the subsidiaries and then about the focus. The most remarkable thing about subsidiaries is the vast range of particulars that can qualify as such. Most basically, there are bodily clues—not simply surface sensations, but also subliminal events of which we have no cognizance. There are marginal clues—clues that do not belong to the object of our attention per se but to its background or context. That these marginal clues are absolutely essential to our understanding is not difficult to prove. Past experiences, preconceived notions, linguistic and scientific frameworks, and foundational beliefs and values also enter into the realm of the subsidiary. This great range of subsidiaries results first of all from the fact that integration is the central activity not only in perception but in scientific discovery, theoretical knowledge, practical or skillful knowledge, and aesthetic judgment. *All* knowing is tacit knowing, Polanyi says, meaning that every kind of act of knowing ultimately relies upon subsidiaries and involves a tacit leap to comprehension. This is the link between the fiduciary program and the structure of tacit knowing, for our deepest-seated commitments function subsidiarily within our integrative acts of knowing, just as bodily clues do. The range of subsidiaries is broad not simply in the sense that there are many kinds of them. It is broad, secondly, in the sense that each particular kind of integration involves the entire spectrum of subsidiaries. Perception clearly relies on bodily and marginal clues. But it relies equally on our theoretical or merely linguistic conceptions of what it is that we perceive. On the other hand, abstract thought can never be divorced from its bodily roots. The fact that it lives, for example, in our speech or our writing (both bodily activities) is demonstrated by the fact that we are rarely able to think without performing one of them.

The second thing that I wish to note concerning subsidiaries is that they are susceptible to two sorts of unspecifiability. Some, but not necessarily all, subsidiaries in a particular integration are unspecifiable because they simply are not known as such by the knower. This is especially true of subliminal clues, but it can be true of marginal and other perceptual clues as well as of our conceptions and convictions. But all subsidiaries are necessarily "logically unspecifiable," meaning that it is impossible to specify them as they are in the course of being relied upon for comprehension within a particular focus. They cannot be specified by our focusing upon them as particulars because such a switch of attention destroys their phenomenal and semantic transformation. They cannot be specified fully in terms of the focus because of the logical gap fixed between them as a result of the integration.

The Focal

Turning our attention to the focus, let me note first that Polanyi has distinguished integrative acts in which the focus is superimposed upon the subsidiaries, such as in the recognition of a face, from those in which the focus lies beyond the clues, such as in the case of the blind man using his stick. Accordingly, he defines physiognostic and telegnostic meaning. The instances of the focus lying beyond the subsidiaries also provide the inspiration for Polanyi's reference to the subsidiaries as the proximal term of the integration and to the focus as the distal term.

Secondly, there is such a thing as what Polanyi calls an empty focus.[11] The concept grows out of the fact that it is possible to integrate clues in terms of a focus that is as yet unknown, or that is in some way insubstantial. The primary examples of integration in terms of an empty focus are universal concepts, and problems. Our ability to function with the concept of man, for example, results from our successful integration of all subsidiary clues

---

11. Polanyi, "Tacit Knowing: Its Bearing," in Grene, ed., *Knowing and Being*, 168.

concerning a variety of men into a joint meaning which is the universal. The universal, the focus, is "empty," especially in contrast to particular men. Yet the integration is possible, enabling us to apply the concept meaningfully, giving significance (in this case, relatively minimally) to the men around us. In the case of a problem, we have in the problem a collection of particulars which are considered significant only with respect to a solution that at present is necessarily unknown. What makes a clue a clue is its relationship to the unknown solution. This empty focus, in contrast to the universal, is meant someday to be filled. The fact that such an integration is possible is absolutely essential to the prospect not only of scientific discovery, but of every form of learning. This will be considered in more detail in chapter 3.

Finally, this last case makes it clear that Polanyi must not intend the focal and the explicit to be coextensive. For the empty focus is in fact tacit. Another case of a tacit focus would be the mastery of a skill such as crocheting, which can be carried on while performing some other activity. Here both subsidiaries and focus are tacit, while attention lies elsewhere. The focus is, of course, more often than not articulable, but what makes it a focus is not this articulability. It is defined in terms of its relationship to subsidiaries by way of an integration—it, like the subsidiaries, is functionally defined. Similarly, "subsidiary" and "tacit" do not mean the same thing. Subsidiaries are what they are by virtue of their function within an integrative focus. The domain of tacit knowledge includes this subsidiary relationship, but includes for Polanyi many other things as well—tacit foci, as we have just seen, the human powers of integration, appraisal, intuition, and imagination.[12]

Indwelling

Finally, we must consider briefly the Polanyian concept of indwelling.[13] We have already noted in passing the fact that all knowing is fundamentally rooted in the human body, for bodily clues are integral to every act of knowing. A person's knowledge of his own body differs from his knowledge of

---

12. It includes the whole realm of what Maurice Merleau-Ponty calls "preobjective experience" (see ch. 11 of this book).

13. Polanyi, *Personal Knowledge*, 59–60, 64–65, 195–96; *Study of Man*, 31, 79; "Knowing and Being," in Grene, ed., *Knowing and Being*, 134, 136; "Logic of Tacit Inference," in Grene, ed., *Knowing and Being*, 148, 149; "The Structure of Consciousness," in Grene, ed., *Knowing and Being*, 211–24, esp. 214 (orig. pub. in *Brain* 88 [1965] 799–810); "Faith and Reason," in Schwartz, ed., *Scientific Thought and Social Reality*, 123 (orig. pub. in *Journal of Religion* 41 [1961] 237–47); "On the Modern Mind," in Schwartz, ed., *Scientific Thought and Social Reality*, 142–43, 148–49 (orig. pub. in *Encounter* 15 [May 1965] 12–20); Polanyi and Prosch, *Meaning*, 36, 37, 145.

any other object, for it is essentially and consistently a subsidiary knowledge. This is not to say that he never focuses on his body nor has explicit knowledge of it. Rather, it is to say that if focal knowledge were all he had of his body, it would not be his body. It is our subsidiary knowledge of our hand, for example, our knowledge of it in its skillful feats of grasping, writing, weaving, and so on that makes us know that it is *our* hand, that makes it feel "lived in." The person whose hand is paralyzed loses such subsidiary knowledge. Thus it is that I dwell in my body via my subsidiary knowledge of it. The Polanyian concept of indwelling consists in the claim that, just as we dwell in the subsidiaries of our body, even so we come to dwell in the subsidiaries of all our integrative acts. We indwell them or we interiorize them—Polanyi uses both concepts. In this way, our being is transformed as our bodies extend out into the world. We come to dwell in the activity of driving a car as we master the skills (i.e., render subsidiary the particulars) involved. After constant practice, the driver no longer needs to focus his attention on the size of his car when squeezing through tight places, parking, etc., for he has gained a working, subsidiary knowledge of the car's boundaries. This knowledge does not—cannot—consist in the driver's continual explicit measurement of the distance in feet between himself and the edge of the car, and between the car and the curb or wall beyond it. Rather, what happens is that we simply drive through and into spaces, making subsidiary allowances for the size of the car as we would our own body. The car is an extension of us, a tool utilized in the achievement of a certain end. We come to live in a foreign language in a similar way. The sign of our mastery of it is that we no longer think *about* it, but rather think *in* or *through* it. Our being is accordingly extended by the interiorization of this framework. Finally, as a scientific community comes to embrace a particular theory in its understanding of reality, together with its values and methods, the particular interpretation comes to appear natural as it is relied upon for the understanding of further events. The community comes to indwell this framework.

In chapter 11, Polanyi's conception of indwelling will receive further scrutiny as an anchoring locus of the justification of his realist claims. Our subsidiary knowledge, in which all knowledge is rooted, can be aligned with the indwelt body and those aspects of the world that we have incorporated subsidiarily. Thus, subsidiary knowing is being and as such is rooted in the world. I will consider whether this furnishes a link with the world that is prior to any distinction between subject and object. Such a link would provide at least partial justification for the realist claim that there exists a world to be known and that man has the capacities to understand it truly.

In Conclusion

In conclusion to this chapter: in his structure of tacit knowing Polanyi offers an epistemic account of both the active participation of the knower in his knowing and the great, foundational expanse of the inarticulate or unspecifiable in knowing. The structure of knowing, subsidiary focal integration, has a broad range of application, since it obtains in all fields that involve any sort of knowing or, for that matter, any sort of human achievement. In the next chapter we will explore its dimensions particularly in scientific discovery.

3

Scientific Discovery

The achievement of discovery constitutes for Polanyi the paradigm of scientific knowing. Discovery, like perception, is the kind of knowing that involves a persistent groping toward an as-yet-unknown solution, and thus it truly represents epistemic achievement in science.[1] Without this sort of achievement, science would not exist. Polanyi demonstrates that the act of discovery is superior to more routine scientific knowing:

> And yet this exalted valuation of strictly formalized thought is self-contradictory. It is true that the traveler, equipped with a detailed map of a region across which he plans his itinerary, enjoys a striking intellectual superiority over the explorer who first enters a new region—yet the explorer's fumbling progress is a much finer achievement than the well-briefed traveler's journey. Even if we admitted that an exact knowledge of the universe is our supreme mental possession it would still follow that man's most distinguished act of thought consists in *producing* such

---

1. Some of the passages in Polanyi's work concerning scientific discovery are these: *Science, Faith and Society*, 14, 35, 36; *Logic of Liberty*, 38–39, 51, 71, 197; *Personal Knowledge*, 64, 104, 120, 121–22, 124–25, 130, 147–48, 148–49, 161, 165, 177, 183, 184, 300, 305, 403; "The Unaccountable Element in Science," in Grene, ed., *Knowing and Being*, 117–19 (orig. pub. in *Philosophy* 37 [1962] 1–14); "Knowing and Being," in Grene, ed., 129–32; "Logic of Tacit Inference," in Grene, ed., *Knowing and Being*, 138–40, 142–43; "Tacit Knowing: Its Bearing," in Grene, ed., *Knowing and Being*, 171–73; *Tacit Dimension*, 23–25, 67–69, 75–81, 89; "Creative Imagination," 85–93; "Science and Reality," 177–96; "Genius in Science," 57–71.

knowledge; the human mind is at its greatest when it brings hitherto unchartered domains under its control.[2]

Scientific discovery is paradigmatic because it reveals most clearly the tacit powers, convictions, passions, and knowledge in which all scientific knowledge, to some extent, is rooted. The fact that Polanyi takes discovery to be paradigmatic of all scientific knowing indicates a dismissal of any distinction between the contexts of discovery and justification. Critical verification requires the same sort of tacit powers and personal appraisal that discovery does.[3]

The structure of tacit knowing is operative in the context of scientific discovery. According to Polanyi, discovery is not qualitatively different from perception; it is the same activity performed by someone with superior perceptive skills and scientific education, and the solution is likely to be farther reaching and more difficult to achieve. But the same tacit integrative skill characterizes both. Scientific discovery involves the search for and reliance upon subsidiary clues in order to achieve by an integrative feat a comprehensive whole on which the scientist focuses. Since this is, in fact, the structure of tacit knowing, all the qualities, descriptions, and implications that characterize the structure per se can be legitimately and fruitfully applied to the process of scientific discovery.

It is clear, then, why Polanyi considers the topic so extensively and why it deserves some consideration in this work. In addition, it merits our attention because of its implications for realism. Most simply put, discovery presupposes that there exists something to be discovered, and that the discoverer possesses the epistemic capabilities to accomplish such a feat. These presuppositions themselves will be examined in later chapters, but at this point we must acquaint ourselves with Polanyi's conception of the process of discovery and the knower's innate abilities.

Recognizing a Good Problem: The Intimation of Hidden Coherence

The process of discovery begins with the recognition of a good problem. The problem comprises the first clues to the hidden coherence. The subsequent search consists of the acquisition (and recognition as such) of further clues. The discovery comprises the focus. It is an "empty" focus prior to the

---

2. Polanyi, *Study of Man*, 18.
3. Polanyi, *Personal. Knowledge*, 13; Grene, "Tacit Knowing: Grounds," 168. Compare Feyerabend, *Against Method*, 145–46, 165–67.

event; that is, it is one that tacitly gives significance to the clues on which we rely especially in the problem stage, despite the fact that we have no explicit understanding of it yet. Discovery is ultimately attained by a sudden integrative comprehension of the solution after much groping and searching. The phenomenal and ontological aspects of tacit knowing are most vivid in discovery, for the particulars that the scientist has perhaps unconsciously relied on in the course of discovery are surprisingly and convincingly transformed in the light of the discovery. The radical character of the comprehension convinces the scientist that he has indeed made contact with reality, which he has brought to light by his discovery of an aspect of reality. More of this in later chapters.

Let us go over this ground again more carefully. A problem, according to Polanyi, is an intimation of coherence among hitherto uncomprehended particulars.[4] This is a strange definition, but one that, under further scrutiny, reveals important Polanyian themes. First, I note what chapter 5 will address in greater depth: an underlying assumption of the ultimate rationality of the universe. Polanyi says the following in a discussion of problems: "These efforts of our eyesight are based on the assumption that any curious things before us are likely to have some hidden significance. Scientists speculating about strange things in nature act on a similar assumption."[5] Polanyi holds unwaveringly and unashamedly to the conviction that the universe is inherently rational, that coherence characterizes our thought because it characterizes nature antecedently, and that anybody who assumes and relies on the possibility of epistemic advance must be convinced of this assumption, whether he admits it to himself or not. Of course, throughout our experience, we encounter collections of particulars that either do not arouse our attention or merely strike us as strange. But there are those that strike us as being curious; what is meant by this is that they cause us to wonder whether they are significantly related. It is this sort of distinction that operates in the different characterizations of data that fail to corroborate a new scientific theory—anomalies, as Thomas Kuhn calls them. An anomaly is perhaps, for a time, dismissed. Later, there may come a time when someone

---

4. Polanyi, "Knowing and Being," in Grene, ed., *Knowing and Being*, 131; *Tacit Dimension*, 21–22. On problems, see also Polanyi, *Personal Knowledge*, 73, 120, 126–27, 130, 300; "Unaccountable Element in Science," in Grene, ed., *Knowing and Being*, 117–18; "Metaphysical Reach of Science," *Duke Lectures* I, 6; "Commitment to Science," *Duke Lectures* III, 12–13, 17; "Creative Imagination," 88–89; "Science and Reality," 188; "Genius in Science," 59–62. There also are several passages which concern problem-*solving*; let me note here only the article devoted to it: "Problem-Solving," 89–103.

5. Polanyi, "Genius in Science," 59. Further documentation of Polanyi's commitment to the ultimate rationality or coherence of nature may be found in ch. 5 of this book.

detects a hidden significance in it or in a set of anomalies. The move to this latter state involves the belief that there exists some meaningful coherence that accounts for and rationally unites the particulars in question and thus implies the belief in the coherence of nature.

It is the recognition of the possibility of hidden significance that constitutes the act of sighting a problem. A problem is, let us note, an *imitation* of a *hidden* coherence: a problem has nothing of its own by which its legitimacy as a problem may be explicitly justified. It cannot even be constituted as a problem except with respect to a hidden focus.

Apart from embracing such an account of a problem, one would be compelled to raise the question of how it is that we ever come to know anything at all—how it is that we can ever make a start toward learning or discovery. As a key part of his argument, Polanyi poses this question, noting that it is essentially the dilemma of the *Meno*: "[Plato] says that to search for the solution of a problem is an absurdity; for either you know what you are looking for, and then there is no problem; or you do not know what you are looking for, and then you cannot expect to find anything."[6] The *Meno* problem turns out to be a dilemma only for those who retain the requirement of explicitness for knowledge. The beginning of a process of discovery and in fact all stages of the advance can hardly be said to involve explicit knowledge. Either the process is wholly explicit, like a deduction—in which case it cannot be considered an advance, and the result does not constitute a comprehension or discovery; or the process does constitute an advance to discovery—in which case knowledge in advance of discovery cannot be wholly explicit.

Rather than to compromise the ideal of explicit knowledge, the bulk of modern epistemology and philosophy of science has simply ignored the question raised by epistemic advance, concentrating its analysis on the context of justification. For example, Karl Popper argues that the question concerning the sources of knowledge should be replaced by the question, "How can we hope to detect and eliminate error?" He replies that we do so by criticizing our own and others' theories and guesses.[7] Such a procedure is no doubt legitimate, but it also does the disservice of obscuring this fundamental epistemological puzzle. The puzzle is fundamental because, first, it besets virtually every form of human achievement that involves advance into the unknown. It besets not simply scientific discovery, but also *all* kinds of learning, from that of the infant to that of the scientific genius. It concerns not only the achievement of pieces of factual knowledge, but also

---

6. Polanyi, *Tacit Dimension*, 22–23.
7. Popper, *Conjectures and Refutations*, 25–26.

other activities that we are more used to thinking of as skills. The puzzle is fundamental because it bears on the existence of something that is an undergirding requirement of all learning which, as such, it would behoove us to comprehend: tacit knowledge.

The *Meno* problem can be solved and the fundamentals of epistemic advance represented more adequately, Polanyi claims, by the accreditation of tacit knowledge. The tacit knowledge that he has in mind at this point is not the knowledge of subsidiaries within an already integrated focus (which falls in my category of "retrospective indeterminacy"), but rather another sort of subsidiary clue: "the intimation of something hidden, which we may yet discover," "a tacit foreknowledge of yet undiscovered things" (what I call "prospective indeterminacy").[8]

In the journal literature concerning Polanyi, there exists a small exchange concerning his use of the *Meno* paradox.[9] Michael Bradie takes issue with what he says is the crucial assumption of Polanyi's restatement of the paradox, namely, that if you know what you are looking for, then there is no problem. Bradie produces a counterexample that employs the well-known Goldbach conjecture. The conjecture claims that there is no even number that is not the sum of two primes. Bradie's point is that the mathematician knows that in order to refute the Goldbach conjecture he must look for a number that is even and is not the sum of two primes. Yet, the mathematician still has the problem of finding that number. On this basis, Bradie dismisses Polanyi's claim for the existence of tacit knowledge.

Polanyi would dispute that even the subsequent search for that number is an exhaustively explicit process unguided by tacit intimations. Mathematicians feel their way to mathematical discoveries. Consider Grene's critique of Descartes: as a mathematician himself he did not follow his own prescribed "method"—if he had, he would not have made the expert mathematical discoveries credited to him.[10] Grene quips acerbically: "He who remains within the clear light of reason goes nowhere and has nowhere to go."

But dilemmas have two "horns," or premises; Bradie has dealt with only one, and falsely represents it as the single major premise of the argument. The other premise, in Polanyi's words, is that if you do *not* know what you are looking for, then you cannot expect to find anything. Marjorie Grene, the expert professional *philosopher* that it may be said that Polanyi never was, embraces and agrees with Polanyi's use of the *Meno* paradox. However,

---

8. Polanyi, *Tacit Dimension*, 22–23.

9. Bradie, "Polanyi on the Meno Paradox," 203; Simon, "Bradie on Polanyi on the Meno Paradox," 147–50.

10. Grene, *Knower and Known*, 78.

she restates the question of the *Meno* in the following way: "That question is, as Meno put it, how can we seek what we do not already know, or, in more modern terms, how can we recognize a problem, how can we advance to discover the unknown?"[11] Grene restates it, not in terms of our ability or inability to define a problem (and then know what we are looking for), but rather in terms of how we can recognize a problem in the first place, how we can *advance* in our discovery of the unknown. This is the question of how learning is possible—which is certainly *Meno*'s problem. Polanyi says this himself more adequately in another place: "We may ask, therefore, how we can ever start and go on with an enquiry without knowing what exactly we are looking for."[12] So the point on which this problem bears in the case of the Goldbach conjecture is the issue of how Goldbach ever came up with the conjecture in the first place. How did he know that it was a legitimate problem? The fact that the problem exists is what causes difficulty for the contemporary epistemologist, for the existence of the problem entails the legitimate use of some sort of non-explicit knowledge of what is to be looked for. Given a criterion of knowledge that it be only explicit, it is certainly the case that if you do not know (in the explicit sense) what you are looking for, then you cannot expect to find anything. That is why tacit knowledge furnishes an alternative to the *Meno* dilemma. It "breaks the second horn," by proposing the existence of knowledge that is not explicit. Tacit knowledge allows for the knowledge of "something hidden," the foreknowledge or intimation of yet undiscovered entities.

Polanyi has, from the beginning, proclaimed the existence and legitimacy of unspecifiable powers belonging to the knower which enable him successfully to achieve comprehension of reality. He speaks constantly of the knower's "anticipations" of the hidden coherence and the "intimations" he senses.[13] Within the structure of tacit knowing, the workings of these powers become a little clearer. The knower's "power" is the power of integration. Polanyi says, "this shaping or integrating I hold to be the great and indispensable tacit power by which all knowledge is discovered and, once discovered, is held to be true."[14] The anticipations and intimations describe the knower's tacit foreknowledge: the as-yet-unlegitimated hints and clues

11. Ibid., 23.
12. Polanyi, "Creative Imagination," 88.
13. Polanyi, *Science Faith and Society*, 14, 33; *Personal Knowledge*, 42, 43, 94, 103, 104, 142, 148, 301, 311,; *Study of Man*, 63, 74, 193; "Logic of Tacit Inference," in Grene, ed., *Knowing and Being*, 143; *Tacit Dimension*, 21–23; "From Copernicus to Einstein," 100; "Faith and Reason," 124; "Science and Reality," 188–91, 195; "Genius in Science," 60–61.
14. Polanyi, *Tacit Dimension*, 6.

on which he relies in his search. Integration involves, once again, the awesome ability of sensing the significance of certain particulars which is theirs only in the light of an as-yet-uncomprehended focus. Such knowledge, since it is unspecifiable, is tacit, and more particularly, subsidiary.

Intuition

Polanyi has further developed his understanding of the process of scientific discovery by exploring two concepts that he has isolated: *intuition* and *imagination*.[15] He elaborates four categories of intuition, the first of which, *dynamic intuition*, just is this integrative skill of tacit foreknowing and is the one on which I will presently focus my attention.

Strategic intuition accounts for the scientist's ability to assess whether the importance of the problem and possible discovery at hand would warrant the investment of the powers and resources requisite for its pursuit. This is intuition in its more practical outworking. Strategic intuition compares its sense of the hidden reality discovered, and its importance, with the general philosophical and economic tenor of the society and time in which the scientist functions, and with the various resources at his disposal. Polanyi's elucidation of this aspect of science compares positively with C. S. Peirce's work on the economy of research.[16]

Creative intuition is the term Polanyi gives to the tacit powers that evoke the final, spontaneous integration that constitutes the discovery. Creative intuition "fills" the empty focus, which has, up to this point, been the unknown center of significance for the subsidiary clues. With the climactic event of discovery, clues are transformed in a focus of meaning, and intimations and anticipations are borne out. In light of the foregoing intimations and anticipations, in fact, the discovery is recognized as such; by the time the discovery appears on the scene, though it may still be surprising, it bears an aura of familiarity as a result of the discoverer's anticipations.

A final form of intuition, which I shall call *"confirmatory"* intuition (Polanyi does not give a name to what he describes), consists of the intuitive recognition of the result as valid. Confirmatory intuition may be heavily relied upon, to the relative exclusion of articulate confirmation, for even years after the discovery, depending upon the relative wealth or poverty of evidence for the claim. It is never wholly eliminated either, given the tacit foundation of all knowledge.

---

15. See in particular "Creative Imagination."
16. Rescher, *Peirce's Philosophy of Science*, ch. 4.

Scientific Discovery

But let us return to dynamic intuition. Dynamic intuition is active specifically in the problem and process stages of a scientific discovery. It is responsible for the very glimpse of a hidden coherence that can be designated a problem; the glimpse that sparks puzzlement and interest in the scientist, and eventually provokes him to sustained research. It operates between the problem and the discovery, actually guiding the scientist's progress, by providing the scientist with what Polanyi refers to frequently as a "sense of the increasing proximity of the solution."[17] Dynamic intuition recognizes clues and somehow "measures the distance" between the present understanding and the intuited focus. Polanyi draws on his own scientific experience as well as everyday experience for the recognition of this sense of increasing proximity. He points out that we have all experienced it in the common attempt to remember someone's name; we know somehow that we are close and then closer to having it; we speak of its being "on the tip of my tongue."[18]

Foreknowledge of a solution and a sense of increasing proximity to it both retain a slight air of paradox, given the inability to explain them in any explicit fashion. But it is, in fact, nothing short of amazing that puzzles and mysteries can be solved, that babies can learn to speak and move through their world, and that scientists can make earthshaking discoveries—all of which involve the tacit recognition of unspecifiable clues. Polanyi captures the appropriate sense of wonder in his citation of Polya:

> The process of solving a mathematical problem continues to depend, therefore, at every stage on the same ability to anticipate a hidden potentiality which will enable the student first to see a problem and then to set out to solve it. Polya has compared a mathematical discovery consisting of a whole chain of consecutive steps with an arch, where every stone depends for its stability on the presence of others, and he pointed out the paradox that the stones are in fact put in one at a time. Again, the paradox is resolved by the fact that each successive step of the incomplete solution is upheld by the heuristic anticipation which originally evoked its invention: by the feeling that its emergence has narrowed further the logical gap of the problem.[19]

Dynamic intuition, unspecifiable capacity that it is, leads to the solution, for it gives rise to a tacit understanding of the focus and of the path

---

17. He also speaks of it as a "gradient of deepening coherence." Polanyi, *Science, Faith and Society*, 32; *Personal Knowledge*, 124–25, 129, 310, 403; "Tacit Knowing: Its Bearing," in Grene, ed., *Knowing and Being*, 171; "Creative Imagination," 88; Polanyi and Prosch, *Meaning*, 193.

18. Polanyi, *Personal Knowledge*, 128–29; Polanyi and Prosch, *Meaning*, 193.

19. Polanyi, *Personal Knowledge*, 128. See also *Science, Faith and Society*, 32.

toward it: "This is how I would resolve the paradox of the 'Meno': We can pursue scientific discovery without knowing what we are looking for, because the gradient of deepening coherence tells us where to start and which way to turn, and eventually brings us to the point where we may stop and claim a discovery."[20]

It may be objected that use of the term "intuition" only serves to fuel the fire of the critic's claim that Polanyi's work sanctions mysticism. The term, of course, may be a little misleading, but its choice can be justified. As for the concept itself, Polanyi does not have a mystical source of knowledge in mind—in the sense of one that provides knowledge immediately or irrationally. The heart of the matter is that intuition is just the ordinary integrative skill that characterizes every form of human achievement: "not the supreme immediate knowledge, called intuition by Leibniz or Spinoza or Husserl, but a work-a-day skill for scientific guessing with a chance of guessing right."[21] Besides, the skill of integration to an as-yet-uncomprehended focus is remarkable enough in itself, especially to those of us raised in a milieu that has set explicit knowledge as its paradigm and ideal and presumed that nothing in addition is required for scientific success.

Does the appellation "intuition" suggest infallibility? If it does, it is not that Polanyi means it to. Human knowledge "comprises everything in which we may be totally mistaken,"[22] and tacit, intuitive knowledge is not exempt. But neither does this imply that there is nothing at all to this so-called faculty of intuition, or that "intuition" really falsely represents an activity that merely is a matter of chance. Polanyi says: "The fact that this faculty often fails does not discredit it; a method for guessing 10% above average in roulette would be worth millions."[23] If no such faculty were operative, a scientist would be left with the overwhelming task of testing an infinite number of alternative solutions to a problem and, more basically, with deciding between an infinite number of possible problems ranging in undetectable potential from good to bad and specious. Finally, if ever the scientist reached the solution, he would fail to recognize it. The fact that this is not what happens in science, that real discovery occurs without an infinite number of attempts and that results are confidently maintained, testifies to the existence of this intuitive skill.

---

20. Polanyi, "Creative Imagination," 88.
21. Polanyi, "Logic of Tacit Inference, in Grene, ed., *Knowing and Being,* 143–44.
22 Polanyi, *Personal Knowledge,* 404.
23. Polanyi, "Creative Imagination," 89. See also *Science, Faith and Society,* 37; "The Structure of Tacit Knowing," *Duke Lectures* II, 25.

Comparing Polanyi's Account with Those of Recent Philosophers of Science[24]

Recent philosophers of science corroborate the existence of intuition or at least recognize the existence of the kind of evidence that points to Polanyi's conclusions concerning the process of scientific discovery. None of the following has more than a little to say, however, and none develops the notion as Polanyi does. Popper's notion of conjectures includes his claim that knowledge progresses only by virtue of unjustifiable anticipations and guesses. He speaks of theories as free mental creations: the result of an almost poetic intuition. But he does not develop the process of scientific discovery to the extent that he develops scientific justification.[25] Imre Lakatos mentions the role of hints and anticipations, particularly in connection with the positive heuristic of a research program: "the positive heuristic consists of a partially articulated set of suggestions or hints on how to change, develop the 'refutable variants' of the research-programme, how to modify, sophisticate, the 'refutable' protective belt."[26] Stephen Toulmin notes that the scientist must look out for deviations that are not yet explained but that promise to be explicable—thereby acknowledging the tacit aspects of a problem: a hidden coherence, an inarticulable promise.[27] Paul Feyerabend says that science contains "vague and incoherent anticipations of future ideologies" alongside of well-developed theories. He also notes that Galileo was convinced intuitively of his conclusions even though confronted with a host of disconfirmatory data.[28] Kuhn also occasionally mentions "anticipations," but it may be that he considers them always to be articulable. But he also speaks of Lavoisier's "sense that something was amiss"—his "advance awareness of difficulties"—concerning the phlogiston theory, which enabled him to see in Priestley's experiments a gas that Priestley himself never recognized.[29] But like the others, Kuhn fails to develop this aspect of scientific discovery.

---

24. In part 1 of this work, thinkers deemed "recent" are writing around 1980. Part 2 selectively engages the work of thinkers writing around 2015. Nevertheless, since current work persists in the outlook formatively shaped by Popper, Kuhn, and Lakatos, this study gives a glimpse of thought that is both closer to Polanyi's own milieu and still germane to ours.

25. Popper, *Logic of Scientific Discovery*, 280; *Conjectures and Refutations*, vii, 38, 45, 192.

26. Lakatos, "Falsification," in Lakatos and Musgrave, eds., *Criticism and the Growth of Knowledge*, 135, 175.

27. Toulmin, *Foresight and Understanding*, 45.

28. Feyerabend, *Against Method*, 97, 145-56, 155, 157,159.

29. Kuhn, *Structure of Scientific Revolutions*, 56, 75, 96.

Part 1: Early Consideration of Contact with Reality

Joseph Rouse has put forward the thesis that the Kuhnian system is to be sympathetically supported and elucidated in terms of Martin Heidegger's thought.[30] At one point, he claims a parallel between Kuhn's constraints that define a puzzle (presumably in chapter 4 of *The Structure of Scientific Revolutions*) and the Heideggerian triad of foundational aspects of interpretation; fore-having, fore-sight, and fore-conception.[31] The parallelism is questionable, I believe, because of a difference that Rouse minimizes: it is that for Heidegger the constraints are tacitly understood. Rouse's discussion serves rather to highlight the similarities of Heidegger to Polanyi. Rouse defines prepossession (fore-having) as one's general familiarity with the sorts of things one is dealing with, how they interact and belong together, and what can be done with them. This compares favorably with Polanyi's conception of latent, or background knowledge. Preview (fore-sight) consists of one's general sense of how to go on, of what is problematic, and how we might proceed to deal with it. Preconception (fore-conception) makes sense only in the light of the possibility of preview, for it is a sense of what would count as a solution to the problem which allows us to know when to stop with it. Concerning these, Rouse argues:

> Philosophers of science have been primarily interested in the retrospective evaluation of the results of scientific research, and such evaluation presupposes that the research has been completed, and that what is to be evaluated has been made fully explicit. But if we are interested in the practice of research, we must consider it prospectively. Research demands that we project possible directions in outline, in advance of their actually having been carried out. To make such understanding fully explicit would be to have already carried out the research activities which the understanding is projecting. A fully explicit preconception would not tell us what would count as a solution to a problem; it would be the solution. A fully explicit preview of how to solve a problem would render its solution merely a technical exercise. It might be argued that we could be fully explicit about what we do know, even though it is not yet fully adequate to solve our problem, but according to Heidegger, this would be to misunderstand the projective character of understanding. Why would it be that just these explicit claims and no other have been projected as our preview and preconception? There must

---

30. Rouse, "Kuhn, Heidegger, and Scientific Realism," 269–90.
31. Heidegger, *Being and Time*, 188–95.

be a not yet articulated understanding on the basis of which any explicit consideration of alternative claims takes place.³²

Rouse quotes from Heidegger: "The character of understanding as projection is such that the understanding does not grasp thematically that upon which it projects—that is to say, possibilities. Grasping it in such a manner would take away from what is projected its very character as a possibility, and would reduce it to the given contents which we have in mind."³³ Rouse concludes: "So long as work remains to be done on a problem, there must be an open-ended, non-thematic understanding of how to go on with it."

Here we see not only testimony to the necessary existence of a foreknowledge that is tacit—non-thematic—but also argumentation very much along the lines of Polanyi with respect to the *Meno* problem. I believe that all of this is not nearly so explicit in Kuhn. Later in his career, Kuhn acknowledges the existence of tacit knowledge; in light of this, perhaps we may take it to have been implied.³⁴

Comparing Polanyian Intuition with Peirce's Abduction

Polanyi's notion of intuition is clearly paralleled, or anticipated, in Peirce's concept of abduction.³⁵ Abduction is the name that Peirce gives to the process of formulating and selecting hypotheses; its counterpart is retroduction: the testing and elimination of the hypotheses selected. The distinction is similar to Popper's, but according to Nicholas Rescher in his helpful exposition, Peirce's well-rounded view of the methodology of science is superior.³⁶ Abduction serves to select from the immense domain of theoretically possible hypotheses a group that is small enough to research profitably in detail and that has a good chance of containing the right answer.

How is the human mind capable of performing such a feat? It has, Peirce says, a natural instinct for truth, a sense of the plausible regarding

32. Rouse, "Kuhn, Heidegger, and Scientific Realism," 274.
33. Ibid., 274; Heidegger, *Being and Time*, 185.
34. Kuhn, "Reflections on My Critics," 270, 274, 275.
35. As far as I have been able to tell, Polanyi refers to Peirce only once ("Sense-Giving and Sense-Reading," in Grene, ed., *Knowing and Being*, 181 [orig. pub. in *Philosophy* 42 (1967) 301–25]), and that in connection with the subject of signs. Thus, it appears that Polanyi was not aware of the affinities between his own concept of intuition and Peirce's abduction.
36. Rescher, *Peirce's Philosophy of Science*, 41–42.

nature. It is the human, cognitive, equivalent of "horse sense," a power of guessing right.[37] Of this instinct, Peirce notes characteristics that, we have seen, describe Polanyian intuition. The faculty has not been acquired "by a self-controlled and critical logic"—i.e., it is not an explicable process.[38] It is like an instinct "in its so far surpassing the general powers of our reason and for its directing us as if we were in possession of facts that are entirely beyond the reach of our senses." It utilizes particulars that possess coherence only in terms of an as-yet-uncomprehended focus.[39] It bears similarities to perceptual judgments, which themselves result from a process that is not sufficiently conscious to be controlled.[40]

The abductive act takes place in a gestalt-like flash: "The abductive suggestion comes to us like a flash. It is an act of *insight*, although of extremely fallible insight. It is true that the different elements of the hypothesis were in our minds before; but it is the idea of putting together what we had never before dreamed of putting together which flashes the new suggestion before our contemplation."[41] Peirce, as seen in this quotation, is quite explicit that the instinct is fallible. "It goes wrong oftener than it goes right," he says, "yet the relative frequency with which it is right is on the whole the most wonderful thing in our constitution."[42]

Finally, we may detect similarity between abduction and intuition in Peirce's statement that abduction is motivated at the outset by "the feeling that a theory is needed to explain the surprising facts"—an intimation of the coherence of as-yet-uncomprehended particulars, i.e., a problem.[43]

Peirce believes that the abductive instinct is born within the human being as a result of the evolutionary process. It has developed as a result of evolutionary adaptation in the struggle for survival. The human mind is a product of the universe; thus, the laws of the universe are incorporated into our being. We are endowed with "a kind of fundamental sympathy for the processes of nature."[44] Even this has its point of comparison within the Polanyian system in Polanyi's notion of human knowledge as one of the highest of a series of emergent levels, a topic that does not fall within the scope of this book.

37. Peirce, *Collected Papers*, 6.530, 7.220, 8.223.
38. Ibid., 5.172–73.
39. Ibid., 5.172–73.
40. Ibid., 5.172–73, 181, 183.
41. Ibid., 5.181, 183.
42. Ibid., 5.172–73.
43. Ibid., 7.218.
44. Ibid., 5.603; also 5.590, 604.

Concerning the justification of abduction, Peirce has the following to say. First of all, the possibility of abduction is itself undergirded by

> ... a fundamental and primary abduction, a hypothesis which we must embrace at the outset, however destitute of evidentiary support it may be. That hypothesis is that the facts in hand admit of rationalization, and of rationalization by us.... We are therefore bound to hope that, although the possible explanations of our facts may be strictly innumerable, yet our mind will be able, in some finite number of guesses, to guess the sole true explanation of them. *That* we are bound to assume, independently of any evidence that it is true.[45]

Thus, the assumption of success in science is fundamentally essential and also ultimately undemonstrable. Polanyi makes this claim repeatedly.[46]

We have already noted the necessity of a belief in the rationality of nature and that it is comprehendable by us. But Peirce fleshes out his justification of abduction by claiming that, if we are ever to understand things at all, it can only be by means of abduction.[47] Thus he urges his readers to accredit it—note the similarities to Polanyi: "We shall do better to abandon the whole attempt to learn the truth, however urgent may be our need of ascertaining it, unless we can trust to the human mind's having such a power of guessing right that before very many hypotheses shall have been tried, intelligent guessing may be expected to lead us to the one which will support all tests, leaving the vast majority of possible hypotheses unexamined."[48]

Finally, the existence of this sort of ability is attested to inductively by the indisputable progress of science, as well as by the historical record that seldom more than two or three attempts have been made before the solution has been uncovered by the work of scientific genius. Abduction is, therefore, "the sheet-anchor of science," without which science would fail to exist.[49] Peirce is obviously more optimistic in his interpretation of science than are the philosophers of science of our day. He is probably more optimistic than Polanyi; the problem of success in science will be given further consideration in chapter 9.

---

45. Ibid., 7.219.

46 Polanyi, *Science, Faith and Society*, 17, 23, 35, 44, 45; *Logic of Liberty*, 38–39; *Personal Knowledge*, 126–27, 305, 316, 403; *Study of Man*, 20; *Tacit Dimension*, 68–70; "Creative Imagination," 86; "Tacit Knowing: Its Bearing," in Grene, ed., *Knowing and Being*, 172; "The Unaccountable Element in Science," in Grene, ed., *Knowing and Being*, 120; "Logic and Psychology," 27; Polanyi and Prosch, *Meaning*, 182–90.

47. Peirce, *Collected Papers*, 5.145, 171.

48. Ibid., 6.530.

49. Ibid., 7.220.

The primary difference between Polanyian intuition and Peircean abduction has to do with the comparative breadth of the two conceptions. Abduction has been elucidated with respect merely to the proliferation and selection of hypotheses. From that point on, according to Peirce, the process of discovery consists of retroduction, the testing of hypotheses, in which, he says, no mysterious guessing powers are required.[50] Intuition, by contrast, accounts not only for the formulation of a good problem but also for the gradual advance by accumulation of clues toward the unknown, for the sudden integration to discovery, and for the conviction of the rightness of the result. There exists for Polanyi no distinction between discovery and justification, and the tacit power of integration is required even for the sustenance of knowledge. Polanyian intuition, by virtue of its development in terms of the subsidiary-focal integrative feat, is a more fully developed notion than abduction.

Intuition and the Creative Imagination

A deeper understanding of Polanyi's account of the process of discovery can be gleaned when we examine the workings of intuition in connection with those of its necessary counterpart, imagination.[51] The creative imagination, by contrast to intuition, comprises the activity, as opposed to the direction, involved in research. It functions by searching out helpful clues in pursuit of the hidden focus. The imagination strives to fill any logical gap extant between present understanding and intuited solution by digging up clues. Imaginative activity consists of a vigorous and persistent brainstorming, a ransacking of our thoughts in search of possible alternatives. Polanyi writes: "But the moment feasibility is obstructed, a gap opens up between our faculties and the end at which we are aiming, and our imagination fixes on this gap and evokes attempts to reduce it. Such a quest can go on for years; it will be persistent, deliberate, and transitive; yet its whole purpose is directed on ourselves: *it attempts to make us produce ideas*. We say then that we are racking our brain or ransacking our brain; that we are cudgeling or cracking it, or beating our brain trying to get it to work." He continues: "And the action induced in us by this ransacking is felt as something that is happening to us. We say that we tumble to an idea; . . . We are actually surprised and exclaim 'Aha' when we suddenly produce an idea. Ideas may come to us unbidden, hours or even days after we have ceased to rack our brain."[52]

---

50. Ibid., 5.197.
51. Also in Polanyi, "Creative Imagination," esp. 89–91.
52. Ibid., 91.

Imagination and intuition are jointly essential, together accounting for the various aspects of scientific discovery. Intuition functions as the necessary guide and arbiter with respect to the products of the imagination. Imagination provides the requisite legwork and force to move the process toward its goal. The former is a spontaneous activity, the latter deliberate, though subsidiary. We can generate a model of the chronological or at least logical development of a discovery on the basis of Polanyi's description:

1. Dynamic intuition formulates problem, setting task to imagination; strategic intuition assesses value of task.
2. Imagination ransacks for clues.
3. Dynamic intuition subsidiarily assesses clues in terms of tacit focus, directs search as it senses proximity to solution.
4. Imagination ransacks for clues (2 and 3 can be repeated alternately a number of times).
5. Creative intuition spontaneously integrates clues into anticipated focus, achieving discovery.
6. Confirmatory intuition proclaims validity of discovery; imagination points to inexhaustible future manifestations (still ransacking for clues!).

Intellectual Passions

One final aspect of discovery must be mentioned if the Polanyian system is to be represented adequately. It is the crucial role played by what Polanyi terms, "intellectual passions."[53] Intellectual passions are necessarily and legitimately exercised in the pursuit of achievement, epistemic or otherwise, human or otherwise. The existence of intellectual passions attests to the personal basis of knowing. They turn out to be essential to the process of scientific discovery. In *Personal Knowledge*, Polanyi delineates three general functions of intellectual passions: selective, heuristic, and persuasive.

Selective passion functions as an index of a scientist's professional interest in a problem and its eventual solution. A scientist becomes interested in and excited about those problems that are potentially of great value to science. Scientific value, Polanyi proceeds to explain, generally results from a combination of three factors: accuracy, systematic relevance, and intrinsic interest. Accuracy concerns the possibility of making information already

---

53. See esp. Polanyi, *Personal Knowledge*, ch. 6.

to some degree in hand significantly more precise. Systematic relevance or profundity concerns a substantial deepening or extension of, perhaps a revolution in, our understanding of experience. Intrinsic interest has to do with whether a certain problem concerns a subject matter that is already intrinsically interesting, such as human life. Thus, intellectual passions in their selective function aid and perhaps to some extent comprise strategic intuition. But the former concept highlights the necessarily emotional aspect of the early problem stage: without such excited interest, a good problem would perhaps never be elucidated in the first place.

Heuristic passion is that which inspires the dogged persistence of the imagination in its ransacking for clues over what may turn out to be a period of years. It is perhaps closely related to Polanyian intuition. Persuasive passions are those that accompany the scientist's conviction of the rightness of his discovery, causing him to maintain and argue for his position in the face of apparently contradictory evidence and the (what is hoped to be temporary) rejection of his colleagues. Thus, the entire integrative process is passionate, and this not only in scientific discovery but also in every manifestation of the integrative achievement.

In Conclusion

In conclusion: Polanyi's central epistemic theses—that all knowing involves the tacit in a subsidiary focal integrative structure—receive their definitive exposition and powerful justification in the exemplifying act of scientific discovery. Polanyi, as a premier research scientist, no doubt felt exceptionally powerfully the mismatch between the prevailing epistemological commitments of the era and his own prodigious experiences in scientific discovery. Embracing scientific discovery as the paradigm of tacit knowing actually places higher stakes on Polanyi's claims, for tacit knowing involves not only present and past subsidiary clues, but also future ones. Coming to know requires that we accredit what we might call anticipative knowledge or half-understanding. The paradigmatic form of scientific knowledge, he actually says, is foreknowledge of an approaching discovery.[54] Laying such a heavy emphasis on discovery, as over against explanation—and thus in utter contrast to the bulk of philosophy of science—not only reveals these dimensions, but also in the process presumes integrally a commitment to realism. With this backdrop of Polanyi's alternative epistemology, we may now turn to consider his "contact with reality."

54. Polanyi, *Tacit Dimension*, 24–25.

4

Polanyi's Realism

In my sketch of Polanyian epistemology in these first chapters, I have purposely given little space to the consideration or even mention of the system's realistic aspects, saving them for treatment in these later ones. This artificial dichotomizing thus far may have been misleading, but the discussion in this section will set that straight. My purpose here is to show that Polanyi does in fact purport to be a realist despite what can seem on the surface an anti-realist epistemology of personal knowledge, commitment, and the fiduciary program. This chapter presents Polanyi's distinctive realism in a preliminary way. The next chapters examine in depth Polanyi's notion of contact with reality and related concepts: the "reality statement," the ontological aspect of tacit knowing, and various criteria of contact with reality. A final section serves to reference other concerns of Polanyi's that corroborate his realism. Further analysis will be the focus of chapters 8, 9, and 10, which give special attention to it in light of categories and issues central to the contemporary realist debate.

Polanyi's Commitment to Realism

To begin with, it can be demonstrated with a few quotations that Polanyi maintains what Joseph Margolis terms, "the original realist thesis," namely, that reality exists external to the knower and independently of any human knowledge of it.[1] Consider the following statements of Polanyi's: "An empirical statement is true to the extent to which it reveals an aspect of reality, a reality largely hidden to us, and existing therefore independently of our knowing it. By trying to say something that is true about a reality believed to be existing independently of our knowing it, all assertions of fact necessarily carry universal intent."[2] Elsewhere Polanyi says: "This is, in fact, my definition of external reality: reality is something that attracts our attention by clues which harass and beguile our minds into getting ever closer to it, and which, since it owes this attractive power to its independent existence, can always manifest itself in still unexpected ways."[3] Also: "The first step is to remember that scientific discoveries are made in search of reality—of a reality that is there, whether we know it or not. The search is of our own making, but reality is not."[4]

The fact that reality is independent is attested to by its potential of manifesting itself in unexpected ways. This signature characteristic, we shall see in chapter 5, forms the core of Polanyi's definition of reality. Reality always remains at least partially hidden so that even when true understanding is achieved, the subject at hand cannot possibly be exhausted, and the actual bearing of our knowledge, to the extent that it does in fact bear on reality, is always indeterminate. Reality as that which manifests itself indeterminately in the future, experience of which signals the knower's contact with reality, is the signature of Polanyian realism with which this inquiry is centrally concerned. I believe that it constitutes Polanyi's distinctive and superior contribution to the realist debate. More of this to come.

Independent Reality is Knowable

Reality, despite its independence, is in fact knowable, according to Polanyi. Truth is not made or invented, but rather discovered, and discovery is the paradigm for all scientific knowledge.[5] Our knowledge is achieved in submission to the real.[6] That Polanyi maintains this thesis despite (actually, pre-

---

1. Margolis, "Cognitive Issues," 373.
2. Polanyi, *Personal Knowledge*, 311.
3. Polanyi, "The Unaccountable Element in Science," in Grene, ed., *Knowing and Being*, 119–20.
4. Polanyi, "Creative Imagination," 92. See also *Science, Faith and Society*, 10, 36; "Tacit Knowing: Its Bearing," in Grene, ed., *Knowing and Being*, 172; "Creative Imagination," 86; *Tacit Dimension*, 32.
5. Polanyi, *Personal Knowledge*, 63, 64.
6. Ibid., 310.

cisely *through*) the active involvement of the human agent in the epistemic enterprise is attested to by Helmut Kuhn, among others:

> Like every analyst of cognitive processes he is impressed by the constructive activity of the mind in achieving knowledge, and in describing this activity he does not shrink from occasionally speaking of entities being "produced" by the knower. [Here Kuhn cites *Duke Lectures*, II, 2.] But not for a moment does he think of following the path of transcendental philosophy in regarding the creative process of the mind in pursuit of knowledge as constituting its object. There is no trace of the Kantian idea of the object having to conform to a rational faculty lodged in man. According to Polanyi, the hallmark of genuine knowledge consists in establishing contact with reality. It is not made but discovered [here Kuhn cites *Personal Knowledge*, 64, 124, 130, 147; *Duke Lectures*, I, 19, 20; *Duke Lectures*, III, 23], and in this respect his point of view is closer to that of commonsense than to the idealist tendency which is characteristic of the bulk of contemporary philosophy of science.[7]

Polanyi never seems concerned to distinguish between reality-in-itself and reality-for-us. Thus, although his constructivism would appear to dictate his classification with Kantian idealism, to say that Polanyi thinks that we never can know reality-in-itself but only reality-as-it-exists-for-us, the two alternatives that Margolis delineates in the above-mentioned discussion, would be utterly misrepresent his thought.[8] The discussions of later chapters should shed light on this matter.

The Polanyian commitment to the knowability of reality is supported by two pillars of his thought. On the one hand, Polanyi argues persistently that the knower is endowed with tacit powers by the manipulation of which he can achieve contact with reality.[9] The participation of the personal in

---

7. Kuhn, "Personal Knowledge and the Crisis of the Philosophical Tradition," in Langford and Poteat, eds., *Intellect and Hope*, 114. See also 121, 129. Further attestations to Polanyi's realism are provided by the following: Buchanan, "Politics and Science," 304; Grene, *Knower and Known*, 50, 52, 240; "Response to MacIntyre," in Engelhardt and Callahan, eds., *Morals, Science and Sociality*, 43, 45; Innis, "In Memoriam Michael Polanyi," 24; "Meaning, Thought and Language," 55, 62; "Polanyi's Model of Mental Acts," 160; MacIntyre, "Objectivity in Morality and Science," in Engelhardt and Callahan, eds., *Morals, Science and Sociality*, 27, 30; Roberts, "Politics and Science," 237–38; Scott, "Polanyi's Theory of *Personal Knowledge*," 358–59. In Polanyi, see also *Personal Knowledge*, 104; "Knowing and Being," in Grene, ed., *Knowing and Being*, 133.

8. Margolis, "Cognitive Issues," 373.

9. See for example Polanyi, *Science, Faith and Society*, 37, 38; *Personal Knowledge*, 37, 114, 265; *Study of Man*, 27; "Logic and Psychology," 30.

knowing poses no threat as far as Polanyi is concerned because of the essential and positive nature of the personal: it is a power that enables man to transcend himself and grab hold of reality in his understanding. In fact, without the personal, such contact would not be possible at all. Chapter 11 of this work will suggest how tacit knowing might be seen to justify Polanyi's realism.

Polanyi's epistemic optimism is undergirded, on the other hand, by his commitment to the inherent rationality of nature, discussed briefly in chapter 3. This of course must be assumed by anyone who believes in the possibility of knowledge that is not entirely of his own making: if we are to make sense of the world, it must be susceptible of having sense made of it—it must itself be reasonably ordered. But the rationality of nature does not imply either its finitude or the possibility of its ultimate elucidation in terms of any single human cognitive structure. Polanyi holds both to the rationality of nature and to its inexhaustibility and consequent indeterminacy. It is what Marjorie Grene terms *systematic* inexhaustibility.[10] Therefore, neither does reality's inexhaustibility preclude its rationality and the prospect of human understanding of it.

Epistemic Realism and More

A great portion of Polanyi's realistic claims may be classified as epistemic realism, in G. H. Merrill's terms, in distinction from metaphysical realism or semantic realism. Merrill defines epistemic realism as the claim that to accept a theory is to believe that it is true, to believe that its terms denote existing entities.[11] But for Polanyi, the realist assumption is essential to more than just the matter of accepting a theory. Belief in the prospect of contact with reality is essential to all kinds of knowing and all stages of discovery. It actually may be seen to guide the search. It is essential to the preservation and accreditation of the scientific community itself and to the preservation of independent thought and academic freedom. It is essential whether it is acknowledged to be so or not. Polanyi believes that this is the testimony both of his own experience as a scientist and of the entire history of science. Statements such as the following are typical: "Such changes [as those wrought by Planck's discovery of quantum theory] have been accompanied

---

10. Grene, *Knower and Known*, 221, in addition to private conversation.

11. Merrill, "Three Forms of Realism," 229. This is not meant to imply the Polanyi is not a metaphysical or a semantic realist; there is a distinctive way in which he is both of these also. See chapter 11.

through the centuries by the belief that they offered a deeper understanding of reality."[12]

That this is what discoverers have believed regarding their work has been evidenced over the centuries by the degree of passion and tenacity with which they have held out for the truth (and not merely the workability) of their discoveries. The length of time Copernicans retained their conviction of the heliocentric system in the face not only of disbelief but also of positivism, and the outbursts of joy recorded by Kepler with respect to his discoveries, are cases in point.[13] Polanyi says that "the enquiries on which Kepler spent his life would have been altogether nonsensical, if the heliocentric system were not real."[14] Thus, it is most directly the presence of intellectual passions in connection with the work of science that demonstrate that the realist assumption is constantly made. For this reason, as well as for others, the realist assumption necessarily attends every stage of scientific discovery. Polanyi says: "This view of science merely recognizes what all scientists believe—that science offers us an aspect of reality, and may therefore manifest its truth inexhaustibly and often surprisingly in the future. Only in this belief can the scientist conceive problems, pursue inquiries, and claim discoveries; this belief is the ground on which he teaches his students and exercises his authority over the public."[15]

Polanyian Realism Justifies Tacit Knowing

According to Polanyi, the problem and process stages of discovery consist essentially of the knower's subsidiary reliance upon clues in the effort to bring to light the integrative focus in terms of which the clues gain their entire significance. Thus, what is required is a tacit foreknowledge of the as-yet-uncomprehended focus. Polanyi has supplied evidence for the existence of such a capacity, as seen in chapter 3. But Polanyi also makes the following remarkable claim: "We can account for this capacity of ours to know more than we can tell if we believe in the presence of an external reality with which we can establish contact."[16] Not only is it the case that his epistemology justifies his distinctive realism; it is also the case that his realism justifies his distinctive epistemology. Each flavors and lends strength to the other. There is a fundamental accord between the two. And that accord

12. Polanyi, *Tacit Dimension*, 69.
13. Polanyi, *Personal Knowledge*, 7.
14. Polanyi, *Duke Lectures*, I, 10.
15. Polanyi, *Tacit Dimension*, 69.
16. Polanyi, "Knowing and Being," in Grene, ed., *Knowing and Being*, 133.

itself displays kinship with the two: the accord is essentially characterized by a fecund indeterminacy, as we will see in coming chapters.

Polanyi doesn't explain, at least in so many words, why realism justifies tacit knowing, specifically, what sort of relationship holds between the prospect of tacit knowing and the existence of a knowable external reality. In other words, he does not expound his realism nor offer justification for it. It is the purpose of my examination to do so. For Polanyi, however, it appears to have been obvious.

But we may note a few implied ways in which realism is necessary to knowing and to the scientific enterprise. First, it is necessary to Polanyian epistemology. On an epistemic model of subsidiary-focal integration as it unfolds in scientific discovery, without the implied contact with reality—that is, the sensed but as-yet-unidentified integrative pattern—any epistemic search would be deprived of its guiding focus. To be a clue, a focus is required. Given the functional aspect of tacit knowing alone, where there is no focus there can be no subsidiaries, and consequently also no possibility of knowing more than we can tell.

For the scientific enterprise, why must the focus be real? Why might it not be simply a convenient summary of the data, as positivists would hold? This matters deeply to Polanyi, as we will see in subsequent chapters. It is a critical question; it will be the effort of later chapters to offer a substantive response. It is clear, however, that Polanyi thinks that, in science at least, the focus must be real, that realism is necessary for the following reasons. First, without such a hope, a scientist's persistence in pursuit over the course of years is very likely to wane or succumb to despair. Secondly, once the discovery has been made, it is impossible for the scientist to believe in and to press upon others the universal validity of his findings unless he is convinced of their reality. His reputation rides on such a claim. Successful contact with the real is essential to the discovery's authority over the scientific community and the public. It is thus essential to the survival of the scientific community as a whole. It is, third, necessary to that community's mutual trust and collaboration. Polanyi believes that commitment to reality is essential to the preservation of the important values of independent thought and academic freedom. And finally, without such a claim, it is impossible to justify our choice of one system over another, or even over a false system such as astrology.[17] Of this last, a little more will be said in connection with Polanyi's critique of positivism.

---

17. See passages listed in n. 39 of chapter 3. See MacIntyre, "Objectivity in Morality and Science," in Engelhardt and Callahan, eds., *Morals, Science and Sociality*, 30; Brownhill, "Scientific Ethics and the Community," 243–48.

Realism in Polanyi's Thought

This, then, in general outline, is Polanyi's realism. How does it fit with and contribute to the corpus of Polanyi's thought? We have already seen ways in which realism serves the Polanyian system. Let us begin by looking at a passage, the first sentence of which has already been noted. The entire paragraph serves as a credo with respect to Polanyi's realism, and it enables us to see what role realism plays in his thought.

> We can account for this capacity of ours to know more than we can tell if we believe in an external reality with which we can establish contact. This I do. I declare myself committed to the belief in an external reality gradually accessible to knowing, and I regard all true understanding as an intimation of such a reality which, being real, may yet reveal itself to our deepened understanding in an indefinite range of unexpected manifestations. I accept the obligation to search for the truth through my own intimations of reality, knowing that there is, and can be, no strict rule by which my conclusions can be justified. My reference to reality legitimates my acts of unspecifiable knowing, even while it duly keeps the exercise of such acts within the bounds of a rational objectivity. For a claim to have made contact with reality necessarily legislates both for myself and others with universal intent.[18]

In the next-to-last sentence, Polanyi articulates two functions of his realism. First, it legitimates acts of unspecifiable knowing—including, as in the first sentence, our capacity to know more than we can tell. We have already examined this issue. But let us note that, if realism does function in this way, then its role in Polanyi's system is absolutely foundational. For his primary motivation has been the legitimation of unspecifiable acts of knowing. Can his form of realism successfully bear such a responsibility? This question will be addressed in later chapters.

Secondly, Polanyi maintains that reference to the real keeps acts of tacit knowing "within the bounds of a rational objectivity." We have met with this curbing action in our discussion of Polanyi's solution to the paradox of self-set standards and his defense against the charge of subjectivity. The following quotation expresses typically the point Polanyi tries to make: "Though every choice in a heuristic process is indeterminate in the sense of being an entirely personal judgment, in those who exercise such judgment competently it is completely determined by their responsibility in respect

---

18. Polanyi, "Knowing and Being," in Grene, ed., *Knowing and Being*, 133.

to the situation confronting them. Insofar as they are acting responsibly, their personal participation in drawing their own conclusions is completely compensated for by the fact that they are submitting to the universal status of the hidden reality which they are trying to approach."[19] The reason that the knower "does not do as he pleases, but compels himself forcibly to act as he believes he must" is that he senses that his specific task exists and will be accomplished only in submission to an external, authoritative reality to which, or on behalf of which, he is accountable.

Finally, the third function that realism serves within Polanyi's epistemology is to counterbalance its inherent activity—the integrative process—with an element of passivity.

Polanyi writes: "The art of knowing . . . is an action, but one that always has an element of *passivity* in it. We can assimilate an object as a tool if we believe it to be actually useful to our purposes and the same holds for the relation of meaning to what is meant and the relation of the parts to a whole. The act of personal knowing can sustain these relations only because the acting person believes that they are apposite: that he has not *made them* but *discovered them*. The effort of knowing is thus guided by a sense of obligation towards the truth: by an effort to submit to reality."[20]

In another place, Polanyi speaks of the "combination of the active shaping of knowledge with its acceptance as a token of reality" as "a distinctive feature of all personal knowing."[21] Passivity joins activity in a two-fold characterization of personal knowledge and realism is seen to lie at its heart.

In Conclusion

Polanyi therefore is a realist in that he holds the following convictions: that reality exists external to the knower and independently of his knowing it, that nevertheless this reality is knowable and that contact with it is the proper epistemic goal, and that this realist assumption is essential to all aspects of the knowing process. Especially significant are three things: on the one hand, Polanyi embraces realism "despite"—surprisingly, it may be thought—his vocal and systematic elucidation of an epistemology that countenances, in fact, accredits, personal, tacit dimensions of all knowing. On the other hand, Polanyi's realist claims move well beyond the pale of the usual, by contrast minimalist, claims of epistemic realism as it is commonly defined. Realism impacts all stages on the way to discovery. And Polanyian

19. Polanyi, *Personal Knowledge*, 310. See also Prosch, "Polanyi's Ethics," 99–100.
20. Polanyi, *Personal Knowledge*, 63. Italics original.
21. Ibid., 132.

realism bears a distinctive, remarkable quality: reality is pregnant and abundant with as-yet-unnameable dimensions and prospects.

Our understanding of Polanyi's realism will be deepened by consideration of the reality statement, criteria of reality, and the concept of contact with reality in subsequent chapters. Also, we shall return to these concepts and explicate them more fully in chapters 8, 9, and 10 in the light of contemporary issues in the philosophy of science.

5

The Reality Statement

> We meet here with a new definition of reality. Real is that which is expected to reveal itself indeterminately in the future. Hence, an explicit statement can bear on reality only by virtue of the tacit coefficient associated with it. This conception of reality and of the tacit knowing of reality underlies all my writings.[1]

The reality statement, as I have come to refer to it, has intrigued me more than any other aspect of Polanyi's thought. Fascination with it has prompted this examination. I am familiar with no one else within the Anglo-American tradition of philosophy who characterizes reality in this way or somehow utilizes the concept—with the possible and comparatively paltry exception of some use of the notion of fruitfulness as a criterion of adequacy. Yet, for all its rarity, the notion captures a legitimate aspect of human experience, from the ordinary day-to-day insight to the once-in-a-lifetime, earthshaking discovery. I believe that it offers critically needed hope for realism. It is the enjoyable task of this chapter to consider the reality statement in greater depth.

---

1. Polanyi, *Science, Faith and Society*, 10.

Polanyi's Various Expressions of the Reality Statement

The statement occurs quite frequently throughout Polanyi's philosophical writings. It is stated almost as an aside, as something obvious; Polanyi never gives it any sort of extended philosophical examination. The reader is left to puzzle over its implications and its relationship to the theory of tacit knowing—some of which we will be doing later on in the chapter. Polanyi most often refers to it as a *definition* of reality, and it typically appears in a definitional form—that is, the phrases are listed as implications of what it means for something to be real. Consider, for example, the following quotations; I have italicized the words that reveal the definitional aspect of the claim:

> For this [comprehensive entity] was always viewed as something real, *which being real*, might be expected yet to manifest itself at some future time in unexpected ways.[2]

> The act of tacit knowing thus implies the claim that its result is an aspect of reality *which, as such*, may yet reveal its truth in an inexhaustible range of unknown and perhaps still unthinkable ways.[3]

> For it [new knowledge] speaks of something real, and to attribute reality to something *is to express* the belief that its presence will yet show up in an indefinite number of unpredictable ways.[4]

Polanyi calls the reality statement a *criterion* only once, to my knowledge: "At whatever level we consider a living being, the centre of its individuality is real. For it is always something we ascertain by comprehending the coherence of largely unspecifiable particulars, and which we yet expect to reveal itself further by an indeterminate range or future manifestations.

---

2. Polanyi, "Tacit Knowing: Its Bearing," in Grene, ed., *Knowing and Being,* 172.

3. Polanyi, "Logic of Tacit Inference," in Grene, ed., *Knowing and Being,* 141.

4. Polanyi, *Personal Knowledge,* 311. The following are the most explicit instances of the reality statement. The asterisked references are those in which Polanyi uses the term "definition," to designate the reality statement: *Science, Faith and Society,* 10*, 22, 23, 29; *Personal Knowledge,* 37, 64, 104, 117, 124, 130, 322; *Study of Man,* 84; "Knowing and Being," in Grene, ed., *Knowing and Being,* 133, 135; "Tacit Knowing: Its Bearing," in Grene, ed., *Knowing and Being,* 168*, 172; "The Unaccountable Element in Science," in Grene, ed., *Knowing and Being,* 119*, 120; "Logic of Tacit Inference," in Grene, ed., *Knowing and Being,* 141*; *Tacit Dimension,* 23, 32, 68; "The Creative Imagination," 86, 88; "Logic and Psychology," 27, 28, 41; "From Copernicus to Einstein," 101; "Faith and Reason," 125; "Science and Reality," 191*; "Genius in Science," 60*; *Meaning,* 58, 97.

Thus the criteria of reality are fulfilled."[5] It should be noted that two criteria are listed here; the latter one consists of the reality statement. The reality statement certainly is amenable to usage as a criterion; we shall see this in chapter 7.

The few commentators who have discussed the reality statement have called it a criterion despite Polanyi's own predominating reference to it as a definition.[6] This has seemed strange to me, but there may be some explanation for this. It may be, first of all, that they felt that Polanyi's use of "definition" was a bit presumptuous in the light of the philosophical overload that the word bears in contemporary discussions. Secondly, to call the statement a definition of reality implies that it is properly a metaphysical concern. But the reality statement falls rather in the interface of the disciplines of epistemology and metaphysics; it has to do more with being as it is apprehended by the knower.

Polanyi does develop a doctrine of levels—see chapter 7—which, by comparison, is more properly metaphysical. Edward Pols distinguishes the issues of the reality statement from those of the doctrine of levels, referring to the two subjects as different "senses" of reality in Polanyi or different ways in which Polanyi deals with reality.[7] He understands the discussion of the reality statement to be "of mixed epistemological and metaphysical import," whereas the doctrine of levels is "clearly metaphysical."[8] Whereas I consider the reality statement's conception of reality to be of greater significance in Polanyi's work, as well as a more viable and helpful notion, Pols prefers the doctrine of levels. As a result, he feels that the reality statement really adds nothing to the teaching of the doctrine of levels and occasionally is even a hindrance to it.[9] Pols finds many difficulties with the reality statement. My belief is that it can be shown that these difficulties stem directly from his prior acceptance of the doctrine of levels with its inherent problems and from his failure to give due study to the reality statement.

Third in this list of possible reasons that these commentators opt to call the reality statement a criterion rather than a definition: these writers, in passing quickly from one to the other, (perhaps unintentionally) blur the

---

5. Polanyi, "Knowing and Being," in Grene, ed., *Knowing and Being*, 135. See also *Study of Man*, 84, and "Science and Reality," 179–85: though the word is not mentioned here, "real" and its characteristics appear to be related criterially.

6. Grene, *Knower and Known*, 220; Pols, "Polanyi and the Problem of Metaphysical Knowledge," in Langford and Poteat, eds. *Intellect and Hope*, 77.

7. Pols, "Polanyi and the Problem of Metaphysical Knowledge," in Langford and Poteat, eds. *Intellect and Hope*, 75.

8. Ibid., 71.

9. Ibid., 78.

distinction between the reality statement per se and its application as a comparative criterion of reality. The comparative criterion consists of the claim that, the more intimations of unforeseen consequences a thing produces within us, the more real it is.[10] A person, therefore, is more real than a cobblestone, to use Polanyi's example, because he intimates a greater range of indeterminate implications than the cobblestone. The comparative application is more clearly criterial. If these writers assume the sole virtue of the reality statement to lie in its comparative application, then it is no wonder that they consider the reality statement a criterion. Finally, as I have noted and as we shall see, the reality statement does in fact function legitimately and crucially as a criterion for Polanyi, independently of any comparative application.

Aspects of the Reality Statement

Let us continue to examine this remarkable reality statement closely. "Real is that which may be expected to manifest itself indeterminately in the future." The consequences, confirmations, manifestations, and implications are, first of all, future: "We have seen already that whenever we make (or believe we have made) contact with reality, we anticipate an indeterminate range of unexpected future confirmations of our knowledge derived from this contact."[11] The reader may have already noted the prevalence of the word, "yet," in these statements. Polanyi is convinced that the history of science testifies to the fact that, at the time a discovery is made and its reality is claimed, the vast bulk of its confirmation and manifestations have not appeared. He is also convinced that the scientist nevertheless persists in maintaining the reality of his claim because he senses the breadth of future implications. Consequences and fruitfulness are important to Polanyi, as they are to pragmatists, but the two systems of thought are qualitatively distinct. For, as Polanyi has so concisely and profoundly put it, the mark of true discovery is not its fruitfulness but the *intimation* of its fruitfulness.[12] The reality statement thus immediately throws us back on the structure of tacit knowing, for what is meant in saying that they are future consequences is that any present knowledge of them can only be anticipatory and hence tacit in character. Thus it is that we meet once again with the strange but true-to-life projective structure of tacit integration.

10. Polanyi, *Tacit Dimension*, 32–33.
11. Polanyi, *Personal Knowledge*, 124.
12. Ibid., 148.

Future manifestations are infinite in number. Polanyi describes them as "boundless undisclosed and perhaps unthinkable experiences." Or at least they are indefinite in number, e.g., "an indefinite number of unpredictable ways."[13] More often, Polanyi speaks of a *range* of manifestations, and the range is characterized as either inexhaustible or indeterminate: "an inexhaustible range of unknown and perhaps still unthinkable ways," or "an indefinite range of future, as yet unknown, manifestations."[14] The notion of a range suggests an array of different kinds of implications. Polanyi has noted, for example, that a good classification reveals its successful contact with reality in a twofold manner. First, it anticipates further instances of itself—i.e., it has an indefinite extension. Extensively, the concept will "validly subsume these future instances in spite of the fact that they will unpredictably differ in every particular from all the instances subsumed in the past." Secondly, its intension is inexhaustible; the classification "anticipates that members of the class will yet be found to share an indefinite range of uncovenanted properties."[15] Thus, it is impossible to determine these future manifestations, not only with respect to number, but also with respect to their character.

Why is this the case? First, of course, is the fact that the knower stands in the present and the confirmations he senses are future, yet to be revealed and articulated. Second, the universe is inexhaustible. Third, as if the universe were not inexhaustible enough in its present state, the higher forms of reality, as "centers of individuality," as Polanyi terms them, are independently capable of *producing* further manifestations for years and possibly centuries to come.

This state of affairs gives rise to a variety of phrases that Polanyi typically incorporates into the reality statement. He speaks of the unpredictability of a real thing's possible manifestations. He calls them unthinkable, uncovenanted, unexpected, unforeseeable, and surprising.[16] It is important

---

13. Polanyi, *Tacit Dimension*, 68; *Personal Knowledge*, 311.

14. Polanyi, "Logic of Tacit Inference," in Grene, ed., *Knowing and Being*, 141; *Meaning*, 97.

15. Polanyi, *Personal Knowledge*, 114; "Tacit Knowing: Its Bearing," in Grene, ed., *Knowing and Being*, 170.

16. "Unpredictable": Polanyi, *Science, Faith and Society*, 22, 23; *Personal Knowledge*, 311; "The Creative Imagination," 86. "Unthinkable": Polanyi, *Science, Faith and Society*, 10; "Logic of Tacit Inference," in Grene, ed., *Knowing and Being*, 138, 141; *Tacit Dimension*, 23, 68. "Uncovenanted": Polanyi, *Personal Knowledge*, 104. "Unexpected": Polanyi, *Personal Knowledge*, 117, 124; "Knowing and Being," in Grene, ed., *Knowing and Being*, 133; "Tacit Knowing: Its Bearing," in Grene, ed., *Knowing and Being*, 172; "The Unaccountable Element in Science," in Grene, ed., *Knowing and Being*, 120; *Tacit Dimension*, 32; "Logic and Psychology," 28. "Unforeseeable": Polanyi, *Personal Knowledge*, 130;

to note once again, however, that unpredictability does not imply irrationality for Polanyi, for it is a *systematic* unpredictability. Such a notion is certainly conceivable.

Reality promises future, indeterminate, surprising manifestations. Additionally, Polanyi claims, paradoxically, that we *expect* them. At the same time, and at least once in the same breath, Polanyi asserts that they are unexpected: the real "might be expected to manifest itself at some future time in unexpected ways."[17] Indeed, the whole point of the reality statement relies on the claim that the knower can in fact expect such confirmations by virtue of his tacit foreknowledge and hence can recognize the real.

But this, I believe, is none other than the apparent paradox that lies at the heart of "knowing more than we can tell." Polanyi is saying that what we sense tacitly is that a certain reality promises a host of future confirmations; this does not imply that we sense what sort of confirmations these will be. Thus, in all probability, we will be surprised. In fact, the more unpredictable (though systematic) the intimations we sense, the greater the depth of reality we attribute to the entity. Conversely, if the future consequences are predictable, we find the entity less intriguing and thus, for Polanyi, less real.[18] Polanyi illustrates systematic unpredictability and superior reality by means of E. M. Forster's distinction between "flat" and "round" characters in a novel. "A character is called flat if its actions are almost wholly predictable, while we say that a character is round if it can 'convincingly surprise' the reader. The fruitfulness of a new mathematical conception betokens its superior reality; and so, in a novel, does the internal spontaneity by which a 'round' personage may unexpectedly reveal new features which nevertheless flow from its original character and are therefore convincing."[19] All of these are notions with which ordinary people function fairly easily and intuitively, especially with regard to their perception of other people.

Future confirmations, because of their indeterminacy, exceed our understanding. What Polanyi has in mind in using this phrase are some instances in the history of science and in scientific practice in which the subsequent applications of a theory either are or would have been rejected by the discoverer. Copernicus, for example, would hardly have recognized Kepler's formulations as confirming his own work.[20] Part of the reason for this is the essential fallibility of our epistemic endeavors, such that

---

"Faith and Reason," 125–26. "Surprising": Polanyi, *Tacit Dimension*, 69.

17. Polanyi, "Tacit Knowing: Its Bearing," in Grene, ed., *Knowing and Being*, 172.
18. Polanyi, *Personal Knowledge*, 117.
19 Ibid.
20. Ibid., 43, 111; "The Creative Imagination," 86; "Logic and Psychology," 28.

more often than not a significant discovery is fraught with error—witness Columbus' discovery of "India." Of this point, more must be said in chapter 6. Secondly, the fact that scientific and technological advance is continuous means that there will inevitably be later developments that shed light on the initial claim and its implications. But the point is that this phenomenon in the history of scientific discovery is just what displays that discoveries make contact with reality, that discoverers rely on a sense of indeterminate future manifestations in order to discern that they have done so, and that what accounts for this is the many-faceted depth of reality itself.

The indeterminate nature of future manifestations gives to an experience the appearance of being at least partially hidden.[21] Hiddenness functions as a token of reality—this is probably a main reason why the reality statement will serve as a criterion of reality. In this it is exactly similar to perception, in which the subject receives subsidiary indication—marginal clues, among other things—that a physical object has another side, a roundness, a permanence, a history, and so concludes its reality: indeterminate future manifestations attest to the full-orbed existence of a prospective or recent discovery. Note Polanyi's realism in speaking of hiddenness: it is not that these nonvisible and unspecifiable aspects do not exist before we know them, and that in knowing them we thereby constitute them; rather, hiddenness implies that something is there that is yet to be discovered. And it could not be that these indeterminate aspects do not exist before discovery, for it is in their very indeterminacy that they serve to testify to the reality of the object. If they did not exist, the "object" in its explicitness would simply fail to convey any sense of its own reality.

What sort of effect do real things, by virtue of their indeterminate manifestations, have on us? Polanyi often speaks of their authoritative character. What Polanyi has in mind here are instances in which the scientist, and the scientific community, once a great discovery has been acknowledged, proceed to rely on the guidance of its new conceptions in subsequent pursuits of understanding.[22] A new discovery "authoritatively speaks for itself," and the scientist is called upon to "submit to its reality." Notice that in all these reality statements the real thing in question manifests *itself* in indefinite future confirmations.

Concomitant to the authoritative character of the real is its effect of attracting us to itself by means of its unspecifiable intimations.[23] This

---

21. Polanyi, *Personal Knowledge*, 64, 124, 311; "The Unaccountable Element in Science," 120; *Tacit Dimension*, 22, 23, 24, 68; "Faith and Reason," 125; *Meaning*, 58–59.

22. Polanyi, *Personal Knowledge*, 5, 104.

23. Polanyi, *Science, Faith and Society*, 14; "The Unaccountable Element in Science," in Grene, ed., *Knowing and Being*, 119–20.

attractiveness is especially clear in the problem and research stages prior to a discovery, where its presence is indicated by the existence of the heuristic and selective passions described earlier, the initial interest and subsequent perseverance in pursuit of the solution.

How Indeterminate Future Manifestations Serve Integration

We have now covered the most characteristic phrases of the reality statement. Although some mention has been made of Polanyi's application of it to the integrative feat, especially within the context of discovery, let us at this point consolidate the information explicitly. Presently, indeterminate future manifestations serve in their capacity of testifying to the reality of a certain object both before and after it is discovered. Prior to discovery, they are just the intimations or clues that guide and inspire the scientist with respect to the discovery. Thus it is that the reality of the discovery is confirmed in advance.[24] But of course the apprehension of unknown future confirmations continues once the discovery has been made, perhaps until the end of time.

It should also be noted that the phrases of the reality statement are applied by Polanyi both to the external object of a discovery and to the conception, the epistemic product that results from the discovery. This is not surprising, even though it leaves us with an ambiguity: for Polanyi, both the object and the conception are real. The conception is real in its own right, as well as by virtue of the fact that it is linked to the object in its contact with reality.[25]

Examples of the Reality Statement in Ordinary Life

That such an understanding of the real and its effect on the knower is a significant and highly applicable notion can be demonstrated simply by examining our personal experience. Some aspects of the reality statement are evident even in the simplest perceptions: my sense, upon seeing a tree, of its roundness and solidity, its other side, its interior, the birds hidden in its branches, its potential for autumn glory and winter starkness, its potential at the hands of a sculptor or builder, even of its history, of the battles or trysts which might well have occurred beneath its limbs. None of this is usually

---

24. Polanyi, *Personal Knowledge*, 130. *Tacit Dimension*, 80; *Duke Lectures*, I, 19; "Tacit Knowing: Its Bearing," in Grene, ed., *Knowing and Being*, 172.

25. Polanyi, *Personal Knowledge*, 94, 104, 133, 150, 317.

explicit in my simple focal apprehension of the tree. These characteristics could, in this case, of course, be made explicit to some extent. But they could be made explicit only piece by piece. You can only ever look at one side of the tree at a time, or experience one season at a time, or either sculpt it or use it for lumber, but not both.

The element of excitement induced by intimations is more evident in cases in which we find ourselves speculating about the potential of an objective state of affairs for the first time: those who contemplate the purchase of an older house are often excited about the potential that they sense that it has. An artist or craftsman experiences similar excitement (and some fear) when confronted with the materials of his work and the prospect of a new creation.

The reality statement seems especially applicable with respect to our involvement with human beings. I find a person intriguing to the extent that he intimates an indeterminate range of future manifestations—I sense that there is much more there for me to get to know. To the extent that a person does not strike me in this way, he strikes me as "unreal" or shallow and uninteresting. Here, we see the Polanyian identification of reality with meaning or significance, a rich notion in itself. Similarly, we often choose a place to live—city or country, shore or mountains—on the basis of the possibilities it holds, even if we never fully explore them.

As for the application of Polanyi's claims to scientific discovery, of course the scientist will be a better judge than the layman. I do, however, remember seeing a television documentary a few years ago concerning a discovery made by some marine biologists of some "vents" deep down on the ocean floor, at the mouth of which plant life survived that should not have survived without the existence of some energy such as sunlight. The implication was that these vents provided some form of sustaining energy. The biologists were childlike in their excitement: in various interviews they kept repeating that the implications of such a discovery, though unknown, were significant and far-reaching, that this was perhaps the greatest biological discovery of the century, and that it opened the door to all kinds of possibilities in research. It was clear that they were being convinced of the reality of their discovery by the promise of presently indeterminate future manifestations.

The Origin of the Reality Statement

As to the origin of the reality statement within Polanyi's thinking, there is little that can be said definitely. The reality statement appears in his earliest philosophical works, and remains throughout the latter ones. It changes imperceptibly, if at all, over the intervening years. Polanyi, as was said, provides the reader with no sustained exposition of the concept or its development. My best conclusion, after much puzzling over this matter, is that Polanyi's notion of reality arose in his thinking hand-in-hand with his conception of tacit knowing: from out of his personal experience and study of the context of discovery. It is apparent to the student of Polanyi's works that his central ideas grow out of scientific experience, rather than resulting, for example, from any sort of philosophical analysis of ideas in the abstract. Marjorie Grene confirms this:

> What distinguishes Polanyi's inquiry ... is that he came to the problem, raised it and grappled with it from within the life of science. It was knowledge in the concrete context of existence, the existence of science and scientists, that he was concerned to vindicate. What resulted was often obscure, sometimes mistaken, and couched in a rhetoric that most professional philosophers find it hard to tolerate; but it was a philosophy rooted in reality, neither the clever gymnastics of analysis, nor the prophylactic debate of a philosophy of science based on a grave misconception of, and almost out of contact with, its alleged subject matter.[26]

That his concept of reality develops out of scientific experience *in tandem with* his concept of knowing is indicated in a passage such as the one quoted at the very beginning of this chapter. It is as if Polanyi takes the characteristic aspects of the experience of discovery and develops them in two directions, one metaphysical, the other epistemological. Just what are these aspects of discovery that have intrigued Polanyi? First of all, he is intrigued by the fact that the scientist commits himself passionately to the truth of his discovery way before he has enough justification to support such a commitment. Secondly, the claim that is made, to the extent that it is successful, implies more than it ever specifies or is able to specify. Third, a great discovery is confirmed in later years in ways that wildly exceed the expectations of even its author. Fourth, the entire process is accompanied by more and greater passion than contemporary philosophy of science would care to admit.

Out of these and perhaps other conclusions concerning discovery, Polanyi generates a concept of knowing that includes and relies on indeterminate knowledge of a reality knowable in spite of indeterminacy—in fact, actually confirmed to be reality by indeterminacy. We ultimately have an

---

26. Grene, "Tacit Knowing: Grounds," 166–67.

epistemic act comprised of an integration of unspecifiable particulars to a hitherto unspecifiable but coherent focus and a reality that is susceptible to such a process: entities that are themselves a focus of a rich spectrum of unspecifiable particulars. Whether, to Polanyi's way of thinking, the nature of reality determines the nature of knowledge or vice versa is not entirely clear, although my preference is to say that for him, ontology ultimately precedes epistemology. It is only clear that the fit is perfect. For a rational yet inexhaustibly rich subject matter implies the possibility of true, but not exhaustive, knowledge. This is knowledge that highlights in a creative synthesis perhaps one aspect of the object, in which many things are indeterminate. The fact of integrative knowledge, on the other hand, implies a creative selection and comprehension of unspecifiable particulars. Small wonder that the achieved focus hints at a host of unspecifiable manifestations.

At the heart of the relationship between knowing and known for Polanyi is another thing that is apparent in that first quotation: explicit knowledge bears on reality only by virtue of the tacit coefficient (the unspecifiable subsidiaries and the unspecifiable integrative act) associated with it. And, what seems like it may be a parallel notion: the real is recognized as such only by virtue of its tacit coefficient: its intimation of future manifestations. Further light will hopefully be shed on these significant but puzzling claims in subsequent chapters.

In Conclusion

In conclusion, reflecting as we have in this chapter over Polanyi's remarkable repeated claims that reality, in the event of our discovering it, is that which manifests itself indeterminately in the future, we can see that, for Polanyi, this is both an epistemological claim and a metaphysical claim. It characterizes successful knowing, but it does so because it characterizes reality itself in the first place. This phenomenon does not occur by virtue of the knower's, as it were, restricted capacities. Polanyi's personal knowledge fundamentally resists the anti-realist posture that casts our capacities as being restricted and our ideal as exhaustively explicit certainty, as we have seen in earlier chapters. It is precisely because of the positive tacit power of our capacities that we contact reality in this intimately indeterminate, fertile way. Personal knowledge is an epistemic posture that allows us to accredit, and therein see, what is true of reality: that it, itself, manifests itself indeterminately in the future.

6

Contact with Reality

We have, in the preceding chapters, already witnessed Polanyi's use of the idea of contact with reality; for example, it was used in the following: "We can account for this capacity of ours to know more than we can tell if we believe in the presence of an external reality with which we can establish contact."[1] In this chapter, I wish to attend more closely to Polanyi's notion of contact with reality and its related concepts. The idea of contact with reality is perhaps no more than a manner of speaking for Polanyi; that is, it does not have the "official status" of a concept such as subsidiary awareness. Yet, as a pattern of speech it occurs frequently and I believe that examination of it will provide us with a clearer sense of the nature of Polanyi's realism—hence the relevance of this chapter and the next, which develops Polanyi's criteria of contact with reality.

---

1. Polanyi, "Knowing and Being," in Grene, ed., *Knowing and Being*, 133. The relevant passages concerning contact with reality are: *Science, Faith and Society*, 37, 40; *Logic of Liberty*, 38–39; *Personal Knowledge*, vii, viii, 5, 6, 43, 59, 64, 86, 104, 106, 116, 117, 124, 137, 144, 147, 148, 189, 251, 310, 313, 315, 316, 317, 403; *Study of Man*, 34; "Knowing and Being," in Grene, ed., *Knowing and Being*, 128, 133; "The Logic of Tacit Inference," Grene, ed., *Knowing and Being*, 141; "Tacit Knowing: Its Bearing," in Grene, ed., *Knowing and Being*, 172; "The Unaccountable Element in Science," in Grene, ed., *Knowing and Being*, 119; "The Growth of Science in Society," in Grene, ed., *Knowing and Being*, 79, 80 (orig. pub. in *Minerva* 5 [1967] 533–45); *Tacit Dimension*, 9, 15, 18, 24, 25, 32, 61, 68, 70, 74, 74–75, 77, 80, 82, 87; *Duke Lectures*, III, 10; "The Creative Imagination," 88; "Science and Reality," 191, 195.

Laying Hold of an Aspect of Reality

Polanyi occasionally speaks of the *bearing* of an idea on reality, or of the knower's *hold* on or *grasping* of reality.[2] I take these concepts to be expressing the same notion of contact in perhaps more picturesque language.

I have also concluded, in the course of my study, that the idea of "an aspect of reality" is closely allied in Polanyi's thought with that of contact. It is an aspect of reality that a discoverer grasps when he has made successful contact with reality. Examine the following: "Why do we entrust the life and guidance of our thoughts to our conceptions? Because we believe that their manifest rationality is due to their being in contact with domains of reality, of which they have grasped one aspect."[3] As far as I have been able to tell, this is the only passage in which both "contact" and "aspect" are used, and thus it is imperative that we pay attention to the relationship as it appears here, if only to learn what is not the case. There is indeed a relationship between the two, such that the grasping of an aspect of reality results from contact with reality.

We would, however, be wrong to push the relationship by saying that the knower's contact is with *only* that single aspect of reality. Here, it says that his contact is with *domains* of reality. The reason that the two do not match in a one-to-one correspondence is that the idea of contact is fraught with Polanyian indeterminacy of the sort generated by subsidiary knowledge, intuitive foreknowledge, and integrative activity. In addition, as we shall see, that "contact" may be of different sorts, that is, that contact may take place both at the subsidiary and at the focal level. "Aspect," it appears, in contrast seems to be related more closely with the focus of the integrative feat, the discovery, and as such is susceptible of being made explicit to some extent.

But my alignment of contact with the notion of an aspect of reality serves to highlight an important feature of contact with reality. It is that successful contact with reality gives rise to knowledge of *merely* an aspect

---

2. "Bearing": Polanyi, *Personal Knowledge*, 251, 315; *Tacit Dimension*, 9, 18, 61, 70, 74, 74–75, 87 (2x); *Duke Lectures*, III, 10; "The Creative Imagination," 88 (2x); "Tacit Knowing: Its Bearing," in Grene, ed., *Knowing and Being*, 172. "Hold": Polanyi, *Personal Knowledge*, 43, 310, 317, 403. "Grasp": Polanyi, *Personal Knowledge*, 104; "The Unaccountable Element in Science," in Grene, ed., *Knowing and Being*, 120. "Touch": Polanyi, *Personal Knowledge*, 106.

3. Polanyi, *Personal Knowledge*, 104. See also *Personal Knowledge*, 313; "The Logic of Tacit Inference," in Grene, ed., *Knowing and Being*, 141; "The Unaccountable Element in Science," in Grene, ed., *Knowing and Being*, 119, 120; "The Growth of Science in Society," in Grene, ed., *Knowing and Being*, 79, 80 (2x); *Tacit Dimension*, 32, 68 (3x); 80, 82; "Science and Reality," 191 (2x), 195.

of reality. The implication of the word "aspect" itself is that reality is never exhausted in our knowledge of it, let alone being exhausted on a single occasion. Polanyi's use of the word reminds the reader of this commitment to the inherent inexhaustibility of reality. It is infinitely rich; thus, there always remains more to be discovered, and no discovery constitutes a final, exhaustive revelation. Yet, contact with reality is necessary even to the grasping of a single strand, or aspect, of reality. This is because of reality's rationality. Thus, the inexhaustibility of reality cannot imply that any random interpretation will do. Contrast all of this with the older and sometimes current belief, engendered by the false ideal of explicitness, that successful contact with reality must entail fully explicit knowledge of the subject matter at hand, and the consequent consternation with regard to instances in which such "knowledge" has proven to be false. More of this in upcoming chapters.

The "IFM Effect" of the Reality Statement and Contact with Reality

Contact with reality, and the successful grasping of an aspect of reality, is accompanied predictably by what I, after writing out "indeterminate future manifestations" too many times, and in facetious deference to the acronymic society of which I am a child, wish to refer to as the "IFM Effect." In coining this term, I am underscoring, first, that the phrases of the reality statement appear time and again in Polanyi's writings in conjunction with either the notion of contact with reality or that of an aspect of reality. But secondly, and more importantly, I mean that Polanyi is saying that the knower's successful contact with reality on any particular occasion is accompanied by the intimation of indeterminate future manifestations. This is the IFM Effect.

A few quotations will suffice to make the point. "Perception has this inexhaustible profundity because what we perceive is *an aspect of reality*, and aspects of reality are clues to yet boundless, undisclosed, and perhaps as yet unthinkable experiences. This is what the existing body of scientific thought offers to the productive scientist: he sees in it an aspect of reality which, as such, is an inexhaustible source of new and promising problems."[4] Note here that the IFM Effect is so far reaching that Polanyi deems an aspect of reality to be itself a clue to indeterminate future manifestations.

---

4. Polanyi, "The Growth of Science in Society," in Grene, ed., *Knowing and Being*, 79–80, or *Tacit Dimension*, 68. See also *Tacit Dimension*, 23, 24.

> We have seen already that whenever we make (or believe we have made) contact with reality, we anticipate an indeterminate range of unexpected future confirmations of our knowledge derived from this contact. . . . But genius makes contact with reality on an exceptionally wide range: seeing problems and reaching out to hidden possibilities for solving them, far beyond the anticipatory powers of current conceptions.[5]
>
> But while in the natural sciences the feeling of making contact with reality is an augury of as yet undreamed of future empirical confirmations of an imminent discovery, in mathematics it betokens an indeterminate range of future germinations within mathematics itself.[6]

In fact, in the preface to *Personal Knowledge*, Polanyi *defines* contact with reality as "the *condition* for anticipating an indeterminate range of yet unknown (and perhaps inconceivable) true implications."[7] Thus the reality statement reappears at center stage with respect to Polanyi's realism, as might have been expected.

Contact with Reality: The Heart of Polanyian Realism

It can be demonstrated that the idea of contact with reality lies at the heart of what Polanyi has in mind by realism. We may take the major points of chapter 4 on Polanyi's realism and document them with quotations employing this phrase. It is, first of all, an independent, external reality that is the object of this contact—this we see in the first quotation above. Secondly, this external reality is knowable by virtue of unspecifiable powers belonging to living beings. In recapitulating the themes of *Personal Knowledge*, Polanyi says the following: "I have expounded the belief that the capacity of our minds to make contact with reality and the intellectual passion which impels us towards this contact will always suffice so to guide our personal

---

5. Polanyi, Personal Knowledge, 124.

6. Ibid., 189. Further relevant passages are: *Personal Knowledge*, 5, 43, 104, 117; "The Unaccountable Element in Science," in Grene, ed., *Knowing and Being*, 120; *Tacit Dimension*, 24, 32, 61, 68; "Science and Reality," 191, 195. It is not the case that in all of these does the reality statement appear as an effect; in many it has the definitional sense discussed in ch. 5.

7. Polanyi, *Personal Knowledge*, vii–viii, emphasis mine.

judgment that it will achieve the full measure of truth that lies within the scope of our particular calling."[8]

Thus, what the Polanyian tacit powers enable the knower to do is to make contact with reality. The following quotation also highlights the role of contact with reality within Polanyi's system to save personal knowing from subjectivity:

> Many writers have observed, since Dewey taught it at the close of the last century, that, to some degree, we shape all knowledge in the way we know it. This appears to leave knowledge open to the whims of the observer. But the pursuit of science has shown us how even in the shaping of his own anticipations the knower is controlled by impersonal requirements. His acts are personal judgments exercised responsibly with a view to a reality with which he is seeking to establish contact. This holds for all seeking and finding of external truth.[9]

Indeed, the true sense in which knowledge is objective, contra those whose false ideal of objectivity Polanyi attacks, is the sense of establishing contact with a hidden reality.[10] The concept of contact with reality therefore never obliterates the fiduciary foundation of knowing; in fact, the reader will notice that the phrase is very often prefaced by fiduciary terminology. Nevertheless, the prospect of making contact with reality drains the personal act of its subjective or arbitrary aspects.

Such a prospect—and this is my fourth in a catalog of aspects of Polanyi's realism for which contact with reality is key—is, for Polanyi, the true goal of science and scientists, whether it is acknowledged to be so or not. In other words, the assumption that what we are after is contact with reality is essential to the scientific enterprise. Polanyi says that "the scientist can conceive problems and pursue their investigation only by believing in a hidden reality on which science bears," and that scientific inquiry "can go on only if sustained by hope, the hope of making contact with the hidden pattern of things."[11] Modification of our conceptual and theoretical framework is effected in the hope of increasing our hold on reality.[12] The fact that science is successful in achieving such contact accounts for the phenomenon of mul-

8. Polanyi, *Study of Man*, 27. See also *Personal Knowledge*, 6, 251, 403.

9. Polanyi, *Tacit Dimension*, 77. See also 87; *Personal Knowledge*, 64.

10. Polanyi, *Personal Knowledge*, vii.

11. Polanyi, *Tacit Dimension*, 74-75; "The Unaccountable Element in Science," in Grene, ed., *Knowing and Being*, 120. See also *Science, Faith and Society*, 40; *Tacit Dimension*, 25, 70, 77.

12. Polanyi, *Personal Knowledge*, 106, 317; *Tacit Dimension*, 74.

tiple, simultaneous discoveries.[13] It also makes possible the prospect of the ultimate reconciliation of apparently contradictory alternative conceptions: "The outcome of a competent fiduciary act may, admittedly, vary from one person to another, but since the differences are not due to any arbitrariness on the part of the individuals, each retains justifiably his universal intent. As each hopes to capture an aspect of reality, they may all hope that their findings will eventually coincide or supplement each other."[14]

The last statements touch on issues of progress and success in science, which hitherto I have ignored. The same is true of the issues of correspondence and truth in Polanyi's thought. I hope to consider all of these in the upcoming chapters on contemporary realist issues. But let me say, as my final point in this introductory reinterpretation of Polanyi's realism in light of the concept of contact with reality, that the Polanyian conception of truth in particular is bound up with and hence best understood in terms of this particular cluster of concepts. We shall return to this at the end of the chapter.

Wherein Lies Contact with Reality?

Contact with reality can occur on either a narrow or a broad range. Polanyi has said, for example, that genius makes contact on an exceptionally wide range. Similarly, the pursuit of knowledge is essentially an effort to expand the breadth of our contact with reality, usually at least minimally by means of the modification of our conceptual framework, impelled by intellectual passions.[15] All of this brings us to the question, wherein lies this contact with reality? At what point of meeting between knowing and being does the contact take place? Polanyi never gives a direct or detailed answer to this question. But it has everything to do with Polanyi's realism and its success, and as such is the focus of attention in later chapters. For now, let us see what Polanyi says about the "location" of contact. What we find is a variety of answers that, after study, I have decided can be related to one another in terms of a spectrum paralleling the process of integration. Consider the following passage:

> Why do we entrust the life and guidance of our thoughts to our conceptions? Because we believe that their manifest rationality is due to their being in contact with domains of reality, of which they have grasped one aspect. This is why the Pygmalion

---

13. Polanyi, *Science, Faith and Society*, 37; *Personal Knowledge*, 315.

14. Polanyi, *Personal Knowledge*, 315. See also 157 for an example of this from the history of science.

15. Ibid., 106, 124, 317, 403; *Study of Man*, 27, 34; *Tacit Dimension*, 74.

at work in us when we shape a conception is ever prepared to seek guidance from his own creation; and yet, in reliance on his contact with reality, is ready to reshape his creation, even while he accepts its guidance. We grant authority over ourselves to the conceptions which we have accepted, because we acknowledge them as intimations—derived from the contact we make through them with reality—of an indefinite sequence of novel future occasions, which we may hope to master by developing these conceptions further, relying on our own judgment in its continued contact with reality.[16]

Looking at this single passage, it is possible to distinguish four different things that Polanyi says about the knower's contact with reality. First of all, our conceptions, to the extent that they are good ones, are in contact with "domains of reality, of which they have grasped one aspect." Polanyi speaks elsewhere of our making contact with reality in our language, our conceptions, our theoretical frameworks, and the current body of science.[17] These items are so many conceptual tools that we have embraced subsidiarily and upon which we rely in the pursuit of further epistemic achievement. That is, they have been subsidiarily incorporated, made part of our extending bodily being. Thus, contact is achieved in the subsidiaries.

Secondly, the passage tells us that we make contact *through* the conceptions—that is, the conceptions enable us to make further contact with reality. In another passage, Polanyi says that personal knowledge in science "claims to establish contact with reality beyond the clues on which it relies."[18] Discovery, the resultant focus of an integration of clues, claims for itself that it has achieved contact with reality: "The pursuit of discovery is conducted from the start in these terms; all the time we are guided by sensing the presence of a hidden reality toward which our clues are pointing; and the discovery that terminates and satisfies this pursuit is still sustained by the same vision. It claims to have made contact with reality: a reality which, being real may yet reveal itself to future eyes in an indefinite range of unexpected manifestations."[19] Thus, contact with reality is located in the integrative discovery and beyond.

---

16. Polanyi, *Personal Knowledge*, 104.

17. Ibid., 116, 104; "Science and Reality," 195; *Personal Knowledge*, 43. See also *Tacit Dimension*, 68, 82; "Science and Reality," 191; "The Growth of Science in Society," 79–80.

18. Polanyi, *Personal Knowledge*, 64. See also "The Creative Imagination," 88; *Tacit Dimension*, 64.

19. Polanyi, *Tacit Dimension*, 24.

Thirdly, it is the *knower* who does the contacting with reality—Polanyi speaks of the contact that *we* make through the conceptions. This almost goes without saying in the Polanyian scheme. The knower himself, in conjunction with the subsidiary and the focal, forms what Polanyi comes to refer to as the tacit triad.[20]

Finally, there is a contact that we make that is not made in the conceptions or even in the focal achievement per se. Our judgment, Polanyi says, is continually in contact with reality; it is in reliance on this contact that we can reshape our conceptions. It is an *intuitive* contact with reality, and it enables us, among other things, to "sense the presence of a hidden reality"—see the last quotation. Now this intuitive contact may be nothing in itself, but only the combined result of the three aspects of contact already delineated. However, there remains one portion of the Polanyian integrative scheme that it may parallel.

We have seen that contact is achieved by incorporated subsidiaries, such as conceptions on which we rely, by the focus of any integration, and by the knower himself. In addition to these, there are also what we may call prearticulate or prethematic subsidiaries: tacit knowledge which is ours prior to any conception and which has never been articulated (in contrast to conceptions, for example). In chapter 11, we will see more fully that this sort of tacit knowledge is ours by virtue of our body's placement in the world.

Thus, Polanyian contact with reality occurs at all stages of the epistemic act. All of these forms of contact are accompanied and legitimated by the IFM Effect. For Polanyi, it seems that contact with reality is more closely bound up with discovery than with the body and its tools, conceptions in particular. Perhaps it seems this way because, in many ways, discovery is the focus of Polanyi's attention. But I think that what is happening is that the integration from clues to discovery always constitutes an advance in contact with reality. Today's discovery becomes tomorrow's clue, to be relied upon in the hopes of making an even more superior contact with reality. We begin in contact with reality by virtue of our bodies; we seek to expand that contact by continually reaching beyond ourselves. I do not mean to imply that this advance is necessarily linear. The Polanyian scheme leaves plenty of room for scientific revolutions or some other metaphor of scientific growth. The result, as we shall see more clearly in chapter 11, is the gradual extension of ourselves out into the world. We will also return, in the end, to the primacy of discovery in Polanyi's contact with reality.

---

20. Polanyi, "Sense-Giving and Sense-Reading," in Grene, ed., *Knowing and Being*, 181–82 (orig. pub. in *Philosophy* 42 [1967] 301–25). See also *Personal Knowledge*, 251. Note that in *Science, Faith and Society*, 37, Polanyi speaks of "intuitive" contact.

Contact and Truth

Finally here I wish to touch briefly on the matter of truth. One of the richest payoffs of exploring the notions of contact with reality and of an aspect of reality is, in my estimation, a clearer understanding of how Polanyi envisions truth. For Polanyi says that "truth lies in the achievement of a contact with reality—a contact destined to reveal itself further by an indefinite range of yet unforeseen consequences."[21] After speaking of "the general anticipations that are intrinsic to any belief in reality," Polanyi says the following: "This defines reality and truth. If anything is believed to be capable of a largely indeterminate range of future manifestations, it is thus believed to be *real*. A statement about nature is believed to be no mere mathematical relation between observed data, but to represent an aspect of reality which may yet manifest itself inexhaustibly in the future."[22] More than once, Polanyi says that the truth of a proposition lies in its bearing on reality.[23]

The fact that truth is related by Polanyi to these notions of contact and aspect gives us a good sense of what truth can and cannot be, to his way of thinking. Any contact with reality is, of course, never wholly specifiable or determinate.[24] To the extent that contact consists of the integrative activity, this must be the case. But it is also the case that the bearing on reality of any conception or discovery that claims contact with reality will always be indeterminate. The indeterminate bearing of knowledge on reality is one of the five indeterminacies that Polanyi explicitly specifies.[25] Polanyi has also referred to this as the indeterminacy of the content of knowledge. We have seen in chapter 2 that knowledge that is wholly explicit would have no bearing upon reality. But now, one reason for this indeterminacy is clear. Contact with reality, for all its breathtaking success, reveals, as far as we know, only an aspect of reality. Much more is implied—I am thinking of the IFM Effect—but we have no way of knowing explicitly the nature of the implications. The next aspect of reality that is laid hold of, even if its discovery is a direct result of the first, may transform our understanding of the situation. Polanyi assesses the relationship of Kepler's to Copernicus' work in this way:

---

21. Polanyi, *Personal Knowledge*, 147. See also "Tacit Knowing: Its Bearing," in Grene, ed., *Knowing and Being*, 172; *Tacit Dimension*, 61, 87; "Science and Reality," 191.

22. Polanyi, "Science and Reality," 191.

23. Polanyi, *Personal Knowledge*, 61; "Tacit Knowing: Its Bearing," in Grene, ed., *Knowing and Being*, 172; *Tacit Dimension*, 87.

24. Polanyi, *Personal Knowledge*, 251, 310.

25. Polanyi, "Logic and Psychology," 27-43.

> Our knowledge of reality has then an essentially indeterminate content: it deserves to be called a vision. The vast indeterminacy of the Copernican vision showed itself in the fact that discoveries made later in the light of this vision would have horrified its author. Copernicus would have rejected the elliptic planetary paths of Kepler and, likewise, the extension of terrestrial mechanics to the planets by Galileo and Newton. Kepler noted this by saying that Copernicus had never realized the riches which his theory contained.[26]

But all of this indeterminacy fails to undermine, but rather positively affirms, the reality of contact with the world. Its presence is, as we have seen, attested to by the experience of the IFM Effect, among other things.

Therefore, the knower's intimations of contact with reality are, like intuition, fallible. Polanyi says that they are "conjectural and may prove false but they are not therefore mere guesses like betting on a throw of dice."[27] The possibility of error accompanies the fact of indeterminacy and thus is necessarily involved in any conception that bears on reality.[28] More often than not, a discovery, even a great discovery, comes to us curiously intermingled with error that is only subsequently filtered out.[29] But once again, this state of affairs is understandable in light of the contact aspect motif—the fact that only an aspect of reality is grasped. What is important, however, is to recognize that despite the admixture of truth and error, contact with reality is still made on a regular basis. For the IFM Effect is experienced on a regular basis. And it is helpful to realize that the IFM Effect comes to the discoverer despite the presence of error; it even comes if the truth that he has got hold of is not the truth he thinks it is—this latter is always the case to some degree. Consequently, the fact that truth is related to contact with reality hardly implies that truth is a one-to-one correspondence of knowledge with reality. But it does imply that there is truth in something more than a conventionalist sense, despite these qualifications of indeterminacy and fallibility. We must keep this in mind as we examine in further detail in chapter 9 Polanyi's conception of truth and the notion of correspondence.

---

26. Polanyi, "The Creative Imagination," 86. Here also is contained one of the more understandable things that Polanyi says about the scientist's "vision of reality": It helps me to understand why Polanyi so often employs that word. Contrast its obscure usage in *Personal Knowledge*, 135.

27. Polanyi, *Personal Knowledge*, 106.

28. Ibid., 315.

29. Ibid., 144.

In Conclusion

This chapter has presented the many dimensions of Polanyi's claim that in successful knowing we make contact with reality, and that it is the sense of the possibility of indeterminate future manifestations—what I term the IFM Effect—that testifies that we have made contact, laying hold of an aspect of reality. The IFM Effect, the signature of reality as that which manifests itself inexhaustibly in the future, becomes the sign of our successful contact with it. Both Polanyi's realism and his understanding of reality itself display this signature. And only Polanyian realism identifies it and pronounces it critically significant to the endeavor of coming to know.

7

Criteria of Reality

According to Polanyi, we know that we have made contact with reality because we sense the possibility of indeterminate future manifestations. Throughout his work, however, he identifies several criteria of contact. But I believe that they can be seen to reduce to two. These are perhaps not criteria so much as mechanisms that underlie and account for all the other criteria he names. In this chapter, as I develop this significant notion of contact with reality, I will show how I arrive at this claim. The discussion will serve to amplify our understanding of Polanyi's expert analysis and the dimensions of contact with reality. And it will deepen our grasp of Polanyian realism.

The Reality Criterion: Prospective Indeterminacy

The two basic criteria of reality are what I will call the reality criterion and the integrative criterion. The reality criterion is just the reality statement in its criterial use: we recognize successful contact with reality in the course of a discovery or other epistemic achievement because of the presence of intimations of indeterminate future manifestations (the IFM Effect), the feeling that the resulting conclusion will go on being confirmed in as yet inconceivable and surprising ways.

Little needs to be said in explanation of this experience by now; it has been a topic of discussion in two chapters already. But let us briefly document the use of the reality statement as a criterion. Polanyi says: "The most daring feats of originality are still subject to this law: they must be performed on the assumption that they originate nothing, but merely reveal what is there. And their triumph confirms this assumption, for what has been found bears the mark of reality in being pregnant with yet unforeseeable implications."[1] The word "pregnant" provides us with a lively metaphor with respect to the reality statement! But the point is made that the IFM Effect accompanies and thereby accredits discovery with respect to contact with reality.

The reality criterion embodies what I have earlier referred to as "prospective indeterminacy." The subsidiary particulars or clues with which it is concerned are not the subsidiaries we rely on in attending to a present focus. Rather, they are clues, or better, intimations, which point beyond ourselves and our present knowledge into the future. They are clues that legitimately belong to as-yet-unthought-of integrative foci. Intimations have the same sort of prospectively indeterminate status with respect to a discovery as they do with respect to a good problem. In each case, what distinguishes them from retrospectively indeterminate clues is simply that they belong to a future (and hence as yet unknown explicitly) focus rather than to the present (and hence focally known) focus.

The Integrative Criterion: Retrospective Indeterminacy

The integrative criterion, in contrast to the reality criterion, involves retrospectively indeterminate clues. Polanyi has distinguished the two criteria in the following passage: "At whatever level we consider a living being, the centre of its individuality is real. For it is always something we ascertain by comprehending the coherence of largely unspecifiable particulars, and which we yet expect to reveal itself further by an indeterminate range of future manifestations. Thus the criteria of reality are fulfilled."[2] The integrative criterion, as stated here, is as follows: contact with reality has been successfully made if the epistemic achievement in question consists of "the comprehension of the coherence of unspecifiable particulars." It was this passage that first called my attention to the presence of a second criterion of reality. But subsequently, I began to realize that the criterial use of the comprehen-

---

1. Polanyi, *Personal Knowledge*, 130. Remember also Polanyi's saying that the mark of true discovery is not its fruitfulness but its *intimation* of fruitfulness (*Personal Knowledge*, 148).

2. Polanyi, "Knowing and Being," in Grene, ed., *Knowing and Being*, 135.

sion of the coherence of largely unspecifiable particulars was pervasive, and that, in all probability, its character was more closely bound up with the character of Polanyian epistemology than was the reality criterion. It can be seen in the phrases of the following passage: "Let me recall that we have already recognized these heuristic powers in a less dynamic form wherever we rely on our awareness of particulars for establishing the presence of a comprehensive entity. For this was always viewed as something real, which being real, might be expected yet to manifest itself at some future time in unexpected ways."[3] Here, our reliance on our awareness of particulars for establishing the presence of a comprehensive entity is taken to imply that the comprehensive entity is real.

This is confirmed by the fact, cited occasionally by Polanyi, that the removal of some of the subsidiaries on which we rely in perception serves to strip the perceptive focus of its apparent reality:

> Observe the way this integration works when we look at an object, for example a finger of our own, through a pinhole in a sheet of paper. If I do this and move my finger back and forth, I see it swelling as it approaches my eye. Psychologists have called this effect a "de-realization." The moving object has lost here some of its constancy, for it lacks confirmation from the periphery of the visual field; and with the loss of its constancy the object has lost some of its apparent reality.[4]

Thus, the presence of unspecifiable subsidiaries in an integrative context contributes crucially to the knower's sense of the reality of the focus.

Next: "Here at last, in the logical structure of such exploring—and of visual perception—we found prefigured that combination of the active shaping of knowledge with its acceptance as a token of reality, which we recognize as a distinctive feature of all personal knowing."[5] Here, it is taken to be the essence of personal knowing that an active shaping of knowledge is accepted as such as a token of reality. The integrative nature of this criterion is clearest in the following passage: "I look at my right hand as I move it about in front of me, and I see a thousand rapidly changing clues as one single, unchanging object moving about at changing distances, presenting different sides at variable angles and in variable light. The integration of

---

3. Polanyi, "Tacit Knowing: Its Bearing," in Grene, ed., *Knowing and Being,* 172. In "Genius in Science," in Grene, ed., *Knowing and Being,* 65–66, the claim to reality is partly what distinguishes Polanyian integration from the standard notion of gestalt.

4. Polanyi, "Logic of Tacit Inference," in Grene, ed., *Knowing and Being,* 139.

5. Polanyi, *Personal Knowledge,* 132.

innumerable, rapidly changing particulars makes us see a real object in front of us."[6] Integration itself, therefore, betokens contact with reality.

Why Integration Brings the Conviction of Contact

Just what is it about integration that brings the conviction of contact? We may think of personal experiences, say, with puzzles. Perhaps we are to find the hidden pictures within a larger picture. At first, we see nothing. But as we continue to look for, say, hidden musical instruments, a moment will come in which the lines for us are reintegrated as a result of our efforts, and we recognize a musical instrument. The fact that we are now faced with a coherent and significant picture as a result of our efforts testifies to us that we have found a right answer. Also, the fact that we sense that we have arrived at our answer by relying on far more clues than we can specify injects the result with an aura of reality. This would be more pronounced the more complex the example. This is what Polanyi means in speaking of the comprehension of largely unspecifiable particulars as a criterion of reality. Finally, I believe that the integrative criterion involves the fact that the very act of integration itself, the feeling of sudden success after a sustained effort to understand, conveys a conviction of the rightness of our answer. This may be implied in the quotation about the hand. I have just specified three aspects of the integrative context that contribute to integration's functioning as a criterion of reality: 1) the making sense of clues in the discovery of a coherent pattern; 2) the fact that this occurs by means of reliance upon unspecifiable particulars—no doubt the sense is that the knower's conscious contribution is far out-weighed by the depth of the solution; 3) the sudden spontaneity of the integration after a sustained effort in which increasing proximity to the solution has been sensed—the latter aspect of this providing a sense of progress, the former a sense of the externality of the solution. All of these aspects Polanyi recognizes in one form or another as convincing the knower of the reality of his integration. All of these aspects reappear in connection with the three criteria of reality to be examined in the latter part of this chapter.

The proposition that the integrative feat claims for itself contact with reality turns out to be intimately related with the ontological aspect of tacit knowing. Polanyi, in speaking of how "the parts of a whole merge their isolated appearance into the appearance of the whole," which indicates "that we have a real coherent entity before us," says the following: "At the same time, it embodies the *ontological claim* of tacit knowing. The act of tacit knowing

---

6. Polanyi, "Logic and Psychology," 28.

thus implies the claim that its result is an aspect of reality which as such, may yet reveal its truth in an inexhaustible range of unknown and perhaps still unthinkable ways."[7]

The ontological claim is, in fact, the claim of the integrative criterion that the act of integration implies contact with reality. As such, my elucidation of the aspects of the integrative criterion serves to flesh out and provide a rationale for the ontological claim. An examination of the further criteria of reality which develop out of the integrative criterion will provide further insight into the claim as well.

The Problematic "Ontological Aspect of Tacit Knowing"

Before I turn to those criteria, however, I must launch into what amounts to an excursus concerning the ontological aspect of tacit knowing, for this matter in Polanyi's work is problematic. It must be examined in order to substantiate my interpretation of the ontological claim.

There are two reasons why the ontological aspect is a problematic notion in Polanyi's writings. The first is that he discontinues his use of the term. The fact that he does so is obvious, for he continues to define the functional, phenomenal, and semantic aspects of tact knowing, speaking of the *three* aspects of tacit knowing. The claim that it is a discontinuation, i.e., that there was a time before which Polanyi used the term, and that after that time he no longer used it (in contrast to characterizing his use of it as sporadic), can be fairly well documented. The ontological aspect appears in the three lectures of *The Tacit Dimension*, which, although published in 1966, consists to a large extent of the Terry Lectures delivered in 1962.[8] It appears in Lectures II, IV, and V of the Duke Lecture series, delivered in 1964, but these passages virtually duplicate the relevant passages in the lectures of *The Tacit Dimension*.[9] It appears twice in "The Logic of Tacit Inference," which, although first published in 1966, was written by 1964, according to Grene.[10] The passages in which only three aspects of tacit knowing are developed

---

7. Polanyi, "Logic of Tacit Inference," in Grene, ed., *Knowing and Being*, 141.

8. Polanyi, *Tacit Dimension*, 13, 33–34, 55. Polanyi says that the texts of the first two lectures are virtually unchanged (v, x).

9. Polanyi, *Duke Lectures*, II, 21; "The Emergence of Man," *Duke Lectures*, IV (March 1964), 1, 4, 17, 18, (passage on 18 not in *Tacit Dimension*); "Thought and Society," *Duke Lectures*, V (March 9, 1964), l.

10. Grene, "Introduction," in Grene, ed., *Knowing and Being*, vii; 138.

are published in 1965, 1968, and 1972.[11] Thus it would appear that Polanyi's disenchantment with the ontological aspect occurred somewhere around 1964-65.

To place all of this in a larger context, it should be noted that there are several articles in which Polanyi does not mention any of the four aspects, giving instead a more informal exposition of the structure of tacit knowing tailored to the matter at hand. Polanyi's disenchantment with the concept is corroborated by Grene's recollection that Polanyi actually expressed to her his regret at ever having included it in his exposition.[12] It remains for us to determine what it was that he disliked about it, and even more basically, what he thought it was in the first place.

This leads us to the second major problem concerning Polanyi and the ontological aspect. It is that, in the few mentions of the term listed above, Polanyi defines it in two virtually distinct, or at least distinguishable, ways. In the passages originating in 1962, Polanyi means by the ontological aspect that the structure of tacit knowing implies, or at least is duplicated by, a parallel structure in reality. The first passage, though confusingly ambiguous, seems to support the parallel-structures sense of the ontological aspect, if only in speaking of "the proximal term represent[ing] the particulars of this entity."[13] The passage in the second lecture of *Tacit Dimension*, duplicated in the fourth Duke Lecture, is more explicit—in fact, the most explicit development of the parallel-structures sense. Consider the following excerpts:

> The comprehension of this real entity has the same structure as the entity which is its object.
>
> It seems plausible to assume in all other instances of tacit knowing the correspondence between the structure of comprehension and the structure of the comprehensive entity which is its object.
>
> The two terms of tacit knowing, the proximal, which includes the particulars, and the distal, which is their comprehensive meaning, would then be seen as two levels of reality, controlled by distinctive principles.[14]

---

11. Polanyi, "The Structure of Consciousness," in Grene, ed., *Knowing and Being*, 212; "Logic and Psychology," 29; *Meaning*, 34-35 (apparently drawn from "Logic and Psychology," 29).

12. Private conversation. The only problem is that apparently he never said *why*.

13. Polanyi, *Tacit Dimension*, 13.

14. Ibid., 33-34.

All of this Polanyi believes explains better his claim that the question, what it is that we know by understanding a comprehensive entity, makes an *ontological* reference to it. Polanyi proceeds to develop throughout his works a metaphysical doctrine of levels.[15] The central claim of this doctrine is that most comprehensive entities span more than one metaphysical level. For example, a machine spans two levels: the lower consists of its physical and chemical composition; the higher is determined by its function. Living beings are characterized by multiple levels, even as many as six. A higher level is always irreducible with respect to its lower level even though the lower conditions the higher's existence. In the case of the machine, the machine's function and significance cannot, as a result of this irreducibility, be understood solely in terms of its physical-chemical composition—hence the machine itself cannot be so understood. Yet the lower level is also indispensable, since it constitutes the material out of which the machine is made. The parallel-structures sense of the ontological aspect is that the subsidiaries of the act of tacit knowing whereby we comprehend a certain entity parallel or constitute the entity's lower level, that the focus parallels the highest level of the entity itself, and that the act of integration is duplicated in the actual evolutionary emergence of the entity.[16]

Contrast all of this with Polanyi's elucidation of the ontological aspect in 1964, one passage of which has been quoted earlier. The second reference comes in a discussion of universal concepts. Polanyi claims that we come to know universals by means of a feat of integration. We rely on our subsidiary awareness of individual men, for example, to attend to their joint meaning, which is the concept. The joint meaning is, thus, a comprehensive entity. "The ontological claim requires that this entity be real," Polanyi says, and goes on to say that this is confirmed by the IFM Effect: "the members of a species are expected to have an indefinite range of as yet undisclosed properties in common."[17] The ontological aspect in both of these passages consists simply of the claim on the part of the result of the integrative feat of tacit knowing that that result is real, or is an aspect of reality, confirmed by the intimation of indeterminate future manifestations. The contact sense is a comparatively weaker claim answering a "that" question and leaving the "what" question of the parallel-structures sense untouched. It is possible that Polanyi still has in mind the doctrine of levels, for the contact sense

---

15. Ibid., 33–34. See n. 38 for documentation. It occurs in a later portion of this chapter devoted to the discussion of levels.

16. The parallel-structures sense is reflected in the title of Polanyi's essay in Grene, ed., *Knowing and Being*, 123–37, as the essay whose title Grene's collection employs as its own.

17. Polanyi, "Logic of Tacit Inference," in Grene, ed., *Knowing and Being*, 149.

of the ontological aspect is not inconsistent with the parallel-structures sense. But if he does have it in mind, there is absolutely no indication in the broader context of these passages.

My problem, therefore, is twofold. It must be shown that I am justified in viewing the contact sense of the ontological claim as the true ontological claim, and it must be shown that I am justified in utilizing it despite Polanyi's own discontinuation of it. I hope to show that what Polanyi rejected was most likely the parallel-structures sense and that the contact sense of the ontological aspect lives on despite the discontinuation of the term. It is interesting to consider the secondary literature on the ontological aspect. All the writers who mention the various aspects of tacit knowing include the ontological aspect in their exposition along with the functional, phenomenal, and semantic aspects.[18] Out of these writers, plus a few others who simply deal with the ontological aspect, only one recognizes both of the term's divergent meanings, and nobody intimates that there is any sort of problem, not even noting its discontinuation. What is more, the number is divided concerning which sense is considered the ontological aspect: five define it in the parallel-structures sense, three in the contact sense.[19] Thus, I am left with little precedent with respect to the issue.

My belief that what Polanyi rejected was the parallel-structures sense is justified primarily because I myself find the parallel-structures sense problematic and can only guess that Polanyi eventually did so as well. The idea of a one-to-one correspondence between the structure of knowing and the structure of being as Polanyi develops it is something that I have never been able to find convincing. Let me elaborate three difficulties. First of all, given how Polanyi himself has developed the structure of tacit knowing, it is impossible that all the subsidiaries on which we rely in knowing an entity are actually part of the entity. I have in mind here marginal clues in particular, some of which are clues precisely because they are not included

18. Gelwick, *Way of Discovery*, 74; Grene, "Tacit Knowing and the Pre-Reflective Cogito," in Langford and Poteat, eds., *Intellect and Hope*, 38; "Introduction," in Grene, ed., *Knowing and Being*, xv; Innis, "Logic of Consciousness and Mind-Body Problem in Polanyi," 82, 90; "Polanyi's Model of Mental Acts," 157; Manno, "Polanyi on the Problem of Science and Religion," 48.

19. Parallel-structures sense: Bennett, "The Tacit in Experience: Polanyi and Whitehead," 41–42; Innis; "Logic of Consciousness and Mind-Body Problem in Polanyi," 82, 90; Kuhn, "Personal Knowledge and the Crisis of the Philosophical Tradition," 115–19; Pols, "Polanyi and the Problem of Metaphysical Knowledge," 71; Prosch, "Biology and Behaviorism in Polanyi," 183. Contact or Criterial Sense: Gelwick, *Way of Discovery*, 74; Manno, "Polanyi on the Problem of Science and Religion," 48; Scott, "Polanyi's Theory of Personal Knowledge," 359; "Tacit Knowing and *The Concept of Mind*," 26. Grene is the one who notes both senses: Grene, "Tacit Knowing and the Pre-Reflective Cogito," in Langford and Poteat, eds., *Intellect and Hope*, 38.

in the entity and thereby help to define its boundaries. A second aspect of Polanyi's thought that mitigates against an inclusion of subsidiaries in the entity in question is the following claim: that, in some cases, such as the recognition of a familiar face, the subsidiaries do make up the entity that constitutes their focus, but that in other cases, such as the blind man's use of a probe, the focus lies beyond the subsidiaries that point to it. In the latter case, there can be no correspondence between the subsidiaries and any components of the entity.

The second difficulty with the parallel-structures sense of the ontological aspect is related to the first. The stronger claim is made that the subsidiaries, in addition to all being included within the relevant entity, are included within or parallel the lower levels of that entity. But this cannot be the case either, for Polanyi has indicated that we rely subsidiarily on a broad range of clues, even in the act of trying to understand something so metaphysically simple as the solar system or a machine. The point can be illustrated with regard to the machine. If I as an archaeologist discover what I take to be a tool, I do not seek to understand it merely by examining its physical and chemical properties. These may shed some light, of course. But even the doctrine of levels itself, in specifying irreducibility of the higher to the lower level, concludes that the higher cannot be understood merely in terms of the lower. Rather, I rely heavily on my beliefs concerning the character and activities of the society whose implementation I am considering, and I probably also rely on any similarities it might bear to tools whose function I understand. Together, these clues may span: levels of function; technical, intellectual, and aesthetic (and therefore human) achievement and values; and perhaps even ethical and religious convictions. Therefore, they cannot all be said to correspond to the lower level of the tool.

A third difficulty with the parallel-structures sense of the ontological aspect has been tentatively suggested to me by Dr. Grene as being, perhaps, the reason why Polanyi rejected his own ontological aspect. It is that the parallel breaks down with regard to subsidiaries in yet another way. In his proposed stratification of reality, Polanyi explicitly recognizes a low*est* level, namely, the level of physics and chemistry. A lowest level, by definition, has no levels that are respectively lower. At the same time, Polanyi does not question or rule out the possibility of focal knowledge of physical or chemical entities, even though such knowledge would necessarily rely on subsidiary clues that should correspond to a lower level. Thus, there would have to be a level lower than that of physics and chemistry; what is more, there could in principle be no lowest level. Polanyi's alternatives are either to deny that we have focal knowledge of physics and chemistry (rather a difficult thing to ask of someone who has been a professional physical chemist!), reject the idea of a lowest metaphysical level (which he never seems to do), or, finally, to reject the idea of a one-to-one correspondence between the structures of knowing and being. The last seems less costly.

The rejection of an exact parallel between structures of knowing and being need not rule out any relationship between them at all. If reality is stratified and emerges as Polanyi describes, then the similarities are striking. But there is nothing in this that says that the structure of knowing is such that it claims that reality is like this—which is what I take the ontological claim in its parallel-structures sense to be saying. The relationship between knowing and being is ultimately close for Polanyi, not because knowing parallels being, but because knowing in fact *is* being. In the final chapter of *Personal Knowledge*, for example, Polanyi says that ontology ultimately extends into epistemology: that the "noosphere," the realm of intellectual and cultural conceptions, is the most recently emerged level of being. The notion of indwelling, as we shall see, ultimately blends knowing with being. Perhaps, in the end, we shall have on our hands another sense in which tacit knowing makes an ontological claim. But if we do, it will not be the parallel-structures sense that Polanyi himself has called the ontological aspect.

It remains to us to consider the legitimacy of maintaining the contact or criterial sense of the ontological aspect in the face of Polanyi's own discontinuation of the term. It is legitimate to maintain this sense of the ontological claim, because, I believe, the ontological aspect itself lives on despite the discontinuation of its name. For one thing, its content appears to be absorbed into the phenomenal aspect of tacit knowing in the 1964 passage—let me now reproduce the passage in full:

> We have seen that by attending from the proximal to the distal, we cause a transformation in the appearance of both: they acquire an integrated appearance. A perceived object acquires constant size, colour and shape; observations incorporated in a theory are reduced to mere instances of it; the parts of a whole merge their isolated appearance into the appearance of the whole. This is the *phenomenal* accompaniment of tacit knowing, which tells us that we have a real coherent entity before us. At the same time it embodies the *ontological claim* of tacit knowing. The act of tacit knowing thus implies the claim that its result is an aspect of reality which, as such, may yet reveal its truth in an inexhaustible range of unknown and perhaps still unthinkable ways.[20]

---

20. Polanyi, "Logic of Tacit Inference," in Grene, ed., *Knowing and Being*, 141.

If the phenomenal aspect of tacit knowing, the fact that particulars are transformed in appearance as a result of their integration into a focus, serves to tell us "that we have a real coherent entity before us," nothing need be added in order for there to be an ontological claim as well. The same thing may be said, although Polanyi does not say it, with respect to the semantic aspect also. This leads me to make the second related point that the ontological aspect lives on in the integrative criterion and in the related criteria yet to be described; the criteria, unlike the ontological aspect, are not discontinued. The ontological aspect just is the claim of tacit knowing to have made contact with reality. This provides added motivation for examining the remaining criteria of contact with reality.

Other Criteria of Reality

Polanyi speaks persistently of three additional criteria of reality: coherence, rationality, and intellectual beauty. As far as I can tell, none of them is qualitatively distinguishable from the two criteria I have already considered; all, rather, seem to grow out of them. This leads me to speak of the reality and integrative criteria as revealing what might be called the underlying "mechanisms" upon which we rely for recognizing reality. In fact, perhaps because of this common base, it becomes at times almost artificial to distinguish the three criteria (coherence, rationality, and intellectual beauty) from one another. Thus, an exposition of each in turn should, perhaps, be better understood as the threefold development of a single subject: how we recognize contact with reality.

Rationality in Nature

At the outset, let us note again Polanyi's underlying assumption that the real is meaningful, significant, and orderly, and that that which is meaningful, significant, and orderly is real. We have already discussed Polanyi's foundational commitment to the rationality of nature; the claim that that which is meaningful is real is obviously a form of this commitment. That he holds such a belief is indicated in the "cobblestone" passage, as he speaks of the comparative reality of cobblestones and minds: "I shall say, accordingly, that minds and problems possess a deeper reality than cobblestones, although cobblestones are admittedly more real in the sense of being *tangible*. And since I regard the significance of a thing as more important than its tangibility, I shall say that minds and problems are more real than cobblestones."[21] One of the passages in which the assumption is clearest is the following: "We can ask then why the general appearance of the heliocentric system made Copernicus and his followers believe that it was real—why its close coherence, its intellectual harmonies had such power to convince them of its reality. And to this we reply that the existence of a harmonious order is a denial of randomness, and order and randomness are mutually exclusive. Moreover, anything that is random is meaningless, while anything that is orderly is significant."[22]

Polanyi never says explicitly here that he identifies the significant and the real. But his very silence shouts to the reader that the hidden premise is so basic that everyone assumes it, and as such it goes without saying. Polanyi, I'm sure, acknowledged that some philosophical systems, such as existentialism and positivism (for different reasons) would seek to deny such a claim. But they do so in the face of their own ordinary, day-to-day practices, and perhaps to their peril, he would say. He would persist in maintaining that science, par excellence, proceeds on the basis of such an assumption. What Polanyi says in this passage calls to mind the things he says in the early chapters of *Personal Knowledge* concerning order and randomness, giving fresh insight into the significance he attaches to the presence of order. I believe that this assumption also serves to ground the criteria of contact with reality.

Coherence

This is especially clear with reference to coherence and rationality. Polanyi says that "it is the coherence of a thing that makes us attribute reality to it," and that as such: "coherence is a token of reality."[23] Of Copernicus, he says that he claimed the discovery of the heliocentric system in these very terms: "He showed that his system included a parallelism between the solar distances of the planets and their orbital periods, and on this coherence he based his insistence that his system was no mere computing device, but a real fact."[24] The fact that the anticipations Copernicus felt with regard to his

---

21. Polanyi, *Tacit Dimension*, 32–33.

22. Polanyi, "Science and Reality," 191. Polanyi adds the note: "I disregard here statistical laws, as they apply to another level of reality. (See my *Personal Knowledge*, 390.)"

23. Polanyi, "Logic and Psychology," 28. See also 30, 38; *Duke Lectures*, I, 12–13, 16; *Duke Lectures*, II, 2, 16, 24; "The Creative Imagination," 86; "Science and Reality," 185, 187, 191; "Genius in Science," in Grene, ed., *Knowing and Being*, 60, 61, 65–66, 68.

24. Polanyi, "Genius in Science," in Grene, ed., *Knowing and Being*, 60.

findings were later discovered by other astronomers legitimates the conclusion that, "in nature, the coherence of an aggregate shows that it is real and that the knowledge of this reality foretells the coming of yet unknown future manifestations of such reality."[25] That our perception of coherence functions as a token of contact with reality is quite a natural notion, especially given the coherence of nature itself and man's innate capacity to recognize it, upon both of which Polanyi insists.[26]

What does Polanyi have in mind by coherence? Coherence, I believe, has to do with appearance—shape, pattern, order, and so on. Consider the following: "Whence can we guess the presence of a real relationship between observed data, if its existence has never before been known?" He continues: "We must go back to the process by which we usually first establish the reality of certain things around us. Our principal clue to the reality of an object is its possession of a coherent outline. It was the merit of Gestalt psychology to make us aware of the remarkable performance involved in perceiving shapes."[27] He proceeds to speak of the capacity of scientists to guess the presence of *shapes* as tokens of reality, concluding that the difference between this and ordinary perception is not qualitative.

If coherence can be properly linked with appearance and pattern, then two helpful conclusions can be drawn. First, the idea of coherence aligns itself nicely with the phenomenal aspect of tacit knowing, and the fact that coherence is a token of reality infuses that aspect with the ontological import necessary to maintaining the concept of the ontological aspect discussed above. Second, it becomes a bit easier to distinguish between the criteria of coherence and rationality. Although the two probably cannot be ultimately separated, it is helpful to see coherence as having appearance as its focus and rationality as having more to do with significance.

The kind of coherence that Polanyi envisions is different from the connotation usually associated with the word, not simply by virtue of its reference to appearance, but also because it is superior in a sense that can be described by saying that it is generally richer. "Coherence" does not describe an aggregate of particulars or even an explicitly deducible and uniform

---

25. Ibid.

26. Coherence in nature: Polanyi, "Science and Reality," 193, 195; "Logic and Psychology," 28, 29, 31, 37, 38, 41; "Genius in Science," in Grene, ed., *Knowing and Being*, 62, 66, 68. In "Logic and Psychology," 28–29, Polanyi distinguishes between coherence and true coherence in nature. The distinction between the two depends ultimately upon the unspecifiable power of the mind. Capacity of the mind to sense coherence in nature: Polanyi, "The Creative Imagination," 89; "Science and Reality," 195; "Logic and Psychology," 29, 38; "Genius in Science," in Grene, ed., *Knowing and Being*, 62.

27. Polanyi, *Science, Faith and Society*, 24.

arrangement. We must remember that coherence results from the integrative feat. As such, it comprehends particulars of which the agent may not even be conscious. It constitutes an achievement that could never have been deduced from the particulars as premises. Most importantly, as the phenomenal aspect tells us, the particulars are transformed within the resulting coherent focus, such that they do not even appear as they did previously. And finally, this coherence, by virtue of its intimations of indeterminate manifestations, testifies to the agent that it extends in reality far beyond that aspect which he has to date been able to comprehend. It is thus an inexhaustibly rich coherence.

Of course, the implication of personal knowledge is that it is impossible to specify any explicit criteria for determining the presence of coherence. This indeterminacy with regard to the assessment of coherence is one of the five indeterminacies that, Polanyi claims, characterize all of knowing.[28] The coherence perceived in a discovery can perhaps be only vaguely defined, Polanyi says. As a result of his inability to articulate the breadth and the depth of the coherence he senses, the discoverer is likely to resort to emotive, metaphorical language in the attempt to convey the greatness of the coherence. The problem in specifying coherence explicitly stems not only from the inexhaustible character of the coherence at hand. It also stems from the fact that the presence of coherence cannot be determined by a logical test. Instead, the scientist must rely on his own personal skill and judgment in drawing a conclusion. This is the message of the early pages of *Personal Knowledge*.

Let us note, finally, two things with respect to coherence. First, coherence plays a role in all stages of discovery. A good problem is the intimation of a hidden coherence of unspecifiable particulars. The process and progress of discovery utilizes a gradient of deepening coherence as a gauge and guide. And coherence in the solution proclaims its validity to its author, immediately upon discovery, and for years to come. Second, the affinity that the criterion of coherence has for the integrative criterion is obvious. Integration lies at the heart of coherence and is responsible for the peculiarly rich character that it has for Polanyi. The act of integration and its success gives rise to the sensation of coherence.

Rationality

Concerning rationality as a criterion for contact with reality, Polanyi says the following: "Copernicus anticipated in part the discoveries of Kepler and

28. Polanyi, "Logic and Psychology," 28.

Newton, because the rationality of his system was an intimation of a reality incompletely revealed to his eyes." He continues: "Why do we entrust the life and guidance of our thoughts to our conceptions? Because we believe that their manifest rationality is due to their being in contact with domains of reality, of which they have grasped one aspect."[29]

Rationality as a criterion, as is the case for coherence, is quite natural in the light of Polanyi's insistence upon the inherent rationality of nature. And whereas coherence picks up the themes of the phenomenal aspect, rationality falls nicely in line with the semantic aspect of tacit knowing. Thus, the semantic aspect as well, by virtue of this alliance, contains ontological import. The criterion of rationality, since it emphasizes meaning more than appearance, is more clearly tied to Polanyi's underlying assumption concerning the correspondence between meaning and reality.

We can guess, as a result of our study of coherence, how it is that the apprehension of rationality comes about and what it is like. It results, once again, from the integrative feat. Isolated particulars are relatively meaningless, but as a result of their integrative comprehension, they are imbued with significance, pointing beyond themselves to their focus. Whereas, before, the particulars had no special sense or relationship within the focus, in the integration they acquire rationality, a reasonable relationship among themselves. The kind of rationality involved is not restricted to some sort of formal consistency but rather exceeds the understanding of its discoverer. As such, it claims authority over him.

Finally, this rationality is not fully determinate. Polanyi, at one point, distinguishes between the "precise predictive content" of the heliocentric view, which was not any more extensive than that of the Ptolemaic view, and a surplus of meaning which exceeds the content more radically in the case of the former than in the case of the latter.[30] This surplus of meaning is tied directly to the "anticipatory powers of the new image," that is, to its indeterminate implications. As a result, rationality of a Polanyian sort is ultimately unspecifiable.

---

29. Both quotations are from *Personal Knowledge*, 104. Polanyi does not explicitly refer to rationality as a criterion or token of reality the way he does for coherence and intellectual beauty. Its use as a criterion is, however, clearly implicit here, as well as in "Science and Reality," 191, where he speaks of "intellectual harmonies" rather than of rationality. He does, however, speak often of rationality in nature, as he does coherence in nature—see *Personal Knowledge*, 11, 12, 13, 15, 16.

30. Polanyi, "Science and Reality," 189.

Intellectual Beauty

The third criterion of contact with reality is intellectual beauty. Polanyi says, "we recognize intellectual beauty as a guide to discovery and as a mark of truth."[31] Intellectual beauty is an inarticulable element of a scientific theory, conception, or discovery, which makes us respond to it with excitement and appreciation—that is, with what Polanyi terms intellectual passions. Thus, the presence of intellectual passions in connection with a discovery actually betokens its contact with reality. If it was difficult to describe coherence and rationality, it is even more difficult to capture the sense intended by intellectual beauty. We can get at least a feel for it by considering Polanyi's use of it by describing Einstein's work:

> Brushing aside the protest of common sense as the complaint of mere habit, he adopted a vision in which the electro-dynamics of moving bodies were set beautifully free from all the anomalies imposed on them by the traditional framework of absolute space and time. Accepting this intellectual beauty as a token of reality, Einstein went on to generalize his vision further and to derive from it a series of new and surprising consequences. This was an unfamiliar beauty in science, for it accepted a new conception of reality. . . . The new beauty inaugurated the modern view of a mathematically defined reality.[32]

If we could capture the essence of beauty, no doubt we would put aestheticians out of business. Yet the existence of this element of beauty and its role in science is affirmed by philosophers of science other than Polanyi—Quine, for instance.[33] To some extent, a theory is beautiful by virtue of its coherence and rationality, thus binding the three criteria intimately together. The sudden success of an integrative feat would quite believably overwhelm us with a sense of the beauty of its result. Intellectual beauty is also related to the indeterminate future manifestations which a discovery hints at, for

---

31. Polanyi, *Personal Knowledge*, 300. See also 133, 143, 144, 145, 146, 149, 189, 201, 320.

32. Ibid., 144. Just as there is a need to distinguish between coherence and true coherence, Polanyi explains that we must distinguish between true intellectual beauty and mere formal attractiveness. He devotes an entire section in chapter 6 to this matter (145–50). But the conclusion is that, though it is vitally important to distinguish between them, it is a delicate, difficult, and baffling thing to attempt to do so, and that such a decision must ultimately be made on unspecifiable personal grounds.

33. Quine, *The Ways of Paradox*, 242. See also Kuhn, *Structure of Scientific Revolutions*, 152–58; Lakatos, "Falsification," 175; Feyerabend, "Consolations for the Specialist," in *Criticism and the Growth of Knowledge*, 228; Toulmin, *Foresight and Understanding*, 81.

we have seen that these fill the discoverer with excited anticipation and a sense of the profundity of his discovery. Thus, the concept of intellectual beauty fleshes out what has turned out to be single clusters of concepts and experience surrounding the experience of making contact with reality.

We can recognize successful contact with reality, therefore, by means of the accompaniment of various experiences that thus function as criteria of such contact. The criteria, most basically, consist of the experience of a sudden, far-reaching integration of unspecifiable clues, and of the experience of intimations of indeterminate future manifestations of the result at hand. The fact that Polanyi claims both that contact with reality is possible and that it is recognizable by means of certain characteristics attests to his thorough-going realism. And Polanyian realism is distinctive for its reliance on an indeterminate, inexhaustive surplus of meaning—something only an epistemology that accredits the inarticulable is prepared to countenance.

There are three other rather sizeable topics of discussion contained in Polanyi's work that deserve at least a brief mention. His critique of positivism, his metaphysical doctrine of levels, and his speculations concerning what sorts of things are real are of interest in this context primarily because Polanyi's concern with them indicates his commitment to realism. They do not, however, lie close enough to the heart of what I have taken to be my central concern in this book to merit any more than this brief description.

Critique of Positivism

Polanyi takes positivism to be the position that scientific claims, rather than being true assertions concerning the nature of things, are instead merely descriptions of the observational data; that science, rather than concerning itself with indemonstrable contacts with reality, limits its interest to "establishing functional relations between the data observed by our senses."[34] Polanyi does not confine himself to a critique of positivism only in this form; he also opposes what he takes to be other anti-metaphysical tendencies such as reductivism, logical positivism, linguistic nominalism, and, in particular, pragmatism (in its standard sense of a theory of truth). The positivistic trend in general refuses to acknowledge the possibility (and actuality) of contact with an external reality and a reality-based truth in scientific claims. Thus, it stands in opposition to various forms of metaphysical realism (see chapter 10), including Polanyi's understanding of realism. Also, positivism refuses to acknowledge the presence and foundational role of the personal

---

34. Polanyi, "Scientific Beliefs," in *Scientific Thought and Social Reality*, 72 (orig. pub. in *Ethics* 61 [October 1950] 27–37); "Science and Reality," 178.

and tacit in human knowledge, except, perhaps, in a conventionalist form. We can thus understand Polanyi's concern to criticize it.

In support of his claim that scientists themselves refuse to regard their discoveries as convenient or helpful organizations of data, Polanyi frequently cites Copernicus' persistence in maintaining the truth and greatness of his discovery in the face of pressure from positivists of his day, Osiander in particular, to bill it as a helpful alternative description, and in spite of substantial social pressure in favor of its retraction.[35]

In addition to this, three general criticisms can be found in Polanyi's work. First, Polanyi argues that positivism is untenable because, on its assumption, we would have no grounds for accepting science as a legitimate enterprise and rejecting the similarly simple and fruitful field of astrology, for example, as illegitimate.[36] Polanyi argues, secondly, that any positivistic claim to the validation of scientific statements in terms of the statements' usefulness in the prediction of future consequences is untenable also.[37] It is logically impossible to base one's present acceptance of a claim on that claim's future usefulness. If the claim can only be validated by future consequences, then it can never be validated at the time it is made but only after predictions have time to be borne out. But the historical record is that great discoverers such as Copernicus did not wait for the actualization of future consequences to claim the truth of the discovery at hand. Polanyi's third and most developed attack upon positivism is to expose its usage of terms such as "simplicity" and "fruitfulness" as examples of what he calls pseudosubstitution.[38] The gist of his claim is that when the positivist substitutes "simple" for "true," he must redefine "simple" in order for it to be able to do its job. In actuality, it is redefined to imply truth, and therefore no genuine substitution is taking place after all.

Metaphysical Doctrine of Levels

A second sphere within the Polanyian system that embellishes his realism is his metaphysical doctrine of levels, the bare outlines of which have already been noted in connection with the parallel-structures sense of the

---

35. See for example Polanyi, *Personal Knowledge*, 145–50, and "Science and Reality."
36. Polanyi, "Scientific Beliefs," 72; *Logic of Liberty*, 18.
37. Polanyi, *Personal Knowledge*, 145–49.
38. Ibid., 15–16, 147, 166, 169–70, 233n., 308, 309n., 371–72; "Scientific Beliefs," 73; "From Copernicus to Einstein," 113–14; see also Grene, *The Knower and the Known*, 220–21.

ontological aspect.[39] Polanyi has, in effect, developed his own vision of reality: one that he believes to be compatible with the personal, tacit, dynamic character of knowledge, and one that would legitimate a realist claim by portraying a rational, knowable, world. Reality for Polanyi consists of multiple levels, each with a distinctive feature, each related to its neighbors in a distinctive way. A level is characterized by what Polanyi terms an operational principle providing it with a level of achievement, a standard of success, and a related potential for failure. In the case of a machine, the example noted before, the operational principle of its higher level is the function or purpose for which it was created. Polanyian levels are best understood as they are considered in relation to one another. Inter-level relationships must be seen to occur within entities rather than between them. This relationship consists, first of all, of the indeterminacy of the lower level with respect to the conditions under which it will be made to operate, because such conditions, called boundary conditions, lie beyond the control of its operational principle. It is the higher level that will specify those conditions. For example, the laws of physics and chemistry leave open the question of what particular entity will utilize them. They continue to operate indifferently whether, for example, the mechanical function that utilizes them is a spinning wheel or a typewriter. The lower level is, thus, blind to the purposes of the higher level, indifferent to its peculiar success or failure, and thus of incomplete help to the person seeking to understand the entity in question. By contrast, the higher level, if it is the highest level of the entity, embodies in its operational principle the key feature, the understanding of which is essential to the understanding of that entity. In addition, the higher level constitutes the entity's true meaning and supplies joint meaning to the particulars of the lower level—the intrinsic meaning of which is relatively inferior and certainly different. Finally, the peculiarity of the relationship between lower and higher levels is manifested in the fact that a single higher operational principle can be achieved by reliance on different sets of particulars from the lower level. All of these aspects of the relationship between adjacent levels lead Polanyi to speak of the irreducibility of the higher to the lower levels. This is not to imply that lower levels make no significant contribution to the structure. The lower level supplies the material conditions to the entity. It constitutes the medium in which higher purposes are carried out. Thus, the lower level both grants to the higher the very possibil-

---

39. The following are major discussions of the doctrine of levels: Polanyi, *Personal Knowledge*, 327–46; *Study of Man*, 46–55; "Tacit Knowing: Its Bearing," in Grene, ed., *Knowing and Being*, 173–80; "Structure of Consciousness," in Grene, ed., *Knowing and Being*, 216–18; "Life's Irreducible Structure," in Grene, ed., *Knowing and Being*, 225–39 (orig. pub. in *Science* 160 [1968] 1308–12); "On the Modern Mind," 134–38.

ity of its existence and circumscribes the domain in which that principle is operative. These positive and negative roles form the basis for Polanyi's notions of acceptance of calling and the bodily rootedness of all thought.[40] Human thinking in all of its reaches would be nonexistent without bodies and brains. In addition, the failure of these bodies and brains automatically terminates human thinking.

Polanyi applies the doctrine of levels to machines, living beings, and even literary composition.[41] Its most fruitful application, however, is to the relationship between mind and body. The mind is that comprehensive feature on which we must focus in order to understand a human being truly.[42] Knowledge of the mind is achieved by subsidiary reliance on its bodily manifestations—hence by means of an integrative feat. Focal knowledge of these manifestations yields only knowledge of the body; this proposition provides the basis of Polanyi's critique of behaviorism.[43]

40. Acceptance of calling: Polanyi, *Personal Knowledge*, 65, 285, 315, 321–24, 334, 346, 374, 379, 380, 389, 397. Bodily rootedness of all thought: Polanyi, *Personal Knowledge*, 64–65; *Study of Man*, 89; "Knowing and Being," in Grene, ed., *Knowing and Being*, 134; "Logic of Tacit Inference," in Grene, ed., *Knowing and Being*, 146, 147–48; "Tacit Knowing: Its Bearing," in Grene, ed., *Knowing and Being*, 160; "The Unaccountable Element in Science," in Grene, ed., *Knowing and Being*, 115; "Structure of Consciousness," in Grene, ed., *Knowing and Being*, 214; *Tacit Dimension*, 15–16; "Logic and Psychology," 40. Of this, more in ch. 11.

41. Machines: Polanyi, *Personal Knowledge*, 331; "Logic of Tacit Inference," in Grene, ed., *Knowing and Being*, 153; "Tacit Knowing: Its Bearing," in Grene, ed., *Knowing and Being*, 175; "Life's Irreducible Structure," 225. Living Beings: Polanyi, "Logic of Tacit Inference," in Grene, ed., *Knowing and Being*, 155; "Life's Irreducible Structure," in Grene, ed., *Knowing and Being*, 234. Literary Composition: Polanyi, "Logic of Tacit Inference," in Grene, ed., *Knowing and Being*, 154; *Tacit Dimension*, 35–36; "Life's Irreducible Structure," in Grene, ed., *Knowing and Being*, 233; "On the Modern Mind," 136–37.

42. Polanyi, *Personal Knowledge*, 263, 312; *Study of Man*, 65; "Logic of Tacit Inference," in Grene, ed., *Knowing and Being*, 151–52; "Tacit Knowing: Its Bearing," in Grene, ed., *Knowing and Being*, 170; "Life's Irreducible Structure," in Grene, ed., *Knowing and Being*, 238; *Tacit Dimension*, 32–33.

43. Polanyi, *Personal Knowledge*, 262–64, 372; *Study of Man*, 65; "Logic of Tacit Inference, in Grene, ed., *Knowing and Being*, 152; "Tacit Knowing: Its Bearing," in Grene, ed., *Knowing and Being*, 169; "Life's Irreducible Structure," in Grene, ed., *Knowing and Being*, 238; Prosch, "Biology and Behaviorism in Polanyi," 178–91; Hall, "Wittgenstein and Polanyi: The Problem of Privileged Self-Knowledge," 275–76; Scott, "Tacit Knowing and *The Concept of Mind*," 206–7. Polanyi's critique of behaviorism can be anticipated fairly easily given his concept of mind. The point is that focal observation of physical particulars—which is presumably the concern of the behaviorist—reveals something different from subsidiary awareness of the same particulars in terms of a distinct comprehensive focus, namely, the mind. In focal observation of the particulars, the mind is thereby lost from view. Furthermore, it is impossible to isolate mental manifestations except by reading them as pointers to the mind from which they originate. In fact,

The mind, as the comprehensive feature, infuses bodily manifestations with meaning along the lines of the semantic aspect of tacit knowing. Focal knowledge of the same bodily activities is devoid of this meaning. The mind, finally, constitutes a higher level with respect to the body. This notion can be developed into a unique, Polanyian response to the mind-body problem, in which the mind transcends the body but remains rooted in it, and to which all the other characteristics of the relationship of mutual levels apply.[44]

What Sorts of Things Are Real

Finally, Polanyi speculates concerning what sorts of things are real. Of greatest interest are his claims that minds, human achievements (skillful feats, artistic conceptions, theoretical frameworks, intellectual systems, etc.), and human ideals (the moral, social, and intellectual standards of a human culture) are real. Although this work does not analyze these specific metaphysical claims in detail, in each case, their reality is attested to by the accompanying IFM Effect.[45]

---

many of the appropriate particulars are unspecifiable in what Polanyi refers to as the stronger sense—that is, they are simply unknown. The determination and selection of bodily behavior which is "significant" to the behaviorist's study is both impossible apart from reference to an ordinary concept of mind and impossible in the abstract. Thus behaviorism is impracticable.

44. Polanyi, "Structure of Consciousness," in Grene, ed., *Knowing and Being,* 213; "Life's Irreducible Structure," in Grene, ed., *Knowing and Being,* 237–38; "Logic and Psychology," 39, 40; "Faith and Reason," 128; *Meaning,* 46, 47, 51; Grene, "Tacit Knowing and the Pre-Reflective Cogito," 42–43; Langford and Poteat, "Upon First Sitting Down to Read *Personal Knowledge,*" in *Intellect and Hope,* 10; Scott, "Tacit Knowing and *The Concept of Mind,*" 30. Polanyi is confident that his analysis of the relationship between mind and body handles successfully the paradoxes that characterize the issue and, in general, serves to make things more clear. Most commentators agree that Polanyi abandons the mind-body dichotomy and in this way dissolves the mind-body problem. It is therefore bound to be puzzling to the reader that Polanyi refers to his view as a form of dualism. Polanyi, as it turns out, thought of his work as a revival of the traditional mind-body dualism. Grene writes: "No, by the 'problem of Cartesian dualism' he meant, I must reluctantly admit, the problem of *defending* mind's separateness from body" ("Tacit Knowing: Grounds," 169). Grene's response is that this is inconsistent with all Polanyi has been concerned to defend, namely, the integral and internal, nondissectable relation between any "from" and "to," including the body and mind. However, Polanyi's theory of mind, despite his own misguided intentions, did more to refute dualism than to revive it, Grene says. "For the theory of mind mediated by the doctrine of tacit knowing is a theory of mind as fundamentally and irrevocably incarnate."

45. Minds: see note 41 above. Universals: *Personal Knowledge,* 114, 115–16, 349; "Logic of Tacit Inference," in Grene, ed., *Knowing and Being,* 149; "Tacit Knowing: Its Bearing," in Grene, ed., *Knowing and Being,* 168, 170, 170–71; "Logic and Psychology,"

In Conclusion

In conclusion: in this section of chapters I have laid out fully Michael Polanyi's epistemic realism, developing several dimensions of his distinctive claim that we know that we have made contact with reality when we have a sense of the possibility of indeterminate future manifestations. The IFM Effect, as well as testifying to our having made contact with reality, is reality's signature. Indeterminacy can be seen to attest both prospectively and retrospectively to contact.

These claims of Polanyi's are utterly distinctive—as is, in a corresponding way, his epistemology. I believe that what makes them distinctive will also prove to render them superior to other forms of realism. How Polanyian realism compares with other forms will be the focus of the next three chapters. In the process, further dimensions of this realism will come to light along with a growing sense, I believe, of its merit and value.

36; *Meaning*, 53. Meanings: "On the Modern Mind," 137–38; *Meaning*, 182. Language: *Personal Knowledge*, 80, 94, 95, 106, 112, 113, 114, 116, 251, 287. Scientific Theory: *Personal Knowledge*, 94, 104, 133, 150, 317. Mathematics: *Personal Knowledge*, 46, 104, 116, 184–85, 189, 192, 201, 202, 302. Art: *Personal Knowledge*, 117, 133, 201, 202, 348; *Meaning*, 65–68, 92, 98, 99, 101, 102, 145, 149. Human Ideals: *Science, Faith and Society*, 73; *Logic of Liberty*, 5, 46, 47; "On the Modern Mind," 148; *Personal Knowledge*, 231, 234, 244; *Meaning*, 24.

8

Polanyi and Contemporary Realist Issues (I): Progress

In these next chapters, I want to locate Polanyi's distinctive realist theses within the broader context of a complex and detailed discussion in contemporary philosophy of science.[1] In doing this, I am attempting the sort of engagement that Polanyi never did for himself extensively. Partially in virtue of the less than enthusiastic welcome of his work into it, he worked and spoke from outside the prevailing philosophical conversation. Polanyi never adopted the rigorous style of analytic philosophers, nor would he have valued it as much as other approaches, given his epistemology. But more importantly, he does not fit seamlessly into the discussion because his epistemology and realism challenge some of the discussion's defining assumptions and supply a positive alternative. In fact, Polanyi's epistemology, in accrediting the scientist's reliance on more-than-specifiable clues which may be anticipated and continue to manifest themselves surprisingly over

---

1. These chapters engage the discussion current in the 1970s. In chapters 12 and 13, I will bring the discussion up to date. But this older conversation remains valuable, because it engages the work of philosophers of science who were Polanyi's contemporaries and whose formative claims remain in play and form a critical backdrop to the conversation now. Popper, Kuhn, Lakatos, and Feyerabend all receive due treatment in the history of philosophy of science as it told today (see Godfrey-Smith, *Theory and Reality*). If we can locate Polanyi's contributions with respect to them, we can gauge in some measure how it relates to current discussions. And it will help us understand why his work continues to matter now.

time, actually reconciles the two sides of a major debate in the philosophy of science. His epistemic proposals ground his view of the nature of science with respect to matters of progress and, in turn, are supported by it.

The mismatch of fundamental vision and approach between Polanyi and better known thinkers in philosophy of science, and the innovative nature of his contributions, render relating his work to contemporary developments in realism and philosophy of science a somewhat tedious and artificial exercise. But it is important to make this effort. It enables an evaluation of each in light of the other and consequently a better understanding of both. But what we will see, I believe, is that what Polanyi offers is not a paste of pieces from this side and that side of the debate but an integratively synthetic re-rendering of them. In this, it exemplifies the very thing it proposes. Overall, I believe that this undertaking sets Polanyian realism off to advantage.

For the sake of this comparison, I have concentrated my attention on two slightly different clusters of contemporary concepts: first, the work of such thinkers as Karl Popper, Imre Lakatos, T. S. Kuhn, and Paul Feyerabend on the nature of science, and second, that of Hilary Putnam, Alan Goldman, and related thinkers on realism. And for purposes of a linear organization, I intend to separate out the various issues for consideration one by one. It is, of course, impossible to package each issue entirely separately, and to the extent that such separation is achieved, the result will be arbitrary, for the nexus of their interrelationships and overlappings is complex.

In the present chapter, then, I will consider the cluster of concepts generally related to the idea of progress in science. Chapter 9 will attend to questions concerning truth. The final chapter in this cluster is devoted more directly to realism. In each chapter I will lay out representative theses prevalent in the contemporary discussion. I will then compare and contrast Polanyi's claims to the extent that this is possible.

The task in this chapter about progress is threefold. First, I will elucidate the relevant issues. Second, I will assess their relationship to realism. Third, I will determine how Polanyi would stand on these issues and what to think of his realism as a result.

Definitions and Issues in the Contemporary Discussion

There is a cluster of closely related but distinguishable concepts surrounding the idea of progress. *Progress, success, continuity, growth,* and *convergence* are terms frequently employed in contemporary philosophy of science that all bear on the matter of the nature of science.[2] Defining these is, of course, integral to developing a position with respect to them. Perhaps the most elemental of these is *continuity*, for the question of whether or not scientific change is continuous could conceivably be answered without reference to any sort of development of direction. But in fact, continuity is taken to imply continuous growth and thus cannot be separated out so easily. *Growth* introduces a directional element: the question becomes one of whether science is change in a certain direction, presumably for the better. *Progress* picks up this notion and, for the most part, is identical to it. For some, however, it seems to also imply the idea of a goal toward which science moves and in terms of which its change is evaluated. The question of *success* in science seems to be treated interchangeably with that of progress in the literature, and I will treat them accordingly. It seems to me personally that success is concerned more with particular scientific endeavors, discoveries, and their ability to further our understanding, rather than with the supersession of one theory by another. In the end, the two questions may be answered simultaneously. Finally, *convergence* clearly concerns the presence of a goal and science's development toward it. However, most often it is specified as having to do with the more immediate question of whether a newer theory retains the approximate truths of its ancestors, attempting to explain them in the light of its new theses. Thus, it actually falls in line with questions of continuity and progress.

All of these questions in contemporary debate have, to a large extent, been made to turn on the issue of whether or not successive scientific theories are *commensurable*. Two scientific theories are commensurable if they can be in some sense compared. Such a comparison would seem to entail a rational standard of comparison. The existence of rational criteria or a rational methodology for comparison constitutes a twin issue for that of commensurability. Since those who would defend the continuous growth, progress, and convergence of science do so on the grounds of their elaborations of a rational methodology for the comparative assessment of successive theories, generally speaking, a denial of the possibility of such a methodology and of the existence of commensurability would appear to

---

2. My primary sources for this overview are: Brown, *Perception, Theory and Commitment*; Feyerabend, *Against Method*; Goldman, "Realism," 175–92; Kuhn, *Structure of Scientific Revolutions*; various contributions to Lakatos and Musgrave, eds., *Criticism and the Growth of Knowledge*; Margolis, "Cognitive Issues"; Popper, *Logic of Scientific Discovery*, and *Conjectures and Refutations*; Putnam, *Meaning and the Moral Sciences*; Rouse, "Kuhn, Heidegger, and Scientific Realism"; Skagestad, "Pragmatic Realism: The Peircean Argument Reexamined," 527–40.

jeopardize the possibility of scientific growth. And, of course, those on each side appeal to the history of science in defense of their position.

How the Question of Progress Connects to Realism

Most significantly for our purposes here, it would seem that progress in science is intimately bound up with the realist claim. Proponents of scientific progress tend to be realists; opponents tend to oppose realism to some extent. Alan Goldman renders the general line of reasoning as follows:

> If (1) there is no theory-free observation; if (2) theories specify different ontologies with different principles of individuation for picking out what is real; if (3) there is no convergence or preservation of reference and truth across theories; and if (4) there is nevertheless an independent world with autonomous structures of individuation which all theories are attempting to describe; then (5) it seems gratuitous to believe that our present theory has succeeded in correctly specifying what is real, where earlier theories failed. Furthermore, there seems no straightforward factual way to say that one theory is superior to another if theories are incommensurable. But there should be this possibility of comparison if theories are true or false by corresponding or failing to correspond with a fixed reality.[3]

If we take Goldman's rendering as representative of the problem, then the reason that incommensurability threatens realism is that successive theories, if incommensurable, specify different, mutually incompatible things as real. Thus, the existence of a single independent reality that is accessible to understanding, and that is the standard of the legitimacy of our knowledge and the goal of our epistemic pursuit, is called into question.

In this chapter, our concern is with incommensurability; I mean to reserve most of the questions concerning truth for chapter 9. However, we can also note the relevance to our discussion of the further issues of the co-existence of mutually incompatible descriptions in science, the question of the legitimacy of the causal theory of reference, and Putnam's principle of charity in reference. The existence of mutually incompatible alternatives in science is akin to the incommensurability of scientific theories to the extent that the alternatives comprise conflicting ontologies that, as such, pose a similar threat to the interests of realism. The *causal theory of reference* is the claim that the referent of a term is determined, not by whatever satisfies

---

3. Goldman, "Realism," 177–78.

most current beliefs about it, but by causal connections between actual entities picked out and subsequent usages. The *principle of charity* is the admonition to construe, as much as is reasonably possible, the intentions of the proponents of earlier theories as being to refer to the same entities as those referred to by more recent theories. Both of these concepts attempt to counteract the charges of incommensurability and the threat to realism.

Positions on Progress

Popper and Lakatos

Sir Karl Popper was a contemporary of Polanyi's; an Austrian, Popper, like the Hungarian Polanyi, eventually settled in the United Kingdom. Popper's well-known *Logic of Scientific Discovery* appeared in 1959, the same year as the first edition of *Personal Knowledge*. Popper's work was better received because it accorded better with the prevailing perception of the nature of science, rather than challenging some of its fundamental parameters as did Polanyi's. It is ironic, I believe, that Polanyi's theses offer a logic of scientific discovery in a way that Popper's do not. Imre Lakatos, a Hungarian a few decades younger than Polanyi, was a colleague of Popper's. He brought a sophistication to Popper's theses that improved them significantly and which brought them more in line with what is sometimes felt to be the opposing approach of Kuhn and Feyerabend. We will see that Polanyi's stance shares some commonality with both sides of the debate, but also contrasts them in distinctively significant ways.

Let us begin with Popper's position concerning scientific growth and with Lakatos' development of it. Both Popper and Lakatos maintain, in contrast to Kuhn and Feyerabend, what Lakatos calls *the rational reconstructibility of scientific change*. The main difference, Popper says (and Kuhn agrees), between himself and Kuhn is that, for Kuhn, no rational discussion is possible between scientific frameworks.[4] For Popper and Lakatos, a rational methodology and logical criteria exist in terms of which two theories can be rationally compared. Such a rational method is essential to the possibility of progress in science, or at least to a rational explanation of progress in science.[5]

---

4. Popper, "Normal Science and Its Dangers," in Lakatos and Musgrave, eds., *Criticism and the Growth of Knowledge*, 57; Kuhn, "Logic of Discovery or Psychology of Research?" in Lakatos and Musgrave, eds., *Criticism and the Growth of Knowledge*, 19.

5. Lakatos, "Falsification," in Lakatos and Musgrave, eds., *Criticism and the*

Popper is commonly known to have developed a general conception of the course of scientific discovery as a twofold process of *conjecture and refutation*. His own concern, on the whole, is to elucidate refutation, for it alone is, as far as he is concerned, susceptible to rational explanation, and it alone furnishes science with its rationality. Science begins with the proliferation of hypotheses. The source of these hypotheses and the method of their production is irrelevant; what is important is the critical scrutiny to which they are subjected subsequently. The proper scientific method is to attempt to falsify each hypothesis, falsification being superior logically to corroboration. Attempted falsification involves the comparison of the hypothesis in hand with relevant evidence resulting from any number of tests performed with a view to refuting that hypothesis. A falsified hypothesis is abandoned; those which withstand the scrutiny are allowed to remain. On one interpretation of Popper, this constitutes the basic outline of the scientific enterprise.

But on such an interpretation, it would be difficult to see that any sort of progress, let alone rational or continuous progress, could be claimed for science. In actual fact, Popper supplements his own theory first of all with the positive notion of corroboration:

> In the first place, I contend that further progress in science would become impossible if we did not reasonably often manage to meet the third requirement [that the theory pass some new and severe tests]; thus if the progress of science is to continue, and its rationality not decline, we need not only successful refutations, but also positive successes. We must, that is, manage reasonably often to produce theories that entail new predictions, especially predictions of new effects, new testable consequences, suggested by the new theory and never thought of before.[6]

Thus, he introduces a factor that supersedes that of continued avoidance of refutation: a factor of positive success. The passage testifies explicitly to his belief that, without this additional element, it would be impossible to conceive of progress in science.

In addition to this, Popper maintains a notion of truth as non-epistemic, objective, and the proper goal of all scientific efforts. On the strength of his understanding of Alfred Tarski's contributions regarding truth, Popper affirms the idea of correspondence, or of truth as agreement with the facts.[7] He attempts to capture the original sense of this concept in his

---

Growth of Knowledge, 114, 115–16.

6. Popper, *Conjectures and Refutations*, 231. See ch. 9 regarding Tarski's theory of truth.

7. Ibid., 232.

notion of *verisimilitude*. Verisimilitude has, however, a more comparative connotation: it has to do with whether one theory approximates the truth more closely than another. Thus we are brought back to the issue of a rational methodology for the comparison of successive theories of science. Popper elaborates the concept as follows:

> Assuming that the truth-content and the falsity-content of two theories t_1 and t2 are comparable, we can say that t_2 is more closely similar to the truth, or corresponds better to the facts, than t_1, if and only if either
>
> 1. the truth-content but not the falsity-content of t_2 exceeds that of t_1.
> 2. the falsity-content of t_1, but not its truth-content, exceeds that of t_2.[8]

How do we know whether t_2 has a higher degree of verisimilitude than t_1? We apply something akin to the method of conjecture and refutation: we guess that it is, and then we examine that guess critically. If our guess withstands severe testing, we can conclude that t_2 is closer to the truth than t_1.

This formulation births a host of questions, not the least of which is how truth-content and falsity-content are to be assessed. The whole notion of moving closer to the truth, rather than being assumed, should be considered part of the problem at hand. As such, its consideration in this work belongs properly to chapter 9. It is helpful to note in passing, however, that criteria (a) and (b) tend to move the notion of verisimilitude away from the question of agreement with facts. Lakatos, in a helpful note on verisimilitude, distinguishes "intuitive verisimilitude," or the intuitive truthlikeness of a theory, from "empirical verisimilitude," which is "a quasi-measure-theoretical difference between the true and false consequences of a theory which we can never know but certainly may guess."[9] Lakatos says that empirical and not intuitive verisimilitude comprised Popper's contribution, although Popper's mistaken belief that his verisimilitude captured the classical sense of truthlikeness obscured the distinction between them. As Lakatos notes, most instrumentalists could agree with empirical verisimilitude while rejecting intuitive verisimilitude. He also notes, interestingly, that while Popper's empirical verisimilitude does something to promote the idea of cumulative growth in science, it does so at the expense of intuitive verisimilitude, for the driving force of cumulative growth in the one is

---

8. Ibid., 233.

9. Lakatos, "Falsification," in Lakatos and Musgrave, eds., *Criticism and the Growth of Knowledge*, 188–89.

revolutionary conflict in the other. If Lakatos is right concerning Popper, it causes one to wonder about the strength of the connection between progress, in particular verisimilitude, and realism—a puzzle that remains to be explored.

Lakatos develops what he believes to be the true sense of Popperian falsificationism, and he calls it *sophisticated methodological falsificationism*. Verisimilitude is replaced by the notion of a *"progressive problemshift."* For the sophisticated falsificationist,

> "a theory is 'acceptable' or scientific, only if it has corroborated excess empirical content over its predecessor (or rival), that is, only if it leads to the discovery of novel facts" and "a scientific theory T is falsified if and only if another theory T' has been proposed with the following characteristics:
>
> 1. T' has excess empirical content over T: that is, it predicts *novel* facts, that is, facts improbable in the light of, or even forbidden by, T;
>
> 2. T' explains the previous success of T, that is, all the unrefuted content of T is included (within the limits of observational error) in the content of T'; and
>
> 3. some of the excess content of T' is corroborated.[10]

The most obvious factor here is that scientific growth and even convergence are built into both the definition of "scientific" and the definition of "falsification"; they are given, Lakatos notes, a historical character. Thus, falsification takes place only after and in the context of the emergence of a better theory, not simply, and in fact not even, whenever conflicting evidence is produced. Falsification also incorporates the notion of convergence: the idea that a superior theory includes the refuted content of the inferior one along with its own additions. Falsification is thus thoroughly transformed; in fact, after reading Lakatos, one wonders whether it isn't missing completely in any significant sense. But at least it can be said that Lakatos' system does away with the curiously supplemental character of the framework supporting scientific progress, installing it instead in a central location.

Lakatos is quite candid concerning the role of decisions in scientific assessment. Falsification, as was noted, is no longer attached to refutation by conflicting evidence. Falsification now becomes a matter of deciding what evidence to retain and what to ignore: what scientific propositions to protect and what to expose to all forms of criticism. Lakatos specifies these considerations nicely in his methodology for scientific research programmes.

10. Ibid., 116.

As it turns out, a decision is even necessary with regard to a proposition's falsification in the sense described above, for even an apparently degenerating problemshift may stage a comeback, once again to claim supremacy.

Lakatos places less emphasis on notions of objective truth and agreement with the facts. His chief concern is with the elaboration and defense of the rational reconstructibility of scientific progress. His assessment of Kuhn and Polanyi is that they have abandoned efforts to give a rational explanation of the success of science because of their reading of the history of science. Instead, he says, they have tried to explain *changes* in paradigms in terms of social psychology.[11] This alternative Lakatos deems irrational, speaking of Polanyi's work as a "'post-critical'-mystical message"[12] Of this evaluation, more must be said at a later point.

Kuhn and Feyerabend

Thomas Kuhn was an American physicist turned historian of science. While the ongoing debate remains inconclusive, Polanyi felt that his own encouragement and work had influenced Kuhn's in a way that Kuhn did not accurately represent nor properly credit. Kuhn's *Structure of Scientific Revolutions* appeared in 1962: the same year as Polanyi's corrected edition of *Personal Knowledge*—the substance of which is his Gifford lectures given a decade earlier. Ironically, Kuhn's book and thought became widely known and influential, well beyond the philosophy of science. Polanyi's remains substantially eclipsed. Austrian Paul Feyerabend knew well all these key players in the discussion. Some of his career he spent in California, in proximity at that time to Kuhn. His thought eventually shifted from a Popperian approach to a more Kuhnian one. His "epistemological anarchist" work appeared in 1976.

Kuhn and Feyerabend, in contrast to Popper and Lakatos, emphasize the more discontinuous aspects of the history of science. They have both been considered to be irrationalists with respect to the growth of science. Kuhn attempts to contest this, and in fact, the charge is questionable as we shall see; Feyerabend embraces the label, "anarchist," with respect to his own contribution. The crux of their difference from Popper and friends is their conviction that the history of science demonstrates that successive or rival theories are incommensurable. It has already been noted that Popper and Kuhn agree that the major difference between themselves concerns the existence or non-existence of logical criteria that transcend theories and can

---

11. Ibid., 115.
12. Ibid., 93, 163n.

therefore be utilized in their direct comparison. Kuhn also believes that they differ regarding the existence of a neutral language or vocabulary which, Kuhn says, is essential to a Popperian comparison of successive theories.[13] No such language exists, for the transformation wrought by a paradigm change extends even to the ways in which words attach to nature, that is, to their meanings and the conditions of their applicability.

Is incommensurability thoroughgoing? For Kuhn, as a matter of fact, it does not seem to be. No neutral language exists for the sake of recourse, but this does not mean that no recourse is available.[14] There must be some recourse, he reasons, because not everything changes. Scientists deal with the same world before and after. They are equipped with generally the same neural apparatus. Most of their "programming" remains the same—because of shared culture and everyday life, and shared human history. And finally to a large extent, language remains intact, and even many of the scientific instruments and manipulations. Kuhn enumerates steps that might be taken to reinstate communication between paradigms. The first step consists in isolating, by means of experiment or armchair experiment, the area in which communication breakdown has occurred. Secondly, scientists must resort to shared everyday vocabularies to elucidate the problems. Third, each side must develop good predictions of one another's behavior—that is, learn to translate one's theories into the other's language and vice versa. This process enables communication; please note that it does not effect logical compatibility or render the successor a refinement of the first theory. Thus, this process does not erase the incommensurability of the two theories. It merely provides guidelines for communication to go on in spite of it. If, as a result of this communication, a scientist was to change camp, his decision would be more in the line of a conversion than any sort of reasoned inference.

Feyerabend provides a graphic picture of the nature of incommensurability. He opposes what he calls the "Swiss Cheese Theory" of theory change: add the missing elements to cosmos A, the missing terms to language A, the missing structures to the perceptual world of A, and the result is cosmos B, language B, perceptual world B.[15] Rather, along with Kuhn, he characterizes the relationship between two scientific theories in terms of a gestalt switch. This comparison captures the "at-odds" character of the relationship. When two theories are incommensurable, it is not simply that

---

13. Kuhn, "Reflections on My Critics," in Lakatos and Musgrave, eds., *Criticism and the Growth of Knowledge*, 266–67.

14. Ibid., 268, 276–77; Kuhn, *Structure of Scientific Revolutions*, 129–30.

15. Feyerabend, *Against Method*, 265–66.

the one rejects the truth of the other; it even rejects the presumption that an alternative has been presented.[16] Just as changing the rules of a game would change the game, so in science "the principles involve something like a 'closure': there are things that cannot be said, or 'discovered', without violating the principles (it does *not* mean contradicting them). Say the things, make the discovery, and the principles are suspended."[17] Thus, incommensurability obtains if a discovery occurs which suspends some of a theory's universal principles. Feyerabend does not share Kuhn's optimism concerning interim, transitory periods. Such an irrational stage is overcome, he says, by "the determined production of nonsense until the material produced is rich [and regular, he says later] enough to permit the rebels to reveal, and everyone else to recognize, new universal principles."[18]

What are the consequences of incommensurability for the rationality of science, according to Kuhn and Feyerabend? In contrast to Popper and Lakatos, Feyerabend concludes:

> If we interpret both theories in a realistic manner, then the "formal conditions for a suitable successor of a refuted theory" which were stated in Chapter 15 [it has to repeat the successful consequences of the older theory, deny its false consequences, and make additional predictions], cannot be satisfied, and the positivistic scheme of progress with its "Popperian spectacles," breaks down. Even Lakatos' liberalized version cannot survive this result; for it, too, assumes that content-classes of different theories can be compared, i.e. that a relation of inclusion, exclusion or overlap can be established between them.[19]

No methods remain for rationalizing scientific change. What is left, according to Feyerabend, are "aesthetic judgements, judgements of taste, metaphysical prejudices, religious desires, in short, *what remains are our subjective wishes.*"[20]

Kuhn's conclusion concerning the rationality of science is somewhat less extreme. In fact, he protests that Feyerabend's description of his argument as a defense of irrationality in science strikes him as "not only absurd but vaguely obscene." He writes: "I would describe it, together with my own, as an attempt to show that existing theories of rationality are not quite right

---

16. Ibid., 224.
17. Ibid., 269.
18. Ibid., 270.
19. Ibid., 276.
20. Ibid., 284.

and that we must readjust or change them to explain why science works as it does."[21]

However, Feyerabend is not as irrational as he at first sounds. In a most helpful passage, he responds to the question of whether science is irrational with the standard philosophical answer, yes and no. Yes, he says, in the sense that no single set of rules exists for science. No, because each episode is rational by virtue of the fact that some of its features are explainable in terms of reasons that are either accepted at the same time as the episode's occurrence or invented in the course of its development. Yes, in the sense that even these changeable reasons are not sufficient to explain all the important features of the episode. No, because, if we ourselves lived during that period, we also would "rationalize" the decision made so as to overcome accidents and discrepancies.[22] Rationality exists for Feyerabend, but he conceives of it quite differently. To this we will return in connection with Polanyi.

What consequences result from incommensurability for the prospect of progress in science? For Feyerabend, it seems, the prospect is grim. To the extent that progress is bound up with convergence, Feyerabend characterizes the "growth" of knowledge as "not a series of self-consistent theories that converges toward an ideal view," but rather as "an ever increasing ocean of mutually incompatible (and perhaps even) incommensurable alternatives."[23] If we take progress to be bound up with convergence, then we may infer that Feyerabend is pessimistic about the prospect of progress in science. Similarly, we may reasonably infer that his beliefs concerning the assessment of progress in science most likely parallel what he says concerning the assessment of success. Success turns out to be, for Feyerabend, manufactured by a theory, because facts come to be interpreted in terms of the theory. The alternatives and empirical content are eliminated, for either the facts agree with the theory or they are removed.[24] The judgment of verisimilitude can be made, he says in criticism of Popper, only within a particular theory.[25]

Kuhn's response is not dissimilar. Progress does occur during normal science. And, from the perspective of the victorious one of two battling paradigms, progress has occurred through the revolutionary period. What

---

21. Kuhn, "Reflections On My Critics," in Lakatos and Musgrave, eds., *Criticism and the Growth of Knowledge*, 263–64. The ultimate determining factor in scientific change is the decision of the scientific community.

22. "Consolations for the Specialist," in Lakatos and Musgrave, *Criticism and the Growth of Knowledge*, 216.

23. Ibid., 30.

24. Ibid., 43.

25. Ibid., 284.

happens is that the newly established paradigm brings about the reinterpretation of the preceding history of science so that it will represent progress toward the present point. There is, perhaps, a more conservative note in Kuhn in contrast to Feyerabend, for Kuhn does affirm progress, in the sense, he says, that later scientific theories are better than earlier ones for solving puzzles.[26] He compares scientific development to evolution, concluding that it is unidirectional and irreversible.[27] What he rejects is the idea of progress toward truth: that a successive theory embodies progress because it constitutes a better representation of what nature is really like. Kuhn believes notions like these to be illusory. Further, he feels that they are not representative of scientific history: Einstein's theory, for example, in important respects more closely resembles Aristotle than it does Newton. Finally, he believes that such notions of truth are not really necessary: the existence and success of science can be understood without them and rather in terms of the peculiar nature of the scientific community. These views must be examined in greater depth in the next chapter.

What are the consequences of these positions for the possibility of realism? Alasdair MacIntyre, citing some of Kuhn's statements concerning the impossibility of a goal of truth or correspondence with nature, says that Kuhn's incommensurability leads him to repudiate realism. This is not surprising, he claims, because the possibility of realism is bound up with "a certain view of the continuity of science," such that the two questions must be answered together.[28] Joseph Margolis speaks of Kuhn's position, not as a repudiation of realism, but rather as a modified realism: a realism based on pragmatic considerations. Kuhn wishes to retain some idea of the acquisition of knowledge of nature, as we ourselves have seen. Because of the difficulty of reconciling this with incompatible ontologies, Margolis concludes that "[i]n short, Kuhn wishes to hold that our knowledge is (realistically) *of* the (mind-independent) world but is not knowledge of the world as it is mind-independently. He wishes, therefore, to incorporate within a modified realist position what, in an earlier era, had been thought to be part of the opposing idealist thesis."[29] What is more, Margolis notes, since success for Kuhn is something that must be construed internally with respect to paradigms, and since success boils down to a question of survival value for Kuhn, Kuhn's realism turns out to rest on pragmatic issues: we must be in

---

26. Kuhn, *Structure of Scientific Revolutions*, 205–7.

27. Kuhn, "Reflections On My Critics," in Lakatos and Musgrave, eds., *Criticism and the Growth of Knowledge*, 264.

28. MacIntyre, "Objectivity in Morality and Objectivity in Science," 30.

29. Margolis, "Cognitive Issues," 375.

touch with nature because we survive.[30] Whether a modified pragmatic realism is realism at all remains to be seen.[31]

But two other questions bear on this question of realism for Kuhn. Kuhn clearly rejects a correspondence theory of truth. If correspondence is part and parcel of realism, then we will be able to conclude that Kuhn rejects realism. But the assumed relationship between correspondence and realism must first be scrutinized. Secondly, we have yet to examine the presumed relationship between progress and realism and, hence, the inverse relationship between incommensurability and realism. Alan Goldman has been most helpful in this regard; I hope to consider his arguments in connection with his discussion of convergence later in the chapter.

We have seen that Popper and Lakatos, and Kuhn and Feyerabend, come to represent opposing sides of a major debate in philosophy of science regarding the nature of science with respect to progress and related notions that bear on the question of realism. Now, let us return to Michael Polanyi in the hope of locating him with respect to this discussion. My foremost goal is to see whether Polanyi's approach offers the debate a distinctive grounding for realism.

Polanyi, Kuhn, and Progress

Before comparing Polanyi's claims with those of Kuhn with regard to progress, I think it is helpful to note that, while both appeal to the history of scientific discovery, Kuhn does so more as a historian of science to offer an account of the nature of science. Polanyi, first and foremost, is doing epistemology. He taps the history of science repeatedly to exemplify his epistemology. The innovative epistemology he offers both makes sense of that history and shapes an understanding of the nature of science. It is good to keep their distinctive agendas in mind as we examine texts and reflect on them regarding the matter of progress and related issues.

Polanyi actually says very little either for or against progress in science. More often than not, when he speaks of progress, he has in mind the progress of a scientific discovery from problem to completion stages. Passages exist in *Personal Knowledge* that express a Kuhnian sort of incommensurability, as we shall see. Yet, by contrast, Polanyi's outlook seems to be more positive with respect to progress. Take, for example, the following passage:

---

30. Ibid.

31. Subsequent discussion in this chapter will shed some light on the question, and the matter can be taken up once again in chapter 10.

Part 1: Early Consideration of Contact with Reality

> I may observe then, as I have done already, that the modern physical sciences went through three stages, each of which had its own scientific values and its corresponding vision of ultimate reality. Scientists of the first period believed in a system of numbers and geometrical figures, the next in one of mechanically constrained masses, the last in systems of mathematical invariances. In attaching themselves to the pursuit of these successive fundamental guesses about the nature of things, the intellectual passions of scientists underwent profound changes—changes similar in extent, and perhaps even not unrelated, to those which the appreciation of visual arts underwent from the Byzantine mosaics to the works of the Impressionists and from these to Surrealism. But there was a similar transcendence of an enduring passion in both cases. Granted that many of the arguments of Copernicus, Galileo and Kepler, and even of Newton, Lavoisier and Dalton, seem misguided today, and that their presuppositions have led to conclusions which we now consider to be false; and granted also that these giants of the past, if they returned today, might not readily accept relativity and quantum mechanics as satisfying systems of science; yet so much of earlier science has remained true, and has even revealed as true ever more of its deeper implications, that the pioneers of science have kept growing through the centuries in our respect. In this sense then science embraces a consistent pursuit of gradually changing, and—I believe—on the whole, ever more enlightened and elevated intellectual aspirations.[32]

While careful to name respects in which older work no longer remains true, Polanyi emphasizes that, in the history of scientific discovery, not only does much remain true, but it has demonstrated its truth specifically as further and deeper implications have continued to come to light. This is recognizably the centuries-long playing out of the very IFM Effect that testifies to the scientist that he has made contact with reality—the signature of Polanyian realism.

Since what Polanyi is doing is innovative epistemology, there are several aspects of the rest of Polanyi's thought that suggest that he would give a positive response to the question concerning progress in science as a whole, and, I believe, make it possible for him to do so. There is, most basically, Polanyi's resolution of the *Meno* problem. The question of whether there is progress in knowledge assumes and, in fact, includes the question of whether we can actually succeed in knowing at all. The question of the

---

32. Polanyi, *Personal Knowledge*, 164–65.

Meno is how it is possible to advance into the unknown. Polanyi's exposition of subsidiary foreknowledge explains this possibility. Polanyi, therefore, conceives of the achievement of scientific knowledge as an advance into the unknown. A second aspect of his thought that implies some kind of progress is the irreversibility of the integrative leap and the effect of successive integrative leaps in extending and transforming our understanding. We have, thirdly, the well-documented "sense of deepening coherence," the "sense of increasing proximity to a solution," experienced by scientists in the interim phases between problem and discovery, which guides them towards their goal. Clearly, at least progress toward discovery over short or lengthy periods of time, exists for Polanyi. But we may note that the nature of the integrative leap is such that this is not a linear, additive understanding of progress, but rather that it is progress precisely because it is not linear and additive.

Polanyi presumes rather than questions progress in science; he then takes it to have major implications for the nature of knowledge and also the nature of reality. The *sine qua non* for progress is the personal skill and commitment of the knower. Progress accredits these tacit powers. "Progress in science," he says in description of his own philosophical system, "is determined at every stage by indefinable powers of thought."[33] Consider also the following passage about reality: "The continued pursuit of science is possible, because the structure of nature and man's capacity to grasp this structure, can be such as is exemplified by this sequence of discoveries covering two millennia. It does happen that nature is capable of being comprehended in successive stages, each of which can be reached only by the highest powers of the human mind."[34] This passage presents two implications of the continued existence and growth of science. One is the capacity of humans to grasp the many-dimensioned structure of nature; the other is, more basically, the fact that nature has a structure amenable to being comprehended, in fact, amenable to comprehension in successive states. Here, Polanyi avers the overall coherence of a sequence of transformative discoveries—Copernicus through Einstein, for example. Kuhn, by contrast, would not consider this a coherent sequence—and he doesn't presume progress, or possibly even knowledge. Polanyi attests to progress in science and does so on the grounds of the distinctive components of knowing that his epistemology uniquely expounds. It is progress, but in a different epistemological key. Where knowledge and rationality are no longer restricted along "standard" lines to focal and linear, progress and incommensurability may coexist.

33. Polanyi, "Logic of Tacit Inference," in Grene, ed., *Knowing and Being*, 138.
34. Polanyi, "Science and Reality," 192.

The element of the knower's skill, as well as Polanyi's interpretation of the history of science, are further evidenced in the following passage:

> But here we meet a strange fact. In accepting the task of pursuing a problem, the scientist assumes it to be a *good* problem, a problem that he can solve by his own gifts and equipment and that it is worth undertaking in comparison with other available possibilities. He must estimate this; and such estimates are guesses.
>
> But such guesses have proved sufficiently good to secure the progress of scientific enquiry with a reasonable degree of efficiency. It is rare to come across years of futile efforts wasted, or else to find that major opportunities were patently missed. Indeed, the opportunities for discovery are so effectively exploited that the same discovery is often made simultaneously by two or three different scientists. There is no doubt therefore of the scientist's capacity to assess in outline the course of an enquiry that will lead to a result which, at the time he makes his assessment, is essentially indeterminate.[35]

He proceeds in subsequent paragraphs to explain this "capacity" in terms of the claim to know reality and the nature of anticipation. Again, we glimpse the progressive light in which Polanyi views history and his utilization of that testimony to undergird his attribution of personal skills and unspecifiable anticipatory capacities to the knower.

Finally, let us note Polanyi's claim that "the progress of scientific discovery depends on heuristic commitments which establish contacts with reality."[36] Presumably, what is said about the progress of scientific *discovery* would be at least partially true for the progress of the whole of science also. Here again, then, is the responsibly personal factor cited as undergirding progress. But here, the emphasis is on its fiduciary aspect—the element of personal commitment which enters with the selection of a good problem and the submission to the guidance of intimations, through which contact is established with reality.

We may postulate a parallel commitment on the level of the whole of science: a commitment that transcends the goals and achievements of specific discoveries, and in terms of which the general progress and continuity of science would be understood. Does such a transcending commitment exist for Polanyi? According to MacIntyre, just this sort of transcending commitment distinguishes Polanyi from Kuhn and Feyerabend and is

---

35. Polanyi, "Genius in Science," 60.
36. Polanyi, *Personal Knowledge*, 316.

implied by the historical continuity of science. MacIntyre compares science to art and law, in which there exist purposes that transcend styles and codes. Natural science, he says, is a set of projects that embodies a moral task. That moral task is partially but importantly defined by the *commitment* of science to realism.[37] He reiterates this in the following passage: "The scientific community is one among the moral communities of mankind and its unity is unintelligible apart from the commitment to realism. Thus the continuities in the history of that community are primarily continuities in its regulative ideals, and the realism which informs those ideals appeals to standards of truth and understanding which are pre-Tarskian (although not necessarily inconsistent with Tarski's theses)."[38] Although his concern is with continuity of science, it would seem reasonable to suppose that, if a transcending moral commitment to realism was essential to the continuity of science, it would also be essential to its progress.

Polanyi, Kuhn, and Incommensurability

How does Polanyi stand on the incommensurability question? We will see that much of what he says accords with Kuhn's views. But Polanyi's work evidences an overarching, we may say principled, commitment to a profounder continuity.

First, Polanyi's account appears to agree generally with the evidence that Kuhn cites in support of incommensurability and even with Kuhn's interpretation of the relationship between paradigms. In fact, it is difficult to believe, despite the absence of acknowledgement, that Kuhn did not derive his inspiration on these matters from Polanyi's decade-earlier work, with which Kuhn was familiar. Kindly bear with my lengthy quotation of selections from a section that Polanyi titles, "Scientific Controversy," in his chapter called, "Intellectual Passions":

> Like the heuristic passion from which it flows, the *persuasive passion* too finds itself facing a logical gap. To the extent to which a discoverer has committed himself to a new vision of reality, he has separated himself from others who still think on the old lines. His persuasive passion spurs him now to cross this gap by converting everybody to his way of seeing things, even as his heuristic passion has spurred him to cross the heuristic gap which separated him from discovery . . .

---

37. MacIntyre, "Objectivity in Morality and Objectivity in Science," 30.
38. Ibid., 37.

Each of the four authors mentioned here [Freud, Eddington, Rhine, and Lysenko] has his own conceptual framework, by which he identifies his facts and within which he conducts his arguments, and each expresses his conceptions in his own distinctive terminology. Any such framework is relatively stable, for it can account for most of the evidence which it accepts as well established, and it is sufficiently coherent in itself to justify to the satisfaction of its followers the neglect for the time being of facts, or alleged facts, which it cannot interpret. It is correspondingly segregated from any knowledge or alleged knowledge rooted in different conceptions of experience. The two conflicting systems of thought are separated by a logical gap, in the same sense as a problem is separated from the discovery which solves the problem. Formal operations relying on *one* framework of interpretation cannot demonstrate a proposition to persons who rely on *another* framework. Its advocates may not even succeed in getting a hearing from these, since they must first teach them a new language, and no one can learn a new language unless he first trusts that it means something. ... Proponents of a new system can convince their audience only by first winning their intellectual sympathy for a doctrine they have not yet grasped. Those who listen sympathetically will discover for themselves what they would otherwise never have understood. Such an acceptance is a heuristic process, a self-modifying act, and to this extent a conversion. It produces disciples forming a school, the members of which are separated for the time being by a logical gap from those outside it. They think differently, speak a different language, live in a different world, and at least one of the two schools is excluded to this extent for the time being (whether rightly or wrongly) from the community of science.

We can now see, also, the great difficulty that may arise in the attempt to persuade others to accept a new idea in science. We have seen that to the extent to which it represents a new way of reasoning, we cannot convince others of it by formal argument, for so long as we argue within their framework, we can never induce them to abandon it. Demonstration must be supplemented, therefore, by forms of persuasion which can induce a conversion. The refusal to enter on the opponent's way of arguing must be justified by making it appear altogether unreasonable. ...

The great scientific controversies which I have just recalled were conducted in passionate accents, as was inevitable between contestants who shared no common framework within which a more impersonal procedure could be followed. Kolbe could not argue against van't Hoff. He quoted with ironical glee van't Hoff's description of the disposition of atoms in spirals, which to him was sufficient evidence that the new theory was a tissue of fancies. And from his own point of view he was right in refusing to enter into any detailed argument on these lines, since he denied that one could argue rationally in terms of such wild ideas. The ironical caricature by which Wohler and Liebig replied to the papers of Caignard de la Tour, Schwann and others, who claimed that fermentation is a function of living yeast cells, sprang from the same view that an argument believed to be wholly specious cannot be seriously discussed point by point.[39]

Additionally, in a later chapter, Polanyi avers that "antagonists on either side of a great scientific controversy do not accept the same facts as real and significant."[40]

Throughout all of this, Polanyi never uses the term "incommensurability." Even so, the preponderant presence of what are commonly known as Kuhnian themes render their concurrence obvious. Two visions are separated by a logical gap. No form of reasoning or framework exists that transcends and can thus unite the thought patterns of the two visions. The difference is so radical that proponents of the two visions speak a different language and disagree concerning facts. Nevertheless, there is recourse, as Kuhn says, and this is Polanyi's whole point. But Polanyi's assessment of the recourse in this passage resembles Feyerabend's more closely than it does Kuhn's. Persuasive passions, another facet of the pervasive tacit component of knowing, strive to convert everyone to the new way of thinking. And since no more impersonal procedure exists, other forms of persuasion are utilized to bring about the prerequisite intellectual sympathy: each side "must inevitably attack the opponent's person."[41] A similar sort of interpretation holds for conflicting, coexistent alternatives. In contrast to both, Polanyi identifies and accredits responsible personal commitment and trust as essential even to understanding another's discovery.

Incommensurability and alternative persuasion would seem to spell a radical rejection of continuity in science, according to the prevailing discussion in philosophy of science. It would thus seem to undermine progress and realism. Incommensurability prevails in this passage from Polanyi, but in others we have already examined, we noted elements of continuity.

39. Polanyi, *Personal Knowledge*, 150, 151, 157–58.
40. Ibid., 240.
41. Ibid., 151–52.

Polanyi elsewhere expresses commensurability and even convergence over a sequence of discoveries. Also, we have MacIntyre's thesis that, for Polanyi, science is characterized by a transcending moral commitment that is, at least partially, a commitment to realism. Thus, incommensurability and continuity cohere in Polanyi in a way they do not in Kuhn and others. Grene, in review of MacIntyre, confirms this and offers her perspective regarding Polanyi in relationship to Kuhn. She concurs that Polanyi shares with Kuhn an emphasis on the dimension of discontinuity between theories, but implies that Polanyi differs from Kuhn in "taking cognizance of the continuity in the growth of scientific knowledge much as MacIntyre describes it."[42] She cites Polanyi's example of the gradual change in the meaning of the term "isotope," in which the original definition of the term is enlarged by virtue of its application to a slightly different case despite protestations on the part of the actual author of the concept. This exemplifies Polanyi's understanding of the continuity of scientific change.[43] Grene's assessment of the relationship between Polanyi's and Kuhn's work is therefore as follows: "Kuhn's relativism, in other words, appears to result rather from an overemphasis on one aspect of Polanyi's theory of science: the logical gap, both between evidence and theory and between one conceptual framework and another, than from a negligent or vulgar reading of the whole of what Polanyi has to say."[44] Grene proceeds to concur with MacIntyre's analysis of the ethical commitment of science. Incommensurability implies discontinuity for Kuhn, but not for Polanyi.

While it may be true to speak of Polanyi having a transcending ethical commitment to progress in scientific knowledge, I believe that we can also discern something far more imminent and ordinary: the workaday patience not to settle for incommensurability and thus distrust of science and reality, but rather to wait for and seek creative resolution that we have not yet discerned. I also think that this is common sense; it is also the characteristic manifestation of a fundamental human drive to make sense of our world. In fact, we humans are not inclined to settle with finality for ultimate incommensurability. The coexistence of incompatible alternatives should never be considered a final state of affairs; rather, we should hope and strive for their reconciliation, perhaps in a fresh scientific vision that would capture the correct aspects of both alternatives and sift out their incorrect aspects. If Polanyi is right regarding our reliance on clues we anticipate but cannot specify, we may properly accredit them in our hope of yet future resolution.

---

42. Grene, "Response to MacIntyre," 46.
43. Polanyi, *Personal Knowledge*, 111.
44. Grene, "Response to MacIntyre," 46.

In this may also be sensed the manner in which Polanyi's approach really doesn't raise a concern about progress but rather presumes confidence and hope.

Polanyi says: "The possibility of error is a necessary element of any belief bearing on reality, and to withhold belief on the grounds of such a hazard is to break off all contact with reality. The outcome of a competent fiduciary act may, admittedly, vary from one person to another, but since the differences are not due to any arbitrariness on the part of the individuals, each retains justifiably his universal intent. As each hopes to capture an aspect of reality, they may all hope that their findings will eventually coincide or supplement each other."[45] Polanyi illustrates such superseding integration from the history of science. He describes a controversy in the 1800s over the question of whether fermentation is caused by living cells or by inanimate catalysts. The controversy raged for over fifty years but was finally resolved. The further discovery of enzymes revealed that yeast cells possessed an inanimate catalyst that operated in fermentation. Thus, he says, in a way, both sides had been right. In a note, Polanyi restates his point: "I have illustrated before how an apposite new conception can reconcile two alternative systems of interpretation which hitherto violently opposed each other."[46] Notice that Polanyi does not suggest that the relationship between the two alternatives and the superseding theory is additive. It reconciles precisely because it does not add to the previous scientific vision but presents a different one. Only because the new vision is qualitatively distinct can it provide a reconciliation of the two alternatives.

The existence of incompatible conceptions concerning the world need not be, and ordinarily is not, taken as damaging evidence with respect to realism, i.e., with respect to the success of our contact with the world; it need not and is not taken to spell relativism. What the existence of incompatible alternatives does imply, at least in the cases in which each alternative makes a legitimate claim to truth, is that more work remains to be done, and that the true state of affairs has yet to be revealed. What is more, that fact that a new conception appositely reconciles previously opposed ones particularly testifies to its having made contact with reality profoundly. It is an example of what I have called the retrospective criterion of reality. For the realist, then, presently incompatible alternatives present no problem in principle.[47]

---

45. Polanyi, *Personal Knowledge*, 315; see also 157; "The Growth of Science in Society," 80.

46. Polanyi, *Personal Knowledge*, 157.

47. This is part of my problem with Putnam's construction of metaphysical realism. See the discussion in chapter 10.

Part 1: Early Consideration of Contact with Reality

Before concluding this discussion regarding incommensurability, let us contrast Polanyi and Kuhn in one more respect. Polanyi would not concur with Kuhn in Kuhn's deletion of questions of truth and correspondence from the notion of progress in science. As we have seen, Grene uses the term, "relativism," with respect to Kuhn, in contrast to Polanyi. Also, we may note that Polanyi's language often hints that he retains the goal that Kuhn rejects. Recall his talk concerning achieving closer contact with reality, for example. Recall his affirmation of the human being's capacity to adapt his framework while applying it so as to increase its hold on reality. Consider the following statement: "Indeed, any modification of an anticipatory framework, whether conceptual, perceptual or appetitive, is an irreversible heuristic act, which transforms our ways of thinking, seeing and appreciating in the hope of attuning our understanding, perception or sensuality more closely to what is true and right."[48] Polanyi thus appears to espouse some notion of a goal of truth or reality towards which science progresses. This must be explored in further depth in chapter 9.

To conclude regarding Polanyi and incommensurability: Polanyi reveals his commitment to the continuity and progress of science despite—in fact, precisely by means of—his acknowledgment of what Kuhn calls incommensurability. And he is able to do this on the basis of his distinctive epistemological thesis. As we go on to engage other contemporary realist theses in subsequent chapters, additional light will be shed on these matters.[49]

---

48. Polanyi, *Personal Knowledge*, 106.

49. Other similarities between Kuhn and Polanyi's earlier work may be noted. Kuhn has, for example, followed Polanyi in utilizing the idea of gestalt switch in describing the relationship between successive theories, although Kuhn has not developed the notion of focal and subsidiary awareness and of dynamic integration (Kuhn, *Structure of Scientific Revolutions*, 120–22). Secondly, Kuhn actually eventually develops what Polanyi has insisted upon all along, the tacit and unspecifiable foundation of knowledge, in explanation of just why it is so difficult for proponents of incommensurable theories to communicate (Kuhn, "Reflections on My Critics," in Lakatos and Musgrave, eds. *Criticism and the Growth of Knowledge*, 270–75). Third, Kuhn has also referred to a person's switch from one framework to another as a conversion. What is more remarkable is that Kuhn elucidates conversion by employing a description substantially the same as Polanyi's explanation of how premises of science come to be changed. After enumerating the steps to communication between opponents described earlier, Kuhn notes that the possibility of translation does not make the term "conversion" inappropriate. He continues; "In the absence of a neutral language, the choice of a new theory is a decision to adopt a different native language and to deploy it in a correspondingly different world. That sort of transition is, however, not one which the terms 'choice' and 'decision' quite fit, though the reasons for wanting to apply them after the event are clear. Exploring an alternative theory by techniques like those outlined above, one is likely to find that one is already using it (as one suddenly notes that one is thinking in, not translating out of, a foreign language). At no point was one aware of having reached a decision,

Polanyi and Popper's Falsificationism

Now let us bring Polanyi's thought to bear upon the various related positions and issues, identified so far in this chapter, of the four philosophers of science. Let us begin with Popper's falsificationism. Polanyi has frequently criticized Popper, and thus we can get some idea of how Polanyi would respond to Popper, as well as to Lakatos, with respect to issues of progress and rationality. Polanyi, along with others, has criticized Popper's understanding of science, sometimes capitalizing on potentially inconsistent claims by Popper himself. We have already noted the two sides of Popper—the strict falsificationism and the more modified position. Polanyi argues, contra what Lakatos calls naive falsificationism, that rather than conflicting evidence being always acknowledged and the theories in question dropped, in actual fact, some evidence is ignored, considered an anomaly, and allowed to stand unaccounted for.[50] Further, there are sometimes events in science in which the very notion of falsifiability seems inapplicable, such as in the case of crystallography.[51] Here, Polanyi says, standards of perfection were generated, such that a crystal that varied from those standards, rather than being considered conflicting evidence and hence falsifying the standard, was in fact judged to be an imperfect specimen. Others have argued that, because Popper's basic statements are scientific statements, and hence fallible, absolute falsification cannot be achieved. Polanyi has argued that, since what constitutes evidence must be appraised personally, even Popper's falsificationism cannot uphold the false ideal of strict objectivity.[52] This would be the case par excellence for a personal transition of allegiance from one theory to another. What is more, as we have seen, progress for Popper relies on the possibility of some corroboration—the fact that scientists must manage reasonably often to produce new theories that entail new predictions and consequences. But such a possibility cannot be supported by falsification. Rather, corroboration like this is the sort of thing that is unexplainable apart from a personal element of intuitive foreknowledge. Finally, it may be

---

made a choice. That sort of change is, however, conversion, and the techniques which induce it may well be described as therapeutic, if only because, when they succeed, one learns one had been sick before. No wonder the techniques are resisted and the nature of the change disguised in later reports" ("Reflections on My Critics," 277). Thus Kuhn has apparently benefitted in many respects from Polanyi's earlier work.

50. Polanyi, *Personal Knowledge*, 20. Note that Kuhn was not the first to speak of anomaly.

51. Ibid., 47.

52. Polanyi, "The Creative Imagination," 85. See also Mays, "Michael Polanyi: Recollection and Comparisons," 53; Wiebe: "Comprehensively Critical Rationalism and Commitment," 193.

noted that Popper, at one point, actually says that the possibility of progress in science depends on two additional factors: 1) the world's inherent rationality, and 2) luck. Neither of these elements can be supported by the Popperian approach. But for Polanyi, the world's rationality and its importance to knowledge has been recognized and acknowledged from the beginning. As far as luck is concerned, Polanyi would agree with Popper concerning the serious element of chance and inherent fallibility of any epistemic attempt. However, he has replaced luck with the more rational notion of subsidiary anticipatory powers possessed by the knower, which, if they do nothing else, at least better his odds in the guessing game.

Polanyi and Rationality

Critically interwoven throughout and essential to this entire cluster of theses is—must be—an underlying outlook with regard to what counts as rational. Indeed, each philosopher's rendering of progress, commensurability, continuity, and convergence depends on how they construe rationality. Let us begin this discussion by placing Polanyi's thought in juxtaposition with that of all four philosophers of science with regard to matters bearing on rationality in continuity, progress, and convergence of science.

Comparison of Polanyi and Lakatos is most interesting in light of Lakatos' dismissal of Polanyi as an irrationalist, a mystic, and a sociologist. For Lakatos, despite his self-referential use of the word "rational" in implied contrast to Polanyi, shares much in common with him. Lakatos picks up Polanyian themes such as heuristic power, that is, "the power of a research programme to anticipate theoretically novel facts in its growth," the relative unimportance of individual experiments, the role of intellectual beauty, and even the rationality of partial dogmatism.[53] Most importantly, Lakatos affirms the central role of decision in the scientific process, noting its crucial function in the acceptance of basic statements and the determination of their truth value, the choice of rules of rejection, and a verdict concerning a specific refutation.[54] Lakatos believes this to be a form of conventionalism. In contrast to Polanyi, who would designate and accredit it as responsibly personal, Lakatos opts rather for the arbitrary aspect of decisions in an attempt to maintain a semblance of objectivity in the stereotypical sense. Also missing from Lakatos' approach is the more positive aspects of Polanyian personal knowledge: the emphasis upon the knower's skills, and his contact with reality which enables him to experience a good measure of success in

---

53. Lakatos, "Falsification," 155; also 123, 137, 175.
54. Ibid., 106, 107, 109, 110, 127–31.

his decision-making.⁵⁵ But if rational scientific method includes, as Lakatos says it does, a consistent reliance at crucial points upon the decisions of scientists, then the presence of the responsibly personal element in the scientific enterprise as expounded by Polanyi does not discredit his system as far as rationality is concerned. Indeed, the fact that Polanyian decision is the decision of a responsible person in the context of his commitment to and constraint by standards of intellectual excellence, renders his distinctive understanding superior in rationality to a conventionalist kind of decision.⁵⁶

Regarding Lakatos, Feyerabend concludes that the leeway for rationality that Lakatos builds into his own system is so great that there remains no rational (in Lakatos' sense) difference between Lakatos' and Feyerabend's views.⁵⁷ Only a rhetorical difference remains, and that because Lakatos has not yet become accustomed to his own liberal proposals. For Feyerabend, the claimed result is irrationality. I myself question whether Feyerabend's stance implies any more than a rejection of rationality in the narrow sense. We have already seen that rationality remains for Feyerabend. In contrast to Feyerabend, Polanyi would reject the idea of anarchy or irrationality. Instead, the introduction of human decision spells the broadening of rationality, not its dissolution.

Juxtaposing Polanyi and Popper, we must note that as far as Polanyi is concerned, the canonization of a single set of rational criteria in science, far from being essential to the progress of science, would actually deter it. Polanyi writes:

> When I speak of science I acknowledge both its tradition and its organized authority, and I deny that anyone who wholly rejects these can be said to be a scientist, or have any proper understanding and appreciation of science. Consequently, nothing that I—who accept the traditions and authority of science—may say about science can mean anything to such a person, and this holds also in reverse. Yet I do not enter this commitment unconditionally, as shown by the fact that I refuse to follow both the tradition and authority of science in its pursuit of the objectivist ideal in psychology and sociology. I accept the existing scientific opinion as a *competent* authority, but not as a *supreme* authority, for identifying the subject matter called "science."
>
> This distinction is implicit in the remarks I have just made about Kepler. It is indispensable to any survey of the historic

---

55. Wiebe, "Comprehensively Critical Rationalism," 101.

56. Relevant discussions of rationality may be found in Brown, *Perception, Theory and Commitment*, 130, 147–50; and Wiebe, "Comprehensively Critical Rationalism."

57. Feyerabend, *Against Method*, 185–87.

progress of science. For to limit the term science to propositions which we regard as valid, and the premises of science to what we consider to be its true premises, is to mutilate our subject matter. A reasonable conception of science must include conflicting views within science and admit of changes in the fundamental beliefs and values of scientists. To acknowledge a person as a scientist—and even as a very great scientist—is merely to acknowledge him as competent in science, which admits the possibility that he was, or is, in many ways mistaken.[58]

The tradition of science spoken of here apparently includes "propositions which we regard as valid," "what we consider to be its true premises," and thus can be understood to include standards of rationality. Science's conception of rationality has to be broad enough to allow for real disagreement among people who are rightly deemed expert scientists. Rational science includes conflicting views and radical changes. Polanyi is emphatic, even extreme: retention of a particular set of standards would "mutilate our subject matter." Thus, it also would prevent a proper understanding of progress in science.

Progress, for Polanyi—and this passage comes in the context of a discussion of premises of science and the means of their alteration—involves an unfolding process of the continual replacement of old premises with the new standards of rationality that come to us embodied in profound discoveries. Such an understanding of the rationality, progress, and the history of science would tend to place Polanyi more in Kuhn's camp than in Popper's.

Here, let us attend to Polanyi's position on the question of the rationality of scientific change. Does Polanyi espouse the notion that transcendent logical criteria or methodology are essential to the rationality of science and also to the possibility of progress in science—along with Popper and Lakatos? If he does not, is he thereby an exponent of the irrationality of science—along with Kuhn and Feyerabend? We have already seen that the opposed sides of this discussion are not themselves entirely in opposition but rather affirm claims that array them more along a spectrum. Lakatos, in particular, introduces Polanyian (and hence presumably, from his point of view, irrational) elements into his rational methodology. And Kuhn rejects Feyerabend's description of his work as a defense of irrationality, preferring to describe it as "an attempt to show that existing theories of rationality are not quite right and that we must readjust or change them to explain why science works as it does." Even Feyerabend, as an anarchist, describes just this sort of readjustment of rationality: the senses in which scientific transition

---

58. Polanyi, *Personal Knowledge*, 164.

is a rational affair. Thus, a comparison of Polanyi's claims with theirs must be nuanced.

I believe that Polanyi would agree with Kuhn concerning the need to broaden the reigning notion of what constitutes rationality. Grene says as much in her personal recollections concerning Polanyi's taking a year to write the chapter on articulation in *Personal Knowledge*:

> Although I collected a vast number of extracts to assist in the composition of the chapter, I did not really understand at the time why just this problem: the grounding of articulation in the inarticulate, should need to be spelled out so painfully. But it is indeed the heart of the matter—not, again, because Polanyi was developing an "irrationalism" (a "neo-obscurantism," as one reviewer called it) but because the understanding of understanding, of rationality itself, demands an understanding of the way in which the subsidiary supports the focal, in particular of the way in which the ineffable supports the activities of voice or pen.[59]

In other words, Polanyi was up to what he considered more critically important and more foundational matters—which led to his proposing "an alternative ideal of knowledge quite generally."[60] He was reinventing epistemology, which would qualitatively recast rationality in a new key. We would be remiss, in our comparison of Polanyi with major conversants in the philosophy of science, to forget this foundational context for all that Polanyi says that bears on realism.

Polanyian Rationality, according to Wiebe

Polanyi's role in "broadening" the bounds of rationality has been defended by Don Wiebe. In a 1973 article, he provides a helpful critique of the rationalism of Popper and of the derivative views of W. W. Bartley. He argues that their program of "comprehensively critical rationalism" (CCR), although it might be a logically adequate characterization of abstract rationality, cannot provide a rational account of our knowledge, for it cannot account for either the existence of our knowledge or its growth. This inadequacy, he hopes to prove, can be overcome only by the adoption of a fiduciary element into the characterization of rational procedure—even the rational procedure of scientific method. He maintains that Popper simply evades the problem of

---

59. Grene, "Tacit Knowing: Grounds," 168. The reference is to May Brodbeck's "Review of *Personal Knowledge*," 582–83.

60. Polanyi, *Personal Knowledge*, vii.

how a scientist moves from observation to theory, let alone from observation to problem. Wiebe argues, secondly, that Popper's falsificationism fails to account as it claims to do for the transition of allegiance from one theory to another for, as we have noted, personal judgment is by Popper's own admission involved. Wiebe's conclusion:

> If in the face of such evidence [from the history of science that advances are made not in a logical step-by-step manner but rather in direct contravention of procedures that had been setup as normative for the discipline—thus contra Popper] our scientific knowledge is still to be conceived as having been achieved in a rational manner, one must then deny the necessity of logical procedures. Michael Polanyi does this. He claims a broader realm for rationality than strict logical certainty and goes on to state that the "basis" of both transitions exists in a fiduciary commitment on the part of the scientist.[61]

Just how does Polanyi propose to broaden the realm of rationality? Wiebe argues that the injection of the fiduciary component, essential to the explanation of scientific growth, does not render the whole discipline irrational unless the ultimate commitment involved is ultimate in the sense of not being open to any further assessment or criticism and hence being, in principle, unfalsifiable. Such commitment would be indeed irrational. But commitment can be ultimate in the sense that it "predominates and guides all subsequent decisions made by him who holds it" and can be neither lightly made nor rejected, and yet not be ultimate in the first, pejorative, sense.[62] Wiebe believes this to be the major thrust of Polanyi's work. Rationality is rendered personal, as Wolfe Mays notes.[63]

Polanyian Rationality, according to Brennan

John Brennan also highlights the personal character of rationality for Polanyi.

> If there are no rules to guide a performance, but yet it is accomplished, then it must be done without rules. If, that is, we can discover real features of nature with no rules to guide us and if we can in the same way make correct evaluations of the import of observational data (whether apparently confirming or

---

61. Wiebe, "Comprehensively Critical Rationalism," 194.
62. Ibid., 196.
63. Mays, "Polanyi: Recollection and Comparisons," 55.

falsifying), then there obviously is a difference between rationality and formal inference. If there is such informal (or "tacit") rationality, then it must be a capacity of people, since its lack of explicitness means that it cannot share the sort of impersonal objectivity which is possessed, say, by a mathematical formula. In other words, our acceptance of science entails that we must accredit persons with the rational powers that are necessary to make science possible. Following this line of reasoning, Polanyi frequently refers to the "responsible decisions" incumbent upon scientists and to the scientific "conscience," for since it is the case that scientific judgment cannot be determined by formal rules, the scientist is obliged to form his decisions in relatively unprecedented circumstances somewhat as must a moral agent or a statesman.[64]

Notice that there is no question that the supersession of strict logical criteria implies either the irrationality of science or the futility of the epistemic enterprise. Success is assumed, therefore rationality must be broadened and personalized.

Brown: Strands of Continuity—Polanyian?

But there is more to be said concerning Polanyi and rationality. Even if, in a sense, nothing is more basic to rationality than commitment, the picture is larger than that. It is helpful to ask how Polanyi replaces the notion of a strict rational methodology that Popper and Lakatos believe is essential to the progress of science. What room remains for rationality and rational standards if incommensurability of Polanyi's sort is acknowledged? How can scientific change and growth be rational in any sense of the word? Harold Brown, in his discussion of just this question, argues that "the thesis that a scientific revolution requires a restructuring of experience akin to a gestalt shift is compatible with the continuity of science and the rationality of scientific debate."[65] Brown's approach may illuminate the middle road that Polanyi wishes to take. Brown contends that the discussion of transition between theories has been confused because of failure to distinguish between the following theses: "the thesis that if we are to have a rational basis for choosing between rival theories at a particular moment in the history of science, we must have some standard to appeal to which is accepted by

---

64. Brennan, "Polanyi's Transcendence of the Distinction Between Objectivity and Subjectivity," 142.
65. Brown, *Perception, Theory and Commitment*, 167.

proponents of both theories, and the thesis that if scientific change is to be rational there must be some eternal standard against which we can compare any theories."[66] Brown's point is that, even though the second thesis of an eternal standard is ruled out by incommensurability and other factors, the first thesis remains a viable alternative and enables us to conceive how change might proceed rationally.

Brown supplies a description of scientific change that he believes suits the requirement. A theory is a theoretical web, with strands composed of concepts and observations, all in the context of definite problem situations. In the course of a dialectical (as he calls it) change from one theory to another, the theoretical web is reorganized, some strands are removed, and some are added. Since strands derive their meaning from their location in the web, reorganization of the web shifts the strands and, hence, their meaning. Nevertheless, strands that are retained provide continuity of development and grounds for the comparison of the two theories. In a manner reminiscent of Kuhn, Brown notes that many observations, techniques, and principles are retained. In a manner perhaps more consistent with Kuhn than Kuhn himself, he explains that this is so even as their meaning is transformed. The strands provide standards to which both theories can appeal in the effort of comparison even though their role in the different theories might be different. In one of Brown's examples from the history of science, there exists a class of observed entities that both theories agree must be accounted for, although each's reasons for thinking this differ—that is, the observations are taken to be instances of very different laws. Even so, the mutually acceptable observations furnish a point of comparison. Thus, the standards of rationality operative during a particular period of scientific transition are not eternal but rather arise perhaps only in conjunction with the two theories in question. They are not theory-free. But still, they provide points of comparison and hence of continuity.

Would Polanyi find himself at home with Brown's analysis? The answer, at least to some extent, is yes. All of this compares favorably to Polanyi's description of particulars and their appearance before and after an integration. The particulars, at least the ones that we know about beforehand, are themselves the same before and after the integration. But, by virtue of the phenomenal and semantic aspects of tacit integration, their appearance and meaning are transformed. Thus, dynamic integration and gestalt switch presuppose some continuity of particulars. Thus, even Kuhn, to the extent that he remains consistent in his use of the gestalt metaphor, must acknowledge some sort of continuity.

66. Ibid., 140.

I question whether Polanyi would entirely concur with Brown's approach. The distinction between them reveals the heart of Polanyi's understanding of rationality in science. My question stems from looking at the epistemic act of scientific discovery as Polanyi describes it. I do not believe it is apt to say that the continuity of particulars—particular observations, particular concepts—are the sources of rationality during a period of scientific change for Polanyi as they are for Brown. Reflecting back over the structure of tacit knowing, we can see that it is never the particulars, but always the integrative, focal whole that is the source of meaning, rationality, sense of reality, and so on; it is the focal that provides meaning for the particulars.[67] Thus, if we are to discover standards of rationality in a Polanyian scheme of the growth of scientific knowledge, it would seem that we must attend to the parallel, in scientific knowledge, not of the particulars about to become subsidiary, but of *the integrative focus*. The parallel feature is, of course, the discovery itself. Can it be that Polanyi finds standards of rationality within a new scientific discovery? As a matter of fact, this is exactly what Polanyi does in his exposition of the premises of science and their change. The premises of science comprise the most basic commitments, assumptions, and standards of science at any particular time. By virtue of their foundational character and role, they are relied upon acritically and subsidiarily, even though it may be possible to specify them. These premises do change; they are replaced especially at the time of a profound discovery. The change transpires because the discovery itself embodies and implies premises of its own. The discoverer comes to embrace the new premises in the course of his search for the solution to his problem; indeed, he must embrace them beforehand, else the discovery will be impossible for him to achieve. But this is not to say that the scientist is focally conscious of this personal shifting of bases. It comes about as a result of the efforts of his imagination straining to acquire and reorganize so as to achieve the as-yet-unrealized focus to which he attends. Polanyian epistemology is well equipped to handle the possibility of the strange notion of embracing new premises before being conscious of them, because it acknowledges and describes the possibility of tacit foreknowledge. Only after the discovery is in place does it become possible to spell out and confront the implications of the discovery, the new premises of science; and by then, they have been part of day-to-day operations for perhaps quite some time.

All this must be supplemented by another aspect of Polanyi's thought if we are to understand his conception of standards of rationality. What I have

---

67. The particulars have an "existential" meaning, some more than others, Polanyi says. But their more important meaning is that which they gain in terms of the focus.

in mind here is the rationality criterion of contact with reality, examined in chapter 7. A new discovery testifies to its contact with reality by virtue of its superior rationality. What makes it *superior* rationality is precisely the fact that the discovery is rational in terms of standards other than the currently explicit standards of rationality. These standards are just what Polanyi has in mind by the premises of science. Polanyi speaks at one point of Einstein being confronted by an "unfamiliar beauty"—a beauty that he could not have predicted and was not used to because it did not fall in line with the standards with which he was familiar. Yet the discovery possessed its own standards of beauty, standards to which Einstein and the rest of the scientific community were compelled to adjust.[68] Brennan discusses the important notion of the intrinsic rationality of theories, his intention being to show that, for Polanyi, it is a theory's intrinsic rationality that gives it its objective standing. But in the course of this discussion, he picks up on Polanyi's argument in "Science and Reality" and explains how this rationality grows out of the new theory itself. Brennan recapitulates Polanyi's discussion of Copernicus as follows:

> A striking example of this [intrinsic rationality] in the case of Copernicus is provided by the way in which his theory explained the fact that all the Ptolemaic major epicycles were of one terrestrial year's duration. Ptolemy himself was aware of this, but he accorded it no significance; since there was no reason in his system why epicycles should be of any particular size, and it would not have materially affected anything if one or the other were different, this noteworthy correlation was passed off as a coincidence, just as we now pass off many equally strong correlations. For the Copernican system, of course, not only did this make sense, but it was a necessary consequence. Further, because their apparent oscillations were of different amplitudes, Copernicus was able to predict the sequence of the orbital radii, and it was this latter achievement with which he himself was most impressed because it showed that he had discovered an order, a coherence, in nature. This exemplifies what Polanyi means when he speaks of the rationality of scientific theory . . .[69]

Copernicus' discovery did not conform to the standards of rationality implicit in the Ptolemaic system; Brennan says that Ptolemy *accorded* uniformity of the epicycles *no significance*, even though he was aware of it; that his

---

68. Polanyi, *Personal Knowledge*, 144.

69. Brennan, "Polanyi's Transcendence of the Distinction Between Objectivity and Subjectivity," 148.

system contained no reason why they should be any particular size. Thus, what made their uniformity not only rational but necessary was the presence of standards of rationality intrinsic to the heliocentric system, i.e., to Copernicus' discovery. Of course, as we have seen, and as Brennan stresses, for Polanyi the intrinsic rationality of theories is bound up with the rationality to be uncovered in nature.

Thus, on the matter of the nature of the rationality of science and scientific change for Polanyi, especially in light of his acknowledgment in some sense of incommensurability, let us summarize what we have gleaned. Brown, in contrast to Kuhn and Feyerabend, modifies the alleged effect of incommensurability by arguing that scientific change is always provided with some standards of rationality, some standards held in common by successive theories, although the domain of these standards may fail to reach beyond the context of a single scientific controversy. Such a position on the rationality and continuity of science he believes to be consistent with an understanding of scientific change along the lines of a gestalt. Polanyi agrees with Brown that a period of scientific change is always provided with a set of standards of rationality, but rather than growing out of points of commonality between contending theories, they are furnished by the new discovery which lies at the heart of the new theory. Old standards of rationality are superseded by superior ones. The scientist in pursuit of discovery anticipates this rationality. Thus, Polanyi's view of rationality, rather than undergirding continuity in science, at least in comparison with Brown's thesis, actually embodies discontinuity. But for Polanyi, discontinuity does not spell the demise of progress in science. Science is discontinuous because it involves supersession—one theory being replaced by one of superior rationality. How does Polanyi know that the rationality of Copernicus is superior to that of Ptolemy? This question can be answered in a non-circular way that transcends a fiduciary framework—a claim that Polanyi has both articulated and embraced. But the answer, positively and precisely in virtue of indeterminacy, seems to be bound up with the possibility of contact with reality.

In conclusion: a key difference between Polanyi and even these defenses of his approach is his, by contrast, entirely positive construal of what the discussion has presumed to be inadequacy. It has attempted to compensate for the disappointing way scientific discovery appears to "fall short of" rationality. Polanyi refuses to accept the negative presumption in which the discussion is cast. This is because of his alternative epistemology, as I said at the outset. The following passage evidences his outlook:

> I suggest that we transform this retreat [philosophy of science gradually admitting less than exactitude regarding scientific

explanation] into a triumph, by the simple device of changing camp. Let us recognize that tacit knowing is the fundamental power of the mind, which creates explicit knowing, lends meaning to it, and controls its uses. Formalization of tacit knowing immensely expands the powers of the mind, by creating a machinery of precise thought, but it also opens up new paths of intuition; any attempt to gain complete control of thought by explicit rules is self-contradictory, systematically misleading and culturally destructive. The pursuit of formalization will find its true place in a tacit framework.

In this light, there is no justification for separate approaches to scientific explanation, scientific discovery, learning and meaning. They ultimately rest on the same tacit process of understanding.[70]

Thus, the very thing that the larger discussion presumes is a problem is just what Polanyi, the premier scientist, is calling us to celebrate, accredit, and employ to our advantage as knowers.

Realism, Convergence, and the Causal Theory of Reference—and Polanyi

Now let us consider in more detail the notion of convergence, specifically in connection with the work of Hilary Putnam. To the extent that the concept of convergence overlaps those of continuity and progress, much of what has been said is applicable. In particular, the problem of incommensurability would appear to threaten the prospect of convergence. Putnam, however, addresses convergence directly.

Putnam, in the early chapters of *Meaning and the Moral Sciences*, has developed and defended what he calls an *empirical realism*. What makes realism empirical is that, he believes, realism functions as an explanation, and hence as a scientific hypothesis, for the empirical fact "that science succeeds in making many true predictions, devising better ways of controlling nature, etc."[71] Peter Skagestad elaborates in commentary on Putnam: "The empirical purport of the realist hypothesis is this: by explaining past scientific progress, the hypothesis predicts future progress. Should scientific progress come to a halt, this hypothesis would be empirically refuted."[72] Putnam believes that the realist argument turns on the success of science.

70. Polanyi, "Logic of Tacit Inference," in Grene, ed., *Knowing and Being*, 156.
71. Putnam, *Meaning and the Moral Sciences*, 19.
72. Skagestad, "Pragmatic Realism," 529.

Progress

For Putnam, success, and even realism itself, are defined in terms of the more specific notion of convergence. Skagestad writes: "What the realist hypothesis states, according to Putnam, is that science converges towards truth, in the sense of correspondence with facts."[73] The notion of *convergence* consists of the claim that "later theories often imply the approximate truth of the earlier theories in certain circumstances," that later theories have earlier ones as limiting cases.[74] Thus, convergence is a notion very similar to Popper's verisimilitude.

Putnam's view is distinctive, however, because of its emphasis on what he terms the principle of benefit of the doubt, or the *principle of charity*, which he specifies in order to counterbalance apparent incommensurability. The principle of charity functions as a constraint placed upon later theories, enjoining them, wherever rationally possible, to assign referents to the terms of an earlier theory from the standpoint of the later theory.[75] The principle of charity is possible only on the basis of a theory of reference that does not restrict the reference of terms simply to their description. Putnam himself embraces a *causal theory of reference*, which defines the reference of a term in light of causal links to actual entities. According to Goldman: "The causal theory holds that the referent of a term is determined not by whatever satisfies most current beliefs about it, but by causal connections between actual entities originally picked out and subsequent usages."[76]

Preservation of reference from theory to theory is, for Putnam, essential to the possibility of progress and convergence and to the possibility of measuring them. Preservation of reference is possible, Putnam believes, despite the transformation of descriptions due to the onset of new theories. For example, Dalton referred to the same entities, when he spoke of atoms, as are referred to within the contemporary context of quantum mechanics, despite the radical difference of current understanding of the atom from that of Dalton's time. By contrast, Kuhn and Feyerabend, holding a more description-oriented theory of reference, accordingly deny that reference is preserved through theory change. Thus, convergence is not a possibility for them and incommensurability indeed spells doom for realism. Another byproduct of such a stance is the conclusion that past theories failed to refer at all—at best an uncomfortable position to hold.

Just what relationship do convergence and the causal theory of reference have to realism? For Putnam, they are part and parcel of realist

---

73. Ibid., 529.
74. Putnam, *Meaning and the Moral Sciences*, 20, 25.
75. Ibid., 21–22.
76. Goldman, "Realism," 181.

philosophy of science. However, Alan Goldman, in his article, "Realism," criticizes the claims of both convergence and the causal theory of reference to being central to realism. Goldman contests both whether realism implies convergence and whether convergence implies realism. Realism can only begin to imply convergence, Goldman says, with the supplementation of something like the following theses: "that there is a comprehensible reality with denumerably many types of entities and properties, and that our practices and science is strongly adaptive toward this world ('strongly adaptive' meaning that there is a single best way in which to adapt, that we are adaptive in that way, and that such adaptation generates a correct representation of reality)."[77] Therefore, other perhaps weaker forms of realism afford no implication concerning convergence.

To approach this from the other side, Goldman discusses several ways in which it is possible to be a realist without espousing convergence. If, for example, one holds reality to be infinitely propertied, it is quite possible for different theories to be nonconvergent and yet compatible, because they describe reality at different levels or in different domains. When different ontologies do conflict, three things may be the case. First, the ontologies may concern entities that scientists take to be ideal and so there is no conflict with respect to what is real and, hence, no threat to realism. Secondly, if a conflict arises between what are taken to be real descriptions, and one theory succeeds the other in current acceptance, it is proper to respond by denying non-realist criticism, saying that whereas earlier scientists failed to pick out what is real, sufficient progress has been made that we are now able to do so. Third, when faced with multiple conflicting ontologies, it is acceptable to reserve judgment; to admit ignorance of the true description of the state of affairs; to claim that both ontologies afford possible descriptions perhaps of different levels of the real; and still to maintain that there is a true description and an ultimate reality with respect to the matter at hand. These three alternatives, Goldman implies, are consistent with a nonconvergent science, even though all three espouse realism.

Goldman describes as follows the usual defense of the other half of the equivalence, i.e., that convergence implies realism:

> It is sometimes suggested that realism underlies a normative ideal in science, even if it is not implied by the history of prior development. The ideal is precisely that of convergence to a unified theory which incorporates predecessors as approximations. In light of this ideal, the presence of apparently equally serviceable theories would be considered an impetus to develop

---

77. Ibid., 178.

a single more comprehensive theory, which will explain the success of prior contenders. Realism is considered the ground of this normative principle, since the notion of correspondence to a single reality is held to be incompatible with the idea of two contradictory theories both being true (although they might have equal instrumental value).[78]

Goldman argues that both the fact of convergence and this normative principle can also be explained from idealist premises. The normative ideal is actually capable of being generated by the goal of coherence, because one encompassing theory has greater coherence than two incompatible theories. As far as convergence is concerned, it becomes even more crucial for theories to converge, in the sense that later theories incorporate the approximate truth of earlier theories, when there is no notion of a correspondent, explanatory reality. It is crucial for the sake of overall coherence, because theories will be all that there is left to explain. Goldman thus supplies the idealist explanation of convergence, which Margolis indicates exists in a similar criticism of Putnam's claims to empirical realism.[79]

The reason that the causal theory of reference is taken to support realism is that it emphasizes the connection between words and objects independent of our beliefs. Goldman argues, first, that the causal and descriptive theories of reference are both correctly applicable at different points throughout science, depending upon what sort of explanatory account is envisioned.[80] Secondly, he points out that in any case "there is never a question of literally tracing causal links from utterances back to primeval dubbing acts which occurred under the influence of verifiable perceptual causal chains from independent objects."[81] Instead, "it is always the case that we assign referents to explain past utterances or theories in relation to our current beliefs" regarding a certain object. Thus, thirdly, the causal theory of reference could be viewed in application as a kind of coherence test for assigning reference. Thus, a causal theory of reference need not be construed realistically. Therefore, a causal theory of reference does not imply realism. Goldman supplies little argument against the other half of the equivalence: that realism implies a causal theory of reference. He simply says that the realist thesis does not imply the existence of the requisite links between language and reality.

78. Ibid., 180.
79. Margolis, "Cognitive Issues," 380–82.
80. Goldman, "Realism," 182.
81. Ibid., 183.

What then is to be concluded concerning realism, convergence, and the causal theory of reference? Goldman's primary thesis is that realism cannot be necessarily true, for it cannot be entailed by any particular conceptual scheme.[82] Goldman has not discussed the legitimacy or illegitimacy of convergence in and of itself—although he does intimate that he himself believes that science evidences progress.[83] But nevertheless, he makes it clear that the realist thesis is not jeopardized if we happen to conclude that convergence and a causal theory of reference are not justifiable. Goldman's arguments, I believe, also render the same verdict with respect to verisimilitude as a notion similar to convergence and with respect to progress and continuity in science. This is by virtue of the fact that they are comparatively weaker or at least more general notions than convergence. If a thesis as strong as convergence can be interpreted idealistically, normative ideal and all, then certainly progress could be interpreted idealistically as well; and since nonconvergence implies discontinuity of some sort, discontinuity would pose no threat to realism either. Thus, incommensurability may not imply an anti-realism.

Polanyi, as it turns out, relates quite nicely to the category that Goldman develops of those who are realists without taking realism to be essentially equivalent to convergence. Polanyi does not have a great deal to say on the specific subject. We have noted comments of his that indicate a sense of ever more closely approximating the truth. And, of course, we have yet to explore Polanyi's understanding of truth. There perhaps is to be found a sympathy with Putnam with respect to reference, at least in the sense that reference may be preserved even if descriptions are transformed—witness the isotope example.

But a Polanyian parallel to the central aspect of convergence, i.e., the idea of retaining the approximate truth of earlier theories as limiting cases, though it is not denied, seems to be lacking. Harkening back to our earlier conversation about Polanyi and Peirce, it may also be inferred that Peirce's notion of convergence in the long run is not espoused by Polanyi. For Peirce, the domain of human inquiry is finite; he apparently believed, at that time, that current science had almost exhausted it. Polanyi's world is inexhaustible. Thus ultimate, explicit, convergence would appear to be principally impossible. But, as we have seen, he still resembles Peirce to some extent in his optimism concerning our prospects of true understanding and the eventual agreement of opposing schools of scientific thought (see, for

---

82. Goldman believes that the argument for realism must be an inductive one. See Chapter 10 of this work.

83. Goldman, "Realism," 179.

example, the quotation of n. 77 above). But this is not because of the finitude of reality; it is rather because of its rationality, as well as the knower's tacit powers for comprehending it.

Comparing Polanyi to what Goldman says: reality for Polanyi may certainly be called "infinitely propertied"; if, as Goldman implies, this rules out convergence in Putnam's sense, then Polanyi does not espouse convergence. Yet, thanks to the logical independence of realism from convergence, as demonstrated by Goldman, Polanyi's realism, in light of the prevailing discussion, would nevertheless remain viable.

In Conclusion

As we bring this wide-ranging inquiry regarding progress in science to a close, we may note that Polanyi's distinctive engagement of the question of the nature of science on the basis of his prior innovative work in epistemology allows him to synthesize features of both sides of the prevailing debate in a fresh key that resists conceding its defining presuppositions. In Polanyi's proposals in this discussion, we have marked just the sort of integratively distinct synthesis that Polanyi is claiming occurs in science. It is not a pasted-together compilation so much as a logical leap. Polanyi is positive about progress while also affirming incommensurability. He redefines rationality in terms of how it plays out in actual research and discovery, rather than forcing a restrictive rationality on the process, and rather than rejecting this restrictive rationality. Thus, he simultaneously affirms discontinuity and rationality. In connection with Putnam and Goldman, we have seen that he remains committed to a goal of truth and to realism, not so much in spite of, but precisely in virtue of, nonconvergence. This "apposite new conception" of science both results from and in turn supports his distinctive epistemic proposals and his robust confidence in contact with reality.

9

Polanyi and Contemporary Realist Issues (II): Truth, in Particular Correspondence

Historical and Philosophical Background

This chapter takes a selective look at some conversations concerning truth and Michael Polanyi's engagement of them. In the philosophical literature of Polanyi's time, the discussion of truth was dominated by attention to how "... is true" functions in logic and language.[1] We might speak of this as the question of what "truth" means or of its linguistic function (whether meaning and function are the same or different aspects). In the nineteenth century, the mathematician Gottlob Frege had proposed that "is true" adds nothing to the *assertion* which is being claimed to be true. Additionally, he developed an assertion sign, enabling the logical distinction between an asserted and an unasserted statement. In the early twentieth century, F. B. Ramsey propounded what was known as the *redundancy theory of truth*: To say that the statement, P, is true, is simply to assert P. Therefore, "is true" is redundant. In this same vein, Max Black proposed a

---

1. I have added to the 1985 dissertation these opening paragraphs of summary in order improve the text for publication. In doing so, I have departed more radically from my policy to let the dissertation stand more or less on its own as Part 1 of this work.

no-truth theory of truth.[2] In the 30s, Alfred Tarski reflected this approach in his own mathematical and logical work when, in the context of set theory, he proposed what he referred to as a semantic theory of truth: "'Snow is white' if and only if snow is white." This is known as the *semantic theory of truth*. P. F. Strawson propounded the *nondescriptive theory of truth*: to say that a statement is true is not to describe the statement. It is, rather, a performative act—as per speech act theory—hence, the *performative theory of truth*. All of these were positions on truth in which truth was deemed a distinctive, intriguing way of speaking, and that failure to see this would lead to wrongheaded philosophical puzzles: even though it sounds as if a person is simply describing adjectivally a quality of the statement in question, that would be a naive and problem-causing way to see it. Since Polanyi himself addresses this, my effort in this inquiry to locate him in the discussion will be easier than in respect to other dimensions of the mainline philosophical conversation.

The logico-linguistic discussion itself took place against the larger backdrop of early twentieth-century analytic epistemology, metaphysics, and philosophy of science. This approach itself represented the zenith of modern empiricism dating back to Locke around 1700. This tradition maintained a progressively more and more anti-metaphysical bias in the very name of empiricism. Empiricism seems to require that the nature of truth must involve the relatedness of our claims to the external world. Yet, it also seems to thwart the very relatedness it requires. An empiricist foundationalist picture of knowledge regards minimally constituted and expressed sensations as foundational to all responsible knowledge. But sensations, by their very constitution, block access to the world beyond or behind them. As a result, claims about that external world would be illegitimate, by definition unsupported by foundational sense experience. Polanyi himself refers to this as radical empiricism; he deems it critical that it be challenged.[3]

The result of these emphases in play in the twentieth century was an ambivalent—to many embarrassing, but deemed necessary—espousal of a minimalist, logic-attuned, objective world. It presumed the correspondence theory of truth: the nature of truth has to do with the correspondence between the statement in question and the independent world. The hope persisted that logical analysis was both necessary and sufficient to resolve this matter and justify the scientific enterprise.

---

2. Cited by Polanyi, *Personal Knowledge*, 255. Polanyi states that his own theory is reminiscent of Black's.

3. Polanyi, *Tacit Dimension*, 81.

As part of its anti-metaphysical penchant, twentieth-century philosophy also often excised from proper knowledge the very knower himself. As this, in turn, impacted philosophy of science, proper science effectively involved an absent knower, or at least a mechanically impersonal one. Proper science was seen to involve an impassive uninvolvement, entirely critical and logic-driven. It is this last expression of the prevailing philosophical winds that Polanyi, as a premier scientist, directly challenges in *Personal Knowledge*. He challenges them by arguing for the essential personal participation of the knower and the tacit component of the epistemic process. And yes, he emphasizes discovery and not justification as the revealing paradigm of knowing. It is in connection with this, it appears, that Polanyi engages the work of Bertrand Russell, Tarski, and others surrounding correspondence and theories of truth, showing against that backdrop how only the knower's/speaker's responsible personal affirmation enables the others' positions to avoid triviality or irresolvability in matters related to truth and correspondence. However, in addition to my engagement here with the debate about truth, we will see in this chapter that what Polanyi affirms about contact with reality can be considered a creative response to the thin correspondence realism that mainline philosophers ambivalently supported.

Truth and Realism

Most generally, there have been thought to be three positive theories regarding the nature of truth: truth as correspondence, truth as coherence, and a pragmatic view of truth. These can be considered to be metaphysical stances as well. The *correspondence theory* says that truth concerns a relation between the knower's truth claim and the world, or the way things actually are. The *coherence theory*, often fueled by the unworkability of correspondence that we have noted, stipulates that truth concerns the internal consistency of all the knower's truth claims. A coherence theory can also be seen to be consonant with an idealism as opposed to a realism: reality just is Idea, as per Hegel, for example. A *pragmatic view of truth* says that truth is a matter of practical value: we claim as true those things that contribute to success and flourishing. This view can be similarly motivated with respect to the problems of correspondence, but also positively finds it worthwhile to place the stress, in matters of truth, on practical value. A fourth theory regarding the nature of truth includes all the logico-linguistic positions I named at the at the beginning of this chapter—the no-truth theory, and so on: if the claim is made that this logico-linguistic functioning is all there is to truth, then that is a claim about the nature of truth.

How do all these theories of truth bear on the question of realism? On the surface at least, it seems obvious that, of these four theories of truth, the correspondence theory alone requires a realist stance. That's because it alone locates truth as having to do with the relationship of our claims *to the world*. There is, at least on the surface, an apparent intent of the others to deny this or at least to deem it impossible and unnecessary. However, it is possible to benefit from the logico-linguistic analyses without espousing the additional claim that this is all there is to truth and that questions of truth stand in no need of connection with reality. One may both affirm Tarski's biconditional and be a realist, and even a correspondence theorist. There can be pragmatic realism as well. Alternatively, there can be an attempt to reinterpret correspondence as being just what we mean by one or the other of the logico-linguistic accounts. But if that is so, surely that is a different understanding of correspondence from one that has been intuitively understood. In contrast, it is one lacking substance or bite.

In order to hold to realism, it is commonly thought, one must hold to a correspondence theory of truth. Thus, it would seem important to realism that a truth-as-correspondence stance could be worked out. Hilary Putnam confirms that realists typically believe in a correspondence theory of truth.[4] Putnam's own understanding of the realist claim is as follows: that science converges toward the truth, truth being in the sense of correspondence with the facts.[5] Alan Goldman defines the realist claim in the following way:

> R2 The physical world consists of entities with (some) properties that are independent of their characterization within any conceptual scheme or theory.[6]

As Goldman develops the implication of this claim, he says:

> The relation between our being justified according to some theory or language in ascribing manifest properties in light of certain experiences, and the ascription's being true, is contingent. Thus also implied is a correspondence theory of truth, according to which empirical truth is a relation between beliefs and objects, rather than between beliefs and other beliefs or experiences. The notion of truth is not reducible to the notion of coherence or justification within some conceptual scheme or language. Of course the truth of any empirical statement

---

4. Putnam, *Meaning and the Moral Sciences*, 18.
5. Skagestad, "Pragmatic Realism," 528–29.
6. Goldman, "Realism," 175. The thesis R1 that "there is a physical world not reducible to classes of experiences or appearances, or to regularities within experience," is, according to Goldman, primarily the statement that phenomenalism is false.

depends upon the meanings of the terms, but according to R2 it always depends upon more than that.[7]

Here, the success of realism appears to be bound up with the success of the correspondence theory of truth, not only in contrast to coherentist and pragmatist alternatives, but also in contrast to any account of truth, or of correspondence itself, as merely a matter of the meaning and function of the term, "true." These minimalist competitors include redundancy (Ramsey), performance (Strawson), and perhaps even the semantic theory of truth (Tarski).[8] It is important, therefore, to see whether Polanyian realism embraces the correspondence theory of truth, and if not, how contact with reality, which it proposes instead, nevertheless succeeds as a realism.

This discussion of truth, in particular, correspondence, matters centrally to the overarching concern of this book. That our claims are true if and only if they correspond to the world is a very natural, commonly presumed, intuition. It seems obvious that, for knowledge to be knowledge, this must be the case. Yet the idea of correspondence, as an idea, appears inherently problematic. This grim prospect threatens our entire hope of knowing the world. On the strength of the problem, whole philosophies have moved away from correspondence to coherence, pragmatism, and even skepticism. Nor is it possible to isolate this concern as a mere parlor game. It can lie, existentially, at the heart of who I am as an individual: am I connected or disconnected from the world? A negative answer impacts endeavors far more preliminary and profound than the important matter of science. It easily bleeds over into deep matters of the self's well-being, perhaps in a way that contemporary mainline discussions downplay along with their antimetaphysical stance. I submit that we need, at the deepest level of who we are, a positive assurance and hope.

Thus, a mass of knotty problems surround and comprise the problem of truth. This chapter will explore some of these. The chapter's general outline is two-fold: first, a discussion of theories of truth in general and correspondence in particular, and secondly, a brief examination of a selection of related concerns regarding truth, especially for philosophy of science. At each point throughout this survey, I will examine Polanyi's writings for his views that bear on the issue under consideration. I will lay his claims regarding truth alongside concerns and proposals in contemporary literature to

---

7. Goldman, "Realism," 176.

8. The following books and book selections provide a main source for this analysis: Pitcher, ed., *Truth*; White, *Truth*; Pap, *Elements of Analytic Philosophy*, ch. 14; Hamlyn, *Theory of Knowledge*, ch. 5.

reveal how Polanyi's approach compares and contrasts. By means of this, we can deepen our grasp of his innovative approach.

What engender the twentieth century's unfortunate puzzlement about truth and reality are, viewed from a Polanyian standpoint, the implicit and presumed parameters characteristic of the prevailing modern epistemic paradigm. As we will see, for Polanyi, truth is intrinsically a fiduciary matter—a matter of the knower's responsibly personal commitment to a claim. This, in turn, is undergirded by the fundamental structure of all knowing, in which explicit claims are always rooted in logically unspecifiable subsidiaries. And for him, the exact match of correspondence is superseded by the qualitatively richer notion of contact with reality. Once again, I believe that we will see that, because of his distinctive epistemology, Polanyi articulates a position on truth and realism in a different key. It is thus difficult to fit into the prevailing discussion, but commendably superior. That different key enables a uniquely sophisticated treatment of the baffling conundrum of correspondence. What is more, I believe we will see that his realism offers the question of truth the existential gravitas it deserves. Thus it offers that much-needed positive assurance.

Some Theories of Truth, and What We Mean by Them

What do we have in mind when we speak of a theory of truth? In light of the foregoing summary, we can see that we can be talking about the question of the nature of truth, the meaning of truth, or the linguistic function of the word, "true." Additionally, these differing senses may be combined to make additional points about truth—for example, one may say that the nature of truth just is its meaning and no more, or the meaning of truth just is its linguistic function.

For example, Strawson, in his performative theory of truth, intends his exposition of "true" in connection with a linguistic performance of agreeing with a certain statement to be an exposition of the meaning of the word.[9] But, as Alan White argues, this cannot be all that we mean or have in mind when we use the word. Rather, Strawson's theory "gives us an important insight into a function of the use of 'true' and 'false,' but not an analysis of their meaning."[10] Thus, it is helpful to distinguish between what we use the word, "true," *to do*, and what we believe it to mean.

---

9. Strawson, "Truth," in Pitcher, ed., *Truth*, 32–53; O'Connor, *Correspondence Theory of Truth*, 113–36; Hamlyn, *Theory of Knowledge*, 126–32.

10. White, *Truth*, 99–101.

Another matter that a theory of truth might concern is that of *criteria of truth*—the sorts of signs we follow in trying to decide what things are true. Finally, in the wake of much contemporary thought, including Polanyi's, we may speak of *standards of truth*. The standards of truth in a particular period and society would be part of a background theory, such as is delineated by Quine, and would lend direction to the search for truths by providing a sense of what sorts of things are to be taken as factual.

The Correspondence Theory of Truth

Let us evaluate the senses in which *the correspondence theory of truth* is a theory of truth in light of these distinctions. Correspondence, more than any other theory of truth, appears to supply us with an understanding of the meaning or nature of truth: to say that something is true is to claim that there is a correspondence between it and an extra-linguistic state of affairs, that things are as the claim says that they are.[11] That this is what all of us mean when we claim the truth of a certain statement seems, on the surface at least, commonsensical.

Correspondence runs into difficulty, however, when it is imagined to be a *criterion* of truth. That is, we do not seem to be able to use it as a guide to actually determine whether or not a certain claim is, in fact, true. It has always been plagued by the obvious fact that it is impossible to check our ideas directly against reality, for the knower has *no direct access* to reality independent of his concepts.[12] To entertain the prospect of checking our words against the world requires, according to Quine, an illicit vantage point.[13] Perhaps under the influence of pragmatism or generally positivist agendas, these difficulties utilizing correspondence as a criterion of truth can lead to its rejection as a theory of truth. The inference would be that any additional "meaning" the theory might be claimed to have that was not embodied in some sort of verifiable activity would not count as meaning at all. A verifiability or warranted assertibility understanding of meaning and truth, it can be seen, could be considered a criterion of truth. It would be positivist if it considered verifiability to be all there is to meaning and truth.

11. White, *Truth*, 102; MacKinnon, "Historical Development of Scientific Realism" and "Systematic Analysis of Scientific Realism," and the Introduction in MacKinnon, ed., *Problem of Scientific Realism*, 55.

12. Rouse, "Kuhn, Heidegger, and Scientific Realism," 270; Grene, "Knowledge, Belief and Perception," 9; Campbell, "The Correspondence Theory," in Ammerman and Singer, eds., *Belief, Knowledge, and Truth*, 401–6.

13. Hauptli, "Quinean Relativism: Beyond Metaphysical Realism and Idealism," 396. Hauptli cites Quine, *Ontological Relativity*, 27.

Despite the conundrum, it would seem that, no matter how we might go about deciding whether a particular claim is true, what we *mean* by claiming that it is true is that it accurately represents the way things really are. Thus, the correspondence theory would retain at least its application to the question of the *meaning* of truth, even if, as it apparently does, its criterial use failed.

Correspondence, as a theory of truth, would not furnish an answer concerning the linguistic function of our claim of truth, as has been supplied particularly by the performative theory. However, from the perspective of the correspondence theory, if not from the perspective of the performative theory, the two are not contradictory but complementary. The fact that we mean by "true" the correspondence of a particular statement to reality does not rule out the fact that we may be using the predicate "____ is true" for the purpose of affirming or agreeing with the statement of which it is predicated. This will be seen as we examine Polanyi's ideas.

Correspondence does not entail but must be complemented by the notion of standards of truth: those basic, constitutive commitments that, in any given society, era, or context, furnish the guidelines for what sorts of things will be taken as true. The fact that truth consists of correspondence with fact would not furnish any particular sense of what constitutes fact. In the apparent absence of any direct access to reality—but even if there is—some such standards are necessary.

Let us also note two characterizations of the correspondence theory of truth that have been made in recent years. Alfred Tarski has claimed concerning his semantic theory of truth that it captures the essence of the classical correspondence theory of truth.[14] Tarski's widely known formulation, "'Snow is white' if and only if snow is white," also appears in Polanyi's discussion of truth; Polanyi contrasts his own theses to it specifically, as we will see. Karl Popper in particular has embraced Tarski's approach.[15] But there are problems with this claim. First, since Tarski's semantic definition of truth relies on strict specification of formal languages, it appears that truth cannot be defined for everyday languages. Yet the notion of correspondence that we have discussed seems very much an everyday affair. Secondly, Putnam has argued that Tarski has captured only the formal properties of correspondence, and that it is possible to retain these formal properties and yet surrender realism (and hence the essence of the classical correspondence theory), replacing it with some idealist notion of truth, such as warranted

---

14. Tarski; "The Semantic Conception of Truth," 341–76.
15. Popper, *Conjectures and Refutations*, 223.

assertibility.[16] Thus, although Tarski provides a nice definition of truth, Putnam says, it does not capture the more realistic meaning of truth.

Secondly, let us note Putnam's own proposal that the correspondence theory functions to provide an account of the success of science.[17] Putnam believes that it is absurd to hold that, in order to learn the meaning of a particular statement, we must learn its truth and conditions, as would be the case if correspondence were required in the analysis of the meaning of a statement. Rather, we learn the meaning of statements as we learn their use in the context of our total linguistic behavior. However, once language is learned, correspondence is talked about as explaining the success of linguistic behavior and science in particular. Science works because our claims correspond to the world. We may understand how to turn a light on without any understanding of electricity. Yet electricity accounts for the success of our flipping the switch to turn on the light. Correspondence serves a similar function with respect to our truth claims. The problem with this, as Rouse points out and as Putnam later recognizes, is that the notion of correspondence is, itself, part of the total theory and thus itself needs to be explained.[18] Correspondence, therefore, provides only a trivial explanation of the success of our linguistic theory.

In addition to its difficulties with direct access, the correspondence theory has been beset in recent years with other problems. There are, of course, all the questions related to the issue of what it is that our beliefs, when true, correspond to—whether objects or facts or propositions.[19] Without delving into this massive subject, at least one thing can be said. It is that if the entities to which beliefs relate in correspondence are facts or propositions, it becomes possible to sidestep the need of direct access to the world. But this would seem to be the case at the expense of the essence of the classical correspondence theory, which is concerned with a relationship that crosses the great divide between words and world as non-linguistically construed. But if, as we have seen, a possible relationship between beliefs and objects is plagued by the apparent absence of the direct access to the objects necessary to confirm the existence of a relationship of correspondence, this may be what remains to us. The result would not be an unqualified realism.

A second difficulty concerns the attempt to make sense of the relationship of correspondence itself. It has been thought that the relationship

---

16. Putnam, *Meaning and the Moral Sciences*, 29.

17. Ibid., 111.

18. Rouse, "Kuhn, Heidegger, and Scientific Realism," 282–84; Putnam, *Meaning and the Moral Sciences*, 129.

19. Pitcher, "Introduction," in Pitcher, ed., *Truth*, 1–15.

could best be described as a matter of picturing or copying—this idea being most thoroughly developed by the early Wittgenstein. But the metaphor breaks down, for example, when applied to negative, conditional, or disjunctive statements that are true.[20] However, it helps to realize that the correspondence theory need not imply a relationship of copying. George Pitcher has distinguished between the kind of correspondence that implies a perfect fit between the relata ("correspondence with," or "correspondence-as-congruity"), and the kind of correspondence that implies simply correlation: some sort of minimal relation or matching ("correspondence to," or "correspondence-as-correlation").[21] If the correspondence theory is characterized in terms of correlation, problems with the metaphor of picturing can be sidestepped. One apparent drawback to such an interpretation would be that we often speak of something's corresponding with the facts. But, as White points out, the facts that we have in mind at that point are not those that correlate with the belief in question but with other surrounding facts. Thus, the actual relationship in view in the correspondence theory is not at issue here. Correspondence-as-correlation is, of course, the weaker of the two relationships. But it may be that it is all that is required by the correspondence theory.

Here is another concern: W. V. Quine has argued that correspondence fails to furnish a legitimate ground for truth and reference.[22] He does this primarily on the basis of his "gavagai" example, in which he demonstrates that on the basis of a correspondence interpretation of truth, it would be impossible to determine whether a native (or a neighbor) did or did not individuate the world in a fashion similar to our own. But in fact, he says, we can distinguish between rabbits and undetached rabbit parts and, thus, truth and reference must be grounded not in unique, determinate word-world relationships, but in a background theory. Quine, in the terms of the distinctions made at the outset of this chapter, focuses the correspondence theory of truth not on the meaning of truth, but on criteria or perhaps standards of truth—how we determine what things are true. In light of the upcoming discussion of Polanyi, I wish to note two things about Quine. First, Quine assumes that correspondence has to do with determinate word-world relations and does not entertain the possibility of indeterminacy and how that would affect the correspondence theory. And secondly, he assumes that correspondence and relativism (in the sense of truth being determined

---

20. White, *Truth*, 106–7.

21. Pitcher, "Introduction," in Pitcher, ed., *Truth*, 9–14; White, *Truth*, 105–8.

22. Hauptli, "Quinean Relativism," 394–96; Quine, *Ontological Relativity*, 27, 47, 48; "Reasons for the Indeterminacy of Translation," 178–83.

by background theory) are mutually exclusive. For Polanyi, these will not be the case.

Polanyi and Truth

While many other problems could be enumerated and examined, what has been sketched here provides a fairly adequate frame of reference for an examination of what Polanyi has to say about truth. Polanyi's claims concerning truth appear to fall along two divergent tracks. On the one hand, he reinterprets truth, like knowledge, in terms of the personal. On the other, he maintains the objectivity of truth and its relationship to reality. Let us examine these two tracks and how they might be reconciled.

The Personal Character of Truth— Fiduciary and Tacit

It may be helpful to organize the Polanyian material concerning the personal character of truth under two somewhat distinct headings, namely, the fiduciary and the tacit. My own sense is that, at least with respect to truth, the former concerns matters that are more structural or formal, while the latter comprises more existential or experiential aspects of the personal. The heart of the fiduciary aspect of personal truth is Polanyi's contention that truth can only be thought of by believing it.[23] Truth is a matter of the personal, first of all, because I cannot speak of something being true unless I myself believe it to be true. Thus, as Polanyi notes, it is nonsensical to speak of a claim being true for someone else and not for myself.[24] I can report that someone else thinks the thing is true, but this is only a report and not an assertion of truth. Thus, the personal character of truth must be distinguished from a subjective or relativistic sort of truth.

The idea that truth is a matter of personal assertion appeals to Polanyi. To say something is true is to endorse or authorize it, like signing one's name on a check.[25] Thus, to assert that p is true is to make an assertion about p, and it is not possible to assert "p is true." "P is true" is not a sentence, but is the assertion of the sentence. Polanyi embraces Frege's idea of having a logical sign for assertion: To say $\vdash$ p is to say, I assert that *p*. This is in contrast to the idea that truth is an impersonal property of statements: this

---

23. Polanyi, *Personal Knowledge*, 305.
24. Ibid., 315–16.
25. Ibid., 254.

cannot be the case because it is impossible to produce any strict criteria for determining if the property is present. I will say more about this later. Thus, Polanyi believes that his own view falls into line with Max Black's no-truth theory of truth, with Ramsey's redundancy theory, and with Strawson's non-descriptive theory. However, I do not believe that Polanyi intends these considerations to constitute the meaning or definition of truth; this is more a question of how we use the word "true" and of its parameters.

Related to the claim that truth is thought of only by believing it is Polanyi's characterization of truth as "the external pole of belief."[26] His point is that the destruction of belief constitutes the destruction of all truth as well. Truth is grounded in belief—this is the fiduciary framework. Polanyi agrees with Tarski to the extent that Tarski captures this asymmetric relationship of assertion and asserted.[27] The problem with Tarski, however, is that his definition appears to equate a sentence with a state of affairs: "Snow is white" is true if and only if snow is white. Polanyi proposes to eliminate this apparent anomaly by inserting the notion of belief: "I shall say that "snow is white" is true if and only if I believe that snow is white." What we are left with, according to Polanyi, is simply a difference in emphasis—the latter part of the formulation stressing the personal character of our knowledge, the former its universal intent. This amplifies Polanyi's claim that the assertion of truth involves a personal endorsement. It also, however, removes any affinity between Tarski's formulation and the classical correspondence theory of truth. Where Polanyi stands on correspondence remains to be seen.

Finally, we may note in these last sentences the relationship of the assertion of truth to Polanyi's notion of universal intent. When a person makes a truth claim or asserts the truth of some statement, he does so with both personal responsibility and universal intent. He claims, in effect, that it ought to be accepted and endorsed by everyone, that everyone is obliged to believe that it is true.

Marjorie Grene believes that the notion of the tacit in Polanyi ultimately undergirds his fiduciary framework.[28] Accordingly, in our discussion of the personal character of truth, the existence of the tacit may be taken to account for the peculiar structural aspects of the concept of truth just noted. Truth is and must be personal because the "determination of truth relies ultimately upon tacit powers." Knowledge, Polanyi says, bears indeterminately upon reality as we ourselves personally participate in knowing and embody an empathetic feel for the aptness of our concepts to the situation. When we

---

26. Ibid., 286; Polanyi, *Tacit Dimension*, 87.
27. Polanyi, *Personal Knowledge*, 255.
28. Grene, "Tacit Knowing: Grounds," 168.

know something, we will therein be unable to tell what all its implications are or even whether there is any admixture of error. To know something is to know more than we can tell; thus to know something to be true is going to involve knowing more than we can tell. Because we cannot fully spell out a claim's implications (we only anticipate that it has them), we cannot determine explicitly the claim's truth.[29]

But it is misleading to present tacit powers as a poor substitute for explicit and impersonal determination of truth. For one thing, Polanyi has demonstrated in *Personal Knowledge* that an explicit and impersonal determination is impossible. In contrast, to the extent that explicit knowledge and procedures do exist, they do so because they are grounded in and aided by our tacit, inarticulate skills. The tacit, far from being a poor substitute for the explicit, is the only way the explicit is possible to the extent that it is. Thus, the declaration of truth emerges as a personal act of appraisal and commitment, implying our own accreditation of our own tacit powers, and justified in the light of personal criteria.[30] Our tacit powers, while they strip—or rather, relieve—truth of its impersonal character, do enable us to recognize truth, not infallibly, but in fact competently—something that an impersonal criterion could never (by virtue of logical impossibility) provide for us. This is the point of Polanyi's discussions of intellectual passions and other criteria for the recognition of truth.[31]

Thus far, then, it appears that Polanyi contributes primarily to what has been referred to as the discussion of the linguistic function of truth. What he contributes is, of course, more than a mere discussion of function, for he provides a full-blown rationale for the personal character of truth in the fiduciary and tacit framework. This is truth as *credo*—*credo*, for Polanyi, as for Augustine and Luther, without which there is no truth.[32]

Polanyi also indicates the existence of criteria and standards of truth that are personal and not fully specifiable. I wish to say a little about these now, although they will reappear in later discussion. What I have in mind by criteria and by standards of truth in Polanyi are perhaps not far apart, but I believe that it is possible and helpful to distinguish them. Polanyi refers time and again to self-set standards: standards primarily of reasonableness and rightness. There are standards for all fields of human achievement—physical skills, perception, scientific discovery. Truth, as the rightness of the action

---

29. Polanyi, *Tacit Dimension*, 23, 87; "Tacit Knowing: Its Bearing," in Grene, ed., *Knowing and Being*, 172–73.

30. Polanyi, *Personal Knowledge*, 311, 70–71; *Tacit Dimension*, 23; "Genius in Science," in Grene, ed., *Knowing and Being*, 57.

31. Polanyi, *Personal Knowledge*, 143.

32. Ibid., 308.

of mental acceptance,[33] itself constitutes a standard for a particular sort of human activity. Self-set standards possess an aura of paradox because of the fact that they are self-imposed: "the criteria of reasonableness, to which I subject my own beliefs, are ultimately upheld by my confidence in them . . . ."[34] Since upholding anything because of my confidence is the function of the tacit component, these standards are personal.

This conception of self-set standards with regard to truth is supplemented, I believe, by Polanyi's notion of scientist's "vision of reality." The scientist's vision of reality is his general understanding of reality, which includes not only explicit information, but more importantly the stock of latent knowledge, intuitions, and anticipations that he has built up over the years of his experience. This dynamic vision of reality itself functions as an interpretive standard of truth, personally indwelt and maintained, and responsibly applied.

> Our vision of the general nature of things is our guide for the interpretation of all future experience. Such guidance is indispensable. Theories of the scientific method which try to explain the establishment of scientific truth by any purely objective formal procedure are doomed to failure. Any process of enquiry unguided by intellectual passions would inevitably spread out into a desert of trivialities. Our vision of reality, to which our sense of scientific beauty responds, must suggest to us the kind of questions that it should be reasonable and interesting to explore.[35]

But in addition to guiding the scientist to reasonable quests, our vision of reality tacitly informs our standards so that we may responsibly determine questions of truth.

> We accept the results of science, and we must accept them, without having any strict proof that they are true. . . . They could all conceivably be false, but we accept them as true because we consider doubts that may be raised against them to be unreasonable. . . . [T]here are no rules for deciding certain factual questions of supreme importance. . . . Having applied to his findings a number of specifiable criteria, [the scientist] must ultimately decide in the light of his own personal judgment whether the remaining conceivable doubts should be set aside as unreasonable.[36]

33. Ibid., 320–31.
34. Ibid., 256; see also 63, 95–97, 100.
35. Ibid., 135; Polanyi, "The Creative Imagination," 86.
36. Polanyi, "Genius In Science," 57. Polanyi proceeds in this article to demonstrate

This scientific vision of reality is rooted in the whole realm of the inarticulate—the kind of latent and skillful knowledge that Polanyi says we share with the animals. Tacit powers function not only to guide intellectual pursuits but also to confirm them.[37] Thus it is that we voice our ultimate convictions "from within the whole system of acceptances that are logically prior to any particular assertion of our own, prior to the holding of any particular piece of knowledge."[38] For Polanyi, then, there exist standards of truth, personal and tacit in character, which render personal judgment "the ultimate criterion of scientific truth."[39] These standards, I have argued, receive their peculiar content or bent by virtue of our inarticulate understanding and our general vision of reality.

What I have in mind by criteria of truth are the particular experiences we have that cause us to believe that we are in the presence of truth. The criteria, of course, will partially, but not determinatively, be informed by our standards of truth. But their formal structure appears to remain the same though the content may be different. The criteria of truth are just what I have referred to as the criteria of reality: we recognize superior rationality and coherence of our integrative pattern and we experience the IFM Effect: the anticipation of indeterminate future manifestations resulting from our claim. More will be said of this matter presently, but now we are faced with a more pressing issue.

Truth as Contact with Reality

It is time to consider the other side of the Polanyian picture of truth. Polanyi refuses to restrict his discussion of truth (and his own use of the word) to its personal and assertive aspects. What seems to be more the case is that Polanyi affirms the distinctions made at the beginning of this chapter, in particular in intending the discussion of truth as personal commitment and assertion to be concerned not with the meaning or nature of truth but with the parameters governing our use of the word. The serious reader of Polanyi is compelled to come away with the conviction that truth, for Polanyi, is ultimately a matter of contact with reality, and that it is this aspect of his conception that constitutes the meaning of the word "true" in his own uses of it. Consider the following quotations:

---

the tacit powers which are an essential part of science.
    37. Polanyi, *Personal Knowledge*, ch. 5, and 132.
    38. Ibid., 267.
    39. Polanyi, "Tacit Knowing: Its Bearing," in Grene, ed., *Knowing and Being*, 173.

An empirical statement is true to the extent to which it reveals an aspect of reality, a reality largely hidden to us, and existing therefore independently of our knowing it.[40]

Actually, both sides [of the Copernicus-Osiander debate] agreed on what they meant by "true"; namely, that truth lies in the achievement of a contact with reality—a contact destined to reveal itself further by an indefinite range of yet unforeseen consequences.[41]

Here we meet the conception of truth. Modern antimetaphysical philosophies, like pragmatism, operationalism, positivism, and logical positivism, have tried to spell out the implications of asserting a proposition to be true. But if the truth of a proposition lies in its bearing on reality, which makes its implications indeterminate, then such efforts are foredoomed.[42]

Even that which we know and can tell is accepted by us as true only in view of its bearing on a reality beyond it, a reality which may yet manifest itself in the future in an indeterminate range of unsuspected results . . . .[43]

A statement about nature is believed to be true if it is believed to disclose an aspect of something real in nature. A true physical theory is therefore believed to be no mere mathematical relation between observed data, but to represent an aspect of reality, which may yet manifest itself inexhaustibly in the future.[44]

To summarize these passages: *for Polanyi a statement is true insofar as it reveals an aspect of reality.* Truth is the achievement of contact with reality. And the truth of a proposition lies in its bearing on reality and concomitant indeterminate implications as signaled by the promise of our conception to manifest itself inexhaustively in the future. In addition to these definitions, we have Polanyi's own use of the word. To cite only one of a host of similar passages: "But the Copernican system did not anticipate the discoveries of Kepler and Newton accidentally: it led to them because it was true."[45] Truth

---

40. Polanyi, *Personal Knowledge*, 311.

41. Ibid., 147.

42. Polanyi, "Tacit Knowing: Its Bearing," in Grene, ed., *Knowing and Being*, 172.

43. Polanyi, *Tacit Dimension*, 61.

44. Polanyi, "Science and Reality," 191; see also *Personal Knowledge*, 43; *Tacit Dimension*, 77, 87.

45. Polanyi, *Personal Knowledge*, 147. The following is only a selection of passages in which Polanyi speaks of truth: *Personal Knowledge*, 16, 43, 94, 106, 112, 113, 114, 147-48, 149, 167, 173; "Knowing and Being," in Grene, ed., *Knowing and Being*, 131,

involves, necessarily, the responsible assertion of personal commitment; but also necessarily, it cannot be only that. It must concern representation of an aspect of reality that is pregnant with indeterminate prospects.

Contact with reality is a *sine qua non:* without there having been contact with reality, there can be no truth. Truth has to do with reality, with the way things actually are. That is why the criteria of reality function as criteria of truth: they indicate successful contact, and contact is essential to truth.

How is this side of Polanyian truth to be reconciled with the personal side? There are at least two things to be said. First, self-set standards, our vision of reality, and our pre-articulate senses themselves grow out of our contact with reality. We need only remember Polanyi's exposition of the premises of science to realize how this works. Our standards of truth are modified subsidiarily in advance of a discovery as our imagination struggles to actualize what our intuition has focused upon. Thus, the discovery, when it comes, Polanyi says, comes claiming its own rightness or truthfulness. For the standards of truth that we now find ourselves to be holding are those that conform to the discovery. Secondly, if truth lies in contact with reality, it is the tacit component alone which enables the knower to decide what is true. For whether or not and to what extent contact has been made—even in what respect it has been made—cannot be explicitly determined. The bearing of truth on reality, by virtue of its indeterminacy, can be recognized only tacitly, Polanyi says. Thus, the personal side of truth, far from being contradictory of this external side, is in fact in harmony with and even essential to it.

Polanyi and Correspondence

The question now becomes one of how to position Polanyi with respect to the correspondence theory of truth. This question is not amenable to a simple, direct answer. Polanyi occasionally speaks of "correspondence to the facts."[46] Only once, I believe, does he address himself to the correspondence theory of truth.[47] This instance falls in the context of his elaboration of the framework of the commitment situation. According to Polanyi, we must distinguish between facts held with commitment and facts not so held. Within the commitment situation, the elements of a truth claim are represented in the following way:

133; "Logic of Tacit Inference," in Grene, ed., *Knowing and Being,* 138; *Tacit Dimension,* 82; "Science and Reality," 192, 195.

46. E.g., Polanyi, *Personal Knowledge,* 136, 187, 304.

47. Polanyi, *Personal Knowledge,* 303–4.

[personal passion] → [confident utterance] → [accredited facts]

When the knower responsibly asserts a claim to truth, passion, utterance, and facts are connected in the knower's accreditation of the facts. The brackets and arrows indicate the orientation of that commitment outward toward the world and the coherence and force of the commitment. By contrast, secession from the commitment situation, as well as representation of it from outside of commitment, looks like this:

subjective belief; declaratory sentence; alleged facts.

Polanyi argues that a subjective belief cannot be accounted for by unaccredited facts, nor vice versa. And a declaratory sentence can never be said to correspond to the facts. The implication is that only a confident utterance can be said to correspond, and what it corresponds to are accredited facts.

At this point in his argument, Polanyi cites Bertrand Russell's definition of truth as a coincidence between one's subjective belief and the actual facts. Here, he says, the "actual facts" are accredited facts and, thus, are viewed from within the commitment situation, while "subjective belief" results from having seceded from the commitment situation. It is self-contradictory, he says, to maintain confidence with respect to the one and not with respect to the other, for "it is nonsense to imply that we simultaneously both hold and do not hold the same belief."[48] The implication of all of this for Polanyi and correspondence is that, yes, there is correspondence between beliefs and facts, but that beliefs and facts both entail the same confident commitment. Thus, as noted before, truth is the external pole of belief.

It can seem, then, that Polanyian correspondence does not quite cross the gap between mind and object. Instead, it anchors on the subjective side of the chasm. But this would be to ignore or reject the very claim he is laboring to establish: that responsible personal commitment is entirely other than uncommitted subjectivity, and that the latter is, in the context of scientific research if not all of life, inaccurate and useless. An approach such as Russell's and the wider analytic tradition his approach epitomizes is actually committing a kind of contradiction—and this is part of the apparent strangeness of the correspondence theory of truth. Better to see humans as responsible to orient toward and make sense of the reality in which they are already embedded. Modern objectivism has rejected both aspects of this stance, leading to epistemic conundrums.

Because of his emphatic emphasis on the role of the personal, it has been mistakenly concluded that Polanyi is an anti-realist. But it is not the case that, in embracing the personal, Polanyi is resigning himself to idealism.

48. Ibid.

For truth, he reiterates, lies in contact with reality. It is my belief that, for Polanyi, the notion of contact replaces the notion of correspondence. We know that we have made contact with reality—grasped an aspect of reality, when we have a sense of inexhaustible, indeterminate, future manifestations.

It is apparent that Polanyi is not envisioning contact as one-to-one match between knowledge and reality. To begin with, such a match presumes that both sides of it are focal and explicit. This is impossible and undesirable. Instead, the epistemic act is rooted at both ends in responsibly embraced indeterminacy: subsidiaries at its root, indeterminate future manifestations at its farthest horizon. For Polanyi, the indeterminacy of reality and of the bearing of knowledge on reality militate against the idea of a concept's specific referral to or denotation of a piece of reality. Polanyi says that our conceptions are *intimations* of reality;[49] he does not say that they are representations of reality. Given the inexhaustibility of reality, this would be out of the question. Successful contact reveals an aspect of reality—and one pregnant with future prospects. Contact does not, therefore, claim or require its object to be exhaustively represented. The exact opposite is the case. The more profound the contact, the more inexhaustive its possibilities. Similarly, where contact is indicated by inexhaustive possibilities, the very truth claim itself is indeterminately inexhaustive. Moreover, a particular contact may be greater or lesser in scale; the accompanying IFM Effect and other tokens of contact with reality will, to some extent, be correspondingly greater or lesser. So Polanyi's idea of contact allows for greater flexibility with regard to truth—and reality.

What is really unique is that the IFM Effect indicates the presence of truth, and not also "the whole truth and nothing but the truth." Thus, as Polanyi is quick to point out, it is rare that there is not an admixture of truth and error. It is impossible to tell exactly what about a discovery sets off the IFM Effect until perhaps years later. This also explains how it is that even false assumptions can, to some extent, be fruitful—they are fruitful to the extent that they are the means to contact with some aspect of reality.[50]

Finally, another advantage of Polanyian contact is that, because truth lies in contact with reality, we may retain our respect for theories such as Copernicus', Kepler's, and Newton's, which now have been superseded. For we may say of them that they did indeed make contact with reality, and to the extent that they got hold of an aspect of reality, they were, and indeed

---

49. Polanyi, see also "Knowing and Being," in Grene, ed., *Knowing and Being*, 133.

50. Polanyi, "Science and Religion," 10-11; "Science and Man's Place in the Universe," in Woolf, ed., *Science as a Cultural Force*, 20-22. It has, for months, struck me as odd that Polanyi discussed these cases without trepidation. But now I see that the notion of truth as contact alleviates the difficulty.

are, true. Contact thus provides the understanding of truth that John Brennan expresses eloquently in his use of Polanyi in his defense, in response to Popper, of the truth of old theories. His conclusions are as follows:

> Copernicus had got hold of reality, even if his articulation of it was in so many respects archaic as well as incomplete and inaccurate.
>
> If the truth of a scientific theory be measured by its grasp of reality, the Copernican theory was true. Only an inordinate love of logical clarity or a reverential empiricism would induce one to say that Copernicus had made a *mistake*, that his theory was *false*.... Considering the indeterminacy of our comprehension of reality, consisting as it does of the vague indication of further possibilities of exploration, rather like the indication of a possible solution which one perceives in a good problem, we ought to be able to frame a concept of truth which is not so utterly dependent upon the absolute correctness of its explicit formulation and a concept of rationality which does not restrict us to formal logic and observable personal knowledge, which frees us from the sterile subjective-objective dichotomy and also gives us access to a richly textured world, takes us a fair way towards the desired goal.[51]

There is another crucial key to the whole problem of correspondence, a topic that I have reserved for the final chapters. It requires at least mention here. It is that if we postulate a gap between ourselves and the world at the outset, it will always remain impossible to cross it. But Polanyi, as will later be argued, repudiates this gap. "Why can't we check our beliefs against reality?" asks Marjorie Grene. "Not, as sceptics believe, because we can't reach out to reality, but because we're part of it."[52] Thus, it appears that the matters addressed in chapters 11 and following will have a bearing on our understanding of Polanyian truth.

One final note about Polanyi and correspondence. There is another aspect of Polanyi's account of knowing that makes sense of how it is that correspondence is a commonsensical notion. There is a kind of matching which takes place within the course of a discovery. We have seen that our tacit foreknowledge precedes the discovery, extending out in advance of our explicit knowledge as our intuition focuses on the unknown comprehensive entity and our imagination scrabbles in search of clues (whose significance can at that point be only tacitly grasped). As a result of this preceding of

---

51. Brennan, "Polanyi's Transcendence of the Distinction between Objectivity and Subjectivity," 152.

52. Grene, "Knowledge, Belief and Perception," 10.

ourselves, when the actual moment of discovery arrives, we recognize it as matching or corresponding with the standpoints and subsidiaries we have attained anticipatively. Thus, discovery comes to us with the conviction of its being true. But even here, the sense is not of an exact match so much as of something which more than confirms. This is because it also surprises us. It is also because it transforms the very clues on which we have been relying—often down to the very questions we were asking.

Is Truth Independent of Our Knowing It?

I wish now to consider a few questions that have been of major concern within the philosophy of science. The first question is this: is truth independent of the human mind and its products? This question is often expressed as being a matter of whether truth is non-epistemic or epistemic. The question has arisen because, in the more recent writings in philosophy of science, the theory-laden character of knowledge, as it has been called, has become more apparent. Scientific knowledge, and what we take to be true, appears to be based on our theories, rather than the theories being based on our information. A theory, it appears, determines to some extent what counts as a legitimate observation. A heliocentric theory, for example, causes us to discredit the apparent fact that the sun rises and sets.

Various conciliatory conceptions have been developed to describe this state of affairs—most notably, Kuhn's paradigms and Quine's background theory. Feyerabend holds an extreme form of concession, such that the successful theory turns into a rigid ideology and, as such, disqualifies the facts that disagree with it. The theory's success, he says, is therefore entirely man-made.[53] Thus, the general belief is that, as Kuhn says, there is no theory-independent way to construct what is really there. We cannot therefore speak of the truth of the theory as a whole, but instead only of intra-theoretic truth.[54]

But not all contemporary thinkers have agreed with these concessions. Popper in particular stands out. He has criticized what he dubs Kuhn's "myth of the framework."[55] The myth, he says, is that the framework (or paradigm) that is currently in control cannot be critically discussed. Popper agrees that we are all caught in a framework, but the myth is dispelled by the fact that we can break out of that framework at any time. We break out, of course,

---

53. Feyerabend, *Against Method*, 43.
54. Kuhn, *Structure of Scientific Revolutions*, 205–7.
55. Popper, "Normal Science and Its Dangers," 55–56.

Truth, in Particular Correspondence

into another framework, but the latter is a better and roomier one. Because of this, a critical discussion and comparison of frameworks is possible.

Kuhn and others have no problem with intra-theoretic truth, where what is considered true is determined within the theory. But they wish to distinguish this truth from the consideration of the truth of the background theory itself. The problem with extra-theoretic truth is the one that plagues the correspondence theory for obvious reasons: this sort of truth seems unattainable. Putnam, who, in earlier chapters of *Meaning and the Moral Sciences* had distinguished truth from warranted assertibility, in the final chapter concludes that it is not possible for our best and ideal theory to be false, conceding that truth is, after all, a matter of warranted assertibility.[56] There, he argues against what he takes to be the distinctive tenet of metaphysical realism (in contrast to his internal realism), namely, that truth is radically non-epistemic in character, that it is possible that a theory that is ideal by all human standards might be false. Putnam no longer sees that the supposition that our ideal theory might really be false is intelligible.

I will not recapitulate Putnam's argument here; let me simply note some difficulties with it. First, as John Koethe has cogently argued, Putnam's notion of an ideal theory, on which the argument turns, is problematic.[57] What Putnam's argument requires is that a theory be ideal in the sense that it is, in principle, unrevisable. But as a matter of fact, we are quite used to the ongoing supersession of theories, such that most people would never consider a particular theory ideal in the sense of being unrevisable in principle. Thus, there is no such ideal theory for the metaphysical realist to question as to its possible falsehood. Nobody presumed that there is such an ideal mapping. Whereas Koethe attacks the claim that the metaphysical realist must accept the existence of such an ideal theory, Raimo Tuomela questions whether metaphysical realists are properly represented in the first place. Dividing realist from non-realist on the basis of their acceptance or rejection of the claim that a statement might be false even though it follows from our best theory is, Tuomela says, in general, a good way to begin. But he continues:

> Yet I would take it to be part and parcel of this very same line of realist thought that at least *ultimately* scientists will learn from their errors and succeed in building up the (or a) correct theory and in finding out "how the world is" so that statements like (A) Venus might not have carbon dioxide in its atmosphere even though it follows from our theory that Venus has carbon dioxide in its atmosphere ... become *false* in the limit. Thus, contra

---

56. Putnam, *Meaning and the Moral Sciences*, 123–40.
57. Koethe, "Putnam's Argument Against Realism," 92–99.

Putnam, the realistic interpretation of connectives need not and indeed does not, entail (A)...[58]

Both Koethe's and Tuomela's arguments pick up on an unrealistic (in the everyday sense) handling of metaphysical realism by Putnam. The reality for the metaphysical realist, as for the scientist, is that the theory we consider our best at a particular time is never thought unrevisable, is always thought to be possibly false, and to the extent that it is false, is expected to be corrected in the light of future discoveries. The metaphysical realist need not fit Putnam's description in order not to be an internal realist. The implication appears to be that truth need not be determinable independently of human conceptions in order for it to be independent and objective.

Polanyi and the Theory-Ladenness of Truth

Let us see what, if anything, Polanyi has to say. To begin with, it is clear that Polanyi would grant the existence and applicability of the idea of a discovery's logical leap to a new vision of reality, theoretical frameworks, background theories, the role of all these in observation, and a lot more besides. For Polanyi developed the notions of the personal, the fiduciary, and the tacit in knowledge a decade before the time of Kuhn's *Structure*.[59] But Polanyi, by contrast, insists that these foundational structures are not arbitrary or conventional; in fact, as we shall see more clearly in the final chapters of this work, they are rooted in the world itself. How does this epistemic bedrock—a bedrock not of certainties, but of responsibly committed, participative, more-than-specifiable indwelling—affect the question of the independence of truth for Polanyi?

Polanyi does not address this question directly. However, he does state unequivocally that reality exists independently of our knowledge of it.[60] It is this independent reality on which the knower focuses in the imaginative, subsidiary efforts that ultimately generate language, discoveries, the premises of science, and his general vision of reality. Polanyi would agree that our present conceptions, be they true or false, shape what we are able to learn concerning reality: unless we expect human blood to play a crucial function in a person's physical health, we will not go looking for positive results from blood transfusions—we won't even think of trying them. Conceptions do not only function restrictively, however. Polanyi calls scientists to lean in

---

58. Tuomela, "Putnam's Realisms," 122–23.
59. See n. 49 in the previous chapter of this book.
60. Polanyi, *Personal Knowledge*, 311.

to the truth of their conceptions, and to trust conceptions that they only anticipate, in the process of research and discovery. But in both negative and positive theory-ladenness, for Polanyi, conceptions condition not truth but understanding, or growth of knowledge.

Polanyi would also affirm the existence of standards (or at least parameters) of truth—as we have seen. But we have also seen that, for him, the determining factor for truth remains whether or not contact is made with reality. If truth is a matter of contact with reality, then to that extent, truth is independent. What we take to be true we do so not on the basis of impersonal criteria or explicit determinations but on the basis of our tacit experience of anticipating indeterminate future manifestations of our claim—a criterion that transcends theoretical boundaries. That is, the manifestations could be, for example, waves, or they could be particles—the IFM Effect does not itself specify which. Of course, if the scientist is barking up the wrong tree entirely, there isn't any IFM Effect at all. Polanyi is not interested in developing a notion of intra-theoretic truth in distinction from an external truth that is impossible in principle to attain. I believe he would reject both alternatives in favor of the more important claim that truth is a matter of contact with reality and, as such, is personally appraised. Explicit determination is not possible, but what is entailed by this is not a conventionalism, but rather a more profound appraisal of truth on the basis of what are legitimate personal and subsidiary factors. Polanyi's whole purpose in writing is to legitimate our holding firmly to what we believe to be true in spite of the fact that our beliefs may turn out to be false. We can never be certain of what we take to be true, and truth comes to us in an unknown quantity, admixed with error, but this does not rule out the ultimate independence of truth. In fact, it displays that truth is not less but more independent than mainline epistemological approaches have led us to presume.

Is There a Single Goal of Truth?

Related to the question of the independence of truth is the matter of whether there is a single goal of truth toward which science must move if it is to be successful. Once again, the problem is posed by Kuhn, and he characterizes the goal as a single, exhaustive, unchanging, attainable account of the way things really are.[61] We have discussed the matter of progress in science in chapter 8; here we are concerned with the goal of truth in particular. Such a goal is crucial to Popper's verisimilitude.[62] But Kuhn believes it to be il-

---

61. Kuhn, *Structure of Scientific Revolutions*, 170–71.
62. Popper, *Conjectures and Refutations*, 229.

lusive in principle. First, there are the related problems of correspondence and independence: there appears to be no way to transcend one's epistemic structures in order to see that one is getting any closer to such a goal. What is more, the history of science fails to indicate that this sort of progressive approximation is actually occurring.[63] And then there is the problem of alternative, incompatible descriptions, the existence of which makes the idea of a single goal appear unlikely. The alternative for Kuhn and other contemporaries is to acknowledge other sorts of goals, which will serve to provide a sense of, and to measure, progress. Kuhn wishes to speak of progress *from* rather than progress *toward*—evolution from primitive beginnings with respect to our ability to meet certain standards: accuracy of prediction, number of problems solved, simplicity, scope, and compatibility with other specialties.[64] Quine's substituted goal is a pragmatic one also: our theories must improve in their efficiency in communication and prediction.[65] These and others conceive of the ultimate goal in terms of the survival of the human race.[66]

Polanyi and the Goal of Truth

Now, as far as can be told, Polanyi retains *knowledge of reality* as the goal of scientific endeavors. However, he could hardly agree to the Kuhnian description of the goal of truth. Reality, Polanyi believes, is inexhaustive. What is more, it is ever-changing, mainly because of the existence of centers of individuality, the most notable and influential of which are human beings. Humans not only change reality and the scope of knowledge by dropping bombs and polluting the environment, they also invent instruments and create ideas that can revolutionize the domain of our inquiries. For example, the field of oil shale research was probably nonexistent before the invention of the automobile and the recent demand for fuel in the face of high foreign prices. The point is that under the circumstances of actual life, it is absurd to characterize our epistemic goal as being exhaustive and unchanging.

Secondly, on Polanyi's interpretation of knowledge, an exhaustive account is in principle impossible to attain by virtue of the necessarily tacit

---

63. See also Feyerabend, *Against Method*.
64. Kuhn, *Structure of Scientific Revolutions*, 170–71, 205–7.
65. Quine, *Word and Object*, 24–25; *From A Logical Point of View*, 79; *Ways of Paradox*, 211; Hauptli, "Quinean Relativism," 399–400.
66. Quine, *Word and Object*, 20; Skagestad, "Pragmatic Realism" 527–28; Toulmin, *Foresight and Understanding*, 111; Margolis, "Cognitive Issues," 374–76; "Pragmatism, Transcendental Arguments, and the Technological," in Durbin and Rapp, eds., *Philosophy and Technology*, 4–6; "Pragmatism Without Foundations," 9–10.

roots belonging to all explicit knowledge. Thus, the sort of goal Kuhn delineates is illusive in principle. But this does not mean that we are left in a morass of subjectivity or even of pragmaticity. For substantial understanding is possible, as would seem to be the implication of Polanyi's continual call for the endorsement of the knower's tacit, personal epistemic skills. We can never be certain, but we can be confident despite the fallibility of our skills and of our truth claims. This substantial knowledge is what should be our motivating goal. A pragmatic goal would be spurned by Polanyi as so much pseudo-substitution. Survival—orientation in one's surroundings—would not be quite so offensive, I believe, although out of the question as an exclusive goal.

Are There Infallible or Indubitable Truths?

A third question concerning truth in philosophy of science is whether or not there are any indubitable or infallible truths. In many ways, this is no longer a live question, especially in the wake of Quine's criticism of the analytic-synthetic distinction. What is more, the history of science testifies rather to the fallibility of our knowledge, for claims that were once held sacred and impregnable have, over the course of time and further discovery, turned out to be false. Thus, there is a general rejection of the possibility of infallible truths and of the related epistemic structure known as foundationalism. Yet, as Joseph Margolis has demonstrated, foundationalism can and has reappeared in altered and subtle forms. Such cryptofoundationalism, he claims, remains even in the works of Quine and Kuhn, specifically evidenced in the references to contact with nature.[67] However, the compelling metaphor at the heart of foundationalism causes us to ask, if there are no foundations, no certainties upon which to build, how is reliable knowledge possible? How can knowledge grow? Are we left with no recourse but rather with relativism?

Polanyi and Infallible Truths

The initial message of *Personal Knowledge* is the illegitimacy of the ideal of certainty, the rejection of the possibility of infallible truths and of strict, explicit procedures. Thus, to this extent, Polanyi is in harmony with much of contemporary thought. Yet, I believe that there is a foundation for knowledge

---

67. Margolis, "Pragmatism Without Foundations," 1–9; "Cognitive Issues," 377–78.

for Polanyi, though it does not consist of indubitable pieces of factual or tautologous knowledge. Consider the following extended quotation:

> The anti-metaphysical analysis of science assumes that the logical foundation of empirical knowledge must be capable of definition by explicit rules. While the difficulties of this enterprise have not gone unnoticed, the reluctance to abandon it in principle still seems universal. My own attempts to acknowledge tacit powers of personal judgment as the decisive organon of discovery and the ultimate criterion of scientific truth, have been opposed by describing these agencies as psychological, not logical, in character. But this distinction is not explained by my critics. Is an act of perception which sees an object in a way that assimilates it to past instances of the same kind, a psychological process or a logical inference? We have seen that it can be mistaken and its results be false; and it certainly has a considerable likelihood of being true. To me this suggests that it is a logical process of inference even though it is not explicit. In any case, to perceive things rightly is certainly part of the process of scientific inquiry and to hold perceptions to be right underlies the holding of scientific propositions to be true. And, if, in consequence, we must accept the veridical powers of perception as the roots of empirical science, we cannot reasonably refuse to accept other tacit veridical processes having a similar structure.[68]

My point here is that Polanyi does not deny the existence of a logical foundation for knowledge. His position is that it is false to say that the foundation is capable of definition by explicit rules. The heart of the Polanyian message is that all knowledge is rooted in the tacit, the subsidiary, the personal. This foundation consists of both acts and knowledge: personal acts, ways of going about knowing, tacit powers, prearticulate understanding, latent knowledge, tacitly held premises, and a vision of reality. The realm of the tacit, at least in regard to these latter items, changes and develops with events of discovery and learning. But a dynamic foundation always remains and in fact grows. It can never be totally erased or even diminished by subjecting it to explicit analysis. In fact, rightly cherished expertise just is an extensive and dynamic subsidiary foundation. Polanyi's foundation is not the same sort of foundation we ordinarily think of in connection with Descartes in that we do not try to reason from it explicitly. We do not even focus on it. Our focus is rather on the world, the problem at hand, and the

---

68. Polanyi, "Tacit Knowing: Its Bearing," in Grene, ed., *Knowing and Being*, 172–73. See also an excellent passage in "Logic and Psychology," 27.

foundation is utilized and developed by the efforts of a subsidiarily functioning imagination. Yet, the tacit component is foundational in the sense that it is the *sine qua non* for all knowledge; it is that in which all knowledge is rooted.

Of course, Polanyi's foundation also differs from the classical one by virtue of the fact that infallibility or indubitability are not claimed for it. Note in the quotation above that tacit inference can be mistaken even as it can prove true. Polanyi says, ". . . again, in accrediting these passions with the power to recognize the truth, we do not assume their infallibility—since no rule of scientific procedure is certain of finding the truth and avoiding error—but we accept their competence."[69] Tacit knowing is fallible but nevertheless reliable. We are not left with relativism as our only recourse. What is more, I do not believe that Margolis's cryptofoundationalism appropriately applies to Polanyian epistemology. His is neither a foundationalism nor a non-foundationalism, but rather a unique and viable third alternative.

Is Truth Unchanging?

A fourth related question: should truth be expected to hold for eternity? Again, the problem results from the experience of scientific development: things that have, in the past, been held to be unquestionable have turned out to be false. This has led to the rejection of the belief that knowledge grows by accretion. Most likely, it is partly responsible for Popper's claims that a theory can never be said to be true, but can only be either ruled as false or considered still not proven false. This leaves Popper, when it comes to verisimilitude, comparing the relative truth of two false theories—which Kuhn finds absurd.[70] The problem concerning the apparent non-eternity of truth presumably leads either to skepticism or to subjective definitions of truth.

Polanyi on Truth as Unchanging

But the whole purpose of *Personal Knowledge*, as has been noted repeatedly in this chapter, is to make it possible for the knower to hold firmly to what he believes to be true even though it may turn out to be false. Polanyi emphasizes time and again the enormous risks that are necessarily involved in any epistemic endeavor. And where there is risk, there is bound to be

---

69. Polanyi, *Personal Knowledge*, 173; see also 143, 214; *Tacit Dimension*, 78.

70. See Brennan, "Polanyi's Transcendence of the Subject-Object Distinction," 146–47.

failure. But it is the old ghost of the possibility of certainty that makes us feel uncomfortable with the notion that knowledge can be fallible. But when we stop to consider it, we realize that fallible knowledge is our stock in trade. Truth that cannot prove false is impossible because of the tacit foundations of all truth and also because of the ever-changing and inexhaustive character of reality. But the point has been made that the possibility of being mistaken does not invalidate knowledge or the skill of knowing. It does sound paradoxical to say that truth can turn out to be false, but to Polanyi's way of thinking, this is because it is a misrepresentation of the case. Truth, he has said, is always going to be indeterminate, because truth lies in bearing on reality. Thus, its implications are indeterminate. Our epistemic endeavors, as a result of our tacit abilities, do bring us into contact with reality, and thus enable us to lay hold of truth. Our experience of the IFM Effect bears witness to successful contact. But that we lay hold of truth does not mean that we lay hold of the *whole* truth and *nothing but* the truth—this matter has been addressed before. The upshot of the fact that truth is indeterminate is that it is not contradictory to claim truth despite the possible admixture of error.

Is Truth a Prerequisite for Knowledge?

One final question: should truth be considered a prerequisite for knowledge? The standard analysis of knowledge—i.e., knowledge is justified true belief—requires truth, truth being that which distinguishes knowledge from belief. But because of the difficulties ascertaining what is true, at least two thinkers have proposed an alternative.

The first, Harold Brown, begins by distinguishing two senses of truth.[71] "$Truth_1$" is truth in the absolute and traditional sense of correct description of reality. Brown says that $truth_1$ "denotes the goal for which scientists strive in constructing theories, but it has no relevance for the evaluation of theories since theories provide the only access we have to reality." The truth or falsity of actual theories must be discussed in terms of "$truth_2$": any proposition that is part of the present body of scientific knowledge is $true_2$. Thus, as Brown sees it, he hereby maintains the traditional link between truth and knowledge; but now, rather than knowledge being defined in terms of truth, truth is defined in terms of knowledge. Such an adjustment takes care of several of the problems we have considered, though not necessarily in a Polanyian way.

---

71. Brown, *Perception, Theory and Commitment*, 153–54.

Marjorie Grene, in her Andrew W. Mellon lecture at Tulane University, provides a readable and cogent assessment of the traditional distinction between knowledge and belief and the justified true belief model.[72] She argues that the most difficult problem with the formula is not really justification, the Gettier discussion notwithstanding. The problem is rather with "true," because of the elusiveness of "a way to check our beliefs against reality and find out, once and for all, whether they *are* true." Now Grene's message, at this point, is very much *not* a skeptical or idealist one but, in fact, a realist one, the possibility of which will be made clearer later on in this work. However, her proposal is that we drop truth and define knowledge as justified belief. Knowledge, rather than being based on truth, is based on the *hope of truth*. She picks up Polanyi's phrase in saying that when we claim a proposition to be true, we do so with universal intent, as she says, "in confidence that anyone with the same evidence and the same standard of objectivity would make the same assertion—and would be correct in doing so."

Polanyi on Truth as Prerequisite to Knowledge

Do either of these positions represent a Polanyian answer to the question? There are some ways in which Polanyi would concur with Brown and others in which he would not. Brown differs from Grene as well as from Polanyi in failing to take into account the basic notion that the known is rooted in reality to begin with—an idea the discussion of which I have been reserving for chapter 11.[73] To a large extent, we must all agree that what we take to be true is, in general, coextensive with what we consider to be the body of scientific knowledge at a particular time. But Polanyi feels no need to emphasize this. Bolstered by his confidence in the enormous tacit veridical powers of the knower, Polanyi emphasizes instead the discovery of, and the criteria by which we recognize, truth, with all the qualifications previously noted. Brown develops his notion of "$true_2$" by saying that, in the case of competing theories espoused by different groups, the one theory is $true_2$ for one group, and the other is $true_2$ for the other group. Relativism, Brown says, is not so bad if there is no absolutist alternative.[74] But Polanyi rejects relativism because of the assertive and fiduciary character of truth claims; the notion of a claim's being "true for so-and-so," as opposed to being "true

---

72. Grene, "Knowledge, Belief and Perception," 1–20.

73. Thus, it is probably the case that Polanyi would disagree with Brown's claim that theories furnish us our only access to the world.

74. Brown, *Perception, Theory and Commitment*, 152–53.

for me," is nonsensical.[75] I can recognize only one truth: the domain of what I hold to be true; and this is not a relativism.

We can legitimately expect Grene's ideas to be generally in harmony with and explicative of Polanyi's. But there is at least a difference of emphasis here. Polanyi does not drop truth out of his epistemological considerations. Truth continues to exist in successful contact with reality, indeterminate as it is, and propositional claims are true to the extent that they reveal aspects of reality. However, the fiduciary aspect of knowledge binds the holding of truth to belief. What Polanyi would say is that truth is, at least proximally, justified belief. He has, in fact, characterized truth as the external pole of belief. Whatever we assert to be true is so asserted and held only within the framework of our commitment. Truth, then, is not so much defined in terms of knowledge, in contrast to Brown, as it is in terms of belief. And, contra Grene, belief does not entirely replace or dispense with truth but maintains it as its external pole.

In Conclusion

Michael Polanyi did deeply consider and respond to some key discussions of truth and correspondence in his time. He did so because they represented telltale anchor points of an overall vision of knowing and of science, which he was concerned to reorient. He felt it critical to the survival of science and of Western culture to do this.

In this chapter, we have seen that Polanyi neither characterizes truth as a property of statements, nor as redundant. It is appropriate to say that he sees it as responsible commitment with universal intent. He resolves some of the characteristic conundrums of the mainline approach by insisting that we never step out of or beyond the commitment framework. In this, his stance is performative, comparing favorably to such theories of truth. But it has its distinctive Polanyi cast. It is no mere performance; it is a *credo* or responsible profession.

Truth, for Polanyi, is always profession.[76] But it is never only profession. Truth involves participative indwelling in logically unspecifiable subsidiaries—which I will consider more fully in later chapters. But truth is, with primacy, about contact with reality. In the event of truth, previous anticipations are "confirmed" precisely because they are transformed, caught up in a larger-than-imagined reality, in which fresh vistas and indeterminate

75. Polanyi, *Personal Knowledge*, 316.
76. This is a way of characterizing it which I have developed in recent years (Meek, *Loving to Know*, 74).

future prospects more than "correspond." Correspondence, if what is meant is a mere one-to-one matching of thought and reality, proves inadequate, not because it is too high of a hope, but because it falls short of actuality. Thus, Polanyi's understanding of truth can be said to reflect the distinctive vision of his epistemology in its entirety. It does so in a way that restores the knower to something more like communion with the yet-to-be-known.[77]

---

77. This is my own language in covenant epistemology (Meek, *Loving to Know*, 465–68, and throughout).

10

Polanyi and Contemporary Realism

The consensus has been that the recent interest in delineating and defending scientific realism has come about as a reaction to three things. First, it comes as a general response to the anti-metaphysical mindset of the early twentieth century. Second, it has grown in response to Alfred Tarski's semantic theory of truth.[1] On the one hand, some, like Popper, saw in Tarski's work an endorsement of correspondence and, thus, a boost to realism. Others, according to Putnam, took his work to have reduced truth to the level of tautology, which they found objectionable. Thirdly, realism has responded to what have been called the *Weltanschaungen* analyses of Kuhn and Feyerabend.[2] Whatever the motivation, the fact is that a variety of fresh analyses of realism have sprung up in recent years. Perhaps the main issue—for them, as well as for our purposes here—is the most basic one of deciding what sort of realism, what specific realist theses, are in this sophisticated philosophical age defensible, and then of course, defending them.

Realism's opponents have been understood to include *positivism* (any sort of anti-metaphysical bent); *conventionalism* (where truth is merely a matter of mutual agreement); *instrumentalism* (the position that theories

---

1. See ch. 9.

2. MacKinnon, "Introduction," in MacKinnon, ed., *Problem of Scientific Realism*, 21–22; Popper, *Conjectures and Refutations*, 27; Putnam, *Meaning and the Moral Sciences*, Introduction; Folse, "Belief and the New Scientific Realism," 37–58. Folse, in connection with this, references heavily Suppe, ed., *Structure of Scientific Theories*, a book that, regrettably, I was never able to obtain. Also, see ch. 8 for more on Kuhn and Feyerabend.

and theoretical entities are valuable and correct only insofar as they are useful in the course of scientific research); *phenomenalism* (the belief that our domain of knowledge is restricted to sensory appearances); *idealism* (where truth and even reality are shaped by the mind's constructs); and *constructivism* (the belief that the pervasiveness of theory-dependence entails that our knowledge is a result of construction rather than discovery). Many of these categories, of course, overlap. In calling these "opponents" of realism, I do not mean to overlook the fact that attempts have been made to reconcile some of them, particularly positivism, idealism, and constructivism, with realism by developing modified forms. Whether such attempts at reconciliation have been successful and whether they have truly preserved the essence of realism is, of course, debatable.

My purpose in this chapter is not to take on all of these issues in the attempt to solve the problems of recent debate, but rather to place Polanyi's realism in the context of contemporary realism. In order to do this, I will first compile and define various realist theses put forth in current literature. This accomplished, I will reexamine Polanyi's realism to see which of these theses he holds and which he doesn't, in hopes of gaining a fuller perspective on his message.[3]

While matters of progress and truth, the topics of earlier chapters in this part of the book, bear critically on questions of realism, this chapter drives to the heart of the matter itself—and to the heart of this consideration of Polanyi's contact with reality. Once again, I believe, this foray will showcase the distinctiveness of Polanyian realism and its value for life and thought.

Versions of Realism in the Contemporary Discussion

Scholastic Realism

Let us begin, not with a contemporary thesis, but with a brief mention of a modern-era form of scientific realism: what E. A. MacKinnon refers to as scholastic realism, or mechanism.[4] Realism from Aristotle to Newton, MacKinnon believes, was characterized by the claim that real laws exist in

---

3. My engagement of contemporary realism is updated in chs. 12 and 13. There, we will see that several thinkers engaging the matter around the 1980s, as represented in this chapter, along with their proposals remain very much in the current discussion.

4. MacKinnon, "Introduction," in MacKinnon, ed., *Problem of Scientific Realism*, 12–19.

nature. The task of science was to uncover and mirror these laws in the laws of physics, etc. The deposition of the Newtonian theory has, according to MacKinnon, done much to threaten the propriety of the claim of scholastic realism. Yet, we may glean from its phrases hints of doctrines being revived and/or debated today, such as the independence of reality, the viability of a correspondence theory of truth, and the success of theoretical terms in referring to trans-theoretical entities.

Scientific Realism

"Scientific realism" appears to encompass a plurality of theses. Consider the following definitions. The first is John Worrall's: "According to scientific realism, scientific theories are to be taken at face value: despite their 'transcendence' of the empirical data, they are to be taken as attempted descriptions of the universe which are true or false in the usual, correspondence sense."[5] Bas Van Fraassen defines realism thus: "Science aims to give us, in its theories, a literally true story of what the world is like; and acceptance of a scientific theory involves the belief that it is true."[6]

Richard Boyd's formulation spells out four theses of scientific realism, at least three of which are implicit in the preceding:

> By "scientific realism" philosophers typically understand a doctrine which we may think of as embodying four central themes:
>
> i. "Theoretical terms" in scientific theories (i.e., non-observational terms) should be thought of as putatively referring expressions; scientific theories should be interpreted "realistically."
>
> ii. Scientific theories, interpreted realistically, are confirmable *and in fact often confirmed* as approximately true by ordinary scientific evidence interpreted in accordance with ordinary methodological standards.
>
> iii. The historical progress of mature sciences is largely a matter of successively more accurate approximations to the truth about both observable and unobservable phenomena. Later theories typically build upon the (observational and theoretical) knowledge embodied in previous theories.

---

5. Worrall, "Scientific Realism and Scientific Change," 201.
6. Musgrave, "Constructive Empiricism *Versus* Scientific Realism," 262.

iv. The reality that scientific theories describe is largely independent of our thoughts or theoretical commitments.[7]

The first of these four theses captures the meat of Worrall's definition: theoretical entities and scientific theories should be taken as descriptions of the world, as referring to the world. The second affirms that theories' approximate truth is confirmed through ordinary scientific work, a claim dear to Boyd and to at least the "early" Hilary Putnam, as we will see presently. Boyd does not mention correspondence as the realist understanding of truth, as Worrall does, and also Putnam. Putnam says, as noted previously, that whatever else realists believe, they typically believe in a correspondence theory of truth.[8]

Boyd's third thesis concerns continuity and progress in science and the possibility of increasingly more accurate approximations to the truth: concepts that we have discussed at length in earlier chapters. Scientific progress involves and confirms approximation of truth. Worrall's and Van Fraassen's definitions do not mention this, but we have already seen that, even if scientific progress is not essential to the definition of scientific realism, it is certainly intimately related. For Putnam, convergence and the principle of charity alone can serve to block the anti-realist's metainduction that "just as no term used in the science of more than fifty (or whatever) years ago referred, so it will turn out that no term used now (except maybe observation terms, if there are such) refers."[9] Convergence and the principle of charity allow for a conception of science as a succession of more accurate approximations to the truth.

Boyd's fourth thesis is what many take to be the heart of realism per se, to the extent that it can be distinguished from scientific realism. Edward MacKinnon says that "realism, in the simplest sense of the term, is a belief that the world exists as known independently of our knowing it."[10] Joseph Margolis defines "the original realist thesis" in the context of the distinction between realism and idealism as "the idea that material objects exist independently of, without any dependence on, mind—in effect, independently of any conditions of cognition."[11] Note, however, that Boyd's thesis is, by contrast, somewhat qualified: he says that reality is *largely* independent of our thoughts.

7. Boyd, "On the Current Status of the Issue of Scientific Realism," 1–2.
8. Putnam, *Meaning and the Moral Sciences*, 18.
9. Ibid., 25.
10. MacKinnon, "Introduction," in MacKinnon, ed., *Problem of Scientific Realism*, 39.
11. Margolis, "Cognitive Issues," 373.

Part 1: Early Consideration of Contact with Reality

Goldman's Realist Theses

Alan Goldman, whose arguments we have examined in earlier chapters, delineates two theses of realism: what he calls a weaker and a stronger version of realism:

> R_1 There is a physical world not reducible to classes of experiences or appearances, or to regularities within experience.
>
> R_2 The physical world consists of entities with (some) properties that are independent of their characterization within any conceptual scheme or theory.[12]

According to Goldman, R_1, the weaker of the two, is simply a denial of phenomenalism, and is almost universally accepted today. R_2 requires further specification. Two claims are implicit in R_2, he says. The first is "that the world is structured or individuated apart from any structure or classification we impose"; "objects themselves and their properties remain unaffected by changes in our theories or ways of describing them."[13] Secondly, "a thing's having a property is not always a matter merely of its satisfying our perceptual or experiential criteria for its having that property." Thus, "the relation between our being justified according to some theories or language in ascribing manifest properties in light of certain experiences, and the ascription's being true, is contingent." A correspondence theory of truth is therefore a necessary (though not a sufficient) condition of R_2. The truth of an empirical statement, Goldman says, does depend upon the meanings of its terms, but the point of R_2 is that it always depends upon more than that. Alternatively, R_1 and R_2 imply that all our beliefs could be false, or that they could be true though not warranted by our current theory. R_1, on the other hand, can be maintained along with a coherence or warranted assertibility theory of truth, in terms of which it makes no sense to think that all our beliefs could be false. R_2, Goldman says, is increasingly rejected today, though he writes for the purpose of defending it, as we shall see.

R_1 does not bear a resemblance to any of Boyd's theses, except to the extent that it is a weaker version of R_2: R_2 resembles Boyd's fourth thesis. As we have noted earlier, Goldman demonstrates that, in actuality, neither causal theories of reference nor the issue of convergence bears a logical relationship to realism. Thus, to the extent that Boyd intends these concepts

---

12. Goldman, "Realism," 175–76.

13. Compare with Margolis, "Cognitive Issues," 373: Margolis says that the irresistible corollary of the original realist thesis is that the independent world has a determinate structure of its own. This is probably what Margolis thinks that the idealist objects to, as opposed to the original realist thesis.

to be implicit in theses (i) and (iii), Goldman would reject them as being definitive of realism.

Merrill's Forms of Realism

Yet another categorization of forms of realism is offered by G. H. Merrill. He distinguishes semantic, epistemic, and metaphysical realism as follows:

> *Metaphysical Realism*: The entities postulated by a (good or acceptable) scientific theory really exist. Alternatively: theoretical terms of science denote actually existing entities.
>
> *Semantic Realism*: We must interpret scientific theories realistically—i.e., we must take the theoretical terms of science to function as denoting terms.
>
> *Epistemic Realism*: To accept a theory is to believe that it is true, to believe that its terms denote existing entities. Alternatively: to have good reason for holding a theory is to have good reason for holding that the entities postulated by the theory really exist.[14]

Merrill proceeds to explore the logical relationships between these three—certainly not a simple task. Instrumentalism, he says, is the rejection of all three forms of realism. What is more, it turns out that a rejection of semantic realism requires rejecting both epistemic and metaphysical realism as well. Merrill writes to contest a claim by Dudley Shapere that the acceptance of semantic realism requires the acceptance of the others as well. Metaphysical realism, it is clear, concerns the actual existence of the entities in question. Semantic realism, by contrast, Merrill claims, does not require a theory-transcendent sense of the word "exists." Rudolf Carnap, for all his distinction between internal and external questions, is a semantic realist. Existence may be relative to the theory at hand. Now, epistemic realism is apparently meant to represent the position held by Wilfrid Sellars. But what Merrill says about epistemic realism renders the category far from clear. My sum of what he says is that the logical affinities of this form of realism vary with the sense given to the word, "exists," contained in the definition. If, when we accept a theory, we believe that its terms denote actually existing entities, then epistemic realism stands or falls with metaphysical realism. However, it is possible to interpret it along the lines of a semantic realism, taking existence in the theory-relative internal sense; in this case, epistemic realism does not stand or fall with metaphysical realism. But interpreted in this fashion, Merrill says, the thesis devolves into somewhat of

---

14. Merrill, "Three Forms of Realism," 229–35.

a triviality. As far as I am concerned, if the category of epistemic realism can vary in its logical status so dramatically with the various interpretations of a component concept, then the real issue is the distinction involved in that component concept. The three-way delineation of realism devolves into a two-way delineation, the real distinction lying between semantic and metaphysical realism. However, to return briefly to Merrill's critique of Shapere, beginning with the assumption of semantic realism, Shapere must and indeed does attempt to specify the meaning of the word "exists" in such a way that, in the end, it has a trans-theoretic sense. This he must do if he is to demonstrate that semantic realism implies metaphysical realism. However, the specification that he offers is in many respects amenable to construal as internal statements, but in another respect is question-begging. Thus, Shapere fails in his attempt to show that semantic realism logically implies metaphysical realism. Merrill, in conclusion, hails semantic realism as an "anti-realist" alternative to instrumentalism and to positivism. Thus, oddly, and perhaps tellingly, semantic realism is anti-realist.

Merrill's formulation of semantic realism is akin to Boyd's first thesis, at least as it is written; it is possible that Boyd intends or himself is committed to something more substantial, i.e., to a trans-theoretic notion of existence.[15] Indeed, the notion of independence that he introduces in the fourth thesis clearly indicates that this last is the case. For the fourth thesis, by virtue of its relationship to a correspondence theory of truth, noted by Goldman, falls in line with metaphysical realism as defined by Merrill. Goldman's R_2 is, thus, akin to metaphysical realism. I do not believe, however, that Merrill's formulation is identical with Boyd's and Goldman's, most notably because it fails to mention the notion of reality's independence of human conception. Any formulation which includes this concept thereby stands opposed to idealism. Merrill mentions phenomenalism as an opponent of metaphysical realism, similarly to Goldman; he also mentions, of course, theory-relative interpretation of what it means to exist. But he does not mention idealism as an opponent. Thus, it may be incorrect to identify Merrill's metaphysical realism with Goldman's R_2 or with Boyd's fourth thesis.

---

15. Merrill's semantic realism also appears to be the same thing as MacKinnon's "functional realism": MacKinnon, "Introduction," in MacKinnon, ed., *Problem of Scientific Realism*, 57–58.

Putnam's Empirical Realism

Finally, I wish to examine terms introduced by Hilary Putnam and various other proponents, specifically, internal realism, empirical realism, and pragmatic realism. I will also examine Putnam's definition of metaphysical realism. Putnam is noted most prominently for his empirical realism. "Without a doubt," Margolis says, "Hilary Putnam's account represents the most sustained effort to date to construe realism as confirmed on empirical grounds."[16] Indeed, empirical realism is not so much another form of realism; it stands rather for the claim that realism is confirmable and confirmed empirically. What renders realism empirical is, apparently, two-fold. First, Putnam says the following: "That science succeeds in making many true predictions, devising better ways of controlling nature, etc., is an undoubted empirical fact. If realism is an explanation of this fact, realism must itself be an over-arching scientific *hypothesis*. And realists have often embraced this idea, and proclaimed that realism is an empirical hypothesis."[17]

Realism thus explains the success and progress of science. Peter Skagestad, on the basis of this passage, concludes the following: "The empirical purport of the realist hypothesis is this: by explaining past scientific progress, the hypothesis predicts further progress. Should scientific progress come to a halt, this hypothesis would be empirically refuted. . . . Any evidence for this metainduction [i.e., the one noted earlier] will count as evidence against realism, which thus turns out to be indeed an empirical hypothesis."[18]

The other sense in which realism is empirical is revealed in Putnam's espousal of Boyd's claims:

> Boyd tries to spell out realism as an over-arching empirical hypothesis by means of two principles:
>
> 1. Terms in a mature science typically refer.
>
> 2. The laws of a theory belonging to a mature science are typically approximately true.
>
> What he attempts to show in his essay is that scientists act as they do because they *believe* (1) and (2), and that their strategy works because (1) and (2) are true. In fine, my knowledge of the truth of (1) and (2) enables me to restrict the class of

---

16. Margolis, "Cognitive Issues," 379.

17. Putnam, *Meaning and the Moral Sciences*, 19.

18. Skagestad, "Pragmatic Realism," 529. Skagestad does not take cognizance of Putnam's own note to this passage, in which he states that he had previously demonstrated why belief in the external world cannot be a *hypothesis*.

candidate-theories I have to consider and thereby increases my chance of success.[19]

Realism is empirically confirmed, therefore, first by virtue of its capacity to explain the success and progress of science, and second by its superiority in increasing chances of success in the laboratory.

Putnam's Pragmatic Realism

Especially in this latter sense, it becomes apparent why Skagestad, at least, refers to Putnam's views as pragmatic realism. Here, once again, we do not have in pragmatic realism a different form of realism but rather a reference to the kind of argument by means of which realism is established. We may in addition see it as an espousal of semantic and epistemic realism for pragmatic reasons—as opposed to metaphysical commitments. Putnam's realism is pragmatic realism because it adequately explains scientific success, and because it proves a more fruitful hypothesis when it comes to singling out the most likely candidate-theories.

MacKinnon also develops a pragmatic realism, calling it analytic pragmatism. But analytic pragmatism also speaks of more than simply a certain kind of argumentation for realism. It sounds very much like Quine: "Both common-sense realism and the functional realism operative within the scientific tradition are pre-critical. They are based on the ontic commitments and the conceptualization of reality operative within a linguistic framework and on the pragmatic decision, whether implicit or explicit, to accept such a framework as the basis for further development. The questions considered are internal, in Carnap's sense, rather than external."[20] (Putnam's position, for similar reasons, is also known as internal realism.) MacKinnon goes on to say that it is a further external question whether our ontic commitments or any other system actually represents reality as it exists independently of our knowing it. Thus, MacKinnon's analytical pragmatism is of a piece with Merrill's anti-realist semantic realism and his distinction between "actually exists" and "exists" in its theory-relative construal.

---

19. Putnam, *Meaning and the Moral Sciences*, 20–21. The reference is to Boyd, "Realism, Underdetermination and a Causal Theory of Evidence," 1–12.

20. MacKinnon, "Introduction," in MacKinnon, ed., *Problem of Scientific Realism*, 58–66.

Putnam and Metaphysical Realism

This brings us to a consideration of Putnam's distinction between internal and metaphysical realism. First, let me say that I do not believe that it is at all clear in the early lectures of *Meaning and the Moral Sciences* that Putnam considers empirical realism to be internal realism. Here, I concur with John Koethe and others who believe that "Realism and Reason" comes as a rather substantial retraction of Putnam's earlier claims.[21] "Empirical" realism, as I have said, I take to refer to a particular sort of argument for realism with little if any reference as to which form of realism it is an argument for. The same is the case for pragmatic realism in Skagestad's and presumably Putnam's sense. Thus, Putnam's identification of empirical realism with internal realism in his last essay comes as a surprise. Internal realism, as Putnam develops it, falls into line with those forms of realism in which the meaning of "exists" is intra-theoretically determined, as per Merrill and MacKinnon, Carnap and Quine. What distinguishes metaphysical realism, according to Putnam, is that a determinate relation of reference must exist between terms in our language and objects or pieces of the actual world, and that the world is independent of any particular conceptualization we might have of it.[22] The key consequence of metaphysical realism, Putnam says, is that for it truth is radically non-epistemic. I have already discussed in chapter 8 some of the problems with Putnam's rejection of metaphysical realism. Let us simply note here how Putnam's representation of it accords with Goldman's R_2, Boyd's fourth thesis, and Merrill's metaphysical realism. The world's utter independence of our representation of it brings Putnam's representation of it in line with Goldman's R_2 and Boyd's fourth thesis, although Boyd, as we have noted, takes the radical edge off of the independence thesis. Putnam, like Goldman, picks up on the possible falsehood of even our ideal theory. Correspondence is obviously a feature, as is the main characteristic of Merrill's version: that our terms denote actually existing entities—as Putnam says, pieces of THE WORLD. Thus, Putnam's version of metaphysical realism appears to collect up all the theses of realism that there are to collect. It is realism in its most unqualified form.

It may be helpful to note, in conclusion to this survey of forms of realism, that Putnam distinguishes this metaphysical realism from two additional forms of realism. First, he distinguishes it from "the mere belief that there *is* an ideal theory"—which he takes to be the form of Peirce's realism. Second, it is to be distinguished from the even weaker claim "that

---

21. Koethe, "Review of Meaning and the Moral Sciences," 460.
22. Putnam, *Meaning and the Moral Sciences*, 125.

an ideal theory is a regulative ideal presupposed by the notions 'true' and 'objective' as they have classically been understood."[23] This last sounds very much to me like the kind of interpretation that Alasdair MacIntyre gives to realism.[24] It may prove helpful to keep these distinctions in mind.

The Form of Polanyi's Realism

Now, the task is, to the extent that it is possible, to assess the nature of Polanyi's realism in the light of the categories delineated in the first part of this chapter. This is a challenge, since he uses few, if any of these terms. The concepts, however, may be gleaned, sometimes constructed, out of his own particular pattern of thought. Perhaps the problem is not so much that he is a realist as it is that he assumes his realist position and does not see that it is necessary to defend it. That is, Polanyi does not defend realism except against the anti-metaphysicians, the positivists.[25]

Scientific Laws Actually Exist in Nature

Beginning, then, with MacKinnon's scholastic realism, let us note that Polanyi is committed to the thesis that real laws exist in nature. Consider the following: "To hold a natural law to be true is to believe that its presence may reveal itself in yet unknown and perhaps yet unthinkable consequences; it is to believe that natural laws are features of a reality which as such will continue to bear consequences inexhaustibly."[26] To hold a discovery to be true "is to believe that it refers to no chance configuration of things, but to a persistent connection of certain features, a connection which, being real, will yet manifest itself in numberless ways, inexhaustibly."[27] And "A true physical theory is therefore believed to be no mere mathematical relation between observed data, but to represent an aspect of reality, which may yet manifest itself inexhaustibly in the future."[28]

---

23. Ibid.

24. MacIntyre, "Objectivity in Morality and Objectivity in Science."

25. Consider, among many other passages, the opening paragraphs of "Science and Reality." Polanyi defends realism by demonstrating science's commitment to reality throughout the history of discovery.

26. Polanyi, "Logic of Tacit Inference," in Grene, ed., *Knowing and Being*, 138; *Science, Faith and Society*, 10.

27. Polanyi, "The Creative Imagination," 86.

28. Polanyi, "Science and Reality," 191.

Polanyi and Contemporary Realism

Besides these more explicit passages, Polanyi has inundated us with references to rationality in nature, and to coherence in nature. Not only are there laws in nature, but they are knowable and in fact known as a result of scientific inquiry. Polanyi, therefore, appears quite classical in the modern sense, as if he had never been confronted with the implications of the downfall of Newtonian science. We need only recall Polanyi's epistemology, however, to understand how this can be. Polanyi is able to retain regard for the dimensions of truth in Newton because he has shed what other current epistemologists have retained: an epistemology that presumes atemporal, exact articulation for there to be knowledge. For Polanyi, the reality and proto-truth of Newton's discoveries is not undermined but rather confirmed precisely because of their subsequent, surprising implications. These include even the discoveries of Einstein.[29]

Theoretical Entities Actually Exist

How does Polanyi's thought compare with Boyd's scientific realism? First of all, we can be sure that Polanyi wholeheartedly embraces the claim that theoretical entities actually exist. The ontological aspect of tacit knowing requires that the comprehensive entity that results from subsidiary-focal integration is real. Of course, however, this means that a theoretical entity need not have a physical counterpart to which it refers in order to be real. Tunes are real, so is the number π, and all of those concepts created by scientists that were never meant to be considered as actually existent. But we may supplement this thesis with Polanyi's exhortation to the scientist that he submit to his own conceptions, that he take them *literally*.

> [Columbus] triumphed by taking literally, and as a guide to action, that the earth was round, which his contemporaries held vaguely and as a mere matter of speculation. The egg of Columbus is the proverbial symbol for such breath-taking originality guided by a crudely concrete imagination. I remember having this feeling when first hearing of Einstein's theory of Brownian motion. The idea that the meandering oscillations of small floating particles seen by a botanist under the microscope, should reveal the impact of molecules hitting the particles in tune with the highly speculative equations of the kinetic theory of gases, impressed me as grossly incongruous. I experienced the same shock of a fantastic idea, when I heard Elsasser suggesting (in 1925) that certain anomalies observed in the scattering of

---

29. This is the main example of Polanyi's "Science and Reality."

electrons by solids may be due to the optical interferences of their de Broglie waves. We had all heard of these waves since 1923, yet were astounded by the fact that they could be taken literally as Elsasser did.[30]

Einstein's return to a mathematical interpretation of reality in the early twentieth century holds a similar significance for Polanyi in his analysis of the Copernican revolution and objectivity in chapter 1 of *Personal Knowledge*. Thus, we return to a familiar passage: "Why do we entrust the life and guidance of our thoughts to our conceptions? Because we believe that their manifest rationality is due to their being in contact with domains of reality, of which they have grasped one aspect. This is why the Pygmalion at work in us when we shape a conception is ever prepared to seek guidance from his own creation; and yet, in reliance on his contact with reality, is ready to reshape his creation, even while he accepts its guidance."[31] The indeterminacy of reality and of the bearing of knowledge on reality militate against the idea of a concept's specific referral to or denotation of a piece of reality. Polanyi says that conceptions are intimations of reality, not representations of reality.[32] Thus, this indeterminacy sets his position apart from the contemporary understanding of theoretical entities and their reference to real things.

No Static, Complete, Ideal of Truth

We have already discussed in some detail Polanyi's understanding of truth, concerning which various conclusions regarding approximate truth and historical approximations to the truth can be and have been drawn. Reality is essentially indeterminate; Polanyi defines it as that which may yet inexhaustibly manifest itself.[33] Thus, there can be no *fixed* account, or *complete* picture, which we gradually approximate. Even so, the concepts resulting from successful discovery grasp hold of the truth as they make contact with reality.

---

30. Polanyi, "Science and Reality," 193.
31. Polanyi, *Personal Knowledge*, 104.
32. Polanyi, see also "Knowing and Being," in Grene, ed., *Knowing and Being*, 133.
33. Polanyi, "Logic of Tacit Inference," in Grene, ed., *Knowing and Being*, 155; see also Roberts, "Politics and Science," 235–41.

Progress in Science Evidences Realism

Comparing Boyd's second and third theses in particular with Polanyi's thought yields the following reflections. First, as far as Polanyi is concerned, the key factors in the confirmation of scientific theories are, of course, the much-discussed criteria of reality, in particular the IFM Effect: the anticipation of indeterminate future manifestations. These confirm both contact with reality and truth. "Scientific evidence" and "ordinary methodological standards" are, I believe, actually important but subsidiary considerations for Polanyi. Polanyi does say something that sounds like Boyd's third thesis:

> The continued pursuit of science is possible, because the structure of nature and man's capacity to grasp this structure, can be such as is exemplified by this sequence of discoveries covering two millennia. It does happen, that nature is capable of being comprehended in successive stages, each of which can be reached only by the highest powers of the human mind. Consequently, to discover a true coherence in nature is often not only to discern something which, by the mere fact of being real, necessarily points beyond itself, but to surmise that future discoveries may prove the reality of the thing to be far deeper than we can at present imagine.[34]

Polanyi speaks of successive stages of discovery, and the sort of thing he has in mind here appears to grow out of his understanding of the sort of contact a discovery makes with reality and the nature of its intimations. Thus, what he says need not imply strict continuity or convergence, except, as Kuhn says, when a string of historical developments is evaluated in retrospect. No doubt, Polanyi could concur that later theories typically build upon the (observational and theoretical) knowledge embodied in previous theories: he stresses that Kepler, working on the assumption that Copernicus was right, discovered surprising confirmations of the heliocentric view. However, he also emphasized that Copernicus would hardly have recognized and perhaps may even have rejected Kepler's findings. (This is what he has in mind when he says that each successive stage of discovery can be reached only by the highest powers of the human mind.) These aspects of Polanyi's understanding suggest that Polanyi would not consider Boyd's (ii) and (iii) as being essential to the successful elaboration or assumption of realism.

---

34. Polanyi, "Science and Reality," 192–93.

Part 1: Early Consideration of Contact with Reality

Reality Exists Independently of Our Thought of It

When it comes to Boyd's fourth thesis, which concerns reality's independence of our conceptions of it, there is more than one angle of comparison to be explored. In general, let us note once again that Polanyi speaks of reality existing independently of our knowledge of it, as evidenced by its hiddenness, that it is reality's independent existence that empowers it to "attract our attention by clues which harass and beguile our minds into getting ever closer to it," and that nature exists beyond our control.[35] The fact of its independence means, further, "that its consequences can never be fully predicted."[36] Independence, thus, entails indeterminacy rather than determinacy, as classical objectivists might have thought. "What Copernicus believed of this system was what we all mean by saying that a thing is real and not a mere figment of the mind. What we mean is that the thing will not dissolve like a dream, but that, in some ways it will yet manifest its existence, inexhaustibly, in the future. For it is there, whether we believe it or not, independently of us, and hence never fully predictable in its consequences."[37]

Now, we noted that for Goldman, a necessary implication of R_2 (which also concerns reality's independence) is that all our beliefs could be false. Although Polanyi does not explicitly confirm this relationship, his own attitude concerning falsehood should function as testimony to his compliance with this aspect of realism. It has already been demonstrated that Polanyi assumes all knowledge to be fallible to the point that he defines our cultural heritage as "the sum total of all in which we may be mistaken."[38] What is important here is that he says that: "The possibility of error is a necessary element of any belief bearing on reality, and to withhold belief on the grounds of such a hazard is to break off all contact with reality."[39] The possibility of error, of course, goes hand in hand with the indeterminacy that, of necessity, characterizes the bearing of knowledge upon reality. Totally explicit, precise, and certain knowledge, in addition to being non-existent, would have no connection to reality at all. Thus, the possibility of falsehood, for Polanyi, signifies not so much reality's independence of our cognition as it does the successful contact of our cognition with reality. But though these extremes seem contradictory, for Polanyi at least they are not mutually exclusive. This is because falsehood and indeterminacy signify contact because they evi-

---

35. Polanyi, *Personal Knowledge*, 311; "The Unaccountable Element in Science," in Grene, ed., *Knowing and Being*, 119–20; *Science, Faith and Society*, 10.

36. Polanyi, "The Creative Imagination," 86.

37. Polanyi, "Science and Reality," 191.

38. Polanyi, *Personal Knowledge*, 404.

39. Ibid., 315.

dence reality's independence of our finite conceptions, its inexhaustibility and its capacity to reveal itself in ever-surprising ways in the future.

Polanyi and Idealism

The question of idealism, the prospect and extent of human conceptual contribution to that which is known, cannot be ignored, for Polanyi, of course, assigns a significant, basal role to the responsibly personal.[40] The more general question that must be posed first is how to distinguish, indeed whether it is possible to distinguish, between realism and idealism. At one extreme, realism would be defined as brooking no conceptual influence whatever, and idealism, thus, would be the massive category that collects up the entire spectrum from slight human input to total human determination of the objects of knowledge. At the other extreme, idealism would be restricted to representing a position of total conceptual determination of the known, and realism, in turn, would be viable so long as external reality had some input, no matter how minimal. And, of course, the truth of the matter may be represented by any one of a number of combinations in between.

But as noted in chapter 4, Helmut Kuhn addresses the matter directly, contrasting Polanyi to Kant: in no way does Polanyi draw Kantian conclusions from an obviously similar respect for the constructive activity of the mind. The mind does not constitute its object; reality does not conform to the knower's rational faculty. Instead, "the hallmark of genuine knowledge consists in establishing contact with reality." This reveals that Polanyi's stance is closer to common sense than to the prevailing idealist tendency in contemporary philosophy of science.[41] Nor does Polanyi consider reality an unknowable noumenon so independent of mind that the knower is left only with "the world-as-it-impinges-on-us."[42] Polanyi declares himself "committed to the belief in an external reality gradually accessible to knowing."[43] Finally, contra idealism in its most extreme form: if extreme idealism were true, it would not be possible to speak of falsehoods and correctability. Nor would it be legitimate to believe that the natural implication of all successful

---

40. We will see in chs. 12 and 13 that the label, "idealism," comes to be replaced with "anti-realism" in more recent discussions.

41. Kuhn, "Personal Knowledge and the Crisis of the Philosophical Tradition," 114. See also Innis, "Polanyi's Model of Mental Acts," 160n.

42. Scott, "Polanyi's Theory of Personal Knowledge: A Gestalt Philosophy," 358–59. Cf. Margolis, "Cognitive Issues," 373.

43. Polanyi, "Knowing and Being," in Grene, ed., *Knowing and Being*, 133.

discovery or contact with reality is that we may make further discoveries about its nature or behavior.[44]

Polanyi's cognizance of and concern with the role of theory, personal judgment, and the vast realm of the tacit and subsidiary in scientific knowledge has not brought him to a rejection of realist assumptions. On the contrary: it has brought him to argue for the legitimacy and reliability of these more-than-explicit factors, and to the realization that, far from detracting from realism, the realm of the personal and the tacit is the only ground upon which successful realism can stand at all. And what is more, it has brought him positively to embrace the responsibly personal subsidiary as a beachhead from which to launch into reality itself. Mental concepts, as carefully examined and consciously embraced or as half-understood intimations, can limit our engagement of the real. But on the other hand, they can be the keys to unlock its transformative ingression. This is not idealism, nor is it, I believe, even "critical" realism.[45]

In all knowing, cast as subsidiary-focal integration, those subsidiaries include not only the beguiling clues of the place of our puzzlement. They also include the knower's felt body sense. Third, they include all subsidiarily indwelt linguistic and theoretical frameworks which the knower has appropriated in search of the pattern. At one point in his argument in *Personal Knowledge*, Polanyi offers a distressingly persuasive argument that the "virgin mind" free of such appropriations would be imbecilic and useless.[46] Elsewhere, Polanyi contends that, in his own account of "the unaccountable element of science," he is fingering the very "mother wit" that Kant noted and then failed to take seriously: "Perhaps both Kant and his successors instinctively preferred to let such sleeping monsters lie, for fear that, once awakened, they might destroy their fundamental conception of knowledge. For, once you face up to the ubiquitous controlling position of unformalizable mental skills, you do meet difficulties for the justification of knowledge that cannot be disposed of within the framework of rationalism."[47] Putting these two complementary aspects together in subsidiary-focal integration means that, in contrast to Kant in every respect, for Polanyi knowledge may be the search for the not-yet-known which responsibly entrusts itself to hitherto appropriated concepts subsidiarily embodied, while enacting

---

44. Prosch, "Biology and Behaviorism in Polanyi," 185.

45. This will be expanded more fully in Part 2. See also Meek, *Loving to Know*, 397–402.

46. Polanyi, *Personal Knowledge*, 295–97.

47. Polanyi, "The Unaccountable Element in Science," in Grene, ed., *Knowing and Being*, 105–6.

humbly delighted confidence that reality itself may at any point more profoundly confirm them or radically supersede them.

Together, all these factors indicate rather strongly that, in Polanyi's mind, realism has the upper hand.

Semantic Realism, Fiduciarily Construed, Is Legitimate

If we compare Polanyi with Merrill's three forms of realism, what conclusions can be reached concerning the specific form of his realism? First, I believe that we may safely assume Polanyi's commitment to semantic realism, given his vehement denouncement of all anti-metaphysical tendencies or positivism. Throughout his works, Polanyi repeatedly criticizes Osiander, Poincare, Duhem, and Mach as incorrectly attempting to interpret science as being after only empirical adequacy, fruitfulness in scientific calculation, and prediction, rather than truth and contact with reality. For example, he says:

> The modification of our intellectual identity is entered upon in the hope of achieving thereby closer contact with reality.[48]

> Man's whole intellectual life would be thrown away should this interpretative framework be wholly false; he is rational only to the extent to which the conceptions to which he is committed are true.[49]

> Modern writers have rebelled against the power exercised by words over our thoughts, and have expressed this by deprecating words as mere conventions, established for the sake of convenient communication. This is just as misleading as to say that the theory of relativity is chosen for convenience. We may properly ascribe convenience only to a minor advantage in the pursuit of a major purpose.

> Our choice of language is a matter of truth or error, or right or wrong—of life or death.[50]

In contrast, Polanyi's own view accredits "the speaker's sense of fitness for judging that his words express the reality he seeks to express."[51] All these quotations come from an extended discussion concerning the development and modification of mental conceptions. Yet, with his discussions of the

48. Polanyi, *Personal Knowledge*, 106.
49. Ibid., 112.
50. Ibid., 113.
51. Ibid.

Copernicus-Osiander debate, Polanyi draws corresponding conclusions with respect to scientific entities and theories.[52] Osiander, of course, urged Copernicus "to acknowledge that science can only produce hypotheses representing the phenomena without claiming to be true."[53] Thus, we can easily conclude that Polanyi would side with semantic realism as over against instrumentalism, conventionalism, or any other form of anti-metaphysical positivism.

Semantic Realism Isn't All There Is

However, it can hardly be said that Polanyi is merely a semantic realist.[54] Indeed, it appears that only those people are semantic realists who have espoused some form of Carnap's distinction between internal and external questions, which, I am confident, Polanyi has not done. Merrill's definition of epistemic realism sounds very much like something Polanyi would say. Merrill, we must remember, concluded that the definition was ambiguous, gravitating more toward semantic realism once "exists" was interpreted internally (thus producing a triviality), or gravitating toward metaphysical realism if the word was given the sense of actual existence. Polanyi would reject the former and presume the latter, stronger, version of the two. The assumption that there is something there to be discovered, Polanyi repeatedly has told us, is essential to all scientific inquiry.[55] The scientist operates his faculties of personal judgment in submission to reality. "Personal knowledge in science is not made but discovered, and as such it claims to establish contact with reality beyond the clues on which it relies."[56] We trust our conceptions because we believe them to be in contact with various aspects of reality.[57] Indeed, the very essence of a scientific proposition is to be concerned with reality.[58] Compare the following statement of Polanyi's with the phrases of Merrill's formulation: "A statement about nature is believed to be true if it is believed to disclose an aspect of something real in nature. A true physical theory is therefore believed to be no mere mathematical

---

52. Ibid., 145–50; Polanyi, "Science and Reality."
53. Polanyi, "Science and Reality," 178.
54. Grene, "Response to MacIntyre," 43.
55. Polanyi, "Tacit Knowing: Its Bearing," in Grene, ed., *Knowing and Being*, 172, among many other passages.
56. Polanyi, *Personal Knowledge*, 64.
57. Ibid., 104.
58. Polanyi, *Science, Faith and Society*, 23.

relation between observed data, but to represent an aspect of reality, which may yet manifest itself inexhaustibly in the future."[59]

But for Polanyi, there is an additional dimension of realism, which serves to distinguish his position from most of contemporary philosophy. That is that knowers are deemed to have the capacity to make contact with reality, as we have discussed at length before.[60] This confidence, of course, comes on the grounds of the skills of subsidiary knowledge. Thus, realism is not relegated to matters of convention, to what we decide is true or real, but may assume a full-blooded significance by virtue of knowers' capacities.

Metaphysical and Epistemic Realisms are True

To the extent that metaphysical realism constitutes the thesis of reality's independence, we have already discussed Polanyi's position with respect to it in connection with Boyd's fourth thesis and Goldman's R_2. For Merrill, however, the definition of metaphysical realism is more a statement of the external counterpart of semantic realism. Michael Polanyi can, I believe, be thought of as concurring with the thesis that "the entities postulated by a (good or acceptable) scientific theory really exist," with some important and quite commonsensical qualifications. Polanyi, of course, has explicitly rejected the possibility of complete explicitness and of certainty in scientific knowledge. We can never be fully aware of the implications of our claims, so we can never be exhaustively certain that they are true. Thus, it is quite possible that our claims turn out to be false; the testimony of history is that even the most successful and far reaching discoveries, as articulated by their discoverers, have proven to be an admixture of truth and error. What is easier to be sure of on a Polanyian scheme—though I do not say that it is foolproof—is that contact has been made with reality. It is easier to know that there has been contact than to know the nature and extent of that contact, i.e., *to what extent* our surmises are true. At the same time, Polanyi's faith in the intuitive capacities of humankind allows him to remain unphased by skeptical doubts. Here, Tuomela's point against Putnam, mentioned in the last chapter, provides us with a helpful way to think. A realist, Putnam has said, must be able to accept the truth of statements like

> (A) Venus might not have carbon dioxide in its atmosphere even though it follows from our theory that Venus has carbon dioxide in its atmosphere.

---

59. Polanyi, "Science and Reality," 191.
60. Polanyi, *Study of Man*, 27, and elsewhere.

Tuomela says, "I think that it represents in principle a good way for a realist to proceed. Yet I would take it to be part and parcel of this very same line of realist thought that at least *ultimately* scientists will learn from their errors and succeed in building up the (or a) correct theory and in finding out "how the world is" so that statements like (A) and (B) become *false* in the limit."[61] Now Polanyi has no concept of ultimate limit. But his confidence in human skills operates in a similar fashion. The Polanyian thesis of the accreditation of the human mind's capacity to make contact with reality thus proves to be an essential pillar within his realism, compensating in substantial measure for the absence of certainty in the face of skeptical doubts.

Polanyi and Putnam's Realisms

We turn now to Putnam's categories of empirical and pragmatic realism, and internal and metaphysical realism. Polanyi, as we have said, spends little time attempting to justify realism in the manner of contemporary discussions, but rather assumes it to be a *sine qua non* of a proper interpretation of the scientific enterprise.[62] If Polanyi offers any justification of realism, it is the existence of the phenomenon of the IFM Effect. Helmut Kuhn concurs with this, referring to Polanyi's justification of the claim of knowledge to reveal reality "such as it is by itself" as "the argument from fecundity." In the course of research, "eventually our experience will come to resemble that of a gold digger who has struck a mine rather than that of an architect. The initial guess, an idea daringly posited by an act of will, develops into a process with a momentum and a direction of its own. And through this process the object, at first vaguely perceived, takes on sharp contours and discloses ever new aspects. Inexhaustible depths of truth open up to our quest, and we would run counter to its meaning should we try to see in it anything but a manifestation of reality."[63] This is perhaps an empirical argument since it appeals to our experience, but it is not the sort that Putnam employs.

With regard to the sort of pragmatic realism that has to do with the pragmatic choice of ontic commitments, we may note some superficial similarity between Polanyi and, say, Quine. But the word, "pragmatic" is highly inappropriate as a description of Polanyi's position with regard to choice, given his own aversion to the concept and the amount of energy he devoted to attacking it. True, *Personal Knowledge* emphasizes the foundational

---

61. Tuomela, "Putnam's Realisms," 122–23.

62. Innis, "Meaning, Thought and Language in Polanyi's Epistemology," 62.

63. Kuhn, "Personal Knowledge and the Crisis of the Philosophical Tradition," 114. Here he references *Duke Lectures*, I, 11f., 19f.; and *Duke Lectures*, III, 20, 23.

character of belief and commitment for all kinds of knowing. But Polanyi came to believe that his reliance upon the necessity of commitment was reduced by working out the structure of tacit knowing.[64] And throughout his career, he acknowledged the unique way in which the premises of science which we embrace come to be embraced by us. They grow out of significant discoveries; they are thrust upon us by our new understanding of the world. We embrace and submit to them, at first subsidiarily in advance of the discovery, such that by the time that we do articulate them, we are already living by them. Even "choice," as a stark or arbitrary action, falls short of Polanyi's understanding of commitment. It would thus be better to describe his position as "fiduciary realism," though even this is not quite right.[65]

As far as internal realism is concerned, it is unlikely that Polanyi would agree to or feel the need of such a category. The distinction between internal and external questions may be seen to be but another manifestation of the subject-object distinction, of which Polanyi was trying to rid philosophy. True, we cannot escape our historical, bodily, and conceptual situation entirely; this is what Polanyi has in mind when he speaks of acceptance of calling. Our particular calling limits us, but at the same time, and more importantly, it is not meant to. Instead, "it offers me my opportunity for seeking the truth."[66]

Polanyi and Underdetermination

In conclusion, I want to note briefly how Polanyi handles the problem of equivalent descriptions, or of underdetermination—an objection that causes a great deal of concern among contemporary realists. Boyd states the argument fully; I will give Worrall's description simply because it is shorter:

> Suppose that T is the presently best available theory in some field. The realist enjoins that we take T's "transcendent" part as an attempt to describe the reality hidden behind the phenomena. The underdetermination argument threatens to demonstrate that there are always rival theories, T', T'', ... which stand on a par with T so far as the evidence is concerned but which tell quite a different story about "hidden reality."

---

64. Polanyi, *Tacit Dimension*, x.
65. MacIntyre, "Objectivity in Morality and Objectivity in Science," 27.
66. Polanyi, "Knowing and Being," in Grene, ed., *Knowing and Being*, 133.

Boyd concludes: "Therefore no scientific evidence can bear on the question of which of these theories provides the correct account of unobservable phenomena; ... knowledge of unobservable phenomena is thus impossible."[67]

The Polanyian response to the problem of underdetermination should be obvious. On the one hand, he readily admits the inadequacy of explicit empirical information as a basis for true understanding; in fact, of course, he was among the first to espouse and proclaim such an idea. But, on the other hand, full cognizance of this limitation did not lead him to anti-realism. It led him rather to endorse, first, the amazing role of personal judgment, responsible indwelling, and scientific intuition in coming up with the truth, and secondly, the indeterminate but far-reaching "surplus of meaning" contained in a substantial new integration.[68] His analysis of the geocentric and heliocentric views is as follows:

> The celestial time-table set out by Copernicus was not markedly different from that of Ptolemy. Close on to a century following the death of Copernicus, all efforts to discriminate convincingly between the two systems on the grounds of their observable quantitative predictions had failed. ... Yet all this time the theory of Copernicus was exercising heuristic powers absent in the system of Ptolemy. We are faced with the question then how one of two theoretical systems, having virtually the same explicit content, could vastly exceed the other in its anticipations. ... Its anticipatory powers lay in the new image by which Copernicus recast the content of the Ptolemaic system. It is in the *appearance* of the new system that its immense superiority lay; it is this image that made the Copernican revolution. ... While the functional relations remain the same, the surplus of meaning which goes beyond them may vary, as manifested in this case by the appearance of the theory.[69]

In this way, Polanyi turns the counterattack to his own advantage, dispensing with strict empiricism along with the attempted anti-realism.

---

67. Worrall, "Scientific Realism and Scientific Change," 214–16; Boyd, "On the Current Status of the Issue of Scientific Realism," 5.

68. Worrall is also helpful at this point—"Scientific Realism and Scientific Change," 221.

69. Polanyi, "Science and Reality," 189.

In Conclusion

In this chapter, I have taken note of or developed Polanyi's position on several realist claims: the reality of scientific laws and theoretical entities, his perception of progress in science testifying to realism, his understanding of truth as more deeply objective than merely a static, exhaustively explicit ideal. We have marked his commitment to semantic realism and beyond—to epistemological and metaphysical realism as well. And we have seen that his as less a pragmatic realism and more something like a fiduciary realism. Raising our sights from this close scrutiny of the details of current discussions of realism and how Polanyi's thought corresponds to them, let us take a more synthetic view.[70] The heart of Polanyi's own realism lies in his vision of reality as that which manifests itself indeterminately in the future, and thus of any successful contact with it being indicated by an unspecifiable sense of indeterminate future manifestations. There is a three-dimensionality, a fecundity, an indeterminacy, a surprise, and an ongoing transformativeness about this that, itself true to this Polanyian signature of the real, more than matches and confirms; in contrast, it outstrips and redefines, redrawing the very question of realism itself. Analogous to how the integrative focal pattern suddenly congeals in a discovery, reinterpreting and revaluing all its clues, his realism reorders and supersedes the current debate regarding realism.

Ontic commitment, to use one philosopher's phrase, very well is prelinguistic. But it isn't only prelinguistic once the knower has sustained any discovery or act of insight. In fact, according to Polanyi, ontic commitment is what sustains the entire act of coming to know. Of course, qualified skepticism about the existence of possible entities is at times judicious, but it would only be judicious in view of a wider conviction to responsibly hope for and trust the surprisingly more-than-objective real.

If Polanyi's vision of reality distinctively anchors his realism distally, his understanding of unspecifiable, subsidiary rootedness anchors his realism proximally—subsidiarily. We have seen throughout these three chapters that the distinctive nature of his epistemology plays in to his realism. We can't "check our beliefs against reality" because we are already rooted in it, as Grene has said. Knowing is already intrinsically a matter of orientation within as well as toward the world. Chapter 11 will explore this aspect more closely, tapping and comparing the thought of Maurice Merleau-Ponty.

In this cluster of chapters, we have examined common loci of debate in recent philosophy regarding matters pertaining to realism: progress, truth,

---

70. These final paragraphs reflect my more recent assessment and will be fleshed out more fully in Part 2.

and realism itself. Throughout, Polanyi's distinctive proposals have proved difficult to connect to the mainline discussion, precisely because they expose and question and move beyond its tacitly presumed parameters. More than the discussion calling Polanyi's position to account for itself, the opposite is true. However, the exercise has proven valuable for gaining a deeper grasp of Polanyian realism and why it matters. The wider debate is conducted entirely from a stance that calls reality into question. It does so because of a deeper metaphysic which opposes knower to known and a correspondingly deeper epistemic vision that installs the knower as the sole repository of requisite explicit certainty. Polanyi's work, taken as a whole, engages the discussion at the level of these fundamental presumptions. Polanyi's approach, quite literally, shifts the focus outward. It renders the real the anchor of realism. It does so in no naïve way, but rather with a sophisticatedly perceptive understanding of how it is that we know. It is reasonable to affirm that, while this fundamental reorientation renders these chapters' agenda of detailed comparison difficult, real engagement and reformation may, nevertheless, therein be seen to be under way.

11

Grounding Polanyi's Realism: Merleau-Ponty

It is, by now, evident that Michael Polanyi's thought is pervaded by realism, or by what Innis refers to as realist intent. There is the repeated claim that the scientist must be committed to the pursuit of the real, the external world, in order for his work to be successful. He must and does claim truth and reality for his discoveries. There is Polanyi's conviction that reality exists independently of our knowledge of it, and that, even so, it is knowable: the external pole of our tacitly rooted integrative activity. We have the repeated definition of reality as that which inexhaustively and indeterminately manifests itself in systematic yet surprising ways. Then, there is the whole nexus of concepts surrounding the ontological aspect and other criteria of reality—among them, that integration proclaims the reality of its product, and that coherence and the Polanyian sort of rationality are tokens of contact with reality. Finally, we have the notion of contact itself, the topic of discussion in chapter 6—Polanyi affirms its possibility without qualification.

The problem is that it remains difficult to see just what ultimate justification exists in Polanyi's work for these various realist claims. With respect to the definition of reality, for example, we have seen that it is virtually impossible to find any clue to its origin in Polanyi's own thinking, and hence, it is difficult to know on what grounds he characterizes reality in this way. Why integration should indicate successful contact with reality, how it is that he believes the world to be knowable, that the gap between knower

Part 1: Early Consideration of Contact with Reality

and known is crossable in the first place, let alone how such an assumption can be the *sine qua non* of scientific discovery—we have yet to be sure what basis exists for these claims. Such a basis appears essential to the success of Polanyi's realism.

What I propose to do in this chapter is to follow a different path into Polanyi's proposals by way of a brief consideration of the work of twentieth-century phenomenologist Maurice Merleau-Ponty. Merleau-Ponty's thought is, in many ways, strikingly similar to Polanyi's, despite his Continental, phenomenological approach. Polanyi and Merleau-Ponty share very basic goals in common. They share the goal of exposing the bankruptcy of the Cartesian tradition and the inadequacy of the contemporary theory of knowledge and philosophy of science that has stemmed from it. And they share a concern to demonstrate the fact of the existence of tacit knowledge and the necessity of its foundational role for all knowledge. Merleau-Ponty, it may be hoped, will provide us with a more extensive development of the area that may constitute the foundation of and justification for Polanyi's realism.[1]

Polanyi briefly compares his own findings with the work of the phenomenologists Edmund Husserl and Merleau-Ponty. He regards Husserl as having mounted a "systematic attempt to safeguard the content of unsophisticated experience against the effects of a destructive analysis."[2] He quotes from Merleau-Ponty's *Phenomenology of Perception* typical phrases that display the way we experience our body in knowing and being. These, he says, foreshadow his own analysis of the body-mind relationship. However, he says, "I find among them neither the logic of tacit knowing nor the theory of ontological stratification, which I regard as indispensable for the understanding of the phenomena described by Merleau-Ponty."[3] These comments indicate both the kinship and the difference that Polanyi himself felt with respect to Merleau-Ponty's phenomenology of perception.

---

1. In ch. 12, as I reflect on the same tack as taken by Charles Taylor and Hubert Dreyfus in 2015 to look to Merleau-Ponty for ultimate justification of realism, I adjust my position to one of preferring Polanyi's own realism as superior in nature and as justificatory. Nevertheless, as will be seen, Merleau-Ponty offers vast riches to the overall realist stance that roundly confirm and elucidate Polanyi's rich understanding of the subsidiary and of indwelling.

2. Polanyi, "The Structure of Consciousness," in Grene, ed., *Knowing and Being*, 221.

3. Ibid., 222.

Polanyian Themes in Merleau-Ponty

Maurice Merleau-Ponty labors extensively in *Phenomenology of Perception* to uncover the true nature of the knower's initial perceptual experience.[4] The phenomenological method involves the effort to attend to the very experience of, in the case of this book, perception, describing it in a manner that exposes rich layers of generally overlooked, concrete involvement and significance.

Shared Material

In the course of this enterprise, much of Merleau-Ponty's considered material, that is, the psychological experimentation from which he draws many of the examples from ordinary life, coincides uncannily with cases that Polanyi has considered: optical illusions, figure-ground problems, the findings of Gestalt psychology, the experience of the body, the phenomena of phantom limbs and forgotten limbs, tools, skills, the blind man's probe, and, of course, perceptual experiences in general—this list results from a cursory glance through only the first 150 pages.[5] In addition, Merleau-Ponty's interpretation of this material resembles Polanyi's. Polanyi attends extensively to perception to uncover the ever-present structure of knowing as subsidiary-focal integration. It is no wonder that he considers some of the same cases that Merleau-Ponty does in his study of perception.

Tacit Knowledge

Most notably, Merleau-Ponty continually emphasizes the pervasive existence of tacit knowledge—backgrounds, subliminal clues, the knowledge we have of our own bodies, and our reliance upon tools. Here is just one of several such passages: "In the same way, the objects interposed between me and the thing upon which I fix my eyes are not perceived for themselves; they are nevertheless perceived and we have no reason for refusing to recognize that this marginal perception plays a part in seeing distance, since,

---

4. Merleau-Ponty, *Phenomenology of Perception*. I have limited my study of Merleau-Ponty's writing to this work. A fresh, superior, translation of this work, by Donald Landes, appeared in 2012. I strongly suggest that the reader wanting to continue on to read this work, rather than follow out the copious citations of the older translation, simply take up that one. I would also note that I heartily concur with Marjorie Grene's stated penchant, with respect to "being captivated by Merleau-Ponty's enterprise," to "lapse into quoting purple passages" (*Philosophical Testament*, 80–81).

5. Ibid., 6, 15, 47, 52, 76, 91, 142, 143.

when the intervening objects are hidden by a screen, the distance appears to shrink."[6] In this comment, Merleau-Ponty affirms marginal perception and the critical role it plays in seeing objects as distant. There is and must be more to perception than what we focally perceive.

Subsidiary-Focal Integration

Merleau-Ponty affirms the subsidiary-focal relationship also, though not in so many words and not with the same degree of significance as Polanyi. For example, he writes:

> What makes part of the field count as an object in motion, and another as the background, is the way in which we establish our relations with them by the act of looking. The stone flies through the air. What do these words mean, other than that our gaze, lodged and anchored in the garden, is attracted by the stone and, so to speak, drags at its anchors? The relation between the moving object and its background passes through our body.... Now what precisely is the anchorage and how does it constitute a background at rest? It is not an explicit perception. The points of anchorage, when we focus on them, are not objects. The steeple begins to move [as opposed to the cloud moving behind it] only when I leave the sky in the margin of vision. It is essential to the alleged fixed points underlying motion that they should not be posited in present knowledge and that they should always be "already there." They do not present themselves directly to perception, they circumvent it and encompass it by a preconscious process, the results of which strike us as ready made.[7]

This passage displays a moving beauty, characteristic of phenomenological description, which doesn't characterize Polanyi's elegant but more scientific or epistemological accounts. But, as in the previous extended quotation, the knower anchors what Polanyi calls the focal in the subsidiary, marginal clues. For Merleau-Ponty, however, marginal perceptions are "preconscious," rather than subsidiary.

With regard to our knowledge of our own bodies, he says that, "in their first attempts at grasping, children look, not at their hand, but at the object;

---

6. Ibid., 48; see also 11, 43, 49, 58, 60, 78, 81, 90, 95, 101, 128, 129–30, 134, 140–41, 152, 165, 169, 180, 198, 213, 214, 233, 238, 241, 242, 251, 257, 277, 279, 280, 283, 296, 303, 309, 310, 311, 312, 314, 321, 322, 340, 361, 365, 369, 371, 381, 391, 395, 401, 404.

7. Ibid., 278–79; see also 30, 49, 68, 111, 116, 119, 128, 133, 134, 135, 149, 150, 221, 238, 242, 250, 253, 264, 275, 278, 279–80, 281, 289.

the various parts of the body are known to us through their functional value only, and their co-ordination is not learnt."[8] This identifies body awareness as functionally valued and not directly focused on.

The process of integration is also affirmed, vividly, by Merleau-Ponty, though again, not with the degree of formality that characterizes Polanyi's analysis:

> If I walk along a shore towards a ship which has run aground, and the funnel or masts merge into the forest bordering on the sand dune, there will be a moment when these details suddenly become part of the ship, and indissolubly fused with it. As I approached, I did not perceive resemblances or proximities which finally came together to form a continuous picture of the upper part of the ship. I merely felt that the look of the object was on the point of altering, that something was imminent in this tension, as a storm is imminent in storm clouds. Suddenly the sight before me was recast in a manner satisfying to my vague expectation. Only afterwards did I recognize, as justifications for the change, the resemblance and contiguity of what I call "stimuli."
> ... But these reasons for correct perception were not given as reasons beforehand. The unity of the object is based on the foreshadowing of an imminent order which is about to spring upon us a reply to questions merely latent in the landscape.[9]

This passage conveys the palpable feel of anticipating and then undergoing the transformative shift that is integration. Elsewhere, Merleau-Ponty says that, "attention is neither an association of images, nor the return to itself of thought already in control of its objects, but the active constitution of a new object which makes explicit and articulate what was until then presented as no more than an indeterminate horizon.... This passage from the indeterminate to the determinate, this recasting at every moment of its own history in the unity of a new meaning, is thought itself."[10] It is evident here that Merleau-Ponty shares with Polanyi the conviction that thought, at its core, involves a repatterning that remakes what has previously been experienced and held. This is integration. In light of Polanyi's own assessment, noted earlier, of the necessary logic of tacit knowing being absent from Merleau-Ponty, I believe that it is appropriate to say that subsidiary-focal integration, as we know it from Polanyi's work, can be seen to be at least described phenomenologically in that of Merleau-Ponty. This, of

---

8. Ibid., 149.
9. Ibid., 17.
10. Ibid., 30–31.

course, is what you would expect if Polanyian tacit knowing is accurate. Taken together, these passages offer rich phenomenological descriptions of the dimensions of perceptual knowing that Polanyi delineates: the anchoring, subsidiary backdrop, the involvement of the body, the feel of actual integration, and the transformative reorientation it induces.

The Reality Statement

There are several other points of similarity between the two thinkers, exploration of which, though most intriguing, is not germane to our subject. These include the inevitability of indeterminacy or ambiguity, the phenomenal aspect of integration, the problem of the *Meno* paradox, the impossibility and undesirability of the totally explicit and of certainty, the notion of acceptance of calling, and the analysis of language, especially denotation and its modification.[11]

What is especially pertinent to this inquiry is that Merleau-Ponty's work also contains passages that echo the Polanyian definition of reality, as well as his concepts of the world's inexhaustibility and hiddenness, the coextension of meaning and reality, the ontological aspect of tacit integration, and, to some extent, Polanyi's realism.[12] Consider the following passages:

> When I see an object, I always feel that there is a portion of being beyond what I see at this moment, not only as regards visible being, but also as regards what is tangible or audible. And not only sensible being, but a depth of the object that no progressive sensory deduction will ever exhaust.[13]
>
> [Perception] throws me open to a world, but can do so only by outrunning both me and itself. Thus the perceptual "synthesis" has to be incomplete; it cannot present me with a "reality" otherwise than by running the risk of error. It is absolutely necessarily

---

11. Indeterminacy/ambiguity: ibid., 5, 6, 11, 169, 189, 208, 318, 390; phenomenal aspect: ibid., 297; *Meno* problem: ibid., 28, 142, 178, 371; contra the explicit and certain: ibid., 60, 133, 142, 143, 295, 297, 322, 343, 391, 396, 398; acceptance of calling: ibid., 84, 85, 147, 171; analysis of language: ibid., 175–83, 186, 193, 388, 389.

12. Definition of reality: ibid., 153, 185, 216, 217, 233, 238, 281, 297, 317, 323, 333, 338, 339, 361, 377, 386, 387–88, 389, 390; Spiegelberg, *Phenomenological Movement*, Vol. II, 548; Bannan, *Philosophy of Merleau-Ponty*, 51, 106, 107, 108, 110, 114; inexhaustibility: Merleau-Ponty, *Phenomenology of Perception*, xvii, 219, 233, 238, 240, 324, 330, 390; hiddenness: ibid., 208, 217, 277; coextension of meaning and reality: ibid., 184, 323, 324; ontological aspect: ibid., 233, 279, 374, 376; Polanyi's realism: ibid., 297.

13. Ibid., 216.

> the case that the thing, if it is to be a thing should have sides of itself hidden from me.[14]
>
> It is thus of the essence of the thing and of the world to present themselves as "open," to send us beyond their determinate manifestations, to promise us always "something else to see."[15]

Phenomenological attending to our perception reveals that to sense an object is to sense a portion of being that is beyond what I sense, a depth that perception cannot ever exhaust. The world I perceive is that to which my effort has thrown me open, and that outruns me and it. A completely exhaustive perception risks error. Hidden sides are absolutely necessary. The thing and the world send us beyond the particular event of perception; they always promise more. "Indeterminate future manifestations" aptly designates what Merleau-Ponty is describing as he talks about perception.

Merleau-Ponty affirms both the systematic and the unpredictable character of the real:

> The experiences of other people or those which await me if I change my position merely develop what is suggested by the horizons of my present experience, and add nothing to it. My perception brings into co-existence an indefinite number of perceptual chains which, if followed up, would confirm it in all respects and accord with it. My eyes and my hand know that any actual change of place would produce a sensible response entirely according to my expectation, and I can feel swarming beneath my gaze the countless mass of more detailed perceptions that I anticipate, and upon which I already have a hold.[16]
>
> Like every other perception, this one asserts more things than it grasps: when I say that I see the ash-tray over there, I suppose as completed an unfolding of experience which could go on *ad infinitum*, and I commit a whole perceptual future. Similarly, when I say that I know and like someone, I aim, beyond his qualities, at an inexhaustible core which may one day shatter the image that I have formed of him.[17]

Merleau-Ponty goes on to speak intriguingly of "a violent act which is perception itself." Taking these two passages together, they can appear contradictory: the first on the surface suggests that complete confirmation

---

14. Ibid., 377.
15. Ibid., 333.
16. Ibid., 338.
17. Ibid., 361.

is possible. If that were the case, however, it would contradict not only the second passage, but all the others we have already inspected. It is important to note, however, that the first passage here also contains phrases that suggest indeterminate excess of prospects as essential to my perception. One way to make sense of this, I believe, is to see this passage as underscoring systematicity and reliability in our perception even of the indeterminate possibilities. In addition to systematicity and unpredictability, we also find in these lines the essential indeterminacy of the resultant comprehensive entity, the existence of hidden sides, and the inexhaustive character of future manifestations, all of which are essential parts of what it means to be a thing, the unavoidable possibility of error, and the fact that future manifestations are anticipated. Let us note, however, that Merleau-Ponty does not follow Polanyi in the application of these concepts to the process of scientific discovery, but whereas Polanyi was concerned to explore perception as consonant epistemically with discovery, Merleau-Ponty devotes this particular exploration to perception.

It should be noted that, on his own terms, Merleau-Ponty is not a realist.[18] This is difficult to believe, given the material that we have just examined as well as those concepts that will be our main concern in this chapter. But this apparent concern is cleared up by Marjorie Grene, who herself believes that Merleau-Ponty's thought paves the way for a post-Kantian restoration of reality, a renewal of ontology.[19] She says: "By realism he plainly means psychological realism, primarily the causal theory of perception, a realism which would exile significance from any ontological status. And to such an exile Merleau-Ponty is emphatically opposed."[20]

Heidegger's Being-in-the-World

I will examine more closely, first, Merleau-Ponty's notion of preobjective experience and its role in the structure of knowledge, and secondly, the nature of the body and the relationship of the body and the world. These concepts provide explanation and justification for virtually all of the aspects of his own thought that we have noted above; the hope is that they may do the same for Polanyi. But prior to this examination, it will be help to consider briefly a concept of twentieth-century philosopher Martin Heidegger's, namely, Being-in-the-world. Merleau-Ponty utilizes the notion

---

18. Ibid., 10, 32, 47, 49, 263, 369.

19. Grene, "The Paradoxes of Historicity," 22, 28–32; "Merleau-Ponty and the Renewal of Ontology," 605–25.

20. Grene, "Merleau-Pontyand the Renewal of Ontology," 606.

Grounding Polanyi's Realism: Merleau-Ponty 213

of Being-in-the-world, and Polanyi, in his later years, came to believe that his own concept of indwelling was identical to Heidegger's Being-in-the-world.[21] Although there is some reason in each case to suspect that the term is not being used in entirely the same way, nevertheless significant affinities exist, and it is thus worthwhile to attend to it as part of this inquiry.[22]

Being-in-the-world is the primary mode of human Being, or Dasein.[23] We do not become acquainted with Being-in-the-world "ontically," that is, by means of experience of things, but rather "ontologically," or in ourselves in advance of experience. "The world" here is therefore not the planet in the solar system, but rather that in which one finds oneself prior to experience. It is that in which Dasein dwells, not as water dwells *in* a glass, but more like, as Grene says, as one is *in* business. The world is not simply there, opposite me, but it is the environment in which I feel at home because it affects me and I affect it. The matter becomes clearer to the reader of Polanyi when Heidegger delineates the world in terms of that which is "ready-to-hand" equipment (not things yet) which I use. To revert to Polanyian terms—and indeed it is difficult to believe that Polanyi in his formative stages was not a student of Heidegger's—we therefore have, not focal or explicit, but rather subsidiary knowledge of the world. To be in a world is, thus, to be surrounded by usable equipment, in which surroundings one feels at home.[24] This is a primordial, non-thematic experience, and it is that without which Dasein is not Dasein.

Finally, Being-in-the-world is the necessary foundation for all thematic knowledge.[25] To quote commentator Michael Gelven:

> To-be-in-a-world is the ultimate presupposition of knowledge. (This puts ontology prior to epistemology—a move that incurs the wrath of all neo-Kantians and positivists.) The bases of epistemology are the knower and known: but prior to the distinction between knower and known (or subject and object) is the fact that the subject can relate to a known, which means that the presupposition of the very subject-object distinction is grounded in an already admitted basis of relationship—i.e., that the subject *has a world* in which the object can occur. Knowledge

---

21. See the Preface to the Torchbook ed. of *Personal Knowledge*, x, xi.
22. See Grene's note in "Tacit Knowing and the Pre-Reflective Cogito," 44; and Spiegelberg's note in *Phenomenological Movement*, 522.
23. Heidegger, Being and Time, 24–40, 78–148; Gelven, *Commentary on Heidegger's Being and Time*, 52–61.
24. See especially Heidegger, *Being and Time*, 95, 99.
25. Ibid., 90.

does not occur in isolation from one's world of concern and environment.[26]

Given the way we learn about it, as well as given the nature of language, our "natural" tendency is to understand the world as a collection of objects known by a disconnected subject. But this is to abstract; in order for such abstractions to exist at all, there must be a primordial experience: a unitary phenomenon in which the subject has a world. In this way, Gelven continues, "certain philosophical 'problems' are 'solved.' The mind-body problem, for example, and the problem of the reality of the external world [the topic of this work] are misleading *abstractions* from the necessary characteristic of Dasein's Being-in-a-world. . . . Once one admits the apriority of the existential structure, then such *ontic* considerations as the nature of external objects can never undermine the work of fundamental ontology."[27]

It thus becomes clear what this concept offers to our subject. There exists an experience of the world prior to thematic (abstracted, articulated) experience, a mode of being that is also a form of knowing. There exists a fundamental level at which no dichotomy exists between knower and known, and the problem of the reality of the external world is not a problem. This is the theme which Merleau-Ponty develops; let us now return to consider it.

Preobjective Experience

As I said, I want to attend here to two general concepts in the *Phenomenology of Perception*, namely, preobjective experience and the body. We will see that it is highly artificial to treat these concepts separately, for in actuality they coalesce. Nevertheless, I think that there is some value in handling the one and then the other, if only to emphasize how each displays the other. I do not here show how Merleau-Ponty himself develops and justifies these notions; I merely attend to his pronounced statements of them:

According to Merleau-Ponty:

> The first philosophical act would appear to be to return to the world of actual experience which is prior to the objective world, since it is in it that we shall be able to grasp the theoretical basis no less than the limits of that objective world, restore to things their concrete physiognomy, to organisms their individual ways

---

26. Gelven, *Commentary on Being and Time*, 55. See also Rouse, "Kuhn, Heidegger and Scientific Realism," 273–74, concerning the possibility of learning.

27. Gelven, *Commentary on Being and Time*, 55.

of dealing with the world, and to subjectivity its inherence in history. Our task will be, moreover, to rediscover phenomena, the layer of living experience through which other people and things are first given to us, the system "Self-others-things" as it comes into being; to reawaken perception and foil its trick of allowing us to forget it as a fact and as perception in the interest of the object which it presents to us and of the rational tradition to which it gives rise.[28]

Two introductory observations: First: the rediscovery and elaboration of preobjective experience appears to be what Merleau-Ponty takes as his primary task in the *Phenomenology of Perception*.[29] He even speaks, as we shall see, somewhat paradoxically, of making it explicit.[30] But this phenomenal layer, he says, even though it is not thematized, can be recognized, identified, and talked about, and it has a significance—a point well made also in defense of Polanyi's subsidiary knowledge.[31] Secondly: Merleau-Ponty, in contrast to Polanyi, identifies "perception" with this preobjective layer. Commentator Herbert Spiegelberg speaks of perception as our privileged access to this stratum; but I think that it is more appropriate to say that, for Merleau-Ponty, perception is the preobjective experience itself.[32] Perception, for Polanyi, is integration; thus, although it is critical to his account to identify and accredit the subsidiary, his account extends beyond the subsidiary to its necessarily tandem counterpart, the focal. However, since both philosophers labor to "foil the trick" of our penchant to attend only to the focal object, the impact of this distinction is minimal. Indeed, carrying out the actual inquiry that Merleau-Ponty enjoins requires attending indwellingly to our experience, which is behind and under the object; thus, the attending itself suggests the from-to structure.[33] What may prove to be more significant is the absence in Merleau-Ponty of the subsidiary-focal integrative structure.

Merleau-Ponty describes the object of his inquiry by means of a series of "prior to"s, "pre-"s, and "non-"s. This experience is primordial—simply

28. Merleau-Ponty, *Phenomenology of Perception*, 57.
29. Ibid., 275; Spiegelberg, *Phenomenological Movement*, Vol. II. 545.
30. Merleau-Ponty, *Phenomenology of Perception*, xvi.
31. Ibid., 274.
32. See ibid., 242, 252, 254.
33. It is helpful and necessary to distinguish this from what Polanyi calls "destructive analysis," in which the knower reverts to focus on subsidiaries, temporarily attending to them focally. Merleau-Ponty's inquiry involves attending subsidiarily to subsidiaries—something I believe is as important to do as temporary destructive analysis.

first. It is pre-conscious, pre-personal, and pre-reflective. It is pre- or inarticulate, pre- or non-thetic, pre-thematic, non-positing, ante-predicative, and tacit (pre-explicit). It is preobjective—meaning prior to our objectifying, prior to the object. Finally, it is, as such, prior to scientific knowledge.[34] Merleau-Ponty has examined perceptual experience, both normal and abnormal, in an attempt to uncover the nature of this primordial sort of experience that we have. He concludes that there is indeed experience that is prior to all those things listed above—i.e., prior to knowledge as it has traditionally been conceived.

Preobjective experience includes the variety of things that readers of Polanyi have come to identify as subsidiary, latent, or marginal knowledge. To give only one example, Merleau-Ponty says that

> in order to be able to assert a truth, the actual subject must in the first place have a world or be in the world, that is, sustain round about it a system of meanings whose reciprocities, relationships and involvements do not require to be made explicit in order to be exploited. When I move about my house, I know without thinking about it that walking towards the bathroom means passing near the bedroom, that looking at the window means having the fireplace on my left, and in this small world each gesture, each perception is immediately located in relation to a great number of possible coordinates. When I chat with a friend whom I know well, each of his remarks and each of mine contains, in addition to the meaning it carries for everybody else, a host of references to the main dimensions of his character and mine, without our needing to recall previous conversations with each other. These acquired worlds, which confer upon my experience its secondary meaning, are themselves carved out of a primary world which is the basis of the primary meaning.[35]

Preobjective experience is not non-cognitive. Not all knowing is thetic: this is the distinction, Grene says, between Jean Paul Sartre, on the one hand, and Polanyi and Merleau-Ponty on the other.[36] It has an expressive significance of its own, perhaps comparable to Polanyi's existential as

---

34. Primordial: Merleau-Ponty, *Phenomenology of Perception*, 184, 254, 256, 370; pre-conscious: ibid., 242; pre-personal: ibid., 84, 254; pre-reflective: ibid., xiv, 241, 242; prearticulate: ibid., 404; pre-thetic or pre-thematic: ibid., xv, 96, 242, 275; non-positing: ibid., xvii, 242, 281, 291, 321, 365; ante-predicative: ibid., xviii, 129, 322, 343; tacit: Merleau-Ponty, *Phenomenology of Perception*, 60, 129, 295, 403; preobjective: ibid., xvii–xviii, 12, 57, 60, 79, 80, 96, 242, 267, 274, 314–15; pre-scientific: ibid., viii, 242, 301–2, 343, 350.

35. Ibid., 129–30.

36. Grene, "Tacit Knowing and the Pre-Reflective Cogito," 33.

opposed to representative meaning.[37] It is not irrational, anti-logical, or magical. Rather, Merleau-Ponty states emphatically: "We are not asking the logician to take into consideration experiences which, in the light of reason, are nonsensical or contradictory, we merely want to push back the boundaries of what makes sense for us, and reset the narrow zone of thematic significance within that of non-thematic significance which embraces it."[38] The phenomenal layer—this layer of phenomenological investigation—is rather "literally prelogical." Its significance for rationality is accentuated by the fact that, as we shall see, it forms the necessary foundation of all that which is overtly logical and rational. Here again we note the affinity with Polanyi.

Non-thetic knowledge differs from thetic knowledge in that it is not so much "thought" as it is "lived." This is Merleau-Ponty's way of capturing the true quality of preobjective experience. "But the system of experience is not arrayed before me as if I were God, it is lived by me from a certain point of view; I am not the spectator, I am involved."[39] He also says: "Natural perception is not a science, it does not posit the things with which science deals, it does not hold them at arm's length in order to observe them, but lives with them; it is the 'opinion' or the 'primary faith' which binds us to a world as to our native land, and the being of what is perceived is the antepredicative being towards which our whole existence is polarized."[40] Again, we note that the concept of "lived" knowledge provides an apt description for Polanyi's subsidiary knowledge. Both concepts contrast to the usual understanding of "subjective" as per the subject-object dichotomy. Neither is the disembodied pinpoint of the modern Cartesian heritage. Both express an intimacy of apprehension that is unarticulated but for that reason palpable and felt.

Let us also note that, here, we begin to see the affinities between Merleau-Ponty and Heidegger: preobjective experience "binds us to a world as to our native land." Merleau-Ponty, in fact, identifies preobjective experience with Being-in-the-world.[41] We have already seen in a quotation that he says that, to be in a world or to have a world, the subject must "sustain round about it a system of meanings whose reciprocities, relationships and involvements do *not* require to be made explicit in order to be exploited." Thus, preobjective experience furnishes the human being with a primordial contact with the world—not the planet, but rather the encompassing environment of all that is ready-to-hand. "To be a consciousness, or rather

---

37. Merleau-Ponty, *Phenomenology of Perception*, 291.
38. Ibid., 275; see also 274, 365.
39. Ibid., 304.
40. Ibid., 321–22; see also xvi–xvii, 60, 129.
41. Ibid., 79, 80, 129.

to be an experience, is to hold inner communication with the world, the body, and other people, to be with them instead of being beside them. To concern oneself with psychology is necessarily to encounter, beneath objective thought which moves among ready-made things, a first opening upon things without which there would be no objective knowledge."[42]

Merleau-Ponty speaks of "a communication with the world more ancient than thought," "a certain indissoluble link between things and myself," "a pre-conscious possession of the world," of an "inescapable link with phenomena," and of "a comprehensive and inarticulate grasp upon the world."[43] The world, as a result, is that which is there before any analysis of mine.[44] It is my situation or environment, my setting.[45] It is (ante-predicatively) self-evident, permanent, constant, a great unity.[46] It is independent and inexhaustible. Finally, as seen in the quotation above, the world for Merleau-Ponty includes both primary and acquired (i.e., human, cultural) worlds.[47]

The major ramifications of this concept of preobjective experience are immediately apparent. First, it proves to be the necessary foundation of all thetic knowledge. Preobjective experience is not to be found only temporally prior to objective thought, but rather it permeates and envelopes all subsequent knowledge.[48] It is that "first opening upon things without which there would be no objective knowledge": the basic experience of the world of which science is the second-order expression, upon which the whole universe of science is built.[49] "It is in the experience of the thing," Merleau-Ponty says, "that the reflective ideal of positing thought will have its basis."[50] For Merleau-Ponty, similarly to Polanyi, preobjective experience provides the solution to the *Meno* Problem (which Merleau-Ponty, like Polanyi, addresses): if no non-thetic knowledge exists, it is impossible to say how we even get a start on conception.

More importantly for our purposes, preobjective experience, as it has been explicated by Merleau-Ponty, enables us to surmount any ineradicable distinction between knower and known, between subject and object.

---

42. Ibid., 96.
43. Ibid., 254, 256, 298, 304, 404; see also 84, 96, 117, 129, 191, 261, 281, 303–4, 313, 321, 343, 370.
44. Ibid., x, xvii, 92.
45. Ibid., 267, 321.
46. Ibid., xvi, xvii, xviii, 129, 297, 313, 328, 375, 383, 397.
47. Ibid., 129–30.
48. Ibid., 254, 275.
49. Ibid., 96, viii.
50. Ibid., 242.

Remember that a return to preobjective experience is a rediscovery of "the system 'Self-others-things' as it comes into being," that it "restores to subjectivity its inherence in history."[51] Merleau-Ponty says that: "It is because it is a preobjective view that being-in-the-world can be distinguished from every third person process, from every modality of the *res extensa*, as from every *cogitatio*, from every first-person form of knowledge—and that it can effect the union of the 'psychic' and the 'physiological.'"[52] The object of science and the subject that posits it are terminal concepts "no nearer than on the horizon of primordial experience."[53] By virtue of preobjective experience (and hence subsidiary knowledge), the knower is inserted into the world prior to any abstractive distinction between the two. The knower has a world; he finds himself always already in and with the world. How this can be the case becomes a little clearer as we consider Merleau-Ponty's notion of the body, to which I shall now turn.

The Lived Body

The body in which Merleau-Ponty is interested is not the physical object but rather the body as we know it in its use—what many people have come to refer to as the "lived" body.[54] Already, we begin to see a parallel between the body and preobjective experience, which is also said to be lived. The parallel is extended by virtue of the fact that the kind of knowledge that we have of our bodies when we know them as lived is, to revert to Polanyian terms, subsidiary knowledge. Merleau-Ponty writes, "Now, as we have seen, the perception of our own body and the perception of external things provide an example of *non-positing* consciousness, that is, of consciousness not in possession of fully determinate objects, that of a *logic lived through* which cannot account for itself, and that of an *immanent meaning* which is not clear to itself and becomes fully aware of itself only through experiencing certain natural signs. These phenomena cannot be assimilated by objective thought."[55] He states: "The body is the habitual body, rather than the objective body."[56]

---

51. Ibid., 57.
52. Ibid., 80. On the subject-object distinction, see also xix–xx, 87, 88–89, 94, 95, 122n., 132, 154, 174, 198–99, 212, 256, 293, 320, 322, 373.
53. Ibid., 242, 219.
54. Ibid., 198, 206, 232, 301.
55. Ibid., 49; see also 82, 90, 95, 101, 149, 150, 314, 322.
56. Ibid., 104–6.

The body, Merleau-Ponty insists, partly for this reason, is not primarily an object. I am not conscious of my body as an object except when my body fails to function. Rather, my body is that for which there are objects:

> In so far as it sees or touches the world, my body can therefore be neither seen nor touched. What prevents its ever being an object, ever being "completely constituted" is that it is that by which there are objects.... Not only is the permanence of my body not a particular case of the permanence of external objects in the world, but the second cannot be understood except through the first: not only is the perspective of my body not a particular case of that of objects, but furthermore the presentation of objects in perspective cannot be understood except through the resistance of my body to all variation of perspective.[57]

Somewhat paradoxically, however, we are dependent upon the world for the knowledge that we do have of our bodies: "I am conscious of my body via the world, that it is the unperceived term in the centre of the world towards which all objects turn their face."[58] The paradox can be resolved in terms of Polanyi's focal-subsidiary relationship: we are subsidiarily aware of the proximal term (our bodies) in terms of the distal term (objects in the world). The proximal subsidiary acquires its meaning in terms of the distal. This is Polanyi's functional aspect of tacit knowing. At the same time, focal awareness of the distal term is simply not possible apart from reliance upon the proximal term—and thus our understanding of the world is dependent upon our bodies as lived. Thus: "When I transfer my gaze from one object to another, I am unaware of my eye as an object, as a globe set in an orbit, of its movement or state of rest in objective space, or of what these throw upon the retina. The figures for the alleged calculation are not given to me. ... My eye for me is a certain power of making contact with things, and not a screen on which they are projected."[59] In view of this last sentence, contact with reality in its primordial aspect, so to speak, just is body-knowledge.

Given this conception of the body, it is not surprising to hear Merleau-Ponty speak of the body itself as having knowledge.

> If habit is neither a form of knowledge nor an involuntary action, what then is it? It is knowledge in the hands, which is forthcoming only when bodily effort is made, and cannot be formulated in detachment from that effort. The subject knows where the letters are on the typewriter as we know where one

---

57. Ibid., 92; see also 90, 91, 94, 149, 153, 198, 278, 322, 352, 387.
58. Ibid., 82.
59. Ibid., 278–79.

of our limbs is, through a knowledge bred of familiarity which does not give us a position in objective space.[60]

This bodily knowledge parallels Polanyi's conception of skills. It hints strongly also of his notion of bodily extension, which, it turns out, is also embraced by Merleau-Ponty. Compare the following passages with relevant ones in Polanyi's works:

> But habit does not *consist* in interpreting the pressures of the stick on the hand as indications of certain positions of the stick, and these as signs of an external object, since it *relieves us of the necessity* of doing so. The pressures on the hand and the stick are no longer given; the stick is no longer an object perceived by the blind man, but an instrument *with* which he perceives. It is a bodily auxiliary, an extension of the bodily synthesis.[61]
>
> It shows that conversely those actions in which I habitually engage incorporate their instruments into themselves and make them play a part in the original structure of my own body.[62]
>
> There is no question here of any quick estimate or any comparison between the objective length of the stick and the objective distance away of the goal to be reached. The points in space do not stand out as objective positions in relation to the objective position occupied by our body; they mark, in our vicinity, the varying range of our aims and our gestures. To get used to a hat, a car, or a stick, is to be transplanted into them, or conversely, to incorporate them into the bulk of our own body. Habit expresses our power of dilating our being in the world, or changing our existence by appropriating fresh instruments.[63]

These passages present profoundly and beautifully, in elegant phenomenological description, not only the concept of bodily extension, but also those of indwelling and interiorization—concomitant aspects of bodily extension developed by Polanyi. Merleau-Ponty's word for interiorization is, appropriately, incorporation. The notion of indwelling is captured in the quotation immediately above in the phrase "transplanted into them." Merleau-Ponty gives voice to yet another point of Polanyi's: namely that, in consequence, bodily extension amounts to a transformation, a "dilation" of our being in the world. So important is this concept that Merleau-Ponty

---

60. Ibid., 144; see also 143, 233.
61. Ibid., 152.
62. Ibid., 91.
63. Ibid., 143; see also 132, 133, 145, 153, 180, 185, 193, 327, 403.

actually defines the body in terms of it: "But the human body is defined in terms of its property of appropriating, in an indefinite series of discontinuous acts, significant cores which transcend and transfigure its natural powers."[64] This passage also sounds a theme we have already noted: indefiniteness. This suggests an IFM effect attending the lived body itself.

There is perhaps a more basic notion than bodily extension in Merleau-Ponty, one that I am prepared only to sketch, but which appears to be a fundamental theme. This concept is intentionality, or the propensity of the human being to project himself beyond himself toward the world. Merleau-Ponty actually defines humanness in these terms: he says, "The essential point is clearly to grasp the project towards the world that we are."[65] He says that the human body "has running through it a movement towards the world itself."[66] This active, defining drive has a variety of manifestations: human being is always oriented toward a world, perception stretches beyond the lived to the unknown, the body extends itself, and thought outruns itself. Thus, we are always already in a world, but we are also oriented toward the world. In fact, both of these are constitutive of being human.

Polanyi himself connected his work with this notion of intentionality. Speaking of subsidiary-focal integration, he writes: "Hence thinking is not only necessarily intentional, as [phenomenologist Franz] Brentano has taught: it is also necessarily fraught with the roots that it embodies. It has a from-to structure."[67] Much more could be said concerning this formative concept of phenomenology, but I have only introduced the matter so as to be able to refer back to it in connection with Polanyi. For it is this intrinsic, vectoring, out-beyond-itself of the lived body that, I will presently argue, is an additional touchpoint between the two and, furthermore, that it holds promise of justifying realism.

We are now in a position better to understand the various phrases that Merleau-Ponty employs to define the body. We have already encountered some of his definitions. In addition to these, we find that the body is "an implicit or sedimentary body of knowledge" and "a familiarity with the world born of habit." It is "an expressive space," "a nexus of living meanings." It is our "point of view on things," our "situation in a certain physical and human setting," "a certain setting in relation to the world"; it is "my general power of inhabiting all the environment which the world contains." It is the

---

64. Ibid., 193.
65. Ibid., 405.
66. Ibid., 327; see also xvii–xviii, 106, 130, 137, 243, 303, 327, 387, 391.
67. Polanyi, *Tacit Dimension*, xviii.

"potentiality of a certain world."[68] As might be guessed upon reflection on these phrases, the lived body is tied intimately with, once again, being-in-the-world: "The body is the vehicle of being in the world, and having a body is, for a living creature, to be intervolved in a definite environment, to identify oneself with certain projects and be continually committed to them."[69]

Time and again, the words, "environment," "situation," and "setting," not to mention "world," crop up in connection with the body. The notion of the body is, by way of being-in-the-world, brought resoundingly in line with the concept of preobjective experience. Merleau-Ponty makes it clear both that the body is that entity that experiences preobjective experience, and that the primary sort of experience that the body has of the world is practical, preobjective.[70] Thus, it may be legitimately inferred that we have preobjective experience only insofar as we have a body—indeed, therefore, that we have knowledge only insofar as we live a body. In the other direction, we find a mutually implicatory relationship between the body and the world, a necessary coexistence, in addition to a *de facto*, antepredicatively self-evident one. Given this coalescence of the concepts of preobjective experience and the body, it is not surprising to find affirmed concerning the latter what was affirmed concerning the former, namely, that the body is our means of communication with the world.[71] It is—and here is yet another definition—"our general medium for having a world"; "to be a body is to be tied to a certain world."[72] The world is given to me along with the parts of my body, he says, "in a living connection comparable, or rather identical, with that existing between the parts of my body itself."[73] The body, he says time and again, is rooted in the world, has a hold on the world.[74] The clarity of this relationship between body and world also, by reason of the intimate connection between body and preobjective experience, serves to shed light on the claims made for the latter concerning its contact with the world.

We should not be surprised to find that the body is also proclaimed the foundation of knowledge. It is the *sine qua non* of all experience of the world—not only of objective knowledge of things in the world, but first and

68. Merleau-Ponty, *Phenomenology of Perception*, 238, 206, 235, 151, 197, 301, 388, 340, 303, 311, 106.

69. Ibid., 82.

70. Ibid., 254, 140–41.

71. Ibid., 92.

72. Ibid., 146, 148.

73. Ibid., 205.

74. Ibid., 101, 139, 141, 144, 206, 275, 297, 303, 320.

foremost even of our antepredicative experience of the world.[75] But in addition to this, as Merleau-Ponty argues cogently in his chapter on the cogito, even the apparently purest thought of a geometrically perfect triangle is rooted ultimately in the geometer's bodily hold on and experience of the world.[76] He concludes: "Our body, to the extent that it moves itself about, that is, to the extent that it is inseparable from a view of the world and is that view itself brought into existence, is the condition of possibility, not only of the geometrical synthesis, but of all expressive operations and all acquired views which constitute the cultural world." To repeat Merleau-Ponty's statement of the obvious: "But if there had been no mankind with phonatory or articulatory organs, and a respiratory apparatus—or at least with a body and the ability to move himself, there would have been no speech and no ideas."[77]

To round out the concept of the body, it must be stated that Merleau-Ponty rejects any dichotomy between the subject and his body. "I am my body," he often says; "we are incarnate beings."[78] Also: "Insofar as, when I reflect on the essence of subjectivity, I find it bound up with that of the body and that of the world, this is because my existence as subjectivity is merely one with my existence as a body and with the existence of the world, and because the subject that I am, when taken concretely, is inseparable from this body and this world."[79] Thus, "experience of one's own body runs counter to the reflective procedure which detaches subject and object from each other."[80] For I, as identified with my body, am in touch with—indeed, am rooted in—the world. Yet again, Merleau-Ponty's two concepts, preobjective experience and the lived body, are brought into line with one another. But the latter—the lived body—goes farther, for it transcends not only the gap within the knower himself but also the one between knower and known. Before anything else can be said, I am in the world.

Polanyi in the Light of Merleau-Ponty

Let us now return to Michael Polanyi. The hope is that our foray into Merleau-Ponty will prove helpful in the attempt to locate grounds for Polanyi's realism. Thus far, it has become clear that Polanyi's work and

75. Ibid., 82, 102, 142, 203, 204, 235, 237, 303, 311, 351.
76. Ibid., 381–88.
77. Ibid., 390–91.
78. Ibid., 106, 170, 198, 206, 403. Also, 83, 137, 138–39, 185, 193.
79. Ibid., 408.
80. Ibid., 198.

Merleau-Ponty's share much in common. The points of greatest coalescence are those that we examined in greater depth, namely, the pervasive existence of tacit knowledge, which serves as the necessary foundation for all explicit knowledge, and the concept of bodily extension. With regard to the first, Merleau-Ponty tends more to emphasize the layer of tacit or preobjective experience itself in his attempt to uncover perception as it really is. He pays less attention than Polanyi to the role this layer plays in the subsidiary-focal relationship and in integration. As for the second, Merleau-Ponty spends far more time than Polanyi examining and defining the body itself as well as its situation in the world, thus filling out and grounding what, in Polanyi, are not very well amplified although crucial and unequivocal concepts of bodily indwelling, extension, and interiorization. He does this in characteristically rich phenomenological description in contrast to Polanyi's elegant but more scientific way of speaking. So Merleau-Ponty's description communicates both the articulated claims and the subsidiary feel of them.

Subject-Object Distinction

What help, then, does Merleau-Ponty give us in grounding Michael Polanyi's realism? On the basis of their similarity, the following can legitimately be said about Polanyi. The subject-object dichotomy, both with respect to the knower and his body and with respect to the knower and the world, has its wings clipped, so to speak. Merleau-Ponty identifies knower and body; Polanyi espouses the bodily rootedness of all thought. Of course, we have to recall the difficulty concerning Polanyi and the mind-body problem to which Marjorie Grene points us: that Polanyi believed his work to be supportive of dualism. But, as Grene says, dualism can hardly be taken as a legitimate description of Polanyi's understanding of the relation between mind and body as a focal-subsidiary relationship between higher and lower levels. For Polanyi, mental capacities such as articulation arise out of bodily ones—as per his chapter on articulation in *Personal Knowledge*. Since this is so, if he cannot say with Merleau-Ponty that the knower *is* his body, he certainly can say that *we are incarnate beings*. Thus, in the relationship between body and thought, the subject-object dichotomy is already superseded. However, the from-to of Polanyi's subsidiary-focal integration maintains an appropriate duality, such that the knower may never be reduced to his body. This openended duality remains the signature of the lively asymmetric connectedness of the two.

Knower and World

This is further substantiated as we turn to the relationship between knower and world: for each of these thinkers, if there is a distinction between knower and world, the body is already on the hither side of it. But now, as a result of extending subsidiary awareness, the body itself—the body as we know it subsidiarily, in its uses, that is, the true body for Merleau-Ponty—extends out into the world. Our bodily being incorporates the entire realm of the subsidiary, thereby transforming our existence. What we have in this incorporated layer, Merleau-Ponty seems to say, is not however simply "body." It does not relegate "world" to that which still lies beyond the frontiers of our indwelling. Rather, it is "incorporated world." It is the world of Being-in-the-world, our situation or environment, that world in which we are at home already, prior to thematic enterprises. No distinction of subject and object, and no question of the reality of the external world, arise in connection with the act of riding a bicycle, for example. The distinction and the question arise only as we focally abstract to objectivize subject and object. And even this sort of thinking is parasitic upon the fundamental act; it cannot come into existence in the absence of such an experience—this, of course, is just what makes explicit knowledge dependent upon ultimately unformalizable tacit experience. Thus, the knower is already in the world; contact—though the word seems almost artificial in such a primordial state—has already been established prior to the germination of positing knowledge. To the extent that explicit knowledge is rooted in subsidiary, preobjective lived experience, to that extent explicit knowledge presupposes a lived, embedded contact within the world.

Thus, "the problem of the reality of the external world" arises only subsequently to its solution. And it arises, we may surmise, only if something blinds us to this preobjective contact. Merleau-Ponty and Polanyi have both noted our propensity to this blindness in our very legitimate subsidiary-focal integration: we can forget the subsidiaries in our drive for the pattern. Merleau-Ponty has spoken of needing, with respect to perception, to "foil its trick." I would surmise that both philosophers also attribute an excessive propensity to blindness to our Western, especially Cartesian, heritage, which has emphasized the certain, focal, and articulate as alone epistemic and rational. In any case, on one level at least, Polanyi's realism is clearly justified. There is a world, and it is knowable—by virtue of the fact that tacit knowing (preobjective experience) *is* being in the world, that the knower is rooted in the known prior to articulation. The idealist cul-de-sac generated by the Cartesian cogito is, in this respect, actually preempted.

Graham Dunstan Martin: Evoking the Prearticulate to Restore Our Sense of Reality

We are indeed aware of this lived contact with the world, and we can "evoke" it even if we cannot articulate it. Given our propensity, just noted, to run to the focal, we need to evoke it for epistemological and human wholeness. Graham Dunstan Martin engages Polanyian epistemology to offer an account of one way we do this. In a very good article called "The Tacit Dimension of Poetic Imagery," he argues that art—he uses poetry as his primary example—functions to evoke the tacit in experience. A major working premise of Martin's is the great breadth of the tacit and the severely limited character of the explicit in experience.[81] When we focus our attention on a perceptual object, a host of perceptual clues remain subsidiary. When we speak of that experience, even our focal perception of it is tacit with respect to our verbal description of it. Martin's conclusion: "There is, in short, a radical loss of experience in language: language is like a map, schematic. It does not reproduce experience in all its tacit depth."[82] His further conclusion, which alludes to Wittgenstein's well-known claim, is this: "But on the contrary, whereof we cannot speak, thereof we beat on drums, sing, dance round the campfire, paint bison on cave walls, compose symphonies, write novels, plays and poems. Whereof we cannot speak, thereof we create art."

Martin proceeds to demonstrate how poetic imagery works, by various means, to disrupt the ordinarily transparent link between experience and language, thereby collecting up and retaining hitherto forgotten or unconscious meanings and experiences. Metaphor possesses its great force by virtue of the fact that it stirs up toward consciousness the emotional depths of our lives.[83] He makes it clear, however, that poetry does not replace the hitherto tacit experience with explicit and abstract statements, but rather evokes the experience itself:

> The explanation for the great power of metaphor is therefore as Polanyi says: it is because we are indeed personally involved, in Polanyi's own deep sense of these words. We draw upon our own flesh and blood to provide the poet's words with their proper tacit depth. Instead of experience being formalized into

---

81. Martin, "Tacit Dimension of Poetic Imagery," 101–3. Martin works especially with Polanyi's last book, *Meaning*, written with the help of Harry Prosch. Marjorie Grene strongly advised me to steer clear of this book of Polanyi's since "he was senile when he wrote it." (Personal conversation, ca. 1979.) For the most part, I followed her counsel.

82. Ibid.

83. Ibid., 100, 107–8.

explicit and therefore abstract statements and detached from its tacit roots, the density of remembered reality is evoked. The streetplan is replaced by the city, the map by real fields and mountains. And the city, these fields and mountains are *ours*, for they are created by *our* remembered experience.[84]

Martin uses a single sample of poetry, showing how it evokes Polanyi's three levels of tacit elements—readily specifiable properties, known but not readily specifiable properties, and the indeterminate range of anticipations expressed in designating something.[85]

Therefore, Martin says that tacit experience is the link between ourselves and the real world.[86] The function of poetry is "to evoke the pre-articulate and restore to us a sense of reality." Martin's work affirms that we are in fact aware of this rich, prearticulate realm of experience, for we recognize its existence whenever it is evoked by a work of art. He shows how we may tap it to restore a sense of reality, of connectedness to and within the world.

Orienting toward Reality beyond the Lived Body's Preobjective Experience

It appears, then, that Merleau-Ponty lends confirmation and force to Polanyi's realism by offering a phenomenologically rich apprehension of bodied, preobjective being-in-the-world. One question remains, however. After a careful reading of *Phenomenology of Perception*, one is left wondering whether there is a world for Merleau-Ponty other than the world for me, the world that is my situation. Herbert Spiegelberg, in commentary on Merleau-Ponty, raises this question: he wonders whether "presence within the world" bridges the gap between subject and object only at the price of "a grading down of our concept of the world from something which exists, whether or not we are in contact with it, to something which is nothing apart from our being inserted in it."[87]

Spiegelberg does not draw a final conclusion regarding whether Merleau-Ponty's thought leaves us in this position, and he does not offer any solutions of his own. But if phenomenology expert Spiegelberg's concern proves true of Merleau-Ponty, the possible implications for my project—to use his work to ground Polanyi's realism—are as follows. If there is no other

---

84. Ibid.
85. Martin cites *Personal Knowledge*, 115–16.
86. Martin, "Tacit Dimension of Poetic Imagery," 108.
87. Spiegelberg, *Phenomenological Movement*, Vol. II, 551–52.

world besides the world-for-me, Merleau-Ponty's system fails to provide grounds for realism of the standard sort, for "the original realist thesis" is that there is a world independent of my knowing it. A second implication is that Polanyi's thought, while unable to tap Merleau-Ponty's for grounding, must actually be seen to diverge from Merleau-Ponty's; this is because Polanyi does embrace the original realist thesis. And finally, we would be left with the consequence that Polanyi's realism is justified to the extent that it corresponds with Merleau-Ponty's and, thus, may be retained only in a modified form. This last would hold unless some other justification can be found for Polanyi's realism.

That there is, in fact, some divergence between Michael Polanyi and Merleau-Ponty in this area can be seen by reflecting upon the two thinkers' understanding of two words, "world" and "contact." Consider the following extended passage from *Personal Knowledge*, in which can be glimpsed Polanyi's sense of the externality of the world with respect to the body:

> As a next step I shall try to strengthen and widen the distinction between subsidiary awareness and focal awareness by identifying it with another commonly known and universally accepted distinction, namely that which we feel between parts of our own body and things that are external to it. We usually take it so much for granted that our hands and feet are members of our body and not external objects, that this assumption is brought home to us only in case they happen to be disturbed by disease. . . .
>
> Our appreciation of the externality of objects lying outside our body, in contrast to parts of our own body, relies on our subsidiary awareness of processes within our body. Externality is clearly defined only if we can examine an external object deliberately, localizing it clearly in space outside. . . .
>
> Our subsidiary awareness of tools and probes can be regarded now as the act of making them form a part of our own body. The way we use a hammer or a blind man uses his stick, shows in fact that in both cases we shift outwards the points at which we make contact with the things that we observe as objects outside ourselves. While we rely on a tool or a probe, these are not handled as external objects; . . . the tool and the probe can never lie in the field of these operations; they remain necessarily on our side of it, forming part of ourselves, the operating persons. We pour ourselves out into them and assimilate them as parts

of our own existence. We accept them existentially by dwelling in them.[88]

Here, we observe those concepts that Polanyi shares in common with Merleau-Ponty: indwelling and interiorization, the extension of our being as we rely on tools. We also find that Polanyi identifies the subsidiary-focal distinction with the body-external object distinction. This confirms Polanyi's identification of the body with the extending realm of subsidiaries, a la Merleau-Ponty. However, it also serves to distinguish both from the external object. Externality is defined in terms of focal awareness and in contrast to the parts of our own body. Whatever the world is for Merleau-Ponty, the world for Polanyi is, thus, not simply the world that we have incorporated, but that which stretches *beyond* the incorporated world. And it is this latter upon which we ordinarily focus.

Something similar can be said concerning contact. It takes only a little reflection to realize that Polanyian contact is not restricted to the primordial contact that we have noted in his affinities with Merleau-Ponty. As we saw in chapter 6, there are in fact two general loci of contact for Polanyi, one in the realm of subsidiaries and the other bound up with the integrative focus. Subsidiary contact includes our prearticulate experience of the real and also various incorporated skills and theoretical frameworks on which we rely in pursuit of discovery. The now familiar "Pygmalion" passage on page 104 of *Personal Knowledge* delineates both of these. We make contact with reality throughout the broad spectrum of the subsidiary realm, beginning with our bodies and extending to articulate frameworks, language, and so on. But this and other passages, we have seen, clearly imply that the knower strives to make contact with reality beyond the realm of what is familiar to him by means of unprecedented integrations. This integrative contact has as its token of success the IFM Effect.

Thus, though human beings remain at all times rooted in subsidiaries, and by virtue of the nature of this level, remain ever rooted in the world, human beings focus their attention, center their activity, always beyond the subsidiary level. It is this reaching for contact beyond himself that, perhaps more than his subsidiary roots, may therefore be thought to characterize the knower, even though the other always remains a necessary, qualifying but enriching, condition. That this is the case for Polanyi can be substantiated by the following. Polanyi, in the chapter on articulation, goes in search of the origins or roots of what, at that time, he was calling the personal coefficient or the tacit component of knowledge. I believe he is looking for the origins, perhaps the rationale, of the tacit power of integration—something

---

88. Polanyi, *Personal Knowledge*, 58–59.

to account for "our intensive personal participation in the search for and conquest of our knowledge." At the farthest point of regress, he claims, lies an "active principle":

> The origin of this intellectual striving which (somewhat paradoxically) both shapes our understanding and assents to its being true must lie in an active principle. It stems in fact from our innate sentience and alertness, as manifested already in the lowest animals in exploratory movements and appetitive drives, and at somewhat higher levels in the power of perception. Here we find self-moving and self-satisfying impulses of both purpose and attention which antedate learning in animals and themselves actuate learning. These are the primordial prototypes of the higher intellectual cravings which both seek satisfaction in the quest for articulate knowledge and accredit it by their own assent.[89]

The active principle as it is manifested in perception "seeks to establish a coherence between all the clues of visual perception."[90] This effort "anticipates the manner in which we strive for understanding and satisfy our desire for it, by seeking to frame conceptions of the greatest possible clarity."[91] In summary of the chapter, Polanyi describes the active principle in the following way:

> As far down the scale of life as the worms and even perhaps the amoeba, we meet a general alertness of animals, not directed towards any specific satisfaction, but merely exploring what is there, an urge to achieve intellectual control over the situations confronting it. Here at last, in the logical structure of exploring—and of visual perception—we found prefigured that combination of the active shaping of knowledge with its acceptance as a token of reality, which we recognize as a distinctive feature of all personal knowing. This is the principle which guides all skills and connoisseurship, and informs all articulate knowing by way of the ubiquitous tacit coefficient on which spoken utterances must rely for their guidance and confirmation.[92]

The integrative principle and integrative contact with reality, both of which call us to stretch beyond the world in which we are subsidiarily, preobjectively grounded, are deeply ingrained in all life, and also distinctively

---

89. Ibid., 96.
90. Ibid., 97.
91. Ibid., 96.
92. Ibid., 132.

characterize what it means to be human. Thus, the world, as well as contact with that world, for Polanyi, cannot be restricted to the domain of subsidiary bodily rootedness. The desire to orient toward the world beyond where we are, to make contact with a reality fraught with indeterminate future manifestations, is as much a definitive anchor to humanness and to knowing as is our subsidiary embeddedness in our world.

But rather than this separating Polanyi from Merleau-Ponty, it may be the case that it in fact serves to reveal a further convergence between them. This outward reaching, the drive always to extend ourselves ever beyond ourselves, probably comprises the general notion that Merleau-Ponty has in mind by the word, "intentionality," introduced briefly earlier. While I have chosen, in exploring Merleau-Ponty's phenomenology of perception, to attend to the plethora of its evidence for the lived preobjective rootedness in the world, there is no doubt that the text could be mined for its permeating witness to intentionality. If this is the case, then we may infer that Merleau-Ponty, although he does not dwell upon the notions of integration, integrative contact with the world, and a world independent of us, would nevertheless be sympathetic to them.

Questions such as *why* we should project ourselves outwards, *why* greater coherence, clarity, and greater intellectual control are worthwhile, let alone achievable, *why* we strive for rationality and *why* it is to be preferred over irrationality—questions such as these I believe remain ultimately unanswered by both thinkers, except to reaffirm an unformalizable starting point, *that* we simply *are* this way. But far from seeing this indeterminacy as a holdout or residue left over in the effort to explain and justify knowing in a realist commitment, we may follow Polanyi's insights to affirm its anchoring, shaping role at the core of our being and knowing. Consider, as noted earlier, Polanyi's elegantly understated but devastating remarks regarding Kant's dismissal of "mother wit." Polanyi wonders that Kant and succeeding epistemologists could have dismissed consideration of it with a few random remarks. He comments: "Perhaps both Kant and his successors instinctively preferred to let such sleeping monsters lie, for fear that, once awakened, they might destroy their fundamental conception of knowledge. For, once you face up to the ubiquitous controlling position of unformalizable mental skills, you do meet difficulties for the justification of knowledge that cannot be disposed of within a framework of rationalism."[93]

---

93. Polanyi, "The Unaccountable Element in Science," in Grene, ed., *Knowing and Being*, 206.

Conclusion: Polanyi's Realism Justified

This move to consider the unformalizable indeterminacy of knowing and contact with reality as, not the recalcitrant residue of a fully justified epistemology and realism, but rather the positive core of the matter, additionally reveals that this very unformalizable indeterminacy itself justifies Polanyian realism. It is precisely the unformalizable—to speak oxymoronically—that testifies to the real. It is in the unformalizable that the real shows itself to be independent of the knower. Were we to be able to succeed exhaustively in justifying Polanyi's realism, we would therein have failed, and we would therein have cut ourselves off from the real. This suggests how Polanyian epistemology is key to resolving the philosophical problem of epistemic realism in that it shifts the burden of proof at the most fundamental level. It does so by calling us to accredit epistemically an inarticulable-because-rich indeterminacy at the root of, at the farthest outward reaches of, and throughout the entire trajectory of coming to know. Indeterminacy itself bears convincing witness to epistemic realism. Polanyian realism more than answers the problem of its justification; it calls into question the very question itself. This, I might add, is a signature feature of the IFM Effect.[94]

For all that, it is nevertheless valuable, if not ultimately determinative—if not, in the final analysis, necessary to consider how Michael Polanyi's realism is justified. In this chapter, we have considered the work of Maurice Merleau-Ponty, laying his rich phenomenological analyses alongside Polanyi's accounts. Doing so does corroborate and strengthen Polanyi's claim to realism. And Merleau-Ponty's analysis effectively explores the felt sense of Polanyi's subsidiary—as Dasein, as preobjective experience, as the lived body. The lived body is preobjective and thus prior to the subject-object distinction. As lived and preobjective, it is rooted in the world. The knower's contact with reality occurs primordially and preemptively in his bodily lived and felt, preobjective, communion in and with the real. As lived bodies, we are familiar with the world and with the extension of our understanding of it. The great divide between knower and reality, if it has not been entirely eliminated, has been substantially reduced. As a result, it takes not nearly so great a philosophical step to believe that the world in which I find myself rooted extends *beyond* me, that it does not exist simply for me, but

---

94. In the Star Trek film *The Wrath of Khan*, reference is made to the unsolvability of the "Kobiashi-Maru" simulator test for trainees in the flight program at Starfleet Academy. When asked how he passed the test, the legendary Commander James T. Kirk replies that instead of beating the computer at the prescribed game, he simply reprogrammed the computer. Reality has this way of "replying" to our questions.

rather *precedes* me, that it exists whether I am fully cognizant of it or not and beckons me to extend myself out into it.

Additionally—and perhaps more importantly for Polanyi—knowing is anchored in the prospect of contact with the external world beyond our understanding. This is the world that calls always beyond our current rationality to an ever-deeper grasp of itself. In fact, it would be impossible to explicate phenomenologically the bodily rootedness of all thought without dealing in the essentially defining orientation beyond myself to the world.

The primary substantiation that the realist thesis receives in Polanyi and in Merleau-Ponty is the testimony of perceptual experience. For Polanyi, the claim is additionally substantiated by the history of scientific discovery—which, for Polanyi, is simply a sophisticated extension of perception. Perceptual experience and the history of scientific discovery testify, according to Polanyi, that the human knower has tacit *fore*knowledge of the world that lies beyond and independent of him.

But there is an additional perceptual phenomenon the implications of which are more difficult to dismiss, and it is this phenomenon that captures the fascination and attention of both thinkers. Not only is it of the essence of human beings to project themselves beyond themselves; it is also of the essence of real things to do the same. We have come to know the real, to be familiar with it in at least a subsidiary way, as a result of being situated in the world. Within this primordial world, we recognize that that which claims to be real reveals itself only partially to us. Merleau-Ponty's phenomenological analyses serve to corroborate the Polanyian claim that our perception of, say, a cube, most immediately consists of our perceiving a couple of sides, most likely with variant shading. But what we see hints of other sides, of an interior, a pattern, and a distinctness from the environment in which we find it. The cube as we come to conceive of it results from an integrative feat, and because this integration has incorporated within it aspects of which we are not explicitly aware, it points beyond itself. Perception, Merleau-Ponty says, "throws me open to a world, but can do so only by outrunning both me and itself. Thus the perceptual 'synthesis' has to be incomplete; it cannot present me with a 'reality' otherwise than by running the risk of error. It is absolutely necessarily the case that the thing, if it is to be a thing, should have sides of itself hidden from me...."[95] That which we have come to recognize as real within the realm of our preobjective experience has as its distinctive characteristic this "iceberg" quality. As such, we continue to recognize the real in all our further epistemic pursuits, no matter how far beyond our ken, by virtue of our anticipation of indeterminate future manifestations.

---

95. Merleau-Ponty, *Phenomenology of Perception*, 377.

Grounding Polanyi's Realism: Merleau-Ponty

The IFM Effect testifies that we have made contact with reality precisely because it testifies, as its essential, signature feature, to reality itself. Reality is inexhaustible, fraught with indeterminate future prospects.

Polanyi says as much in the early 1970s, close to the end of his intellectual career. After defining reality in terms of anticipation that a real object will manifest its existence indefinitely hereafter, he says, "For years I have written about this kind of anticipation, but only now can I see an explanation for such anticipations. I see that the anticipations offered to us by good problems should be understood in the same way as the anticipations aroused by all true facts of nature. Thus, when a coherent set of clues presents us with the sense of a hidden reality in nature, we are visited by an anticipation similar to that which we feel in seeing any object already recognized to be real."[96] The presumption is that we are already used to the way real things behave. But the point here is that the real—perceptual experience teaches us—is in essence that beyond which there is always more. As such, even the real that we presently have grasped and incorporated by our integrative feats remains independent of us.

The independence of reality for Polanyi, therefore, ultimately stands or falls with his particular analysis of perceptual experience along with his innovative, philosophical tradition and problem-challenging epistemology of subsidiary-focal integration. This latter is in turn proposed on the basis of, and substantiated by, perceptual and scientific experience. Thus, the Polanyian defense of realism is inductive, as Alan Goldman said a defense of realism must be.[97] Such justification may be deemed insufficient by some, but only insofar as they remain closed to and skeptical of their own orientation within and experience of the world.[98]

---

96. Polanyi, "Genius in Science," 60–61.

97. Goldman, "Realism," 184.

98. This discussion continues as updated in Part 2. It will prove that, in one sense, the entire question of reality should be not so much answered as superseded; the accessibility of reality as a whole is not so much a stance to be justified but a posture to be lived. Hence the slight dissatisfaction one feels with the success of a proof of realism.

PART 2

Re-Calling Contact with Reality

Preface to Part 2

The first part of this work—in substance, my 1985 dissertation—has offered a thorough exposition of Michael Polanyi's notion of contact with reality, his realism, and a cluster of surrounding concepts. It has also conducted a detailed consideration of realist issues abroad in the 1970s, comparing and contrasting Polanyi's claims with those of other prominent philosophers. Part 1 has culminated with an in-depth scrutiny of the phenomenological insights of Merleau-Ponty, comparing and contrasting them with those of Polanyi's in an effort to tap the one to justify the realism of the other.

Part 2 consists of three fresh inquiries that update the earlier work by catching it up in my current, somewhat superseding, understanding and appreciation of Polanyi's contact with reality. This chapter and the next selectively update the still-lively realist vs. anti-realist debate. Specifically, in chapter 12 I offer a critical examination of a recently released work by premier philosophers Hubert Dreyfus and Charles Taylor, *Retrieving Realism*. The discussion also deals in Marjorie Grene's final work on realism. Chapter 13 selectively explores the realist vs. anti-realist debate through the recent efforts of William Alston's edited collection, *Realism and Antirealism*, and Anjan Chakravartty's *Metaphysics for Scientific Realism*.

Again, I pursue this primarily to showcase the distinctive contribution that Polanyi's work, if it were to be admitted to the conversation, would make. However, I also conclude, superseding the work of Part 1, that Polanyi's realism offers its own justification. While Merleau-Ponty's rich insights significantly corroborate Polanyi's independently developed account of knowing as subsidiary-focal integration and the preobjective, bodied contact with reality that humans fundamentally live out, my studied conclusion is that Polanyi's contact with reality is distinctively connected to discovery and beyond. The indwelt, committed pursuit of the approaching discovery and the surprising ingress of a fresh integrative pattern, accompanied by the telltale IFM Effect, is true realism. Reality breaking in, it may be said, itself justifies realism.

If the youthful question that first drove me into this inquiry was, "how do I know that reality exists outside my mind?" that question has transmuted, in my mature years, into, "what is reality like?" Specifically, does the sense of indeterminate future manifestations attest to our having made contact with reality because this just is the telltale signature of reality itself? And if so, I want to explore this aspect of reality. Is reality itself inexhaustive, fecund, generative, and generous? And you would not be mistaken in sensing that this latter question is less critically and more contemplatively pursued.[1]

Polanyi himself, in the plethora of statements we have explored, explicitly affirms that the IFM Effect characterizes both our contact with reality and reality itself. It is reasonable to surmise that, in some way, it led him to his metaphysical proposal of emergent levels of being. But I do not believe that he extensively explores the notion of the inexhaustive generativity of reality itself. In the last chapter of this part, I want to do this, offering a single beginning foray in an area I would be happy to explore indefinitely beyond the publication of this work.

In my further reading over the years, I have found several works that hint—or downright exult in—the abundant real.[2] The more exultant ones are metaphysical and theological works; many hail from a rejuvenated (or never dead) ancient Great Christian Philosophical Tradition. D. C. Schindler's work, the object of my engagement in chapter 14, is an elegant specimen of this lively current conversation.

For my own work, it is deeply appropriate to consider reality as including God as most real Person—or Persons-in-communion, as the Trinity would be. My youthful questions were two: the one about knowing reality at all and the one about knowing whether God exists. I felt that the questions were intertwined—that the answer to one would supply, and be, the

---

1. David Kettle creatively appropriates Polanyi's subsidiary-focal integration and other concepts to develop the fresh understanding of knowing, which modern Western culture (specifically, the Christian church) desperately needs to supplant the "modern betrayal of enquiry." Kettle calls for a "conversion to attentiveness towards God" (*Western Culture in Gospel Context*, 36, and ch 3 in pt. 2). Mary, the Virgin Mother of Jesus, epitomizes the lively attentiveness that is a dynamo of subsidiary-focal integration—in contrast to the critical stance that characterizes the high priest, Zacharias, when he asks the same question as Mary (Luke 1).

2. Oliver Davies' wonderful expression, in *The Creativity of God*. See n. 72 in ch. 14.

answer to the other. I do not at all mean to imply that this inquiry regarding contact with reality is not worthwhile and satisfactory in its own right. But it may be said that it is fraught with religious prospects. In this, I believe it is consistent with a Polanyian understanding of Polanyi's vision.

Nor is it inappropriate to pursue the matter of God in connection with Polanyi's work—although certain stipulations must be made. First: Polanyi did not set out to produce a "Christian work," nor a work in intelligent design.[3] He produced, as is obvious, an alternative epistemology to the end of representing and saving science and Western culture.[4] Second, he felt that his thought held implications for religion along with culture quite generally.[5] *Personal Knowledge* was his Gifford Lectures and thus concerned natural religion. He believed that his work was bordering on religion: touching frontiers about which religion was concerned and to which it ought to respond. However, he sensed that religion in its twentieth-century expression and reception was, perhaps, rather in need of the help of science—and of his discovery-based epistemology.[6] In any case, Polanyi himself was not closed to the prospect of profounder religious dimensions. He would have considered himself a Christian believer.[7] But he did not explicitly build God into his epistemology as a sort of anchoring component. He would have been uncomfortable with religion as a kind of add-on or explicit application of his work. In his work, although Polanyi speaks of God, readers justifiably disagree regarding what he believed and what he was saying, and also regarding the relative consistency or merits of what he professed on matters of religion.

Yet the Christian influence is evident, notably in his appeal to St. Augustine in developing the fiduciary program and his possibly tapping Christ's metaphor of the vine and the branches for the notion of indwelling.[8] And it is surely the case that an epistemology that actually succeeds as a positive third alternative to modernist epistemology and most reactions to it, and which therefore attacks their inherent atheism, is thus also an epistemology that intrinsically opens out afresh to transcending realities. It opens out thus

---

3. This was a topic of discussion at the special Polanyi Society Conference in 2002 at Loyola University.

4. Polanyi, *Personal Knowledge*, vii.

5. Polanyi, "Faith and Reason."

6. Polanyi, *Tacit Dimension*, 62.

7. This is the opinion shared by many in the Polanyi Society. Scott and Moleski, *Polanyi: Scientist and Philosopher*, 163.

8. Polanyi, *Personal Knowledge*, 266; I cannot now recall the source of my understanding regarding the latter.

to matters generally deemed theological—especially from the perspective of the compartmentalization of the modern age.

I suggest that Polanyi is theological in a manner more similar to the Great Christian Philosophical Tradition, than to a modern philosophical (and Protestant) approach. The former is more implicitly metaphysical. It is more an implicit, metaphysical, religious sense that permeates a fundamentally open-ended epistemology and ontology. The modern approach in theology and philosophy is anti-metaphysical—inspired as it is by thirteenth-century William of Ockham's (and others') conceptualism and restriction of apprehension of God to belief in Scripture's revelation.[9] Christianity for Polanyi does not appear to be a matter of divine will verbally articulated, to be focally reconciled to ordinary human truth claims or reverted to away from ordinary knowledge. We may surmise that Polanyi's upbringing and training in the liberal arts contributed to his formation in this respect. So I believe it is appropriate to bring Schindler's work into conversation with Polanyi's. I mean to suggest that this avenue of inquiry may better accord to Polanyi's agenda than does the endless realist vs. anti-realist debate.[10]

I believe that the IFM Effect is what it is because it is also the signature of reality. And I have come to believe that that is the signature of reality just because reality has its source in an endlessly generous and exuberant God. I came to realize, in a sudden, convicting integration of my own some years ago, that this is why Polanyi's repeated claim about contact with reality and its indeterminate future manifestations so tantalized me from the moment I first read it. In any case, this current book ends with the beginning of this opening out, as reality itself answers—supersedes—the problem of realism.

Finally, in this Preface to Part 2, I want very briefly to describe covenant epistemology. Covenant epistemology, my own Polanyi-inspired epistemic proposal, has come about as a direct result of my reflection on Polanyian contact with reality. This itself corroborates what I have been claiming here regarding the intrinsic openness of Polanyi's thought to religion, Christianity in particular. It counts as my development of his realism in the intervening years between the two parts of this book.[11] And describing it here also shows why I sense the fundamental accord between Schindler's work and Polanyi's.

---

9. Or, we should say, not "is," but "strives to be": I would argue that it is ultimately impossible to be successfully anti-metaphysical..

10. For a thorough and thoughtful consideration of the religious dimension of Polanyi's work, and the propriety of tapping his work for theological purposes, see Andrew Grosso's recent *Personal Being: Polanyi, Ontology, and Christian Theology*, 3, 31–33, 56–61, 97–98.

11. It is also a major reason that the dissertation was not published sooner.

The covenant epistemology thesis is that we should take as our paradigm of knowing the interpersonal, covenantally-constituted relationship.[12] Covenant epistemology presumes Polanyian epistemology, specifically subsidiary-focal integration, and, of course, the notion of contact with reality. But it moves on from there to develop the claim that we should deem not only the knower to be personal but, in some sense, *the known*—reality—to be personal as well. Thus, knowing would be like cultivating an interpersonal relationship. Best epistemic practices, then, are those that best cultivate interpersonal relationship: love, pledge, invitation, indwelling—it is easy to develop an extensive "epistemological etiquette." The act of coming to know (discovery) is transformative encounter. The proper end of knowing is not explicit exhaustive comprehension nor something that falls short of that wrongheaded ideal. Instead, the proper end of knowing is communion with the real.

The main task in justifying covenant epistemology is creatively explicating and justifying wherein reality can be said to be person-like. I will not replicate any of that here. But two things pertain to this current book project. First: it is directly from reflection on Polanyi's contact with reality that I developed the idea of reality as responding as if it were a person. And second: for the Christian believer, it is obvious that reality includes the original Person or Persons-in-communion; reality is God and God's "stuff." Although, quite frankly, the fact is that Christian believers, also products of modernity and modernist epistemology, struggle even to get this from their own doctrinal commitments so as truly to be shaped by them.[13] It is emphatically not the case that covenant epistemology claims to describe the knowing only of Christian believers, or that belief in God is necessary to knowing. However, in aptly describing ordinary knowing, I believe that it tacitly signposts or anticipates God's reality. To invite the real, one must anticipate that it—he—might come.

---

12. Meek, *Loving to Know*.

13. This is why I have found repeatedly that Polanyian epistemology and covenant epistemology can be life-transforming.

12

Polanyi and *Retrieving Realism*

The recent release of *Retrieving Realism*, the valuable contribution of premier philosophers Hubert Dreyfus and Charles Taylor, strategically helps my revisiting of Polanyi's realism and my own argument with respect to it.[1] For, like my 1985 dissertation (Part 1 of this work), they take on the current philosophical establishment (in an expert and persuasive way).[2] What is more, like my dissertation, as well as like Marjorie Grene's approach around that time, as reflected in her end-of-century *Philosophical Testament*, Taylor and Dreyfus look specifically to Maurice Merleau-Ponty to demonstrate realism. And finally, all of these, including my original dissertation, while they find in his work rich and deep confirmation for realism, nevertheless acknowledge, in an understated way, that Merleau-Ponty ultimately falls short of delivering proof-positive for realism.

In this chapter, I would like to show this. I would also like to show the comparative superiority of Polanyi's realism in the fresh light of these considerations. I will suggest that Polanyi's realist commitment is not only superior, but really the only kind of realism worthy of the name. In this, I am offering my revised understanding of and appreciation for Polanyi's realism. I will show that hints of the Polanyian solution are evident, though unacknowledged, in Dreyfus and Taylor, and, acknowledged, in Grene. In

---

1. Dreyfus and Taylor, *Retrieving Realism*.

2. And as I too attempt in my later work, they labor to display the damaging wrongheadedness of the philosophical presumptions of modernity in which alone the question of realism is engendered.

the final analysis, Merleau-Ponty does not hold forth a sufficient answer to the question of realism; Polanyi does.

Reconsidering Polanyian Realism

Part 1 of this work dates from the 1980s. Part 2 consists of fresh inquiry and reflection. Here is a brief, current synopsis of and reflection on Polanyi's notion of contact with reality and its implicit realism.

Contact with Reality: Reality Exists Independently of Our Knowing It[3]

Polanyi, who wrote to challenge mid-twentieth-century positivism and strict empiricism, felt that whatever the explicit self-description of scientists, their implicit conviction must be that in their research they are pursuing the presence of a hidden reality with which they seek to make contact. Discovery is making contact with reality; contact with reality is sensed as the unspecifiable sense of indeterminate future manifestations. In fact, reality itself is typified as that which manifests itself indeterminately in future, inexhaustible profundity—that's why this sense justifies any claim to have made contact with it. And our concepts, individually or taken together as science, are claims we hold because we believe them to be clues to reality—and thus themselves are real. All of these sorts of claims Polanyi uttered as obvious assertions in need of no justification. Polanyi, unlike myself and so many in modernity, did not problematize realism; rather, he witnessed to it as its devoted handmaid.

Knowing and Being

Although it is somewhat problematic to specify, there is an evident resonance between Polanyi's view of reality and his epistemology.[4] Both have, as their signature, a pregnant, positive indeterminacy. This is "the unaccountable element in science," which continually intrigued and preoccupied him as key to a fresh understanding of knowing, of being, and of our contact.[5]

---

3. This is what is known in the discussions as metaphysical realism.

4. Polanyi himself endeavored to draw the inference that being, like knowing, exhibits a from-to structure. (See Lecture 2, "Emergence," in *Tacit Dimension*, for example.) While this argument may be only partially successful, it is nevertheless successful.

5. Polanyi, "The Unaccountable Element in Science," in Grene, ed., *Knowing and*

His epistemological claims and his metaphysical claims mutually support each other. Realism justifies knowing as a riskily responsible commitment to submit to reality, to trust our intuitive grasp of things we cannot yet articulate, while at the same time refraining from inappropriately exalting that grasp. By the same token, Polanyian epistemology is requisite to his realism. It takes indwelling subsidiary clues to disclose the hidden contours of a yet-to-be-conceived pattern—just as you must give yourself to look through the telescope if you want to see the moons of Jupiter or take a spin on a bike if you are to achieve the performance. You cannot see the real by focally fixating on its particulars. So to answer the realist question, just as to access the real, you have to be "real-ized," so to speak—indwelling the groove of it subsidiarily. Not only is there no view from nowhere; the view from nowhere is intrinsically anti-realist. Personal indwelling of the clues is the window to the real.[6]

Indwelling

Positively speaking, indwelling opens the world, connecting the knower more deeply in it—something I ponder every time I watch Pirates baseball or Steelers football.[7] Putting this all together, the act of coming to know, then, is anchored in the unspecifiable and orients outward toward the unspecifiable.[8] And this unspecifiable is no lack, but rather is telltale positive surplus of meaning that confirms reality and the proper structure of what we are doing when we know.

Being, 105–22.

6. I state this as directly opposite of Dreyfus' and Taylor's claim (*Retrieving Realism,* 133).

7. This critical dimension of Polanyian epistemology accords with Merleau-Ponty, and thus also with Dreyfus and Taylor's work, about which I will say more presently. The differences are, however, that phenomenology isn't necessary (unless you consider what Polanyi is offering to be, in fact, a phenomenology of knowing and discovery), as Taylor and Dreyfus think; nor, contra their work and Merleau-Ponty's, I believe, can it be accomplished without the idea of subsidiary-focal integration, what Polanyi calls the structure of tacit knowing.

8. In the dissertation (Pt. 1 of this book), I also show that Polanyi suggests that all aspects of subsidiary-focal integration can be seen to be involved in making and sensing contact with reality.

Reflecting on the Reality Statement

Here are a few observations regarding Polanyi's reality statement. First, I haven't ever heard anyone else ever speak quite like this! It seems to have no precedent in philosophy. Nor did I find in his writings anything like an origin of this way of thinking. Apparently, he simply observed the phenomenon and thus presumed it as evidence for other arguments. Plus, Polanyi's claim about contacting reality is remarkable. To this day, I cannot utter the statement or conceive the idea without an automatic sense of wonder and, quite often, with literal chills up my spine.[9]

Second, Polanyi's realism was and is surprising. His epistemology stands in direct challenge to foundationalism, and it was and is widely misheard to represent, at best, a critical realism if not a downright anti-realism. It was presumed that the personal attenuates and impedes contact with reality. But this is a blatant (albeit common) misunderstanding of Polanyi.[10] And Polanyian epistemology isn't non-foundationalist either. As Lady Drusilla Scott argues, referring to Ernest Sosa's famous characterization of foundationalism and coherentism, it isn't a pyramid (foundationalism), nor is it a raft (coherentism).[11] It is a swamp. Scott is endeavoring to capture pictorially the fact that the critical "foundation" for Polanyian epistemology is real but unformalizable and subsidiary.[12]

As it turns out, far from being a modest realist, Polanyi is an immodest realist—sold out to reality with no shame. And far from this being a robust realism, this is realism$_2$—an abundant realism, realism in spades. Grene opts for the phrase, "the primacy of the real."[13] This is the real as systematically but inexhaustively *surprising* and *generous*. Far beyond a one-to-one correspondence of thought and things, this is *a one-to-infinity correspondence*—and it's just the infinity that testifies to the one. But the infinity is always half-hidden and, as-yet, inarticulable. "Pregnant" is a wonderful adjective; it applies aptly both to the real as well as to any true claim.

---

9. I am a very excitement-driven person. It wasn't until years after the dissertation that I realized that I had written a dissertation on excitement—in its perhaps solitary appearance in twentieth-century epistemology!

10. Helmut Kuhn, "Personal Knowledge and the Crisis of the Philosophical Tradition," in Langford and Poteat, eds., *Intellect and Hope*, 114.

11. Sosa, "The Raft and the Pyramid."

12. Drusilla Scott, *Everyman Revived*, 59–61.

13. Grene, "The Primacy of the Real," ch. 6 in *Philosophical Testament*.

Part 2: Re-Calling Contact with Reality

What's Behind the Reality Statement?

What might have motivated Polanyi's distinctive notion of reality? First, it is the primary concern of this chapter to suggest that Polanyi *was* a discoverer. Of all the people I have read frequently and closely, he is the only person writing philosophy who was first a *premier* scientist and whose identity and calling were so forged. Of course, he was attuned to the not-yet-knowns of reality—he banked on them! This was more than his bread and butter: to reality and its birthing, Polanyi was handmaid and midwife. He submitted to it, trusted it, and knew its hidden presence like the back of his hand.[14]

Second, because Polanyi was one of modernity's finest and finest-tuned minds, he modeled the richest of its thought. But he did this while at the same time grasping tacitly and identifying explicitly its denuding and distrusting of reality. He understood that this denuding and distrust intrinsically threatened science and society. He gave intentional expression to that which directly would subvert this deadening proclivity of the age.

Third, his polymathic scholarship and variegated religious commitments exposed him to thought beyond the bounds of the voices of modernism—to the ancient liberal Christian tradition, for example. There is a kind of Platonic eros to being and knowing, for Polanyi. This is evident, to name but one place, in his discussion of intellectual passions, of coherence and beauty as tokens of reality. And there is an unqualified trust in the rationality of nature.

Fourth, in attending (one might say, phenomenologically) to what it is that we do when we know, in ordinary life, in perception, in scientific discovery, and in any critical verification and holding of claims, Polanyi himself was finally not held captive by the Cartesian picture. He saw instead that all knowing has a two-level, from-to structure of dynamic subsidiary-focal integrative insight. There is no grasping of an aspect (only ever an aspect) of reality's inexhaustible profundity apart from the responsible shaping of an integrative pattern fraught with a surplus of meaning. There is no accessing such a pattern apart from trusting yourself to a kind of intuitive foreknowledge carried in the clues. And there is no grasp of the pattern that is not, in turn, pregnant with unforeseeable implications. This last is, of course,

---

14. In comparison with Merleau-Ponty, for the sake of Dreyfus and Taylor and others conversant with his work, perhaps we may see that Polanyi was himself doing phenomenology—phenomenology of discovery. To quote Taylor and Dreyfus quoting Merleau-Ponty, "the thing is presented not as spread out before us but as an inexhaustible reality full of reserves." (*Retrieving Realism*, 61; original quote from *Phenomenology of Perception* [trans. Donald Landes. London: Routledge, 2013, 261]. This, Merleau's reflection on Cézanne's superior artistry, is how the phenomenon of discovery feels to the discoverer.

the reality statement. Where knowing is subsidiary-focal integration, making sense of reality inevitably overflows with exciting unspecifiable future prospects.

Additionally, Polanyi did give thought and expression to a non-reductivist account of being as characterized by levels, in which each higher level can never be exhaustively determined in the grammar of its next lower neighbor. In such an ontology, indeterminacy is the name of the game. There is an intrinsic telltale openness to a higher level or yet-to-be-ascertained further transformative pattern. Reality is characterized by excess.

Finally, and negatively, it must be said that, for Polanyi, the inherent incompleteness of our conceptualization should not be thought to be the sole cause of our sense of the possibility of indeterminate future manifestations, our sense of the fecundity of the real. The knower's finitude is, of course, real. But reality's fecundity is intrinsic—and it holds supervening primacy.

Underscoring Polanyi's Realism: Grene's Primacy of the Real

In a chapter entitled "The Primacy of the Real," in her *Philosophical Testament*, Marjorie Grene recurs to Polanyi's work to add to her own effort to work out the necessary distinctives of human being. From it, we can derive a sense of her late-in-life take on Polanyi's realism. By the primacy of the real, Grene means that we exist within a real world, surrounded by it and shaped by it, and that we ourselves are real instantiations of the world's character.[15] The world "is what obtrudes, fascinates, concerns me from the start and, so far, to the end, and it is also what has made me and continues to make me who I am."[16]

She is contrasting her position with the deflationary "realism" of Arthur Fine's "natural ontological attitude," once he has "proclaimed that realism is dead."[17] She criticizes his methodological presumption that scientific realism must be justified via an argument more accurate and exact than the methods by which the conclusions of science are elicited: this reflects the deeper unexamined presumption that processes of discovery and explanation must be kept strictly separated. Of course, this approach lends itself to the ideal of explicit knowledge, but in circumventing the unsettling messi-

---

15. Grene, *Philosophical Testament*, 114.
16. Ibid., 115.
17. Ibid., 113. This compares favorably to the deflationary realism of Richard Rorty, which is Dreyfus and Taylor's main thrust of attack.

ness of discovery, it also fails to pay attention to what scientists actually do. However, abandoning this strict separation easily allows us to see "the real immersion in reality of the processes of science."[18]

At this point Grene introduces Polanyi as the one who made this point central to his account of scientific knowledge. Here is her succinct summary of Polanyi's claims:

> All knowledge, he argued, necessarily includes a tacit component on which it relies subsidiarily in order to focus on its goal, whether of theoretical discovery and formulation or of practical activity. All knowledge has a 'from-to' structure: it is the groping of embodied beings toward the understanding of something in the world that surrounds them. . . . The primary drive is outward. Indeed, it is through that from-to relation that knowledge is rooted in the reality of the knower and his (her) world.

Grene proceeds to represent what, in her mind, is Polanyi's clearest statement of the move that he is commending—the "changing camp" passage.[19] Of this, she avers that "the move Polanyi called for seems to me indispensable if we are to escape the to-and-fro of realism-anti-realism arguments."[20] But then, she also adds that the admission of a tacit dimension is necessary but not sufficient to establish realism. She also notes, regarding Merleau-Ponty, whose work she also approves and taps, that his great contributions are similarly necessary but not sufficient. I will return to this later.

In her engagement of Polanyi, Grene underscores two essential dimensions of his proposals which are radically significant for the problem of realism. One is the subsidiary-focal integrative structure of all knowing that orients a knower not only within but through and outward from herself toward the world. By contrast, as we will see, Dreyfus and Taylor's proposals evidence that they omit this critical structure of knowing, and that their work is comparatively inferior, I believe, as a result of it.

The other essential dimension, according to Grene, is the critical importance, not to mention necessity, of a shift from the context of explanation to the context of discovery, as a result of which alone it becomes possible to merge them. If we are to talk of the primacy of the real, Polanyi's contribution is to talk of the primacy of discovery. Discovery, not explanation, is the paradigm for all knowing. Discovery highlights the indeterminate as the very thing that testifies to the real. Discovery entails realism and justifies realism against skeptical attack. As we will see, Dreyfus and Taylor call for a

18. Ibid., 121.
19. Polanyi, "The Logic of Tacit Inference," in Grene, ed., *Knowing and Being*, 156.
20. Grene, *Philosophical Testament*, 123.

shift of presumption that significantly weakens the stranglehold of "the picture that held us captive" that is modernist epistemology. But their shift in no way foregrounds discovery. It is a shift, rather, from "mediated contact" theory to "direct contact theory," where the latter consists of a prereflexive engagement with the world. I will show that, for Polanyi's notion of contact with reality and for his realism, discovery is key.

Another aspect of Grene's Polanyi-consonant discussion is especially significant for my purposes in this paper. As her overall argument in the book makes patently clear, it is unnecessary to the establishment of realism that a contact with reality or a proof of realism be prethetic. I say this also in contrast to Taylor and Dreyfus. Polanyi's tacit dimension is not at all relegated to the prethetic, for we dwell in our language and concepts subsidiarily as we dwell in our bodies. It's only as we subsidiarily dwell in our language that language itself means anything, or that it bears on and opens reality beyond us. I would also add that, if perhaps we at some point operated meaningfully prior to learning language—and this is highly debatable given that the baby *in utero* is always already immersed in her mother's conversation even as she is embraced in her nurturing body—once we do learn language, the effect is retroactive.[21] As my then three-year-old daughter said to me, once you can read, you can never not read that the stop sign says stop. Our indwelled language comes to permeate and give shape to all of our experience.

I will return to these matters and draw on them as I complete this argument.

Contact with Reality in Taylor and Dreyfus

The ongoing philosophical debate regarding realism and anti-realism, as well as this effort to update and publish my dissertation, both benefit greatly from Taylor's and Dreyfus's *Retrieving Realism*. The two argue that the entire debate is only viable within what Wittgenstein famously called "the picture that held us captive"—modernist epistemology.[22] This picture views knowledge as mediated by our mental representations in an inner-outer "dualist sorting" that sticks to explicit propositions in justifying beliefs. They trace the picture's persistence through the various "turns" of contemporary philosophy; and they trace its critique beginning with Kant's demonstration of presuppositions requisite to support this supposedly presuppositionless

---

21. Grene argues that humans—unlike animals such as bees—use language *not* for communication but to make worlds in and through which they live. ("Our Way of Coping: Symbols and Symboling"; *Philosophical Testament*, ch. 8).

22. Dreyfus and Taylor, *Retrieving Realism*, ch. 1.

picture.²³ However, Taylor's and Dreyfus's proposal is to replace the picture with a different picture—one of direct rather than mediated contact. This direct contact is located, they say, only by means of phenomenology, beneath explicit reflection in our engaged coping with the things in the world. This prereflexive, self-authenticating, direct grip on the world accomplishes the following: it supplies knowledge the requisite sense-making conditions. It is the locus of the interface of causes and reasons to support justified believings that are connected to the world. And, to the point of the book's title, it furnishes the kind of active-receptive body-world attunement that retrieves realism It furnishes, not just a deflationary realism (effectively an anti-realism—sparring partner Richard Rorty's, to be exact), but a robust realism.²⁴

As central to their argument, Dreyfus and Taylor present Merleau-Ponty's phenomenology of perception: of embodied, engaged coping that continually moves toward an optimal grip on the world. And to shore up a Merleau-Pontyean account against further, perhaps justified, charges of idealism, they appeal to the work of Samuel Todes, in his *Body and World*, to demonstrate that this coping simply has to be seen to be in response to independent reality, as shown specifically in the at once spontaneous and receptive attunement to a vertical field—the phenomenon of balance.²⁵ For Taylor and Dreyfus, this is the determinative proof they are looking for to justify belief in a reality independent of our conceptions of it.

Beyond this, the book further argues for a similar direct contact with other bodied humans; to develop this the authors tap Hans-Georg Gadamer's notion fusion of horizons.²⁶ This traces a second line of argument against the solitary mediationalist picture. They entertain further imagined challenges from a Rortyesque pragmatism,²⁷ and they conclude by developing a pluralist qualification to their nevertheless robust realism.²⁸

A key tenet of *Retrieving Realism* is that shifting the picture regarding contact with reality proves a most effective move in moving beyond the ongoing realist vs. anti-realist debates to retrieving realism. It is most effective because it obviates the entire problem. They recur more than once to Merleau-Ponty's dismissive but profound aside: "To ask whether the world

---

23. Ibid., ch. 2.

24 This is my brief summary of the book's overall argument.

25. Ibid., ch. 7. (Reference to Samuel Todes, *Body and World* [Cambridge: MIT Press, 2001].)

26. Ibid., ch. 6.

27. Ibid., ch. 7.

28. Ibid., ch. 8.

is real is not to understand what we are saying."²⁹ While they do not note it, I feel sure the irony is not lost on these great philosophers that, if the problem is therein entirely obviated, there would have been no need for them to write this book. But, as is sometimes the case in life, it takes an apparently needless great effort and sacrifice to shift opinion away from beguiling falsehood and back to the obvious. So Taylor and Dreyfus's work offers a valuable contribution in a modernity that won't quit.

Despite what I feel to be an unwarranted omission of attention to Polanyi's significant, innovative, and effective insights that resonate deeply with their claims—contributions offered a half century in advance of their own from a premier practitioner of science whom they knew—Taylor's and Dreyfus's influence in this book may serve to clear the way for other dismissive philosophers to give Polanyi's work a more serious hearing. One may hope.³⁰

Their work is highly germane to my own. As I noted, apart from the distinct difference of attentiveness to Polanyi's reality statement in hopes of justifying realism, it takes an approach similar to my 1985 dissertation in engaging contemporary philosophical discussions surrounding realism and tapping Merleau-Ponty as a critical proof of realism. With respect to the contemporary conversation, the work of Taylor and Dreyfus, as premier philosophers, is expertly done and powerfully effective. With respect to the

---

29. Ibid., 53n. Quoted in French from the Gallimard edition of *Phenomenologie de la Perception* (1945), 396.

30. This chapter was first a paper I gave at the 2016 Polanyi Society Conference. Several papers and a panel addressed themselves to Dreyfus and Taylor's book. At the conference, a general sense of frustration prevailed regarding the utter absence of attention to Polanyi's insights. (Actually, *Retrieving Realism* cites Polanyi one time for a four-word dependent phrase, but even this was evidently added in later, since the subsequent footnote on pp. 76–77 was never altered to reflect it.)

The following are factors in our frustration. First: in 2014, the Polanyi Society invited Taylor and his work to be featured at their Annual Meeting. Second, Polanyi's ideas on these matters predate theirs by decades. Third, Polanyi, with the agency of Marjorie Grene, in the 1960s and 70s actually convened several study groups, in which Dreyfus and Taylor were invited to participate, the purpose of which was to extend the influence of the Polanyian vision. (Breytspraak and Mullins, "Polanyi and Study Groups"; see also Grene, ed., *Interpretations of Life and Mind: Essays around the Problem of Reduction.*) At the conference, the counterpoint was made that Dreyfus and Taylor, in *Retrieving Realism*, are in fact carrying Polanyian influence forward in their work, as per the mission of the Study Groups. (Rutledge, "Polanyi's Prescience.") It was noted that Dreyfus and Taylor may well have felt that citing Polanyi, who is quite generally perceived as not being a conversant in the conversation, might hamper the reception of their own work. (Apczynski, "Reflections on *Retrieving Realism*.") However, even if these are true, it remains the case that due consideration of Polanyi's work in regard to the topic of realism is expected of these philosophers. Surely their own reputation would not have suffered, but rather would have exhibited greater integrity—and humility.

use of Merleau-Ponty to prove realism, my dissertation climaxed where *Retrieving Realism* does. So studying this fresh work, now decades later, has served to clarify my maturer thinking regarding realism and Polanyi's contribution. In the remainder of this paper, I want to show how, as I now believe, Polanyi's contact with reality is distinctively superior in offering definitive proof of the one kind of realism that is worthy of the designation.

Contrasting Notions of Contact with Reality

Taylor's and Dreyfus's idea of contact with reality, while sharing much in common with Polanyi's earlier insights, diverges significantly from Polanyi's innovative notion. This divergence, I will argue, is just what allows Polanyi's realism to succeed distinctively.

For Taylor and Dreyfus, contact with reality is located in the prereflexive (and thus non-explicit), engaged coping with the things of the world beneath our verbalization and reasoning. It is therefore direct and not mediated, and it provides the sense-making conditions for all verbalization. *Retrieving Realism's* argument never mentions discovery; the word is absent from the index. By contrast, Polanyi, while he identifies the rootedness of the subsidiary, reserves the phrase, "contact with reality" for what discovery accomplishes. Contact is even located beyond discovery. It is characterized by indeterminate future manifestations. It is not so much a one-to-one correspondence as a one-to-infinity attestation of a similarly inexhaustive independent real. Inexhaustibility does get a mention in Dreyfus's and Taylor's argument[31]; however, I believe that since their argument remains defined by the stipulations of modernity—the context of explanation, correspondence, and confirmation—what is telltale and spectacular to the premier scientist is overlooked by the premier philosophers. Polanyi, by contrast, was a premier scientist; of course the next discovery was for him the all-important focus.

For Taylor and Dreyfus, the telltale clue is the confirmed, determinative, active receptivity in the matter of keeping our balance. For Polanyi, it is the unaccountable element in science—both the inarticulate subsidiary that undergirds and outruns the articulate in knowing and the sense of indeterminate future manifestations which attends discovery as the signature of an independent reality. What it was about Kant that caught Polanyi's attention was not the transcendental deduction, since, as I am about to argue in the next paragraph, subsidiaries are subsidiary—not capable of being focally examined. Rather, it was what Kant calls mother wit—and never attends

---

31. Dreyfus and Taylor, *Retrieving Realism*, 138–39.

to.³² But, for a premier scientist, honing mother wit is key to success. And for Polanyi, indeterminacy, not determinacy, testifies to the real.

While subsidiary-focal integration easily (and without phenomenology) opens and accredits the tacit dimension that Merleau-Ponty explores, and while Polanyian contact with reality is always also rooted in the pre-reflexive, the accent for Polanyi is decidedly not on the "from," but on the "to" and beyond. So in addition to the distinctive difference between Polanyi and Taylor and Dreyfus regarding discovery, there is a distinctive difference regarding those implicit beliefs: Taylor and Dreyfus do not recognize, as Merleau-Ponty did not, the all-important from-to structure of knowing. They display no concept of the subsidiary. But if you emphasize the implicit as the locus of contact, and if you have not rendered the implicit subsidiary, your position continues to drive anti-realism—as the authors' chapter 7 confirms. Continuing to engage the prethetic layer focally gets in the way of the surrender to the real that is true realism, because it implicitly rejects the very indwelling of what is thereby subsidiary that opens us to and launches toward reality.

The notion that all that supports our focal integration is subsidiary, unique to Polanyian epistemology, holds very significant implications highly germane to the matter of realism, implications that directly contrast to Taylor's and Dreyfus's proposal. First, of course understanding is mediated—that's just what humans do in knowing. Second, that mediation is no longer a barrier, but rather a rooting in the world. Third, we indwell—commit ourselves to—subsidiaries in order to seek the real. By definition, we can't be scrutinizing them simultaneously. The language of commitment and submission, far from being an antiquated add-on in a superior modernity, just is what we do when we indwell subsidiaries in hope of contacting reality. Fourth, we meld subsidiaries creatively in anticipation of the as-yet-undiscovered pattern we seek. In contrast to Dreyfus's and Taylor's argument about pluralism, for Polanyi, something like pluralism is the intrinsic working of subsidiary indwelling. For subsidiarily, we creatively meld what focally would appear to be contradictories.³³ That's how we invite the real.

---

32. Polanyi, "The Unaccountable Element in Science," in Grene, ed. *Knowing and Being*, 105–6. Note Polanyi's understated critique: he wonders that a critique of pure reason could have accepted "such a powerful mental agency" without analysis, and how generations of scholars similarly could have ignored it. He suggests that perhaps they were letting sleeping monsters lie for fear of the destruction of their fundamental conception of knowledge.

33. The effort at pluralism which Taylor and Dreyfus make in their last chapter thus tends to confirm that they lack the critical notion of the subsidiary. Dreyfus and Taylor, "Plural Realism" (*Retrieving Realism*, ch. 8).

Fifth, obviously our subsidiary rooting, while it infills and enriches our grasp of the real, is, by definition, *subsidiary* to the focus—the sought-for integrative pattern that lays hold of an aspect of reality. It receives its superseding meaning and status from the real—not vice versa. And the real can and does overwhelm it with transformative meaning. That's why Polanyi calls it integration. The conclusion comes before the premises, as the young Polanyi once told a surprised supervisor;[34] the pattern lays hold of the real and transforms the meaning and appearance of the clues. As such, while we must honor and attend to the subsidiaries, we do so to invite a real that the subsidiaries, though they evoke it, cannot determine and ultimately do not keep out. What is distinctive about the independently real is that it comes—surprisingly and abundantly. Our task is to tend our lamps and wait for the bridegroom. The focus and anchor and confirmation of realism is the fecund real beyond us that nevertheless breaks in transformatively.

We may note here another key difference between robust realism and Polanyian realism: the dimension of hope. Nowhere to be found in Taylor and Dreyfus, hope, that driving distinctive of human persons, is an essential aspect of Polanyi's contact with reality. We humans seek what we hope for, which is generally beyond, not beneath or in, where we are. Confirmation of things never exhausts our desires; we lay hold of the real in our hope. And what testifies to our having made contact with reality, as Grene expresses it, is not confirmation but hope of confirmation beyond what we can, at present, imagine.

Merleau-Ponty Is Not Enough

I am grateful for the fresh work of *Retrieving Realism* precisely because it has helped me identify the distinctive superiority of Polanyi's unique proposals for the matter of realism as over against a Merleau-Pontyean line of argument, which, in the end, falls short of the task. My 1983 work aligns with Grene's later publications on the matter and also now with Dreyfus's and Taylor's important effort. All three concur that what Merleau-Ponty offers is remarkably supportive of realism; Grene and I (and Polanyi himself) aver that it corroborates and expands Polanyi's distinctive proposals regarding subsidiary-focal integration (while not entirely in agreement with them in identifying the crucial two-level, from-to structure of knowing.)

But all three suggest that, in the end, Merleau-Ponty falls short of a sufficient proof of realism. True, all suggest that realism needs no proof, that there is something intrinsically wrong-headed about the entire issue.

---

34. Scott and Moleski, *Polanyi: Scientist and Philosopher,* 43.

However, Merleau-Ponty's contribution somehow doesn't get us the whole way to abandoning the doubt.

Taylor and Dreyfus, for example, acknowledge that Merleau-Ponty's work itself tends to idealism and needs something like Todes' verticality phenomenon to shore it up. But even this, they suggest, does not satisfy a Rortyan bent on anti-realism. Granted, they are stipulating the problem in a manner reflective of the distinctives of the contemporary philosophical debate—as I did in my early dissertation, but which neither Polanyi nor Grene stand on ceremony to do. But to their main argument, Dreyfus and Taylor add the argument about realism conforming with progress in science and being essential to describing what scientists see themselves as doing.[35] And then, in final response to the holding out of an unconvinced anti-realist, they suggest—without any additional consideration or rationale—"there may be phenomena revealed in our scientific practice that show that our true theories correspond to an independently existing universe."[36] I contend that this comment (finally) pinpoints Polanyi's contact with reality, inadvertently, according it the ultimate determinative role in proving realism.[37]

Similarly, Grene declares Merleau-Ponty's work important to a realism worthy of the name, even as she deems Polanyi's shift of context from explanation to discovery and his from-to character of knowledge as necessary (but not sufficient) to it. Like Taylor and Dreyfus, Grene proceeds to suggest that there must be more. She adds a Gibsonian account of perception (which Dreyfus and Taylor also reference),[38] and an account of humans as symboling and promising in their making contact with reality.[39] This leads her to her final words—which, like Taylor and Dreyfus, suggest a Polanyian solution as alone sufficient to support realism. Grene writes:

> We enter into obligations which compel us—not biologically or physically, but personally and morally—to act as we do. The intellectual passions that drive the life of science, the aspirations that compel the artist to paint or write or carve or build or compose: all these strivings express commitments, obligations to fulfil demands made on us by something that both defines and transcend our particular selves.... The point is to recognize

---

35. Polanyi attended deeply to these matters as well, seeing them as obvious evidence that we are in contact with the real.

36. Dreyfus and Taylor, *Retrieving Realism*, 147.

37. These matters Polanyi identified repeatedly as clear evidence of contact with reality.

38. Grene, *Philosophical Testament*, ch. 7; Dreyfus and Taylor, *Retrieving Realism*, 35.

39. Grene, *Philosophical Testament*, ch. 8.

what Polanyi called the paradox of self-set standards. We accept with universal intent principles or patterns of behavior that we have at one and the same time both happened to develop and enacted as responsibly our own.[40]

She amplifies this in her final chapter, whose title, "On Our Own Recognizances," is pregnant with double meaning, and whose argument is too rich and beautiful to capture here. Person, a notion she says is absent from Merleau-Ponty (and from Taylor and Dreyfus), involves a center of agency who freely chooses obligation to something higher than him- or herself. She references Augustine: "This is my freedom, that I am subject to this truth."[41] She fingers authenticity—people living out of a center that is truly theirs—as she tells the story of an illiterate tumbler of Our Lady—to whom alone the Lady graciously appears.[42] Grene repeats that Polanyi was the one who rendered this personhood and this commitment central to human knowing—and, by easy inference, to realism: "The relation of persons as active knowers to the realities they seek to know is just what Polanyi was trying to elucidate."[43]

Only personal, responsible commitment is sufficient to render us realists. But that, I would argue, just is what realism *is*. One cannot be a realist without committing to it. Hence the wrongheadedness of the debate; but positively, commitment to reality beyond our present understanding contributes to the sufficient completion of the argument because it is also the inner structure of the epistemic effort.

As was apparent in chapter 11 of this work, my final assessment in my original dissertation was that Merleau-Ponty's thought fell short of convincing proof of realism. However, I am now in a good position to revise my stance to accord Polanyi's very own notion of contact with reality and his brand of realism the credit it deserves. My conclusion is that Polanyi's contact with reality constitutes its own superior justification of realism. There are three intrinsically intertwined dimensions of this, all three unique to the Polanyi package, as this chapter has displayed: (a) the structure of knowing as two-level, subsidiary-focal integration; (b) the signature of contact with reality present in discovery, the sense of indeterminate future manifestations; and (c) the implicitly presumed dimension of all of knowing as responsible commitment and submission to the real.

---

40. Ibid., 169–70.
41. Ibid., 179.
42. I hear in this the incursion of the fecund real in response to the knower's responsible submission. See Meek, *Loving to Know*, ch. 15.
43. Grene, *Philosophical Testament*, 188.

The telltale signature of independent reality, the sense of indeterminate future manifestations (which Polanyi says testifies to discovery and to the superiority of our conceptions, because it also characterizes reality itself), stands, not in denial of the Todes argument in Taylor and Dreyfus, but in proper complementary emphasis on the real, not beneath, but beyond us. The IFM Effect witnesses to the real's independent agency—its capacity to transform our surmises and our very selves, and to be pregnant with unforeseeable intimations.

Additionally, only responsible personal commitment is sufficient to render us realists. But that is just what it means to be a realist: to be in responsible submission to the real. However, quite positively, pledge is what invites reality most effectively.[44] It is from within the committed posture of indwelling clues anticipatively—something only possible for a knower committed beyond proof of the independence of the real she seeks—that a knower in fact makes contact with reality in discovery.

In this way, Polanyi's realism proves to be its own justification, to offer the superior defense of it, and to be perhaps the only realism worthy of the designation.

In Conclusion

When I gave this chapter as a paper at the 2016 Polanyi Conference, colleague John Apcynski responded quickly and tersely: "Why do you need proof?" Indeed, this response underscores the wrongheadedness of the debate about realism and even of this work. There is a real sense in which a true realist would not perceive it as a legitimate problem to debate. The Polanyian most especially, for whom realism is an indwelt commitment, would follow Polanyi's own inattention to the matter. To ask the question and seek proof of reality is to evidence ongoing implicit commitment to the anti-realism bred into modernist epistemology through its Cartesian inception. Both Grene and the authors of *Retrieving Realism* acknowledge this and seek rather to move beyond it.

But Dreyfus and Taylor nevertheless write and offer the book (and Grene a chapter)—as do I. For a child of modernity, it has been my driving question. And it has taken the effort of a lifetime, if not to answer the question, to move beyond it. The proof may, in the end, be seen to function not as a proof so much as an inducement. It remains critically important for people in modern thought and culture to share the effort with others.

---

44. Meek, *Loving to Know*, ch. 15.

13

The Current Conversation: The Difference Polanyi Would Make

Some decades after this work's inception, the conversation regarding realism and anti-realism continues apace. As with all conversations in the analytic tradition, a myriad of matters are generated and attended to with unwavering commitment to dealing with fine points but with the hope of an overall progression in understanding.[1] I do not mean to suggest that the progress has been evenly linear: in the wake of Thomas Kuhn's *Structure of Scientific Revolutions*, a fresh anti-realism came to the fore in a preoccupation with the sociology of scientific knowledge—the focus not on knowledge in itself but on other, non-epistemic factors that significantly shape it and to which it might make sense to reduce it.[2] While this exploration has produced valuable and legitimate insights regarding knowing, it drove realists at the time to greater determination not only to articulate and defend realism, but to prevent the entire realism discussion (not to mention, putatively, the entire disciplines of epistemology and philosophy) from being swept away.

1. Gary Gutting's thesis expresses this well. Gutting, "Introduction," *What Philosophers Know*.

2. In his 1984 book, *Realism and Truth*, Michael Devitt takes on the then-prevailing challenges to scientific realism. He includes chapters of reply to Bas Van Fraassen, "Davidsonians" John McDowell and Richard Rorty, "the renegade" Hilary Putnam, and "Kuhn, Feyerabend and the Radical Philosophers of Science." See his "Conclusions," ch. 13.

Also, in the interim, there have been other ideational developments that bear on the realist debate. As we have seen, Richard Rorty's anti-essentialism has also prompted fresh efforts to defend realism. Also, positivism, of the sort that so distressed Polanyi, continues apace among scientists.[3] Yet another critically important development—the implications of which, for realism, are not necessarily apparent—is neuroscience, in which epistemic activity is seen to be permeated with brain activity if not reduced to it.[4] Finally, we may note that in a few quarters realism is considered to bear on theism—in which, of course, God is a reality. This is evident, for example, in the Alston anthology I will consider in this chapter.[5] Altogether, the intervening developments at least partially display how the modernist, Cartesian vision of certainty unavoidably teeters on the edge of the abyss of skeptical anti-realism, specifically doubting rather than trusting the knower's (or knowers') connectedness to the real.

As scrutiny of Dreyfus and Taylor's very recent *Retrieving Realism* has made abundantly clear, the conversation ignores Polanyi's work. It happens continually that Polanyi enthusiasts will pick up a book that, on first glance, they deem to hold prospect for responsibly drawing on his insights, yet on checking the index they find no entry. How can this be? we rightly wonder. How can it be changed? Polanyians are committed to this mission. One hope for this book, as for others of our production, is that it might engender a sea change, so that Polanyi's work, which Marjorie Grene considered to be "grounds for a revolution in philosophy," might begin to be given its due attention and yield the healing fruit with which it is pregnant.[6] In the matter of realism and anti-realism, the oversight is acute.

---

3. For a recent overview of the contemporary realism vs. anti-realism debate, see Brock and Mares, *Realism and Anti-Realism*. Richard Rorty's anti-realism functions as primary opponent for Dreyfus and Taylor's robust realism, as we will see.

4. This vision characterizes some recent empiricism, such as Quine's naturalized epistemology. It challenges, not realism directly, but the entire discipline of philosophy. Godfrey-Smith, *Theory and Reality*, 151; Heil, "Introduction," in *Philosophy of Mind*.

5. It was also the point of Thomas F. Torrance's work in theological realism. See *Reality and Evangelical Theology*; *Reality and Scientific Theology*. I look forward to exploring this work in the future.

6. Grene, "Tacit Knowing: Grounds for a Revolution in Philosophy." Andrew Grosso's thorough bibliography in his recent *Personal Being: Polanyi, Ontology, and Christian Theology*, lists these major works by scholars working in the tradition of Michael Polanyi include: Richard Allen, *Polanyi*; John Apczynski, *Doers of the Word*; Joan Crewdson, *Christian Doctrine in Light of Polanyi's Personal Knowledge*; Jerry Gill, *The Tacit Mode*; Martin Moleski SJ, *Personal Catholicism*; Harry Prosch, *Polanyi*; Andy Sanders, *Polanyi's Post-Critical Epistemology*. This is not to mention a wide array of essay and dissertation entries, nor works that implement Polanyi's proposals to other ends. Grosso, "Bibliography," in *Personal Being*.

Part 2: Re-Calling Contact with Reality

In this chapter, I would like to take an extremely selective look at the current discussion and then suggest how Polanyi's distinctive insights regarding contact with reality, were they given a serious hearing, would contribute to it. For purposes of the look at contemporary realism, I have chosen two books representative of it: William Alston's anthology, *Realism and Antirealism*, and Anjan Chakravartty's *Metaphysics for Scientific Realism*.[7] Then, in considering Polanyi's valuable potential contributions, I will also be giving, in part, this work's culminating expression of their significance and power, not only for the ongoing realist debate, but beyond—for Christianity and culture quite broadly.

Alston's Anthology: *Realism and Antirealism*

William Alston has been a key player in the contemporary realist discussion.[8] In his 1997 *A Realist Conception of Truth*, he argued that a realist conception of truth ("alethic realism") is the only conception of truth possible; that is, a merely epistemic conception of truth—that truth by its nature is not about reality, but about its epistemic aspects—is not a serious alternative.[9] In addition to convening the group of scholars and offering a helpful critical introduction, Alston's own contributed essay in this particular collection reflects his work on metaphysical realism: this term can just be the claim that reality exists mind-independently, or it can be a stance regarding what sorts of real things there are.[10] Another of the book's contributions considers semantic realism and anti-realism—whether our language is true by virtue of describing accurately a mind-independent reality (the writer opts for anti-realism here).[11] Taken together, the book considers an array of

---

7. William P. Alston, ed., *Realism and Antirealism* (2002); Anjan Chakravartty, *A Metaphysics for Scientific Realism: Knowing the Unobservable* (2007). Other important books in the field include: Richard Rorty, *Philosophy and the Mirror of Nature* (1980); Bas Van Fraassen, *The Scientific Image* (1980); Michael Devitt, *Realism and Truth* (1984); John McDowell, *Mind and World* (1993); Hilary Putnam, *Reason, Truth and History* (1981); *The Many Faces of Realism* (1987); *Representation and Reality* (1989); and *Realism with a Human Face* (1990); Arthur Fine, *The Shaky Game: Einstein, Realism, and the Quantum Theory* (1986); John Searle, *The Construction of Social Reality* (1995); William P. Alston, *A Realist Conception of Truth* (1996), and *A Sensible Metaphysical Realism* (2001).

8. See n. 7.

9. Alston, "What Metaphysical Realism Is Not," Alston, ed., *Realism and Antirealism*, 115.

10. Ibid., 97–115. Where these things are unobservables, metaphysical realism effectively becomes metaphysics, as we will see with Chakravartty.

11. David Leach Anderson, "Why God Is Not a Semantic Realist," Alston, ed.,

The Difference Polanyi Would Make

stances in metaphysical, epistemic, and semantic realism and anti-realism; additionally, it considers how the matter is connected to theism. Already it is evident that categories persist in the current conversation from that of decades earlier. And it is evident, as Chakravartty will say, that there are about as many realisms as there are realists.[12]

Most synthetically, Alston identifies the central concerns of realism to be conceptual relativity and ontological pluralism.[13] This assessment accords with the Taylor-Dreyfus account. Stemming from Kant, the critical role of concepts in knowing raises the specter of not being able to (or needing to) make sense of a mind-independent reality. Where total anti-realism would be idealism, Kant is not an idealist. Alston names Richard Rorty and Hilary Putnam as contemporary proponents of the Kantian legacy. These two are not idealists, but effectively for them, as for Kant, our understanding of reality cannot be independent of the knower's definitive conceptual activity. Putnam is famous for having asserted that there is no "God's-eye view of reality." In addition to the rise of the sociology of knowledge, the intervening years in the realist debate have been marked by this anti-realism and the effort to respond to it.[14] Many of the essays in the Alston collection concern especially Putnam's claims.

Conceptual relativity concerns the knower; ontological pluralism concerns, at least in some sense, the known. The question is whether competing truth claims can both be true. If the answer is yes, it calls realism into question or suggests that we must develop an account of knowledge and of realism that accommodates pluralism. The matter of ontological pluralism may be seen to connect to the older question of incommensurability of successive and concurrent scientific theories.

Chakravartty's *Metaphysics for Scientific Realism*

While the nuances are detailed, Alston confirms that most of the contributors are realists in some respect.[15] But the anthology offers no sense of consensus apart from this nor of progress in the conversation. Anjon

Realism and Antirealism, 131–47.

12. Chakravartty, *Metaphysics for Scientific Realism*, xii. It is also the case that the designating adjectives do not all function in the same way—similar to the situation with sales (consider the difference between a fire sale and a shoe sale): consider, for example, entity realism, epistemic realism, scientific realism, and robust realism.

13. Alston, "Introduction," Alston, ed., *Realism and Antirealism*, 6.

14. Yet a third force for anti-realism in the intervening decades may be identified: the work of extrinsicists such as Jacques Derrida. Alston, *Realism and Antirealism*, 14.

15. Alston, "Introduction," Alston, ed., *Realism and Antirealism*, 5.

Chakravartty, by contrast, gives the reader a sense of meaningful progress in the discussion and of its philosophical value. Chakravartty's work concerns scientific realism.[16] Scientific realism has to do with the mind-independence of the world, specifically with the question of the interpretation of scientific knowledge: do theories and their entities function truly to identify observable and unobservable features in the world?[17] Chakravartty locates scientific realism as a challenge to a radical empiricism—the claim that scientific knowledge consists of adequate summarizing of data, rather than of a mind-independent world that they cannot help but obscure. In his book, Chakravartty identifies the key dimensions of the debate as part of his overarching effort to trace what he characterizes as an evolution of a responsible scientific realism in response to various anti-realist claims, to propose his own synthetic, "sophisticated," semi-realism, and to undergird this proposal with a metaphysics that will provide a critical piece of its justification. It is a well-done, laudable achievement.

Specifically, Chakravartty identifies three potential sources of concern for scientific realists: the use of inference to the best explanation (which need not be realist); the underdetermination of theory choice by data or evidence (which means that the data may support rival theories); and discontinuities in scientific theories over time, yielding a "pessimistic induction" (which is the matter of incommensurability).[18] Of these three, he deems only the latter to be of real concern, and he frames his account of the evolution of realism in terms of realist responses to it—specifically, "entity realism" and "structural realism."[19] Portions of these he melds to form his own semi-realism. This position involves maintaining both an optimism and a "selective skepticism" regarding differing portions of scientific knowledge: we take some aspects of a theory realistically and not others.[20] Semi-realism also involves the distinction between "detection properties" (those properties the scientist has managed to detect and that thus anchor the theory) and "auxiliary properties" (other properties attributed to particulars by theories).[21] While it will

---

16. Chakravartty, *Metaphysics of Scientific Realism*, xi, 183. Just one essay in the Alston collection addresses scientific realism specifically, Bas Van Fraassen's constructive empiricism in particular (Anne L. Hiskes, "Van Fraassen's Constructive Empiricist Philosophy of Science and Religious Belief: Prospects for a Unified Epistemology" Alston, ed., *Realism and Antirealism*, 238–52).

17. Of note is that Chakravartty distinguishes realists from scientists! *Metaphysics for Scientific Realism*, 69.

18. Chakravartty, *Metaphysics for Scientific Realism*, 5.

19. Ibid., ch. 2.

20. Ibid., 29, 41.

21. Ibid., 47.

be detection properties that link a theory to the world, Chakravartty repeats that one should not, for that reason, not attend to auxiliary properties. These prove valuable heuristically as one continues to search for the presence of hidden variables.[22] This selective approach will characterize Chakravartty's treatment of what there is—his metaphysics. Scientific realists are already thereby involved in making metaphysical claims regarding causal properties and natural kinds—these things have to be there.[23] But a metaphysics substantive enough to corroborate scientific realism need not be onerous, he claims, nor does it need to be complete.[24] Chakravartty wraps up his account by considering matters having to do with how the theory connects to the world—namely, truth. Along the way, he has attended to or developed other very helpful notions, such as, for example, the role of abstraction and idealization in theory making and implementation and how this bears on assessing approximate truth.[25] At the end, he draws on the analogy of truth in art, as per Nelson Goodman's account, to argue that, in the end, there is an informality to the assessment of truth.[26] This is appropriate to the messiness of science, he says. In fact, frequently through the book, Chakravartty cautions that realists must be realistic.

Polanyi's Key Contributions to the Ongoing Realist Debate

Against this admittedly brief backdrop, Polanyi's distinctive approach and potential contributions stand out in sharp relief. Since the conversation continues in the same vein as it has for half a century, these potential contributions are the same as what they were from the time Polanyi first crafted them. However, the gradual reshaping of our overarching zeitgeist, I hope,

22. Ibid., 50, 68.

23. Ibid., 93.

24. Ibid. 150, 179. I believe that, in this, he shares Alston's sentiment that metaphysical realism needs to be divested of add-ons that lead to its unnecessary, unfounded rejection.

25. Ibid., 190–91, 222–23. "Abstraction is a process in which only some of the potentially many factors present in reality are represented in a model or description concerned with some aspect of the world, such as the nature or behavior of a specific object or process." Idealization involves assembling elements in a model in such a way as to differ from the things they represent, not merely by excluding factors, as in abstraction, but by incorporating factors that cannot exist given the actual properties and relations involved.

26. Ibid., 218–34. Goodman's book is *Languages of Art: An Approach to a Theory of Symbols,* 2nd ed. (1976).

renders his proposals that much more germane to our understanding of things.

To imagine Polanyi's contributions to the current debate is to imagine a conversation that, right now, isn't happening, as we have seen. Centrally, the situation is complex because what Polanyi offers is an epistemology that fundamentally challenges key working assumptions of the debate. It is difficult to compare apples and oranges (as I was attempting in the earlier dissertation). Or if you do, you can end up actually over-accommodating Polanyi's distinctives to the parameters of the prevailing debate. On the other hand, you don't want to be dismissive (as I often am) of what is undeniably a major, lively conversation in philosophy. So, in what follows I am motivated by a third, Polanyi-inspired hope: that his contributions, which challenge so deeply, will anticipate an integratively superior configuration to the current conversation, revaluing its various emphases and thus breaking it open to welcome knowing and reality, and to healing and creativity for science and culture quite broadly.

It is perhaps telling to inquire whether Polanyi himself would have wanted to enter this debate. Quite possibly not: the debate itself is spawned and continues in the context of fundamental parameters that he disputes. The question of realism itself is anti-realist and should be moved beyond—an assessment of Grene's and of Taylor and Dreyfus, as we have seen. And we may additionally surmise that, tacitly, Polanyi's own vision, and the more promising direction of his realism, lies elsewhere.

My assessment here presupposes the extensive exposition of Polanyi's work that this inquiry has already offered; thus, it will be brief. Reflecting on the current debate from a Polanyian perspective, I believe that there are four critical features that distinguish his proposals from it and thus hold the potential entirely to reshape it. They are: Polanyi's status as a premier scientist; (thus) his according lively primacy to discovery and to the real; (thus) his preoccupation with the unaccountable element in science; and (thus) his innovative epistemology. I will briefly describe each, noting its implications for the current debate. Then, I will suggest a few additional points of contrast and comparison.

Surely it makes a difference that Polanyi was a scientist. That would seem to render him a supremely qualified contributor to a conversation about scientific realism. It also renders him utterly unique in contrast to just about all the other participants. But as Chakravartty rightly notes, the current debate has focused, not really on reality and discovering it but, in true analytic philosophical fashion, on the question of interpreting and giving a justified account of the nature of scientific claims. It is not exactly a debate that scientists have. Nevertheless, it is a proper further question whether

The Difference Polanyi Would Make

this is the way it should be. Peter Godfrey-Smith, for example, argues in his introduction to philosophy of science that philosophy about science should be naturalist, meaning that it should, where possible, take its lead from what scientists do and uncover.[27] This should not be taken to imply that philosophy simply should close up shop. Polanyi, as a scientist, affirms the inevitability and critical need for doing philosophy; he himself stepped aside from science to address fundamentally philosophical matters critical to the perpetuation of the discipline, and of Western culture in general.

Polanyi was no ordinary scientist; he was a premier research scientist who begat, both literally and figuratively, scientists of Nobel Prize-winning caliber.[28] He trucked in discovery—as has already been emphasized. But it is safe to say that the entire realist debate is framed in the context of, not discovery, but explanation and propositions. To give just one sort of example typical to the conversation: "X is a table."[29] So a second critical contribution Polanyi would make to the current debate is to shift the context from that of explanation to that of discovery—as Grene and many have put it. As we saw, Grene rightly emphasizes that this move would shift the debate to an entirely new, utterly proper key; only such a shift could effectively move us beyond it. Grene sees Polanyi as doing this.[30]

From the perspective of a discoverer, why on earth would you be concerned with the known and stated to the exclusion of the not-yet-known nor stated (as per the current realist debate)? Discovery concerns the latter, not the former. Or better: it concerns the latter focally and the former subsidiarily and anticipatively, as I will note presently. However, when thinking of science, Polanyi distinguishes between the actual explicit beliefs of scientists regarding the institution, and their tacit commitments. He understood that he was identifying and commending the latter in opposition to the former.[31] So in this, Polanyi himself conforms less to the institution of science than other scientists; and other scientists' understanding of science accords more easily with the contemporary realist debate. Many, in fact, are anti-realist.[32]

---

27. Peter Godfrey-Smith, *Theory and Reality*, 149.

28. These include Michael Polanyi's son, John, in 1986. Scott and Moleski, *Michael Polanyi: Scientist and Philosopher*. See also http://www.manchester.ac.uk/discover/history-heritage/history/nobel-prize/ .

29. Alston, ed., *Realism and Antirealism*, 56.

30. Grene, Philosophical Testament, 120.

31. Polanyi, *Tacit Dimension*, 70. Grene notes that "Polanyi used to say, if you want to know about the presuppositions of a given field, spend five years in the laboratory of one of its leaders. In the course of such a process, the very person is altered" (*Philosophical Testament*, 125).

32. I observed this first-hand as I listened to several scientists present at an exclusive

But Polanyi is rightly preoccupied with discovery. For him, the paradigm of all knowledge is knowledge of an approaching discovery. This will lead him, rightly, to develop a discovery-based epistemology—one that actually helps you do the job well.[33] That is what subsidiary-focal integration will be, as I will note presently. But it should also be said that the primacy of discovery also renders the matter of metaphysics in a different light. As Grene puts it, in the context of discovery, you cannot tell, as per Aristotle, which properties are essential and which are accidental.[34] This matter bears, I believe, similarly on Chakravartty's effort to distinguish between causal properties and auxiliary properties: the whole point is that it might not be obvious in the discovery what it is that is engendering the phenomenon and, thus, what exactly the phenomenon is that you are experiencing.[35] So while Chakravartty offers a minimal metaphysics for realism, Polanyi the discoverer, though he might agree in principle regarding causal processes and natural kinds, would be more interested in what specific, as-yet-hidden reality is present and beckoning. In fact, as per the quotation below, Polanyi actually deems the inexhaustible profundity of reality to be the metaphysical feature that grounds science.

This leads to the third distinctive that Polanyi rightly offers to the conversation: attention, not to the explicit and exact but to the tacit and inexact. For a discoverer, Polanyi is saying, what matters is the unaccountable element in science.[36] I noted previously that "mother wit"—and decidedly not the matter of conceptual relativity—is Polanyi's takeaway from Kant. He rightly considered that Kant had overlooked the very thing that would undermine Kant's own entire system. In an extended discussion of incommensurability and progress in science titled, "Science and Reality," Polanyi labors to show that, when compared with respect to accuracy of formulas

---

conference in which I also presented (I was presenting Polanyi's subsidiary-focal integration and his claim, as over against the hope of Artificial Intelligence, that human knowing is intrinsically unformalizable): they always qualified their claims by saying that they were just adequate summaries of the data—not claims about reality. "Epistemology for the Workplace." Talk for TTI/Vanguard's "Understanding Understanding" Conference, Carnegie Mellon University, Pittsburgh, PA, October 2–3, 2012.

33. Meek, *Little Manual*. The central claim is that understanding how knowing works, as subsidiary-focal integration, makes you better at it; if business is your line of work, it will improve your bottom line.

34. Grene, *Knower and Known*, 57.

35. Chakravartty, *Metaphysics for Scientific Realism*, 47.

36. This is something also understood in the Lilly Family Foundation. Around 2000, I received training from Lilly in connection with their stewardship of a grant in which I was involved in assessment. They stipulated that we attend, not to objectives met, but to "significant learnings" and "surprising outcomes."

The Difference Polanyi Would Make

and predictions, the Ptolemaic and the Copernican accounts are exactly the same. It is not the explicit but the unspecifiable and pregnant "surplus of meaning" that is of interest. Such surplus meaning is key to science contacting reality.[37] Polanyi is deeply concerned with "unobservables"—the not yet known—but this not at all in the sense of this word in which the debate typically employs it. It is critical to see that, time and again, the very matters that participants in the current debate consider drawbacks and weaknesses to their realist accounts—the very things that might thus support antirealism—are the very things that Polanyi the discoverer deems to be assets most worthy of our attention.[38] This, of course, presumes and suggests an entirely redrawn epistemology. The fact that Polanyi renders the subsidiary, the tacit, the anticipative, and the intuitive central to discovery challenges the fundamental dynamic driving the current realist debate; this is because the debate entirely presumes that, for our efforts at stipulation and justification in scientific realism to be satisfied, they must be thoroughly, exactly articulated. This is why Polanyi himself might not be interested in the debate: it's not the explicit content, focally considered, that leads you to discovery.[39]

The value of the inexact is what intrinsically implicates Polanyi in realism—again, in contradistinction to the prevailing realist debate. But as this inquiry has displayed, his is no ordinary realism but rather perhaps the only true realism there is, for it accords, committally, primacy to the real (also in decided contrast to Kant) rather than to our articulated statements of it. It understands that such articulations can actually occlude the very thing we desire to contact. This, of course, is the ghost of Cartesianism that haunts modernity.

How do we know that reality is mind-independent, according to Polanyi? The idea that this is impossible *a priori* is a false conundrum; one need only endure a typhoon to see that. We understand reality to be independent because it beckons, breaks in, and trumps us. It "contacts back." The issue is not that it is conceptually free or unfree; the issue is that it, at key times, surprisingly obviates our conceptions—most centrally in discovery. This is the only kind of independence that makes sense.

In connection with several points I am making here, consider the following comment of Polanyi's:

---

37. Polanyi, "Science and Reality."

38. Alston, "What Metaphysical Realism is Not," in Alston, ed., *Realism and Antirealism*, 103. Thus Polanyi summons scientists to "changing camp." "Logic of Tacit Inference," Grene, ed., *Knowing and Being*, 156; quote and commentary in Grene, *Philosophical Testament*, 122.

39. Polanyi, *Tacit Dimension*, 76.

> Perception has this inexhaustible profundity, because what we perceive is an aspect of reality, and aspects of reality are clues to boundless undisclosed, and perhaps yet unthinkable, experiences. This is what the existing body of thought means to the productive scientist: he sees in it an aspect of reality which, as such, promises to be an inexhaustible source of new, promising problems. And his work bears this out; science continues to be fruitful—as I said in my first lecture—because it offers an insight into the nature of reality.[40]

The passage is prefaced by his claim that this expresses "the metaphysical grounds which underlie all our knowledge of the external world." Polanyi's understanding of contact with reality furnishes the key metaphysical feature essential to science—and to the most fundamental perception. And the link is with the unspecifiable dimensions of our knowing. For Polanyi, science, traditioned, apprenticed, and indwelt, just is the body of thought generally deemed inexhaustibly promising of new problems—and thus, itself, real.

The point of this book has been to display Polanyi's unique conception of contact with reality with its concurrent sense of indeterminate future manifestations. What would it be like for the current debate to attend to these actualities? Contact contrasts to correspondence, as I have said, the way 1–1 contrasts to 1-potentially inexhaustive multiplicity; it is the latter that signals the desired, longed-for, and much-sought inbreaking of the real. Polanyi would argue that scientists, if not analytic philosophers, know this and actually live this; it is just that they have not been given permission to accredit it as scientific knowledge.

All this leads naturally to Polanyi's distinctive epistemology. His realism has, as its natural home, his epistemology of subsidiary-focal integration. The converse is equally true. It is difficult to imagine one without the other or either paired with another version of the other. This epistemology directly challenges the overlooked, driving presumptions of the current realist debate. It challenges them, not as a skeptical denial of knowledge, but as a liberation of knowledge to its true form—and a liberation of the knower, and reality, as well.

The current debate presumes that knowledge is exhaustively explicit—or else less than ideal. It is, thus, entirely articulated in statements—or else unqualified for consideration. It aspires to exactitude—nothing less. And perhaps most important and most overlooked: it is wholly focal. Apart from Polanyi, prevailing epistemology has no category of the subsidiary. It recognizes "implicit beliefs," and pretheoretical ones, as we have seen. It also

---

40. Polanyi, *Tacit Dimension*, 68–69.

The Difference Polanyi Would Make

recognizes critical non-cognitive externalist dimensions to knowing. But these acknowledgments in themselves do not identify the from-to structure in which they should be seen to be implicated as subsidiaries. Nor is there any idea of the positive epistemic value of doing so.

Yet, devising this sophisticated epistemology appears effortless to Polanyi; it's just a matter of attending to what you actually do in knowing, starting with perception. Take his oft-cited example of vision: attending focally to the mutually contradictory views of left and right eyes (an experience approximated by covering one eye at a time) is not what yields optimal seeing and contact with the real; it is subsidiarily indwelling them as they both bear on, contribute to, and function as part of the integrative whole that we are able to see, and therein see reality three-dimensionally.[41] And the point is not to eliminate or even minimize this logically unspecifiable undergirding layer, but to accredit and cultivate it. In this widely common example—neither you nor I right now can avoid doing it without our writing and reading grinding to a halt—subsidiary-focal integration is plain, along with the profound surplus of meaning that is reality's telltale signature. So Polanyi draws on the obvious—what we are *actually doing* when we know—to challenge the fundamental parameters of the ongoing prevailing realist vs. anti-realist debate. Surely something so fundamental as this raises the question of the debate's value. It questions its effectiveness: in this blindness is it not utterly predisposed against the primacy of the real? Plus, this matter is the very thing that prevents the debate from even hearing Polanyi. It's why it is difficult to imagine a discussion in which his innovations are, so to speak, merely added in. The accommodation involved in attempting a rapprochement is potentially dangerous.

Other Aspects of Polanyi's Epistemology Germane to the Current Debate

Let me briefly note other aspects of Polanyi's epistemology that are germane to the current debate. Polanyi's subsidiary-focal integration, of course, utterly requires subsidiary indwelling. This entails all sorts of fundamental differences regarding truth. Truth is not so much representation as mediation, as Dale Cannon expresses it. It involves, for Polanyi, believing in.[42] Truth is

41. Polanyi, *Personal Knowledge,* 96–100; "Unaccountable Element in Science," in Grene, ed., *Knowing and Being,* 106–8, 111–18.
42. Dale Cannon writes: "Any scientific theory will indeed for a time and in certain circumstances be considered critically, as subject to critically entertained belief *that.* But in shifting our attention from this *focal attention to* the theory, once we have come

informally assessed, and that only in the context of commitment. This is as true of critical verification, quantification, and precision as it is of discovery. Truth requires indwelling, just as vision and contacting reality do.

Polanyi has articulated a much-needed account of what it is we are doing when we say that our claim is true: we are holding it responsibly with universal intent. While the idea of commitment makes modern Western epistemologists nervous and dismissive, Polanyi has rightly argued that this, his fiduciary programme, is the only responsible way to avoid certain absurdities in epistemology and to describe what we are actually doing when we know.

In contrast to much of the realism abroad for the recent decades, Polanyian epistemology actually honors and explicates some matters brought to our attention and regard by recent anti-realist approaches. These include the embodied and situated nature of human knowers and knowing in the world. Phenomenological approaches amplify this, although they do not replace the idea of the subsidiary. And the idea of the subsidiary is nothing short of a boon for these efforts. Similarly, all efforts to accredit the role of "external" factors such as history, sociology, and community in knowing receive solid explication and affirmation as subsidiaries transformatively incorporated into the integrative pattern of our knowing. Polanyi actually contributed the now-valued components of tradition and apprenticeship to the wider conversation.[43] His epistemology deals directly with the Cartesian predicament that engenders modernity. But unlike many other such efforts, it does so in a way that nevertheless honors the tradition.[44] Polanyi has developed something post-critical that doesn't reject the critical so much as redeem it by revaluing it as subsidiary. He is obviously not post-critical in the usual sense of being anti-realist; nor has he found modernism realist. He

---

to recognize it as true, to *subsidiarily attending from* the theory to aspects of reality to which it provides us clues, we come *a-critically* to rely upon the theory (to believe *in* it) so as to put us in contact with (in a direct, though mediated, acquaintance relationship with) those aspects of reality.... For Polanyi, believing (*qua* believing *in*) as well as knowing (*qua* tacit knowing) are more fundamentally relational than representational. ... Truth, for Polanyi, is thus more than propositional truth ... ; it is *the achievement of connection in the first person (for oneself) with, or rapport with, objective reality (qua recognizable in common to responsible inquirers), a fidelity to it that adheres to it, acknowledges it, and makes it known, appearances and others' unbelief to the contrary notwithstanding*" ("Sanders' Analytic Rebuttal to Polanyi's Critics," 22–23, italics original).

43. Consider the influence he exercised on the thought of Alasdair McIntyre, also a participant in the Study Groups which Grene convened on behalf of Polanyi. Grene, ed., *Interpretations of Life and Mind: Essays around the Problem of Reduction*. See n. 29 in ch. 12.

44. Jerry Gill speaks of Polanyi's work as reconstructive postmodernism. Gill, Introduction," *Tacit Mode*.

The Difference Polanyi Would Make

has instead posed a positive third alternative, rather than a futile compromise. It is my informal but nevertheless wide experience that reality matters more to this current age than its explicit self-ascriptions would lead us to believe. And though we perceive ourselves as an information age, what we long for is not information but encounter with the real.

Polanyi's stated conviction all along has been that it is impossible to substitute anything else for reality and truth. Ideas such as radical or constructive empiricism, reductivism, instrumentalism, internal or pragmatic realism, semantic anti-realism, and coherentism, in addition to being anti-realist, are, more to the point, what he terms pseudosubstitutions. They only seem to work because they presume an underlying commitment to reality. It is noteworthy that Alston suggests that anti-realism appeals to certain people because they have an "intolerance of vulnerability."[45] This rightly suggests the underlying motive of modernity, which has been control or mastery. By contrast, Polanyi understands that understanding requires vulnerability; realism does as well.

Polanyian Epistemology's Treatment of Conceptual Relativity and Ontological Pluralism

Let us consider the matters of conceptual relativity and ontological pluralism, which Alston and others have identified as being central to the prevailing realism vs. anti-realism debate. Polanyi's epistemology creatively and neatly handles the "problem" of conceptual relativity by rendering conceptualization subsidiary—along with embodiment, history, place, training and expertise, and the ways and puzzlements of the world that pertain to the inquiry. In this way, conceptualization—although we always must be careful to think beyond our categories and not let them dictate our perceptions—actually aids our contact with reality. Concepts open surprising doors. Concepts can actually be more pregnant with future prospects than we have yet to realize. This notion, by the way, is entirely omitted from the prevailing debate's treatment of statements as "exact." To treat conceptualization as subsidiary is to accord it its most respectable, freeing, and fruitful place. For Polanyi, the whole point of scientific knowledge is that it too is real; it consists of an inexhaustible fund of promising problems and clues. Again, it is not science's focal exactitude but its pregnant promise that is key. This is in utter contrast to the prevailing realist debate. Far from conceptual relativity being a liability, it is science's critical asset. I do not believe that it

---

45. Alston, "What Metaphysical Realism is Not," in Alston, ed., *Realism and Antirealism*, 122.

would have occurred to Polanyi to be concerned "that there is no God's-eye view."

As Polanyi's category of the subsidiary creatively addresses contemporary realist concern regarding conceptual relativity, along with his notion of contact with reality and its attendant sense of indeterminate future manifestations, it also speaks to the matter of ontological pluralism. Integration, the driving mechanism of knowing, involves creatively melding, subsidiarily, what appear, at first, to be contradictories. Plurality is essential to integration. Also, the simple fact that all knowing involves sustaining a two-level structure (i.e., from-to) renders knowing itself fundamentally plural in a certain sense. Then, the IFM Effect, in testifying to our having made contact with reality in discovery, bears witness to the happy smallness of our nevertheless successful feat in our sense of an inexhaustible supply of future possibilities. It witnesses to a reality that resists reduction to our current categories—and always will. From our vantage point at the moment of discovery, those IFMs include creative resolutions of matters that appear to us now as contradictory. This is plurality also. And we can identify a fourth, implicit but profound plurality in the Polanyian approach: knowing is intrinsically open to the other beyond itself and to the future.

Thus, there are two ways to understand what is behind apparent ontological pluralism from a Polanyian point of view. One is to see that it suggests that we have farther to go in our understanding—and that's fine. The other is to see that it suggests that reality is bigger, richer, and more creatively dimensioned than we grasp. These two, of course, are of a piece. And to understand ontological "pluralism" in this way is not the pseudo-humility that pluralism can involve, but the true humility of patience with the real and our understanding of it.[46] So subsidiary awareness and integration, with its indeterminate future manifestations, are very forgiving with respect to preoccupations and the fine-grained distinctions of the realist vs. anti-realist debate.

Possible Fruitful Touchpoints between Polanyi and the Current Debate

Taken together, these factors and touchpoints amount to a formidable challenge, both to reconciling Polanyian realism with prevailing debate, and to the debate itself. Does no hope remain for a rapprochement? As I said at the outset, my hope would be Polanyian in configuration and actually justified as such by several of the things we have noted about pluralism in particular.

46. This will be a theme of D. C. Schindler's *Catholicity of Reason*. See ch. 14.

The Difference Polanyi Would Make

Might it be possible for the prevailing conversation to evolve even further so as to invite, not a debate so much as a creative melding of complementary lines of sight? Might the apparent conflict itself prove to hold clues to a more profound integration? I scrutinize the conversation for places that hold promise of accord with Polanyi's work. Here, I note a few.

The first, and perhaps primary, one is that much of what the debate might deem to be involved in articulation and defense of a responsible account of scientific knowledge would, on a Polanyian account, be melded into the creatively imaginative, subsidiary scrabbling that a scientist undertakes in pursuit of a discovery. Take, for example, the centerpiece of Chakravartty's semi-realism—a selective optimism and pessimism with respect to different aspects of a theory. Add in the fact that, in pursuit of discovery, it is in principle impossible to tell which aspects warrant optimism and which pessimism—a modification of Chakravartty's claim. But then add in the Polanyian claim that the discoverer navigates anticipatively, relying tacitly on clues to unleash their true meaning, with a sense of increasing proximity to the solution. Integration requires assigning appropriate values to the clues involved—thus it is inherently selective. What cannot be specified nevertheless occurs and occurs artfully for the trained discoverer—or her apprentices.

Not only optimism and pessimism may be so absorbed into and managed in the scientist's anticipative, subsidiary scrabbling. So also can inference to the best explanation, and matters of underdetermination of theories by data, abstraction and idealization, and even the very matter of "how one should understand scientific claims"—where this is fundamentally redrawn to involve the anticipative indwelling of scientists in scientific thought, in search of promising problems. It might be said that Polanyi produced his philosophical thought in an effort to guard the freedom of scientists to pursue this artful, not necessarily justifiable, creative exploration.

Secondly, in Chakravartty's work are some comments that Polanyians identify as telling and hopeful if only they may be accredited more fully and drawn out. For example, those auxiliary properties: Chakravartty says more than once that these, even though they do not provide the causal anchorpoints for the theory, should nevertheless be attended to for the valuable heuristic role they can play.[47] Chakravartty speaks, in this passage, of "the presence of hidden variables"—a comment with decidedly Polanyian cast, that suggests attention to the process of discovery. Another intriguing feature of Chakravartty's argument is actually where it ends, with his claim that the approximation of truth is best understood as intrinsically an informal

---

47. Chakravartty, *Metaphysics for Scientific Realism*, 50, 68.

affair, drawing helpfully on the analogy of art to science.[48] It would not be difficult to develop a conversation around this matter.

A final touchpoint concerns an essay by Christopher Tollefson in the Alston anthology: "Cooperative, Coordinative, and Coercive Epistemologies." Drawing these descriptors from the field of sociology, he poses that they may be helpful to the realist discussion. Specifically, neither a coercive nor even a coordinative approach is optimally suited to "see us through to a broadly realist position."[49] Tollefson's thesis is that a cooperative epistemology is in fact necessary to a genuine realism. But this will be possible "only if the world is a suitable partner in our cooperative knowing venture." Coercion and even coordination, by contrast, thwart realism along with genuine knowing. After identifying various anti-realisms and realisms with his conception of coercive and coordinative epistemologies, Tollefson expounds various dimensions of a cooperative epistemology. Some of these are as follows. How would this include, but not be limited to, involving other persons in knowing as just one aspect of cooperating with the world itself?[50] How is it that cooperative awareness, unlike coordinative awareness, does not merely "meet at an interface"; rather, "my awareness of the other extends right out to take in her reasons for action and make them my own"?[51] How would it be compatible with the mix of activity and passivity that typifies experience?[52] How would inquiry be helpfully guided normatively, including, for example, by respect for the other?[53] And how is this metaphor strengthened in a Judeo-Christian theistic context, in which the world is there for our contemplation?[54] What Tollefson is describing is essentially Polanyian indwelling, I believe. And since I believe that Polanyi's own work opens out into an interpersonally relational epistemology, these features that Tollefson identifies resonate deeply with Polanyi's realism. Thus, this holds promise as a very fruitful, cooperative, discussion.

---

48. Ibid., 219–34.

49. Tollefson, "Cooperative, Coordinative, and Coercive Epistemologies," Alston, ed., *Realism and Antirealism*, 150.

50. Ibid., 161.

51. Ibid., 159.

52. Ibid.

53. Ibid., 160.

54. Ibid., 165.

In Conclusion

In conclusion: with respect to the prospect of bringing Polanyi's insights to bear on the ongoing realist discussion, I believe that the way forward appears daunting if viewed confrontationally. And it is either futile or accommodatively self-defeating if attempted additively. Instead, moving forward in a fashion truer to Polanyi's own non-linear, anticipatively hope-filled integrations by attending to what may be small but pregnant particulars may yet make an opening for his unique vision of knowing and reality to shape the contemporary realist conversation. Why is it worthwhile to persist in this hope? I believe it is worthwhile because Polanyi's epistemology and realism ring true to knowers, knowing, and the known. They ring true even as they bring healing liberation, opening us to greater knowing ventures. They ring true in reintroducing excitement quite literally as an epistemic practice and indicator of contact with reality. They ring true by being fraught with intimations of inexhaustive future prospects.

14

Recovering Reality

The previous two chapters show that Michael Polanyi's distinctive understanding of contact with reality supports a rich realism and suggests a rich reality. In this final chapter, I will pursue the latter further: what do Polanyi's epistemology and notion of contact with reality imply about reality itself? Specifically, do indeterminate future manifestations attest to contact with reality because they characterize reality first? By implication, have we children of modernity done a grave disservice to reality itself through our skepticism—including the very posing of the question of realism? In turn, positive responses to these last two questions not only underscore the distinctive shape of Polanyi's realist commitment, but also show why it matters deeply as a redemptive sally targeting modernity's prevalent, culture-damaging anti-realism. "Indeterminate future manifestations," I believe, are the telltale clues to a wider, truer understanding of knowing and being. They also hold strategic promise of thwarting and healing it.

In recent years, I have become acquainted with the work of Catholic philosopher D. C. Schindler—specifically, with his book, *The Catholicity of Reason*.[1] I find in his more properly philosophical, traditionally grounded account an uncanny confirmation of both Polanyi's claims and of my own covenant epistemology.[2] Although I must do this very briefly, I want to

---

1. Schindler, *The Catholicity of Reason*.

2. With reference to the latter, "confirmation" inadequately represents my sense of standing on the threshold of a wider world opening out beyond my comparatively novice attempts. In essence, I am experiencing indeterminate future manifestations, a

sketch Schindler's overarching agenda. Pervading Schindler's work, as we will see, are studied references to and emphatic confirmation of the significance of certain distinctive features of knowing and being that readily accord with Polanyi's IFMs and Polanyi's claims about them. I propose that Polanyi's epistemology—specifically with all the dimensions of his idea of contact with reality, which we have explored here—is an exceptional specimen of what Schindler calls *ecstatic reason*. In fact, I suggest that Polanyi offers Schindler a valuable "on-the-ground" look at ecstatic reason in action. The profound resonance between Schindler's and Polanyi's accounts allows me further to suggest that we take a serious look, beyond knowing, to being, with Schindler's help—to get a sense of what may well lie behind and beyond Polanyi's contact with reality. Schindler's account actually offers a positive account of the phenomenon of indeterminate future manifestations.

Thus, my inquiry in this book will culminate, beyond retrieving realism, with contacting and recovering the real. Drawing on Schindler's work, I would like to claim that reality itself is characterized by indeterminate future manifestations, given that it can be understood to be gratuitous, generous, generative, abundant, and excessive. As such, reality itself appropriately ends anti-realist skepticism by overwhelming it. And Polanyi's very concept of contact with reality itself proves real (as Polanyi would say) by itself being pregnant with indeterminate future manifestations.

Synopsis of D. C. Schindler's Proposals

David Schindler[3] is a scholar in the extensive work of Swiss theologian Hans Urs von Balthasar. Balthasar (1905–88) is considered one of the foremost Catholic theologians of the twentieth century; he is known for according primacy, among the transcendentals, truth, goodness, and beauty, to beauty, as a way to restore the integral "circumincession" of all three.[4] While Balthasar's agenda is the restoration to vibrancy of theology in the modern age, it is Schindler's agenda in *Catholicity of Reason* to show that Balthasar's

---

pregnancy of future prospects, in my discovering Schindler's work.

3. I am referring to "D. C."—not to his father, "D. L." The younger, incidentally, learned Polanyi "at my father's knee." (Personal conversation, Summer 2014).

4. The "transcendentals," so identified for centuries of Christian philosophy in the Great Tradition, are characteristic marks of all being. As such, consideration of them would anchor any discussion of reality, as well as of knowing and action. "Circumincession" suggests a dynamic interpenetration, similar to *"perichoresis,"* a concept I employ in *Loving to Know*. Hans Urs von Balthasar's main work is a "trilogy" (fifteen volumes) called *The Glory of the Lord*. In the trilogy, part 1 concerns beauty, part 2, goodness, and part 3, truth. I do not directly consult these texts in this brief chapter.

claims may, indeed must, be extended beyond knowing God to knowing anything at all—beyond theology to epistemology quite generally.[5]

Schindler carefully expounds Plato, Aristotle, Augustine, Dionysius, and Aquinas to develop a distinctive Balthasar-inspired approach that nevertheless accords with their implicit intention, and thus with the overarching philosophical tradition. He examines recent greats—primarily Hegel and Heidegger, as well as phenomenology in general—to display their inadequacy, in the final analysis, as responses to modernity, and the need for an alternative account—one that is Balthasarian. Schindler is also acquainted with Polanyi and appears to presume the accuracy of Polanyian insights.[6] Since Schindler's primary agenda is a rehabilitated understanding of knowing and being that directly addresses the conundrums of modernist epistemology and (anti)metaphysics, it is appropriate to see it aligning with Polanyi's own and thus deepening its impact and import.

Schindler argues that reason must be seen to be catholic. By "reason," I take him to mean everything having to do with human knowing. Of course, he means to distinguish it from faith, but reason cannot exclude faith, nor vice versa—that is essential to Schindler's idea of reason's catholicity. By "catholic," Schindler has in mind that reason most always be "of or according to the whole."[7] Schindler delineates multiple ways that reason is of the whole, but a key one, briefly, is that all knowing and understanding contains, implicitly, a reference to being in its totality.[8] This implicit reference is intrinsic to reason. Were reason to deny it, it would implicitly affirm it: to say that reason cannot comprehend the whole is to say something of the whole—something totalizing—and violent.

In fact, the modernist wake of the epistemic presumption of the Enlightenment has been typified by such efforts to render an immanent reason "modest" by setting limits to what reason is able to appropriately do. To conceive of reason as immanent means to see it as entirely determined "from below" as opposed to "from above" or beyond. Here, one can easily recognize the starting point of the Cartesian cogito. Once this standpoint has been adopted, the question is whether such reason can be of any other whole than the absolute mortal self. According to Schindler, Hegel typifies a

---

5. This renders Schindler's project similar to my own in *Longing to Know, Loving to Know*, and *Little Manual*: knowing God is an ordinary act of knowing, and conversely, ordinary knowing is like knowing God.

6. Schindler especially cites Polanyi's essay, "Faith and Reason." Schindler, *Catholicity of Reason*, 16–17.

7. Schindler, *Catholicity of Reason*, xi.

8. Ibid., "Reason as Catholic" (ch. 1).

positive response to this question: the whole and Reason become identical.[9] According to Schindler, Heidegger, along with many who appropriate his insights, typifies a negative response. To do as Hegel has done, according to Heidegger, is to bring "the god" into metaphysics. To do metaphysics is unavoidably to do onto-theology. So, Heidegger concludes, let's not do metaphysics. The only way to respond to this false dichotomy of "unholy zeal and false modesty" that Hegel and Heidegger typify, Schindler argues, is to reject the view of reason that both share in presuming and to replace it with an alternative understanding—an alternative that turns out to prove undeniable. So Schindler's case rests on this alternative epistemic account. In this, it profoundly matches Polanyi's own agenda.[10] In fact, Schindler characterizes Polanyi's epistemology as being, not "from below," but "from above." This is in critical contrast to modernity, and is true of Schindler's own proposal regarding reason.[11]

Just what would make reason catholic in a way that moves beyond the faulty all-or-nothing dynamic? Here lies the heart of Schindler's proposal: reason must be seen to be *ecstatic*—that is, as the heart of what it is, reason is always out beyond itself. Reason is self-transcending.[12] It is of the essence of reason to be beyond itself, leaving its home to find its home. And in so doing, it fulfills its own essence.[13] I will describe his notion of ecstatic reason more fully presently. Schindler's idea of reason as ecstatic, I am convinced, aligns with Polanyi's understanding of knowing as out beyond itself in anticipative clues and indeterminate future manifestations.

The various essays in the book amplify the idea of reason as ecstatic. Schindler argues that the Western philosophical tradition, as it is conventionally interpreted, has offered no epistemology in which it is possible to be genuinely "surprised by truth."[14] Surprise, for Schindler, concerned as he is to restore mystery to the most lucid knowing, lies at the heart of the epistemic act.

Schindler taps Balthasar's identification of the encounter that is "the mother's smile," as the excessively generous self-giving of love, as the event wherein the baby receives the very conditions of possibility and the posture of delighted reach beyond herself to the other. This encounter renders reason ecstatic and actual. In another essay, he develops Balthasar's account

9. Ibid., "The Problem of the Problem of Ontotheology" (ch. 8).
10. Polanyi, *Personal Knowledge*, vii–viii.
11. Schindler, *Catholicity of Reason*, 16.
12. Ibid., 8.
13. Ibid., 105.
14. Ibid., ch. 2.

to show how it pertains equally to philosophy as to theology. He shows that reconnecting goodness and truth, so critically needed in this era, can be accomplished only by beginning with beauty—where goodness, truth, and beauty are the relational transcendentals, or characteristic marks of all being.[15] The unfolding dance of "the acts of the soul" that is the trajectory of knowing just is the "circumincession of the transcendentals": vision, rapture, choice, fidelity, trust, disclosure—and then the joyous cycle begins again as disclosure opens out into further vision.[16]

And in another essay, Schindler engages Aquinas' account of the will and of intellect to reconcile them in a "nonpossessive" account of knowledge—as over against the inherently possessive modernist epistemology.[17] While Schindler works with a conceptual framework different from that developed by Polanyi, nevertheless, each of these discussions resonates with Polanyi's understanding of things and, additionally, with my own covenant epistemology.

Schindler then turns to metaphysics—to being. He offers an extended examination of causality, contrasting the mechanistic causality of the modern age with Aristotle's deeply intertwined four causes. Modernity has wanted to, and succeeded in, eliminating wonder from knowledge. Schindler taps the work of the philosopher/theologian of the early Middle Ages, Dionysius, to show how Dionysius connects this fourfold causality with the Christian God the Creator. Reality's originary causality coincides with both beauty and goodness. Causality is the "excessive erotic goodness of God"—so excessively generous that it accords its desired "other" (creation) its own derivative being and freedom and desire to respond. In this excessively rich account, knowledge does involve causes and, just for that reason, involves ever-deepening wonder.[18] The wondrous mystery of Being lies at the very heart of its intelligibility. The last discussion I will note here comes in the chapter about "overcoming the overcoming of ontotheology," and Schindler titles the section, "A Recovery of Metaphysics."[19] He presents Balthasar's response to Heidegger as involving an epistemology and a metaphysics that

---

15. Ibid., ch. 3. According to Balthasar, beauty is the splendor of the form, where form and its splendor represent two polarities essential to beauty.

16. I have argued elsewhere that this description neatly aligns with covenant epistemology's layout of the moments of the knowing venture in *Little Manual*. I also make the case that Polanyi's repeated reference to beauty, as an intrinsic part of the scientist's sense of contact with reality, accords deeply with Schindler's idea ("Beauty as a Token of Contact with Reality").

17. Schindler, ch. 4.

18. Ibid., chs. 5–7.

19. Ibid., 254–61.

are both not only "from below," *von sich aus* (on the basis of itself), but also simultaneously "from above," *vom Anderern her* (given by another). There is neither limitation nor threat from God as beyond being, because being itself is beyond being. I will explain this more as now I turn to focus on the account that stands out from the backdrop of these multiple, rich discussions of knowing and being as ecstatic.

Reason as Ecstatic

Drawing from these discussions, I now sketch Schindler's idea of reason as ecstatic. As I do so, I want to foreground how its dimensions and those of Polanyi's epistemology align—with a special emphasis on the idea of contact with reality, as well as with an eye to covenant epistemology. Given this profound resonance with respect to epistemology, it only makes sense to consider whether the positive metaphysics that Schindler expounds can be seen reasonably to accord with the Polanyian vision and perhaps be suggested by it.

Reason is structurally ecstatic according to Schindler. Its very nature is to be always already out beyond itself, catching up with its own essence.[20] The soul (that is, the intellect) takes up residence beyond itself; its home is beyond itself.[21] Ecstatic reason thus resolves the problem of the *Meno*.[22] There is real progress in knowledge because knowing is, in some sense, already at the end. "[K]nowing that one does not know is not a skeptical self-limitation of reason *a* priori, but is rather the most comprehensive—most catholic—conception of reason possible."[23] These phrases disclose the fundamental accord of the account Schindler is developing with Polanyi's. The last calls to mind Polanyi's remarkable statement that the paradigm of knowing is knowledge of an approaching discovery.[24]

In one place, Schindler considers what is just the right amount of anticipation of the whole that is proper in knowing. He argues that it is neither no anticipation nor total anticipation—both of which prove to be "possessive." Rather, it must be a balanced amount in which the knower's anticipation is both fulfilled and surprisingly reconfigured.[25] That he actually

20. Ibid., 8.
21. Ibid., 16, 105.
22. Ibid., 21.
23. Ibid., 30.
24. Polanyi, *Tacit Dimension*, 25.
25. Ibid., 5–6.

undertakes an inquiry regarding anticipative knowing stands as an uncanny corroboration of Polanyi's epistemological insights.

Ecstatic reason moves beyond itself toward the whole, toward the "other." It is not simply "inside" intellect, but goes out to meet the other.[26] And reason is intrinsically open to abiding otherness even in its completion.[27] In contrast to a typical phenomenological understanding (and, thus, also in contrast to Taylor and Dreyfus), knowing has two centers, not one: the self, and the other; and reason is of each whole, in different respects.[28] Polanyian ears begin to hear in these claims the characteristic "from-to" and "beyond" of subsidiary-focal integration. Indeed, Schindler claims that Polanyi's tacit dimension is reason's beyond.[29] Additionally, Schindler's—and Balthasar's—persistent reference to a positive abiding other accords with the critical emphasis of my own covenant epistemology—something, by contrast, only implicit in Polanyi's thought. More of the primacy of the real in the next section.

Ecstatic reason is actually two simultaneous movements in opposite directions: reason starts from inside and from the being that is outside, the other, simultaneously.[30] In fact, the outside beginning, the beginning in being, is prior to the inside beginning: when one wakes to an inquiry, one finds herself as having already been beckoned. Modernity has moved away from the medieval conviction that *intellectus* (receptive contemplation) precedes *ratio* (active discursive thought): a receiving precedes an active inquiring as well as accompanying it throughout.[31] According primacy to beauty restores the other priority in the many-staged (as per the circumincession of the transcendentals) knowing encounter.

Knowing is an encounter that fundamentally requires that reason's structure be empathetic. "Empathy is the natural structure of the spirit."[32] He describes this as intimacy of communion, an awareness of reality in its most fundamental sense, where awareness means consent to/with being. It yields a feeling of actual contact, of intimacy.[33] Schindler identifies this empathy with Balthasar's "consent," or feeling-with the other. He also says that

26. Schindler, *Catholicity of Reason*, 10.
27. Ibid., xi.
28. Ibid., 8–9, 74.
29. Ibid., 16.
30. Ibid., 19–20.
31. Ibid., 115.
32. Ibid., 19.
33. Ibid., 12. In this passage Schindler quotes Balthasar: "The soul's most fundamental relation to the world is affirmation and joy in being" (*Glory of the Lord, vol. 1*, 244).

Polanyi's indwelling is Balthasar's consent. Indwelling is not pretheoretical, in contrast to phenomenology and its proponents: rather, "it is reason's taking up residence, so to speak, in a place beyond the mind, and specifically doing so in terms of what Polanyi has elsewhere elaborated as personal involvement.... The tacitness of the tacit dimension, in other words, is not a subconscious feeling or intuition, but instead it is consciousness' self-transcendence in being."[34] So for Schindler, in empathy, or indwelling, reason is ahead of itself already at the destination of its path.[35] It begins its activity already from within the beings it encounters. Also, the primacy of beauty reveals that, as encounter, knowing, like beauty, is epiphanic: it cannot be grasped in detachment but, rather, only in the event of encounter.[36] That is to say, it can only be grasped as we indwell, in hope, the aspects we know to bear on the sought-after pattern, and as we indwell/submit to the object. All of this underscores Polanyi's notion of indwelling as something pretheoretic in the sense of approaching from beyond rather than as already embodied or prior to any understanding at all. I note, however, that Schindler's language of encounter, epiphany, and intimacy explicitly parallels covenant epistemology, while accenting what is more implicit in Polanyian epistemology.

Reason, always already out beyond itself, enjoys an immediate contact, as intimacy with reality.[37] Contact, we may infer rightly, requires that it be apprehended in overflowing unspecifiability. But ecstatic reason (alone) concerns genuine insight and discovery.

> The true begins in trust, a word etymologically connected with "truth," and ends with *disclosure*.... The fruit of one's constancy is a revelation of the reality of that to which one has bound oneself. Knowledge thus understood is anything but abstract; it exhibits something of a "concreteness" that Hegel pursued throughout his speculation, namely, a comprehensiveness that cannot come to light in the discreteness of a mere "result" but instead requires a patient suffering of the object, a laboring and living-through in which disparate aspects of a reality finally reveal how they "fit" together, that is, reveal their otherwise hidden unity.... Because ... the positivity of the givenness is paradoxically one with the negativity of excess (what one grasps is *not* the whole of what is given), the fruit of a faithful dwelling with the object comes to term, as it were, in an abiding spirit of receptive wonder, and the

---

34. Ibid., 17. Regarding personal involvement Schindler cites Polanyi's *Personal Knowledge*.
35. Ibid., 18.
36. Ibid., 71.
37. Ibid., 30.

resulting disclosure thus includes a promise of an inexhaustible "more." The clarity of the perception of truth is one with the hopeful expectation that keeps knowledge endlessly interesting. As Joseph Pieper puts it, . . . an inexhaustible light.[38]

This text, embedded in Schindler's tracing the acts of the soul in encountering reality on the circumincession of the transcendentals, displays multiple matches to the Polanyian account. We can hear the critical role, in advance, of pledge and commitment to the not-yet-known. We can easily hear the creative feat of integration described, as bringing with its sudden *Gestalt* insight the promise of an inexhaustible more.[39] Contact, with its characteristic but surprisingly generous excess, occurs beyond us, not behind us.

Elsewhere, in listing implications of an account of reason as ecstatic, Schindler notes that it means that the operation of the intellect involves a discontinuity: a letting go to take hold of.[40] As a result, surprise and wonder, and Schindler's notion of it as drama, are intrinsic to thought. As noted previously, the knower's anticipation is neither absent nor total, but rather is fulfilled even as it is surprisingly reconfigured. It represents, not a destruction of the knower, but a transformative change in the knower's being. Neither does discontinuity pose a principial threat to reason, since reason, as ecstatic, has this as its natural movement. Finally, knowing as ecstatic does not possess or threaten the form it seeks, because it accords it primacy. The intelligible form governs the intellect's efforts "even if it has not yet fully appropriated that form as such."[41] The act of knowledge, then, can be nonpossessive and thus generous, humble, nonviolent. Knowledge is possible without subordinating it to the self.[42] Also in this passage, Schindler affirms the incredible rest that is possible, on this account, as one trusts oneself to reality—even the reality of the half-understood, anticipated, yet to be known.

Now, here is an intriguing aspect of the account that additionally accords with Polanyi's thought: according to Balthasar, as Schindler presents

---

38. Ibid., 78. The Pieper reference is to his *Unaustrinkbares Licht* (München: Kosel, 1963). Schindler continues in the note: "For Pieper, the inexhaustible truth of things is due to their resting in the unfathomable creative knowledge of God. While Balthasar would ultimately agree, it is significant that he roots mystery more proximately in the very nature of finite being."

39. Further on, I'll say more about the reference to excess.

40. Schindler, *Catholicity of Reason*, 111.

41. Ibid. 112.

42. Ibid., 113.

it, the concrete *Gestalt* is the locus of truth.[43] For Balthasar, as for Polanyi, *Gestalt* aptly identifies the integrated form or pattern. For Balthasar, this *Gestalt* lies beyond the knower, but it also lies this side of the known. I personally believe that it can be seen to coincide with Polanyi's own notion of the comprehensive entity. I believe also that it displays additional, intriguing amplification and corroboration of Polanyian contact with reality with its characteristic IFMs. It accords with Polanyi's saying that our concepts are real as well, as they are clues to the reality they discover and invite. For Balthasar, the act of understanding is not unilateral but a co-act of different activities of the soul and the object in conjunction with one another.[44] Being gives itself, makes itself known, to an appropriately attentive and generous soul. The *Gestalt* is the single fruit of their encounter or reciprocal interaction. It is a third entity distinct from both knower and reality. As such, "a *Gestalt* is a whole greater than the sum of its parts; at the same time, it is itself a part that makes concretely manifest a greater whole."[45] In this, "Balthasar intends to preserve what we might call the 'ever-greater' (*je-mehr*) character of the *Gestalt*. The reality that comes to manifestation in the *Gestalt* is a reality 'beyond' the manifestation."[46] What Balthasar is saying here, to connect it with Polanyi's notions, is that the *Gestalt* (the integrative pattern), the ecstatic locus of truth with roots in the knower, as well as the ecstatic epiphany of the being under consideration, is that through which the inexhaustible depths of the thing itself may be glimpsed—or better, are made manifest. Similar to Balthasar's definition of beauty, the union of splendor and form, the *Gestalt* is the concrete form that manifests the depths of reality. It is as if the comprehensive entity that we integrate, in that epiphany allows us a direct, piercing line of sight into the bottomless depths of the thing's reality. This splendid excess of Balthasar and Schindler's account is identical with Polanyi's indeterminate future manifestations that attend discovery, the epiphanic contact with reality. Thus, "the *Gestalt* is the particular, and thus finite, manifestation of a depth that transcends it, and every *Gestalt* therefore possesses an intelligibility that is inexhaustible." But "it is an intelligibility that the soul can comprehend, and thus include within itself, but which represents more than the soul can articulate (in knowing a *Gestalt*, the soul always knows, as it were, more than it knows)."[47]

---

43. Ibid., 115.
44. Ibid., 105.
45. Ibid., 105–6.
46. Ibid., 107.
47. Ibid. Schindler here notes Polanyi's similar *Gestalt*-founded epistemology.

The closure of a genuine *Gestalt* is also a new kind of openness. This aspect of Balthasar's *Gestalt* accords exactly with the criteria of reality I developed in chapter 7: retrospective and prospective indeterminacy. The latter is the IFM Effect. In a note lies the following delightful claim of Balthasar's that rings true to Polanyi's understanding of integration and its IFMs:

> Truth as *emeth* does two things. On the one hand, it is conclusive, in the sense that it puts an end to uncertainty and endless seeking, to conjecture and suspicion, so that this condition of ever-shifting vacillation can give way to the clearly formed, solid evidence of things that are unveiled as they actually are. On the other hand, this closure of uncertainty and its bad infinity is the unclosing and unsealing of a true infinity of fruitful possibilities and situations. Once truth has become present, a thousand consequences, a thousand insights, spring from it as from a seed. Once being has become evident, this evidence immediately harbors the promise of further truth; it is a door, and entrance, a key to the life of the spirit.[48]

The result, for Balthasar and Schindler, is that "mystery is convertible with truth," in the lingo of Catholic philosophy.[49] For the Polanyian preoccupied with the phenomenon of indeterminate future manifestations, Balthasar and Schindler offer resounding confirmation—an alignment which is itself a *Gestalt* that manifests splendid depths.

It is abundantly evident that Schindler's understanding of reason as ecstatic accords profoundly with Polanyi's with respect to the matters that concern my own inquiry primarily. Polanyi's subsidiary-focal integration, issuing as it does in contact with reality accompanied by a sense of indeterminate future manifestations, is ecstatic reason worked out more concretely in our everyday coming to know. It is also patently evident that Schindler's account is fraught with personal and interpersonal dimensions as per covenant epistemology.

Summarizing Schindler's notion of the catholicity of reason: "To say that reason is catholic is to say, not that it encompasses the whole in itself, but that it grasps the whole only in being called constantly beyond itself to what remains ever greater."[50] This account underscores that Polanyian contact with reality with its sense of future prospects is an integral, essential feature of knowing, not merely a happenstance. An epistemic account that

---

48. Ibid., n. 79, 109–10. Original reference: Balthasar, *Theo-Logic I*, 39. "Convertible" means, in this context, that the all that is true is also fraught with mystery.

49. Ibid., 108.

50. Ibid., 32.

admits neither genuine discovery nor genuine surprise, neither contact as a hoped-for "beyond" nor the anticipation of unspecifiable depths of future prospects, while common in the Western tradition and characteristic of modernity, fails to do justice to what we do as inquiring humans, and would thwart all our efforts to know. Polanyi's distinctive understanding of discovery, contact with reality, and its attendant IFM Effect are essential to his and any responsible account of knowing.

Reality as Ecstatic

We now turn our attention from knowing to being. In *Catholicity of Reason*, Schindler is arguing from the analogy of being for his notion of reason as ecstatic (analogical)—for the Catholics, I surmise; but he is also arguing from ecstatic reason to ecstatic being—for modernity, I surmise. This latter is of primary concern to my inquiry: knowing as ecstatic suggests being as ecstatic.

By now it should be apparent that ecstatic reason requires and in fact presumes that *being itself* is ecstatic also. For knowing to have two centers, it is trivially true, there must be two centers. For ecstatic reason to be what it is, it must be finding its home beyond itself, cleaving to the thing it seeks and desires. It is reasonable to infer that knowing can find its home only in a beyond fundamentally like itself and thus available for the intimacy and communion of knowing's contact with reality.

But Schindler says that the fundamental act of *knowing* is *being's giving itself*.[51] For the human knower this occurs primordially and constitutively in the initiating smile of the mother, which cannot but be responded to in the baby's first smile.[52] In the loving gift of herself in the smile, the mother remains the abiding other, and the baby reaches out toward her in the return smile. This is simultaneously personal and ontological, as "the entire paradise of reality" unfolds around, not the child's "I," but thanks to the gracious favor of the "Thou."[53]

The primordial experience of the mother's smile especially reveals the character of being. Being gives itself to be known; it self-communicates.[54] And in this self-communication, "it does not disappear into the concept."[55]

---

51. Ibid., 13. Italics added.
52. Ibid., 44–47.
53. Balthasar's own description, quoted by Schindler (ibid., 46). The use of I-Thou hearkens back to the work of Martin Buber.
54. Ibid., 10.
55. Ibid.

Even as it is known, reality resists reduction to its knowledge. We may count Polanyi's indeterminate future manifestations as evidence corroborating this claim. The knowing event, says Schindler, is a many-staged encounter with reality's acts of self-disclosure, in which the opening overture is not the knower's but rather that of the yet-to-be-known. Reflecting the transcendentals and inaugurated by beauty, the drama of coming to know has begun with "the splendor [mysterious excess] of the form"[56]—the beauty of the inviting not-yet-known itself. Knowing is inaugurated by being and would betray it in discounting its primacy.

In fact, reason, as ecstatic, is itself a manifestation of being in its own beyondness. For "reason just *is* being, precisely insofar as being is already 'out beyond itself.'"[57] The "rational soul" is itself a specimen of being as ecstatic; as rational beings we share, in a privileged way, in being's being more than itself. The ego itself "is already, so to speak, a manifestation of being, understood not as *phenomenon* here, but as a kind of *focal* point, a concentration of reality simply."[58] So knowing is "genuine ontological communion with the other." And to grasp being as analogical is "*to be* with and in it as it opens unceasingly beyond itself in ever-new beings. To the analogy of being corresponds an essentially ec-static conception of reason . . . reason is in fact the whole soul, the substance of the rational animal, out beyond itself in and with the world."[59]

The "analogy of being" is central to the great Christian philosophical tradition. According to Schindler, it means that "Being is everything . . . and more."[60] Analogy implies continuity in discontinuity, unity in ever greater difference.[61] "To say that being is analogical," Schindler remarks, "is to say that it always also receives its most basic sense from above."[62]—And beyond: "every whole includes what lies beyond it."[63]

---

56. Ibid., 69–70.

57. Ibid., 12. This hints of Polanyi's notion of epistemology as ultrabiology (*Personal Knowledge*, 387).

58. Ibid.

59. Ibid., 21.

60. Ibid., 4, 11.

61. Ibid., 81. Schindler and Balthasar identify the discontinuity, strikingly, with freedom.

62. Ibid., 252, 258. Not only from above; Schindler affirms the claim that Being, as the generous erotic excess of God, also receives its being from below. And as noted previously, Schindler's sees Polanyi's epistemology as also "from above."

63. Ibid., 21. Compare with Polanyi's idea of levels being subject to "dual control" (*Tacit Dimension*, 36).

It could be argued that what Polanyi was attempting in his account of being as multi-leveled, irreducible to lower levels, and anticipatively open to the shaping of higher levels, may be construed as a gesture in the direction of this notion of being as analogical. Although it remains partially elusive, Polanyi's levels of emergence do imply his conviction that reality is irreducibly rich and ever-open to fresh configurations from above as well as his conviction that in this, reality parallels the structure of knowing.

Truth, goodness, and beauty are the *positive relational* transcendentals. As transcendentals, they characterize all being; as relational, they imply "that there *is* something 'in addition' to being, that being has a genuine, positive other to which it relates."[64] Although this is paradoxical, "reality includes a genuine otherness within itself.... [I]t is the nature of being to be more than itself." Since the transcendentals are marks of being, being itself is self-transcendent. This will be characterized as being's excess. Being, like reason, is ecstatic. The "narrative of the acts of the soul" in knowing also furnishes the basic "plot structure of reality."[65]

How is it that reality is like this? What is its source? And why has modernity been studiously blind to it—as especially evidenced in its proclivity to positivism and reductivism? It is in response to these important questions that Schindler develops his extended examination of causality in modernity—causality as force—in wholesale rejection of all four of Aristotle's intrinsically intertwined causes. Although in the final analysis critical of Heidegger, Schindler affirms much of Heidegger's assessment of the adverse impact this inevitably has on culture, including philosophy. But for Heidegger, metaphysics is the forgetting of Being; for Schindler it is the very opposite.

Schindler then returns to an ancient philosophical understanding of being beginning with Plato, developing through Plotinus, and then brought to fruition in the Christian philosophical tradition in a distinctive way in Dionysius.[66] Dionysius brings Plato and Aristotle together in identifying the ultimate cause of all things, a fourfold causality, as the Good which is inherently generative. For the Christian Neoplatonic tradition, "goodness has the character above all of generosity and desirability."[67] For Dionysius, the Good is its activity of self-giving, and in giving it gives rise the world.

---

64. Ibid., 65.

65. Ibid., 67.

66. Schindler works from a Latin version of Dionysius the Areopagite's *Divine Names: De divinis nominibus* (Edited by Beate Regina Suchla; New York: De Gruyter, 1990).

67. Ibid., 204.

This is no pantheism, because it is personal, free self-gift.[68] Causality is "a kind of gratuity, which is not the horror of the nothing [ct. Heidegger], but the positive presence (in transcendence) of generous love."[69] All of created reality, in response, manifests desire (eros) for the Good and gives itself to it. It is in desire that we exist, giving ourselves to the Good. Desire coincides with generosity; the most generous gift to another is to desire the other, says Schindler. By inference, Dionysius concludes that the self-giving of God (for the Creator God is the Good) is identical with eros. In so doing, Dionysius fundamentally alters the notion of eros bequeathed by Plato from one that presumes lack to one that implies the positive excess of love.[70] Created reality is the ecstatic act of another, yet creation also has its own intrinsic freedom, goodness, desire, and generosity. Indeed, the Aristotelian fourfold cause that constitutes a thing just is both the generous self-gift of God and also the thing's "holding itself together" in desire and goodness.[71] The thing, then, is both itself and more than itself; caused of itself and from another.[72] Things, for Schindler, as a result, are both intelligible and full of endless surprise:

> Concretely, this means, for example, that the "what" of a bird cannot be separated from its "that" and its "why." There is no end, in other words, to the surprise of the whatness; one can never "get over" what a bird is, and there is no reason why one should. . . . This is not a mystification; the surprise is not an empty stupefaction. Instead, it coincides with a real, certain, in principle even unshakeable grasp. It is a *deep* knowing of the bird, but a knowing that is always also a receiving, a letting be, and so a wondering[;] . . . the unusualness lies *inside* the usual, even as it unfolds beyond the usual into genuine ontological depth. Whenever one grasps the usual, . . . one does not need to . . . turn in some other direction in order to enter into wonder: one needs instead to deepen one's grasp. . . . This wonder is shot through with desire, and indeed a non-narcissistic desire, because it is constantly brought beyond itself in genuine fulfillment. It is shot through with desire, quite simply, because it is

---

68. Ibid., 206.

69. Ibid.

70. Ibid., 210–11. Schindler remarks that "it is perhaps not too much of an exaggeration to say that this text represents one of the most dramatic moments in the history of Western thought."

71. Ibid., 214.

72. Ibid., 222.

a participation in "excessive erotic goodness," the causality that makes all things be what, how, and why they are.[73]

Thus, Schindler concludes his argument to show that wonder is convertible with knowledge. While this passage is imbued with all the Platonic, Aristotelian, and Dionysian dimensions of Schindler's case for wonder in knowledge, it is impossible not to hear a resounding accordance with Polanyi's vision of reality and our contact with it. Such a reality cannot but be attested to by a sense of the possibility of indeterminate future manifestations, for it is the nature of reality itself to be "excessive erotic goodness." Insights are attended by the IFM Effect because reality itself is pregnant with an inexhaustible fund of future prospects. Polanyian epistemology and vision of reality are equally hospitable to wonder.

Subsequent to the text quoted at length above, Schindler reflects upon two valuable implications of it for thinking in science, of such a refreshed understanding of reality and of knowing as deepening wonder.[74] It would allow within the cause-effect thinking of science "a place that is integrated into the more comprehensive context of meaning rather than isolated from it," a place in which the wonder that scientists typically express only privately may come into their work. Second, it would shift the center of scientific thinking from determinism of mechanistic relations to a kind of self-causality more evident in personhood. A person "is more intelligible than a mechanical event, more completely knowable, not because there is less mystery, but precisely because there is more." It is evident to me that the first of these two implications of Schindler's coincides precisely with what Polanyi, as scientist, modeled, and as epistemologist, taught; the second, I recognize as the intent of my own covenant epistemology.

One might object that this extended argument is a "reverting" to theology and thus fundamentally unfaithful to the discipline of philosophy. Or one might object that it is unscientific. To each, Schindler would respond: "If this sounds strange to our ears, it is arguably the most traditional view of causality, a tradition begun by Plato's association of causality with the good."[75] It is eminently reasonable and fitting to see that, in contrast to modernity's eclipse of reality, reality as ecstatic outruns and relativizes

---

73. Ibid., 223. I savor especially Schindler's argument-culminating reference to the bird since my own *Loving to Know* begins with my story of loving and being loved by a wild cedar waxwing, Bandit (*Loving to Know*, xv–xvi). Also note the title of the first essay of Schindler's that I read: "Surprised by Truth" (ch. 2 in *Catholicity of Reason*).

74. Ibid., 224–25.

75. Ibid., 224.

modernity's own re-realizing agenda. Schindler notes that Balthasar said that the Christian is called to be the guardian of metaphysics of our time.[76]

Nor do I believe that this understanding of being as ecstatic adds more to the Polanyian framework than is consonant with it. To one familiar with Polanyi's life and work, it is evident that he felt the need for metaphysics.[77] On the one hand, it would take more than science to address the inherent and dangerous inversions of modernity.[78] On the other hand, he felt that the religion of the day was not up to the task; he felt that perhaps science as he understood it (as implicitly practiced by all, not as explicitly misperceived by many) might be able to actually help religion at this point in some unspecified way.[79] It is evident that Polanyi felt that his epistemology pointed beyond itself to reality. Also, as we have noted, Polanyi sensed both the dangers inherent in modernity's ideational outlook at the same time that he proudly honored the tradition of thought and culture to which he self-consciously fell heir.[80] All these factors warrant a claim that Polanyi's vision of reality accords, at least implicitly, with the one presented in this chapter of the real as superabundant gift.[81] We may take his notion of contact with

---

76. Ibid., 256. Original reference to Balthasar, *Glory of the Lord* vol. 5, 656. Elsewhere, I have offered a similar exploration of the semiotic cosmology proposed by Oliver Davies in his book, *The Creativity of God: World, Eucharist, Reason* for the same purpose for which I have presented Schindler's work: that of grounding Polanyian IFMs in reality itself. While on the surface the two approaches register fundamental differences, they share a climactic affirmation of reality as divine excess. One of Davies' chapter titles is, "The Abundant Real." His work shares with my own covenant epistemology a preoccupation with the word of the Lord as creative and with the Eucharist as an epiphanic paradigm of the knowing encounter. Davies finally develops an account of reason that he terms, "Eucharistic reason." The fundamental difference between Schindler and Davies concerns Davies' rejection of premodern cosmology as no longer viable in our modern age, and thus his project to offer a fresh cosmology that is scientifically compatible. In place of Schindler's recurrence to the ancient philosophical tradition (with the implied corollary that it can yet accord with modern science), Davies offers his semiotic cosmology: reality just is the ongoing, creative, conversational, word of the Lord. While Schindler's strategy, like my own, has been to begin with epistemology and move to ontology, Davies' is the other way round. For all this, I believe all three can be reconciled; and even if not, offer uncannily similar corroboration for the abundant, excessive real whose signature is indeterminate future manifestations. Taken together, these accounts bear witness to that excessive abundance ("Covenant Realism: The Love at the Core of All Things").

77. Polanyi, *Tacit Dimension*, 68–70.

78. Ibid., 4, 74

79. Ibid., 62.

80. Consider the impact on Polanyi's thought of his mother's salons—the intelligentsia of Europe in the young Michael's home—and a classical liberal education. Scott and Moleski, *Michael Polanyi*, Pt. 1.

81 Ibid., xi. Also, Davies, "The Abundant Real," *The Creativity of God* (ch. 7);

reality and its telltale indeterminate future manifestations as itself a clue—as Polanyi himself avers with respect to discovery—to the nature of reality itself.[82]

In Conclusion

This further confirms my claim in a previous chapter that Polanyi's own proposals in this area outrank other measures taken in hopes of justifying them—specifically, my own in my original dissertation (ch. 11), and the efforts of Taylor and Dreyfus in defense of realism (ch. 12), which share an appeal to the phenomenological work of Merleau-Ponty. My own deep reflection on Schindler's work has led me to the conclusion that Dreyfus and Taylor retain the defective understanding of knowledge—as non-ecstatic, and as a result, possessive—that typifies modernity and thwarts the very recovery of reality that they desire. No amount of appeal, however warranted and true (when transposed into a Polanyian key), to a pretheoretical phenomenon, on its own, will solve and dissolve the problem of realism. What is needed is contact with reality beyond and before us in hope—a reality whose pedigree consists of its coming and superseding even our questions with its indeterminate future prospects. And this is needed for our effectiveness in learning and discovery, for our epistemology, and for the future of our age. As Polanyi says: "My search has led me to a novel idea of human knowledge from which a harmonious view of thought and existence, rooted in the universe, seems to emerge."[83]

Inviting the Real

It is utterly untypical in this day for a "proper" philosophical inquiry to end with an injunction regarding how to live.[84] This book, on the ground of the very notion of contact with reality it commends, stands to challenge that. To recover reality just is to submit to its primacy, both retrospectively and

---

Meek, "Covenant Realism."

82. Polanyi, *Tacit Dimension*, 70.

83. Polanyi, *Tacit Dimension*, 4.

84. We may rightly question the legitimacy of this application of philosophizing. Consider Joseph Pieper's contrasting understanding of philosophy, as wonder, "piercing the dome of the [deadening, World War II producing] workaday world." "Philosophizing is an act in which the world of work is transcended" ("What Does It Mean to Philosophize?" in *For the Love of Wisdom*, 29).

anticipatively. What does that look like? How may we live it out? Recovering reality requires indwelling.

Negatively, we must recognize the ravages of modernity's skeptical, anti-realist proclivity. While no philosopher that I have considered in this inquiry would consider damaging utilitarian conquest of nature a tenet of their anti-realism or realism, I suggest that it is a tacit, thus unrecognized, consequence. Recently, a youthful science student in my philosophy of science class assured me that "we are on the verge of explaining everything!" My first silent thought was: "I pity his future wife." Polanyi made it his business to warn against "unbridled lucidity."[85] By contrast, he offers unspecifiability as clue, and pursuit of it as both savvy and virtuous. This accords with Schindler's call for a nonpossessive account of knowledge.[86]

Positively, Polanyi's understanding of reality as that which we contact, signaled by our sense of indeterminate future manifestation, suggests that those who would discover, understand, and know should assume a posture of radical attentiveness, an anticipative attunement—or attuned anticipation—that we can actually learn expertly to trust ourselves to.[87] Here, I cite only in brief David Kettle's deep reflection on Polanyian subsidiary-focal integration, the radical attentiveness, and the dynamic lively inquiry that is the posture of true openness to the real. As I said in an earlier note, Kettle appropriates Polanyian epistemology to develop the fresh understanding of knowing that modern Western culture (specifically, the Christian church) desperately needs to supplant the "modern betrayal of enquiry."[88] Kettle calls for a "conversion to attentiveness towards God." This is the posture appropriate to apprehending God, or having been apprehended graciously by him. It involves ongoing, riskily trusting, openness to God. Kettle envisions this lively attentiveness—appropriate for God, and, I would argue, also appropriate for reality—as a kind of dynamo of Polanyian subsidiary focal integration. Radical attentiveness is humans' proper epistemic posture. But the Enlightenment's theoretical paradigm, as Kettle terms it, including its pretension to or rejection of "a God's-eye view," has entirely occluded any

---

85. Polanyi, *Tacit Dimension*, 18.

86. Consider also the theme of Wendell Berry's ongoing impassioned critique of a possessive account of knowledge. In a recently published poem, he writes that good forestry involves, not impersonal instruction or methodology, but loving the forest, entering to walk and watch in sympathy. A learning that takes decades, this approach alone leaves the forest whole. Berry, "A Small Porch in the Woods," sec. 10, p. 26.

87. It goes without saying that the prospects to which we attend should not be exclusively utilitarian.

88. Kettle, *Western Culture in Gospel Context*, 36; "Introduction," pt. 1, and pt. 2, ch. 3. See n. 1, p. 240 in this book.

possibility of such a lively, personal engagement of and participation in the real. If lived out consistently by human knowers, not only God is left on the doorstep, but for everyone, reality is as well.[89]

Further, Polanyi's contact with reality, with its telltale sense of indeterminate future manifestations, where it is affirmed and forwarded emphatically, may be the very antidote to heal the ravages of modernity. IFMs directly contradict reductivism and positivism.[90] In Balthasarian language, they open us to depths of mystery in our very understanding of the real. They begin to open a hearing to reality as abundant and fraught with truth, goodness, and beauty, the characteristic marks of all being.

Finally, recovering reality engenders hope—hope, not of total explanation, but of something even better: encounter and communion with the ever-lively real. Discovery and exploration will never get old in a world of continuing, surprising, generous excess. Indeed, this was what science meant to the premier scientist, Michael Polanyi: "This endless delight is what the existing body of scientific thought means to the productive scientist: he sees in it an aspect of reality which, as such, promises to be an inexhaustible source of new, promising problems. And his work bears this out; science continues to be fruitful . . . because it offers an insight into the nature of reality."[91] Nor is the experience restricted to the elite: in the sentence just before this, Polanyi exclaims: "Perception has this inexhaustible profundity, because what we perceive is an aspect of reality, and aspects of reality are clues to boundless undisclosed, and perhaps yet unthinkable, experiences." Recovering reality is hope-filled for us all. Reality beckons and self-attests in its surprising self-disclosure.

This implies, rightly, that this book represents a beginning.

---

89 Meek, "Review of Kettle, *Western Culture,*" 75.

90. Balthasar writes: "All of the perversions that human freedom can inflict upon being and its qualities always aim at one thing: the annihilation of the depth dimension of being, thanks to which being remains a mystery even, indeed, precisely in its unveiling. The formula 'A is nothing other than . . .' typifies this perversion." (*Theo-Logic* I, 16)

91. Polanyi, *Tacit Dimension,* 68–69.

Bibliography

Alston, William P., ed. *Realism and Antirealism*. Ithaca, NY: Cornell University Press, 2002.
———. "*A Realist Conception of Truth*. Ithaca, NY: Cornell University Press, 1996.
———. *A Sensible Metaphysical Realism*. Milwaukee: Marquette University Press 2001.
Apczynski, John V. *Doers of the Word: Toward a Foundational Theology Based on the Thought of Michael Polanyi*. American Academy of Religion Dissertation Series, no. 18. Atlanta: Scholars Press, 1982.
———. "A Polanyian Epistemology Manqué: Reflections on *Retrieving Realism*." Paper for Polanyi Studies: Past, Present, and Future, 2016 Polanyi Society Conference, June 8–11, 2016.
Balthasar, Hans Urs von. *The Glory of the Lord: A Theological Aesthetics; Volume V: The Realm of Metaphysics in the Modern Age*. Edinburgh: T. & T. Clark, 1991.
———. *The Truth of the World*. Vol. 1 of *Theo-Logic*. Translated by Adrian J. Walker. San Francisco: Ignatius, 2000.
Bannan, John. *The Philosophy of Merleau-Ponty*. New York: Harcourt, Brace and World, 1967.
Bennett, John B. "The Tacit in Experience: Polanyi and Whitehead." *The Thomist* 42 (1978) 28–49.
Berry, Wendell. *A Small Porch: Sabbath Poems 2014 and 2015* together with *The Presence of Nature in the Natural World: A Long Conversation*. Berkeley: Counterpoint, 2016.
Boyd, Richard N. "On the Current Status of the Issue of Scientific Realism." Lecture delivered at the Conference on Scientific Realism, North Carolina State, Greensboro NC, Spring 1982.
Bradie, M. "Polanyi on the Meno Paradox." *Philosophy of Science* 41 (1974) 203.
Brennan, John. "Polanyi's Transcendence of the Distinction between Objectivity and Subjectivity as Applied to Philosophy of Science." *Journal of the British Society for Phenomenology* 8 (1977) 141–52.
Breytspraak, Gus, and Phil Mullins. "Michael Polanyi and the Study Group for Foundations of Cultural Unity (SGFCU) and the Study Group on the Unity of Knowledge (SGUK)." Panel for Polanyi Studies: Past, Present, and Future, 2016 Polanyi Society Conference, June 8–11, 2016.

Brock, Stuart, and Edwin Mares. *Realism and Anti-Realism*. Montreal: McGill-Queen's University Press, 2007.

Brodbeck, May. "A Review of *Personal Knowledge*." *American Sociological Review* 25 (1960) 582–83.

Brown, Harold I. *Perception, Theory and Commitment: The New Philosophy of Science*. 1977. Reprint. Chicago: Phoenix, 1979.

Brownhill, R. J. "Scientific Ethics and the Community." *Inquiry* 11 (1968) 243–48.

Buchanan, James M. "Politics and Science: Reflections on Knight's Critique of Polanyi." *Ethics* 77 (1967) 303–10.

Burks, Don M. "Review of *Meaning*." *Quarterly Journal of Speech* 62 (1976) 436–37.

Campbell, Charles A. "The Correspondence Theory." In *Belief, Knowledge, and Truth: Readings in the Theory of Knowledge*, edited by Robert R. Ammerman and Marcus G. Singer, 401–6. New York: Scribner's Sons, 1970.

Cannon, Dale. "Sanders' Analytic Rebuttal to Polanyi's Critics, with Some Musings on Polanyi's Idea of Truth." *Tradition and Discovery* 23.3 (1996–97) 17–23.

Chakravartty, Anjan. *A Metaphysics for Scientific Realism: Knowing the Unobservable*. Cambridge: Cambridge University Press, 2007.

Collins, James. "Review of *Meaning*." *America* 133 (1975) 471–73.

Davies, Oliver. *The Creativity of God: World, Eucharist, Reason*. Cambridge: Cambridge University Press, 2004.

Devitt, Michael. *Realism and Truth*. Princeton: Princeton University Press, 1984.

Dreyfus, Hubert, and Charles Taylor. *Retrieving Realism*. Cambridge: Harvard University Press, 2015.

Erickson, Glenn W. "Beyond Realism and Idealism." *Philosophy Today* 24 (1980) 12–19.

Feyerabend, Paul. *Against Method: Outline of an Anarchistic Theory of Knowledge*. London: NLB, 1975.

Fine, Arthur. *The Shaky Game: Einstein, Realism, and the Quantum Theory*. Chicago: University of Chicago Press, 1986.

Folse, Henry J. "Belief and the New Scientific Realism." *Tulane Studies in Philosophy* 30 (1981) 37–58.

Gelven, Michael. *Commentary on Heidegger's* Being and Time. DeKalb, IL: Northern Illinois University Press, 1970.

Gelwick, Richard. "Science and Reality, Religion and God: A Reply to Prosch." Paper presented at the American Academy of Religion Consultation on Polanyi and the Interpretation of Religion, November 9, 1980.

———. *The Way of Discovery: An Introduction to the Thought of Michael Polanyi*. New York: Oxford University Press, 1977.

Gill, Jerry. "Saying and Showing: Radical Themes in Wittgenstein's *On Certainty*." *Religious Studies* 10 (1974) 279–90.

———. *The Tacit Mode: Michael Polanyi's Postmodern Epistemology*. Albany, NY: SUNY Press, 2000.

Godfrey-Smith, Peter. *Theory and Reality: An Introduction to the Philosophy of Science*. Chicago: University of Chicago Press, 2003.

Goldman, Alan H. "Realism." *Southern Journal of Philosophy* 17 (1979) 175–92.

Goodman, Nelson. *Languages of Art: An Approach to a Theory of Symbols*. 2nd ed. Indianapolis: Hackett, 1976.

Grene, Marjorie. *The Knower and the Known*. 1966. Paperback. Berkeley: University of California Press, 1974.

———. "Knowledge, Belief and Perception." The Andrew W. Mellon Lecture, Tulane University, Fall 1978.
———. "Merleau-Ponty and the Renewal of Ontology." *Review of Metaphysics* 29 (1976) 605–25.
———. "The Paradoxes of Historicity." *Review of Metaphysics* 31 (1978) 15–36.
———. *A Philosophical Testament*. Chicago: Open Court, 1995.
———. "Response to Alasdair MacIntyre." In *Morals, Science and Sociality*, edited by H. Tristam Engelhardt Jr. and Daniel Callahan, 40–47. The Foundations of Ethics and Its Relationship to Science, Vol. III. Hastings-on-Hudson NY: The Hastings Center, 1978.
———. "Tacit Knowing: Grounds for a Revolution in Philosophy." *Journal of the British Society for Phenomenology* 8 (1977) 164–71.
Grene, Marjorie, ed. *Interpretations of Life and Mind: Essays around the Problem of Reduction*. London: Routledge and Kegan Paul, 1971.
Gutting, Gary. *What Philosophers Know: Case Studies in Recent Analytic Philosophy*. Cambridge: Cambridge University Press, 2009.
Grosso, Andrew T. *Personal Being: Polanyi, Ontology, and Christian Theology*. New York: Lang, 2007.
Hall, Ronald L. "Wittgenstein and Polanyi: The Problem of Privileged Self-Knowledge." *Philosophy Today* 23 (1979) 267–78.
Hamlyn, D. W. *The Theory of Knowledge*. New Introductions to Philosophy Series. Garden City, NY: Doubleday, 1970.
Harre, Rom. "The Structure of Tacit Knowledge." *Journal of the British Society for Phenomenology* 8 (1977) 172–77.
Hartt, Julian. "The Realities of the Human Situation: Review of *Personal Knowledge*." *The Christian Scholar* 43 (1960) 231–36.
Hauptli, Bruce. "Quinean Relativism: Beyond Metaphysical Realism and Idealism." *Southern Journal of Philosophy* 18 (1980) 393–410.
Heidegger, Martin. *Being and Time*. Translated by John Macquarrie and Edward Robinson. New York: Harper and Row, 1962.
Heil, John. *Philosophy of Mind: A Contemporary Introduction*. 3rd ed. New York: Routledge, 2013.
Innis, Robert E. "In Memoriam Michael Polanyi (1891–1976)." *Zeitschrift fur allgemeine Wissenschaftstheorie* 8 (1977) 22–29.
———. "The Logic of Consciousness and the Mind-Body Problem in Polanyi." *International Philosophical Quarterly* 13 (1973) 81–98.
———. "Meaning, Thought and Language in Polanyi's Epistemology." *Philosophy Today* 18 (1974) 47–67.
———. "The Triadic Structure of Religious Consciousness in Polanyi." *The Thomist* 40 (1976) 395–415.
Kettle, David J. *Western Culture in Gospel Context: Theological Bearings for Mission and Spirituality*. Eugene, OR: Cascade, 2011.
Knight, Frank H. "Virtue and Knowledge: The View of Professor Polanyi." *Ethics* 59 (1949) 271–84.
Koethe, John. "Putnam's Argument Against Realism." *Philosophical Review* 88 (1979) 92–99.
———. "Review of *Meaning and the Moral Sciences*." *Philosophical Review* 88 (1980) 460–63.

Kuhn, Thomas S. *The Structure of Scientific Revolutions*. 2nd ed. *International Encyclopedia of Unified Science*, Vol. 2, no. 2, edited by Otto Neurath. 1962. Reprint. Chicago: University of Chicago Press, 1970.

Lakatos, Imre, and Musgrave, Alan, eds. *Criticism and the Growth of Knowledge. Proceedings of the International Colloquium in the Philosophy of Science*. Vol. 4. London: Cambridge University Press, 1970.

Langford, Thomas A., and William H. Poteat, eds. *Intellect and Hope: Essays in the Thought of Michael Polanyi*. Durham, NC: Duke University Press, 1986.

MacIntyre, Alasdair. "Objectivity in Morality and Objectivity in Science." In *Morals, Science and Sociality*, edited by H. Tristram Engelhardt Jr. and Daniel Callahan, 21–39. The Foundations of Ethics and Its Relationship to Science, Vol. III. Hastings-on-Hudson NY: The Hastings Center, 1978.

MacKinnon, Edward A., ed. *The Problem of Scientific Realism*. New York: Appleton-Century-Crofts, 1972.

———. "A Review of *Personal Knowledge*," *Modern Schoolman* 36 (1959) 294–96.

Manno, Bruno. "Michael Polanyi on the Problem of Science and Religion." *Zygon* 9 (1974) 44–56.

Margolis, Joseph. "Cognitive Issues in the Realist-Idealist Dispute." *Midwest Studies in Philosophy* 5 (1980) 373–90.

———. "Pragmatism, Transcendental Argument, and the Technological." In *Philosophy and Technology: The Werner-Reimers-Stiftung/Bad Homburg Conference*, edited by Paul Durbin and Friedrish Rapp, 291–309. Dordrecht: Reidel, 1983.

———. "Pragmatism without Foundations." *American Philosophical Quarterly* 21 (1984) 69–80.

———. "Realism's Superiority over Instrumentalism and Idealism: A Defective Argument." *Southern Journal of Philosophy* 17 (1979) 473–79.

———. "Skepticism, Foundationalism, and Pragmatism." *American Philosophical Quarterly* 14 (1977) 119–27.

Martin, Graham Dunstan. "The Tacit Dimension of Poetic Imagery." *British Journal of Aesthetics* 19 (1979) 99–111.

Mays, Wolfe. "Michael Polanyi: Recollection and Comparisons." *Journal of the British Society for Phenomenology* 9 (1978) 44–55.

McDowell, John. *Mind and World*. Cambridge: Harvard University Press, 1993.

Meek, Esther Lightcap. "Beauty as a Token of Contact with Reality: Aligning Michael Polanyi's Epistemic Realism with D. C. Schindler's Account of Beauty." Paper for "The Power of Beauty," Franciscan University Annual Conference on Christian Philosophy, October 24–25, 2014.

———. "Contact with Reality: An Examination of Realism in the Thought of Michael Polanyi." PhD diss., Temple University, 1983.

———. "Contact With Reality: Retrospect and Prospect." Paper for Polanyi Studies: Past, Present, and Future, 2016 Polanyi Society Conference, June 8–11, 2016.

———. "Covenant Realism: The Love at the Core of All Things." Plenary Talk for the Annual Conference of the American Scientific Affiliation, July 26, 2015.

———. *A Little Manual for Knowing*. Eugene, OR: Cascade, 2014.

———. *Longing to Know: The Philosophy of Knowledge for Ordinary People*. Grand Rapids: Brazos, 2003.

———. *Loving to Know: Introducing Covenant Epistemology*. Eugene, OR: Cascade, 2011.

———. "'Recalled to Life': Contact with Reality." *Tradition and Discovery: The Polanyi Society Journal* 26.3 (1999–2000) 72–83.

———. "Review of David Kettle, *Western Culture in Gospel Context: Towards the Conversion of the West;* Theological Bearings for Mission and Spirituality." *Tradition and Discovery: The Polanyi Society Journal* 34:1 (2012–13) 74–76.

Merleau-Ponty, Maurice. *Phenomenology of Perception.* Translated by Colin Smith. London: Routledge and Kegan Paul, 1962.

———. *The Phenomenology of Perception.* Translated by Donald Landes. Abingdon, UK: Routledge, 2012.

Musgrave, Alan. "Constructive Empiricism *Vs.* Scientific Realism: Review of Bas C. van Fraassen, *The Scientific Image.*" *Philosophical Quarterly* 32 (1982) 262–71.

Musser, Donald W. "Review of *Meaning.*" *Zygon* 12 (1977) 259–63.

O'Connor, D. J. *The Correspondence Theory of Truth.* Hutchinson University Library Series. London: Hutchinson, 1975.

Pap, Arthur. *Elements of Analytic Philosophy.* New York: Macmillan, 1949.

Peirce, Charles Sanders. *The Collected Papers of Charles Sanders Peirce.* Edited by Charles Hartshorne and Paul Weiss (vols. I–VI), and Arthur Burks (vols. VII–VIII). Cambridge: Harvard University Press, 1931–35 (vols. I–VI), 1958 (vols. VII–VIII).

Pieper, Joseph. *For the Love of Wisdom: Essays on the Nature of Philosophy.* San Francisco: Ignatius, 1995, 2004.

Pitcher, George, ed. *Truth.* Contemporary Perspectives in Philosophy Series. Englewood Cliffs, NJ: Prentice Hall, 1964.

Polanyi, Michael. "Clues to an Understanding of Mind and Body." In *The Scientist Speculates*, edited by I. J. Good, 71–78. London: Heinemann, 1962.

———. "The Creative Imagination." *Chemical and Engineering News* 44, April 25, 1966, 85–93.

———. Duke Lectures. Lectures delivered at Duke University, Spring 1964. Microfilmed and copyrighted by Pacific School of Religion, 1964.

———. "From Copernicus to Einstein." *Encounter* 5, September 1955, 1–10.

———. "Genius in Science." In *Methodological and Historical Essays in the Natural and Social Sciences*, edited by R. Cohen and M. Wartofsky, 57–71. Boston Studies in the Philosophy of Science, vol. 14. Dordrecht and Boston: Reidel, 1974.

———. *Knowing and Being: Essays by Michael Polanyi.* Edited by Marjorie Grene. Chicago: University of Chicago Press, 1969.

———. "Logic and Psychology." *American Psychologist* 23 (1968) 27–43.

———. *The Logic of Liberty.* Chicago: University of Chicago Press, 1951.

———. "On Body and Mind." *The New Scholasticism* 43 (1969) 195–204.

———. *Personal Knowledge: Towards a Post-Critical Philosophy.* 1958. Reprint. New York: Harper and Row, Harper Torchbooks, 1964.

———. "Problem Solving." *British Journal for the Philosophy of Science* 8 (1957) 89–103.

———. "Science and Man's Place in the Universe." In *Science as a Cultural Force*, edited by Harry Woolf, 54–76. Baltimore: Johns Hopkins University Press, 1964.

———. "Science and Reality." *British Journal for the Philosophy of Science* 18 (1967) 177–96.

———. "Science and Religion: Separate Dimensions or Common Ground?" *Philosophy Today* 7 (1963) 4–14.

———. *Science, Faith and Society*. 1946. Reprint. Chicago: Phoenix, 1964.

———. *Scientific Thought and Social Reality*. Edited by Fred Schwartz. Psychological Issues, vol. 8, no. 4, monograph 32. New York: International Universities Press, 1974.

———. *The Study of Man*. Chicago: University of Chicago Press, 1959.

———. *The Tacit Dimension*. 1966. Reprint. Garden City, NY: Anchor, 1967.

———. *The Tacit Dimension*. Foreword by Amartya Sen. Chicago: Chicago University Press, 2009.

———. "The Value of the Inexact." *Philosophy of Science* 3 (1936) 233–34.

Polanyi, Michael, and Harry Prosch. *Meaning*. Chicago: University of Chicago Press, 1975.

Popper, Karl R. *Conjectures and Refutations: The Growth of Scientific Knowledge*. 1962. Reprint. New York: Harper Torchbooks, 1968.

———. *The Logic of Scientific Discovery*. New York: Basic, 1959.

Prosch, Harry. "Biology and Behaviorism in Polanyi." *Journal of the British Society for Phenomenology* 8 (1977) 178–91.

———. "Polanyi's Ethics." *Ethics* 82 (1972) 91–113.

———. "Review of *The Way of Discovery*." *Ethics* 89 (1979) 211–16.

Putnam, Hilary. *The Many Faces of Realism*. La Salle, IL: Open Court, 1987.

———. *Meaning and the Moral Sciences*. London: Routledge and Kegan Paul, 1978.

———. *Realism with a Human Face*. Cambridge: Harvard University Press, 1990.

———. *Reason, Truth and History*. Cambridge: Cambridge University Press, 1981.

———. *Representation and Reality*. Cambridge: MIT Press, 1989.

Quine, Willard V. *From A Logical Point of View*, 2nd. ed. Cambridge: Harvard University Press, 1964.

———. *Ontological Relativity*. New York: Columbia University Press, 1969.

———. *The Ways of Paradox and Other Essays*. New York: Random House, 1966.

———. *Word and Object*. Cambridge: Technology Press of the Massachusetts Institute of Technology, 1960.

Rescher, Nicholas. *Peirce's Philosophy of Science: Critical Studies in His Theory of Induction and Scientific Method*. Notre Dame, IN: University of Notre Dame Press, 1978.

Roberts, P. C. "Politics and Science: A Critique of Buchanan's Assessment of Polanyi." *Ethics* 79 (1969) 235–41.

Rorty, Richard. *Philosophy and the Mirror of Nature*. Princeton: Princeton University Press, 1980.

Rouse, Joseph. "Kuhn, Heidegger, and Scientific Realism." *Man and World* 14 (1981) 269–90.

Rutledge, David. "Polanyi's Prescience." Paper for Polanyi Studies: Past, Present, and Future, 2016 Polanyi Society Conference, June 8–11, 2016.

Ryle, Gilbert. *The Concept of Mind*. New York: Barnes and Noble, 1949.

Schindler, D. C. *The Catholicity of Reason*. Grand Rapids: Eerdmans, 2013.

Scott, Drusilla. *Everyman Revived: The Common Sense of Michael Polanyi*. Grand Rapids: Eerdmans, 1985.

Scott, William T. "Commitment: A Polanyian View." *Journal of the British Society for Phenomenology* 8 (1977) 192–206.

———. "Polanyi's Theory of Personal Knowledge: A Gestalt Philosophy." *The Massachusetts Review* 3 (1962) 349–68.

———. "Tacit Knowing and the Concept of Mind." *The Philosophical Quarterly* 21 (1971) 22–35.
Scott, William Taussig, and Martin X. Moleski. *Michael Polanyi: Scientist and Philosopher*. New York: Oxford University Press, 2005.
Searle, John. *The Construction of Social Reality*. New York: Simon and Shuster, 1995.
Simon, H. A. "Bradie on Polanyi on the Meno Paradox." *Philosophy of Science* 43 (1976) 147–50.
Skagestad, Peter. "Pragmatic Realism: The Peircean Argument Reexamined." *Review of Metaphysics* 33 (1980) 527–40.
Sobosan, Jeffrey G. "The Tacit Dimension of Faith: A Reflection on Michael Polanyi." *Philosophy Today* 19 (1975) 269–79.
Sosa, Ernest. "The Raft and the Pyramid: Coherence Versus Foundations in the Theory of Knowledge." *Midwest Studies in Philosophy* 5 (1980) 3–26.
Spiegelberg, Herbert. *The Phenomenological Movement: A Historical Introduction*. 2nd ed. Vol. II. The Hague: Nyhoff, 1965.
Suppe, Frederick, ed. *The Structure of Scientific Theories*. 2nd ed. Urbana, IL: University of Illinois Press, 1977.
Tarski, Alfred. "The Semantic Conception of Truth and the Foundation of Semantics." *Philosophy and Phenomenological Research* 4 (1944) 341–71.
Torrance, Thomas F. *Reality and Evangelical Theology: The Realism of Christian Revelation*. 1982. Reprint. Eugene, OR: Wipf and Stock, 2003.
———. *Reality and Scientific Theology*. 1985. Reprint. Eugene, OR: Wipf and Stock, 2002.
Toulmin, Stephen. *Foresight and Understanding: An Enquiry into the Aims of Science*. New York: Harper and Row, 1961.
Tuomela, Raimo. "Putnam's Realisms." *Theoria* 45 (1979) 114–26.
Van Fraassen, Bas. *The Scientific Image*. New York: Oxford University Press, 1980.
White, Alan R. *Truth*. Problems in Philosophy Series. London: Macmillan, 1970.
Wiebe, Don. "Comprehensively Critical Rationalism and Commitment." *Philosophical Studies (Ireland)* 21 (1973) 186–201.
Wittgenstein, Ludwig. *On Certainty*. Edited by G. E. M. Anscombe and G. H. von Wright. Translated by Denis Paul and G. E. M. Anscombe. 1969. Reprint. New York: Harper Torchbooks, 1972.
Worrall, John. "Scientific Realism and Scientific Change." *Philosophical Quarterly* 32 (1982) 201–31.

Name Index

Allen, Richard, 261n
Alston, William, 239, 261–65, 267n, 269n, 273, 276
Anderson, David Leach, 262n
Apczynski, John, 253, 259, 261n
Aquinas, Thomas, 280, 282
Aristotle, 120, 181, 268, 280, 282, 291
Augustine, 160, 258, 280

Balthasar, Hans Urs von, 7–8, 279–90, 294, 297
Bannan, John, 210n
Bennett, John B., 94n
Berry, Wendell, 296n
Black, Max, 148, 159
Boyd, Richard, 182–84, 186–87, 189, 191, 193–94, 199, 201–2
Bradie, Michael, 42
Brennan, John, 136–37, 140–41, 167n, 175n
Brentano, Franz, 222
Breytspraak, Gus, 1n, 253n
Brock, Stewart, 261n
Brodbeck, May, 135
Brown, Harold, 13, 110n, 133n, 137–41, 176–78
Brownhill, R.J., 60n
Buber, Martin, 289n
Buchanan, James, 57n

Campbell, Charles, 154n
Cannon, Dale, 271

Carnap, Rudolph, 185, 188–89, 198
Chakravartty, Anjan, 239, 262–69, 275
Copernicus, Nicolaus, 7, 43n, 65n, 69, 83–84, 97, 99, 103, 122, 140–41, 163, 166–67, 193–94, 198, 202

Dalton, John, 122, 143
Davies, Oliver, 240n, 294n
Derrida, Jacques, 263n
Devitt, Michael, 260n, 262n
Dionysius, 280, 282, 291–92
Dreyfus, Hubert, 1, 206n, 239, 244, 246–59, 261, 263, 266, 284, 295

Einstein, Albert, 1, 19, 101, 120, 123, 140, 191–92

Feyerabend, Paul, 13, 26n, 39n, 47, 101n, 108–10, 112, 116–21, 124, 127, 133–34, 141, 143, 168, 172n, 180, 260n
Fine, Arthur, 249, 262n
Folse, Henry, 180n
Forster, E.M., 69
Frege, Gottlob, 148, 158

Galileo, 47, 84, 122
Gelven, Michael, 213–14
Gelwick, Richard, 16n, 93n
Gill, Jerry, 23n, 261–62n

Godfrey-Smith, Peter, 108n, 261n, 267
Goldman, Alan, 109–11, 121, 143–47, 151–52, 184–86, 189, 194, 199, 235
Goodman, Nelson, 265
Grene, Marjorie, 1, 3–4, 16n, 20–23, 25, 29–30, 32n, 34–35, 38–, 40, 42–43, 45n, 46n, 49n, 51n, 56–59, 61n, 65–66, 68–70, 71n, 73, 75–79, 82–83, 87–88, 90–98, 104–6, 123n, 128, 130, 135, 142n, 154n, 159–60, 162–64, 166–67, 174n, 177–78, 190n, 192n, 194–96, 198n, 201n, 203, 206–7, 212–13, 216, 225, 227n, 232n, 239, 244–45, 247, 249–51, 253n, 255–59, 261, 266–69, 271–72
Gutting, Gary, 260n
Grosso, Andrew, 242n, 261n

Hall, Ronald, 105n
Hamlyn D.W., 152–53
Hauptli, Bruce, 154n, 157n, 172n
Hegel, G.W.F., 150, 280–81, 285
Heidegger, Martin, 48–49, 212–14, 217, 280–82, 291–92
Heil, John, 261n
Husserl, Edmund, 46, 206

Innis, Robert, 57n, 93sn, 195n, 200n, 205

Kant, Immanuel, 4n, 57, 195–96, 212–13, 232, 251, 254, 263, 268–69
Kepler, Johannes, 59, 69, 83–84, 99, 122, 133, 163, 166, 193
Kettle, David, 240n, 296–97
Koethe, John, 169–70, 189
Kuhn, Helmut, 57, 195, 200, 247n
Kuhn, Thomas, 1, 13, 26n, 40, 47–49, 93n, 101n, 108–10, 112, 116–31, 134–35, 138, 141, 143, 168–73, 175, 180, 183, 260

Lakatos, Imri, 13–14, 17, 26–27, 47, 101n, 108–10, 112, 114–21, 130–34, 137
Langford, Thomas, 3n, 57n, 66n, 93n, 106n, 247n
Lavoisier, Antoine, 47, 122
Locke, John, 149
Luther, Martin, 160

MacIntyre, Alasdair, 1, 57n, 60n, 120, 124–25, 128, 190, 198, 201n
MacKinnon, Edward, 154n, 180–83, 186, 188–90
Manno, Bruno, 93n
Mares, Edwin, 261n
Margolis, Joseph, 3, 55–57, 110n, 120, 145, 172–73, 175, 183–84, 187, 195n
Martin, Graham Dunstan, 227–28
Mays, Wolfe, 131n, 136
McDowell, John, 260n, 262n
Meek, Esther, 4n, 11n, 178n, 179n, 196n, 243n, 258n, 259n, 268n, 295n, 297n
Merleau-Ponty, Maurice, 3–4, 6, 12, 35n, 203, 205–35, 239, 244–46, 248, 250, 252–58, 295
Merrill, G.H., 58, 185–86, 188–89, 197–99
Mullins, Phil, 1n, 253n
Musgrave, Alan, 17n, 26–27, 47n, 110n, 112n, 114n, 117n, 119–20, 130n, 182n

Newton, Isaac, 84, 100, 120, 122, 163, 166, 181, 191

O'Connor, D.J., 153n
Osiander, Andreas, 103, 163, 197–98

Pap, Arthur, 152n
Pierce, C.S., 44, 49–52, 146, 189
Pieper, Joseph, 286n, 295n
Pitcher, George, 152–53, 156–57
Plato, 280, 291–93
Plotinus, 291

Name Index

Popper, Karl, 13–14, 23, 41, 47, 49, 108–10, 112–21, 131–37, 143, 155, 167–68, 171, 175, 180
Prosch, Harry, 35n, 45n, 51n, 62n, 93n, 105n, 196n, 227n
Putnam, Hilary, 109–11, 129n, 142–47, 151, 156, 169–70, 180, 183, 187–89, 199–200, 260n, 262–63

Quine, Willard, 101, 154, 157, 168, 172–73, 188–89, 200, 261n

Ramsey, F.B., 148, 152, 159
Rescher, Nicholas, 44n, 49
Roberts, P.C., 57n, 192n
Rorty, Richard, 249n, 252, 257, 260–63
Rouse, Joseph, 48–49, 110n, 154n, 156, 214n
Russell, Bertrand, 150, 165
Rutledge, David, 253n

Sartre, Jean Paul, 216
Schindler, D.C., 8n, 240, 242, 274, 278–96
Scott, Drusilla, 247
Scott, William, 1n, 57n, 93n, 105–6, 195n, 241n, 256n, 267n, 294n
Searle, John, 262n

Sellars, Willard, 185
Shapere, Dudley, 185
Simon, H.A., 42n
Skagestad, Peter, 110n, 142–43, 151n, 172n, 187–89
Sosa, Ernest, 247
Spiegelberg, Herbert, 210n, 213n, 215, 228
Suppe, Frederick, 180n
Strawson, P.F., 149, 152–53, 159

Tarski, Alfred, 113, 125, 149–52, 155–56, 159, 170
Taylor, Charles, 1, 239, 244, 246n, 248–59, 261, 263, 266, 284, 295
Tollefson, Christopher, 276
Torrance, Thomas, 261n
Toulmin, Stephen, 13, 47, 101n
Tuomela, Raimo, 169–70, 199–200

Van Fraassen, Bas, 182, 260n, 262n, 264n

White, Alan, 152–55, 157
Wiebe, Don, 131n, 133n, 135–36
William of Ockham, 242
Wittgenstein, Ludwig, 23, 157, 227, 251
Worrall, John, 182–83, 201–2

www.ingramcontent.com/pod-product-compliance
Lightning Source LLC
Chambersburg PA
CBHW021649230426
43668CB00008B/565